"Right now, at this very moment, we have a mind,
which is all the basic equipment we need
to achieve complete happiness."

—The 14th Dalai Lama

"Happiness is inherent in man and not due to
external causes. One must realize his Self in order
to access the store of unalloyed happiness."

—Ramana Maharshi

"The world's great mythic-religious systems are a
precious human resource, the only ones speaking
to the unavoidable stages of human growth."

—Ken Wilber

HAVE THIS MIND

Supreme Happiness, Ultimate Realization, and the
Four Great Religions—An Integral Adventure

JAMES E. ROYSTER, PH. D.

BALBOA.
PRESS

A DIVISION OF HAY HOUSE

Balboa Press books may be ordered through booksellers or by contacting:

Balboa Press
A Division of Hay House
1663 Liberty Drive
Bloomington, IN 47403
www.balboapress.com
1-(877) 407-4847

Because of the dynamic nature of the Internet, any web addresses or links contained in this book may have changed since publication and may no longer be valid. The views expressed in this work are solely those of the author and do not necessarily reflect the views of the publisher, and the publisher hereby disclaims any responsibility for them.

The author of this book does not dispense medical advice or prescribe the use of any technique as a form of treatment for physical, emotional, or medical problems without the advice of a physician, either directly or indirectly. The intent of the author is only to offer information of a general nature to help you in your quest for emotional and spiritual well-being. In the event you use any of the information in this book for yourself, which is your constitutional right, the author and the publisher assume no responsibility for your actions.

ISBN: 978-1-4525-7274-1 (sc)
ISBN: 978-1-4525-7276-5 (hc)
ISBN: 978-1-4525-7275-8 (e)

Library of Congress Control Number: 2013907849

Print information available on the last page.

Balboa Press rev. date: 09/17/2015

Dedicated

to all who are drawn to religion—

and especially to those who are not.

Contents

Appreciation and Gratitude

Innumerable persons have contributed to this book, directly and indirectly, scholars, students, religious practitioners, family members, and friends, to name the main categories. My first seminar paralleling the content of this book was given at The Western College in Oxford, Ohio in the early 70's. The subject matter of the book has been taught almost annually since that time. Cleveland State University granted two sabbatical leaves devoted to research and writing. Discussion with countless believers while living and traveling in countries where the great religions are dominant contributed to a sense of the religions as actually lived. My gratitude extends to all.

A very special thanks to Yvonne Y. Miller, who read the entire text twice with her eagle eye and grammatical expertise. In addition, her enthusiasm and support for the book provided welcome encouragement. Author Ray Moore, scholar of English composition and literature, also read the full text twice and provided immense help with consistency and proper form. Professsor Christine Naylor of Kent State University gave inestimable help in formatting the text of the book to meet publisher's acceptance requirements. Her command of Microsoft Word is exceptional and the enthusiasm and eager willingness with which she tackled the various issues posed by my text is greatly appreciated.

Several persons assisted with references and documentation. Gibb Webber, Professor Emeritus of Anderson University, located the exact wording of an important quotation and provided the bibliographic data. Dr. Richard R. Lau, San Diego Community Colleges, verified documentation of another quotation, as did Sonny Clark, who drew on his broad knowledge of literary sources.

I am pleased also to express gratitude to Mary Harper, Access Points Indexing, Hood River, Oregon, who undertook the intricate task of preparing a comprehensive index for *Have This Mind,* and with such professional expertise.

My three children, Judy, Samuel, and Steven, plus Steven's wife, Janya, have each been committed throughout their adult lives to the values and ideals discussed here. And each has read portions of the book and given their considered and helpful views. Of all who have had an impact on this book, however, the role of one has been such that without her selfless spirit of giving and giving more, this book would never have materialized. Her feedback on specific features of the book was ever insightful. Her repeated covering of my particular family duties enabled me to have the required solitude and time for research and writing. No word of appreciation is adequate for what my wife of more than half a century, Elizabeth, Beth, Liz, Aleezabet, has done to bring this book to life (each of her preferred names mirrors her unfolding spirituality and a somewhat different quality of her inexhaustible generosity).

Preface

The title of this book deserves comment. As Christopher Bache rightly observes: "Mind is the context within which all knowing arises: it is the frontier which comes before all other frontiers."[1] Without the mind, we would not be aware of anything of which we are aware. Because the mind is so crucial to our very humanness and aliveness, it plays a vital role in the natural process of human development and maturation. This being so, mind is the locus for the transformational process that leads to ultimate realization in each of the world's religions. Because this is less recognized in Christianity than in other religions, and because the book is directed mainly to a Western audience, the title is drawn from a phrase in the New Testament (Phil. 2:5): "Have this mind in you," also translated, "Let this mind be in you."[2] Briefly characterized, this is the unconditioned mind, the mind of universal love and wisdom. The verb, 'have' or 'let,' is absent in the Greek text and therefore supplied by the translator. These are appropriate English verbs since they convey a twofold import: receiving something as a gift, i.e., allowing something to happen, on one hand, and developing something or working to make it happen, on the other hand.

As we will see throughout this study, the transformational process is one of practice and realization, of preparing for, doing the work, on one hand, and receiving the gift, experiencing the result, on the other. The tension and seeming contradiction between work/effort and gift/grace arises in both Eastern and Western religions and will be addressed again in the final chapter, which treats the principles and practices of personal transformation that the world religions, particularly Buddhism and Christianity, have in common and have found most effective.

Mind, as a focus running throughout this study, is interpreted broadly to include all that arises in awareness. What we see, hear, touch, smell, and taste make up the contents of our minds; also our emotions, sensations, and intuitions. The most pervasive contents of our minds are thoughts, the swirling ideas that seem ever-present. Mind also includes specific functions, the rational function, for example. Finally, mind names consciousness itself, i.e., pure consciousness, consciousness without content. In a word, mind represents our inwardness. Context will indicate which of these varied meanings is intended.

Some Eastern languages have a single word that means both mind and heart. Lacking such a word in English, we will occasionally use mind/heart to indicate the arbitrariness of the distinction, particularly when referring to the higher forms of personal realization where a single, integral way of being becomes the mode of life. Mind is a particularly apt concept for a work of this sort since it figures prominently in each of the religions investigated, though more in some than others.

For religion to be authentic, it must be grounded in the full range of human experience, and demonstrate the power to facilitate extraordinary personal transformation throughout this entire range. If not, it tends to become merely conventional, routine, one of many cultural forms that commonly engage human attention. The intent of this book is to show how religion is grounded in profound, universal human experience, grounded in what might be called our spiritual nature. The book argues that our very nature as human beings calls for religion, or something akin to religion, even though many forms fail to exhibit the central features of authentic religion.

The method of investigation is descriptive and normative. It is descriptive because religion as it actually appears in its most noble expressions, i.e., as professed, practiced, and exemplified by its foremost representatives, its saints and sages, is the foundation of what follows. At the same time, we will not avoid calling attention to features of religion that not only fail to lead to higher spiritual realization but sometimes actually forestall personal development. This study is also normative because the focus on the genuinely transforming and transcending features of religion furnishes the objective data from which emerge the criteria for evaluating religion, for distinguishing between nominal, merely conventional religion, often wanting in respect to the noble qualities of human achievement, and those forms of religion that exhibit these qualities. Thus, the norms against which the various features of religion are evaluated arise from within religion itself. These are experientially verifiable standards. They are clearly observable in the lives of those who have devoted themselves most fully to the religious quest, who have ascended to the highest levels of spiritual awareness.

These experientially validated norms, against which all forms and claims of religion must be assessed, consist of at least nine distinguishable but integral qualities: (1) inclusiveness, wholeness, interconnectedness, nothing alienated from anything, recognition of the complementarity of all apparent contradictions and oppositions; (2) spontaneity, creativity, freedom, absence of compulsive or inhibiting behavior; (3) deep contentment, happiness, and tranquility; (4) acceptance, even appreciation, of whatever happens, wholly without any psychic pushing away (frustration, anger, fear) or pulling to (seeking, lust, greed), that is, without avoidance or resistance, on one hand, or craving or grasping, on the other; (5) absence of the need to control others or circumstances; (6) absence of a sense of oneself as separate, especially of oneself as special, that is, absence of repeated self-reference and especially self-preference [in the sense of judging persons and events in terms of one's own (usually narrow and highly conditioned) expectations and standards]; (7) a universally applicable sense of justice, fairness, and equality, wholly uncontaminated by preferentialism; (8) deep concern for the welfare of others, commonly expressed as unconditional love or compassion, that results in selfless and non-discriminating service; and finally (9) an abiding joy, appreciation, and gratitude for life in all its forms as it unfolds and presents itself moment by moment.

These are not the standards that are usually invoked to establish truth; neither are they the common standards of theology as it reflects on the truth of revelation, nor those of philosophy as it seeks to discover truth through reason. Truth is ordinarily pursued by means of the rational mind, an approach that will be shown in the first chapter to be inherently limited and therefore unable to know truth or reality as it is known by those exemplifying the qualities listed above. The truth that is of primary concern here is the truth noted by William Butler Yeats: "Man can embody the truth but he cannot know it."[3] Authentic religion is concerned with experiential truth, truth reflected in the quality of one's life, not just ideas held in the mind, whether theological, dogmatic, creedal, or simply beliefs.

One way of seeing the limitation inherent in the effort to know truth through the intellect alone is that the world's thinkers have not so far produced a view of reality that is anywhere near universal acceptance. Broadly stated, ideologies—understood as systems of thought or ideas about reality—are varied, contradictory, and inconclusive. It is perhaps safe to conclude that humans will never agree on any single worldview, religion, political system, social pattern, or other 'thought up' dimension of our common life together. Therefore, to expect humanity to ever accept a single, universal religion would seem to be an idle and hopeless expectation. Even to search for common notions (ideas, thoughts, perspectives) in the world's religions as they are conventionally understood and practiced is a venture unlikely to succeed. Indeed, all world religions are characterized by texts, symbols, myths, rituals, philosophies or theologies, ethics, ideals, etc. But these are forms and not contents. When investigating the contents of these forms one finds great differences and irreconcilable contradictions.

On the other hand, virtually all humans of reasonable maturity, sound mind, and good faith will recognize the desirability of the nine qualities noted above. Some may regard a few of them as too idealistic to be attainable, but we will see that that is not the case. Others may have reservations or even objections to some of them. These disavowals may stem from personal ideology, from failure to understand properly, and may well disappear on further explanation. William Blake observed: "Truth can never be told so as to be understood, and not be believ'd." That Blake's understanding of truth parallels Yeats is seen in his view that "every thing possible to be believ'd is an image of truth," not truth itself but a reflection.[4] Therefore, it is perhaps not too naive to expect that, with continued personal development along the lines explored in subsequent chapters of this book, even those who presently disagree with the possibility, or even the desirability, of the nine qualities will come to recognize them as indeed the highest desiderata of human life. To do so, however, may require commitment to a psychospiritual practice designed to lead to such realization. To admit the value of these qualities is one thing. To exemplify the qualities is quite another, and most certainly demands full, rigorous, and lengthy commitment to a psychospiritual discipline. This requirement is no different than that requiring anyone who wants to understand and practice medicine to study medicine, or anyone who wants to be an engineer to develop the requisite skills. To attain the exceptional, one must undertake an exceptional practice.

A reader has the right to know something of an author's life experience that bears on the content of his writing. The personalization of a text in this fashion is particularly relevant in a work that treats issues of the deepest personal significance. The author grew up in a conservative Protestant family that was devout to a fault, Sunday school, Sunday morning worship, mid-week prayer meeting, Boy Scouts, choir, youth group, all followed by four years of college and three of seminary in the church's main educational institutions. After ordination to the Christian ministry, an academic year was spent in an inter-denominational and internationally recognized seminary preparing for mission service. Five years were spent in India, Egypt, and Kenya as an educational missionary, after which doctoral study in world religions was completed. The next four decades included: teaching, research, and broad reading in the world's major religions; personal programs and exercises in psychospiritual development, solitary and under guidance; nearly a year of religiously-oriented travel across North Africa, the Middle East, and Asia; and finally, acquaintance and friendship with many practitioners of the world's religions.

Looking back over my lifetime, I recognize two emphases from my early religious heritage that have remained—though now significantly reinterpreted—namely, personal holiness and Christian unity. Personal holiness is now seen as one form of the values found in the saints and sages of the world. Christian unity has expanded to include not only interreligious dialogue and world ecumenical organizations but, more importantly, the harmony, unity, and mutual appreciation found among the world's saints and sages. What was once regarded as unity among Christian churches has become unity among the religions of the world.

These two viewpoints, as they have matured over the years, are reflected in the following pages. The first, personal holiness, is now deepened and expanded to refer to a state of mind and way of being that is marked by unrestricted love, impartial justice, and altruistic wisdom. Humans are able to become pure in heart, i.e., motivated by unconditional love, and clear in mind, i.e., guided by a wisdom founded on the interrelatedness and ultimate unity/nonduality of all that is. This conviction is supported by the view, proclaimed by Pierre Teilhard de Chardin, Jesuit priest, theologian, and paleontologist, that we are essentially spiritual beings having a human experience and not just humans who occasionally have a spiritual experience. The second viewpoint, the ideal of commonality and unity among the multiple forms of the world's religions, is universalized in the contention that all major religions contain—in their essence—authentic, complete, and fulfilling paths to Ultimate Spirit and ultimate realization.

NOTES

1. Christopher M. Bache, *Dark Night, Early Dawn: Steps to a Deep Ecology of Mind.* (Albany, NY: State University of New York Press, 2000), 26.

2. Further comment on this passage occurs in Chapters VI and VII. Jim Marion uses this text and injunction in his groundbreaking study, *Putting on the Mind of Christ* (Charlottesville, VA: Hampton Roads Publishing Company, 2000), which offers a comprehensive and insightful description of inner growth in Christianity.

3. William Butler Yeats, "To Lady Elizabeth Pelham" in Allan Wade, ed., *The Letters of W.B. Yeats.* (London: Rupert Hart-Davis, 1954), 922.

4. William Blake, "The Marriage of Heaven and Hell" in David V. Erdman, ed., *The Complete Poetry and Prose of William Blake.* rev. ed., (New York: Doubleday, 1988), 38, 37.

Consciousness, Ultimacy, and Religion

"Consciousness is both the most obvious and the most mysterious feature of our minds."
—Daniel C. Dennett

Ultimacy precedes all, succeeds all, surrounds all, permeates all, is all.—Anonymous

"Religion is at best a tool to help you train your mind."—The Dalai Lama

The function of religion is to facilitate fundamental transformation in our personality, our character, our inherited sense of who we are, the most basic element of our beingness, in a word, our very nature as human beings. Religion that does not actively foster human transformation—by means of transcendence—is little more than a social convention. If it does not regularly and consistently promote individual change, growth, development, transformation, it fails to operate out of its true base and center. Such religion forfeits its primary purpose and becomes indistinguishable from other noble features that make up social life. By not basing and centering itself in that which is unique to itself, religion loses its authenticity and becomes only one more enterprise among the many that make up society—cultural, educational, recreational, political, commercial, etc.

1

Generic Religion

An initial understanding of the nature of religion can be gained by considering the Latin word from which it is derived, *religio*. Scholars believe that religio in turn is derived from either *religare* or *relegere*. Religare means 'to re-connect', 'to bind to'. Religion is thus a means of rejoining what has become separated. It is the means by which we become re-rooted in that from which we draw our existence; it is the rediscovery of our Source. In most religious traditions, this is understood as returning to God, to the divine. T.S. Eliot, locating the religious thrust in the nature of man to reach into the unknown, may have had this etymological sense of the Latin root, religio, in mind when he wrote in the Four Quartets:

> We shall not cease from exploration
> And the end of all our exploring
> Will be to arrive where we started
> And know the place for the first time.[1]

In this sense, religion represents an essential impulse or orientation in the very core of our nature as a human being.

The second possible root for the word religion, relegere, indicates a way out of the widespread, virtually universal way that we humans unwittingly restrict our engagement with life. A great deal of evidence supports the view that we typically live in self-created, mental-emotional boxes of ideas, thoughts, expectations, fears, desires, etc., that shape and limit our experience of life and the role we play in it. We tend to ignore or deny whatever comes before us that challenges or contradicts our familiar view of self, other, and world. To feel safe, to avoid uncertainty and confusion, to maintain some degree of contentment and happiness, we typically resist whatever disturbs or threatens. Or we do not even allow it to engage our awareness. Through selective attention, we unconsciously filter out much that would disrupt our nominal sense of well being. This second root, relegere, means 'to attend to', 'to observe carefully'. Accordingly, religion is the process of paying close attention to whatever presents itself—emotionally, intellectually, physically, relationally, etc.— without prior evaluation, without closing down or shutting out. If we do not arbitrarily exclude what does not fit our pre-established worldview, if we remain open to new input in the course of life, even when it threatens, we may discover a power and mystery and wonder in life greater than anything previously imagined.

The Chinese are fond of noting that danger is also opportunity, that when we feel threatened by something we are being given an opportunity to engage life more openly and realistically. The letters making up the word 'fear' may be seen as an anagram which means "forever evading another reality." By staying open to life as it unfolds on its own terms, we may in fact experience what the German scholar, Rudolf Otto, calls the *mysterium tremendum et fascinans*, the awe-inspiring, power-filled mystery known as the Holy. Any encounter with the divine that is likely to effect transformation must of necessity entail some degree of apprehension, perhaps even anxiety and trepidation. Only by relinquishing the "tried and true" and venturing into the unknown, with all the uncertainty and fear that this inevitably entails, is it possible to experience the power that transforms. Relegere suggests a sensitive awareness and ready willingness to embrace life on its own terms, as it presents itself to us, without expectation and without denial. Only then is discovery and insight possible. Nothing is revealed to the one who is closed, to the one who thinks he or she already knows.

Both of these Latin roots locate the religious thrust in human nature itself, as if to say: to be human is to be religious. Contrary to naive and simplistic views, authentic religion is not rooted in fear, whether the fear of pain, loneliness, punishment, insecurity, or death. Those who engage religion authentically face these and other exigencies of life with courage and acceptance, seeing personal trials

3

as opportunities for growth and realization. At the same time, it would be foolhardy to deny that many are drawn to religion out of a desire to avoid the perplexities and sufferings of life. Religion does offer explanations and give consolation. But escapist religion, all too common within the ranks of conventional religiosity, goes even further. This is religion marked by unreflective belief, doctrinaire rigidity, shallow emotionalism, and fanciful hope, the kind of religious orientation that is far removed from standing open and attentive to life as it unfolds, accepting and venturing into the unknown as it arises each ongoing moment.

Even as the root meanings of the word religion give no support for an attitude of avoidance, they give no support to a religion of mere conventionality or tradition. A great deal of religion is little more than custom—routine, habitual, repetitive—more concerned with security, comfort, and the *status quo* than with the adventure that leads, often by way of uncertainty and disruption, to personal discovery, growth, and realization. Destiny places most of us in a specific tradition, with all the limitations that inevitably characterize an established way. Only inertia, however, keeps us bound to the customary. To recognize the merely conventional is to glimpse the vital and the authentic beyond the usual and formal. To embrace the newly sensed—however, subtle, elusive, or threatening it may be—is to relinquish infantile and adolescent perspectives and embark on the journey of mature religion.

One reason some people are not religious may be because the only forms of religion they know are seen to be inadequate, are recognized as escapist and/or fantastic in their claims. If only limited or deficient forms of religion are known, one is actually to be commended for refusing to align with them. However, if one's highest intuitions and sentiments are belied by so-called religion, one may be motivated by a deeper, unrecognized but genuine religious sensibility, a sensibility, for example, that refuses to acknowledge a god who would destroy humans because they worship a god of different name and features.

If religion is not presented authentically, one would not expect conscientious, thinking people to be attracted to it. William Blake was of this outlook when he contended, as we saw above, that when truth is truly understood it will be believed.[2]

Another reason why some may not be interested in religion is because they are so captivated by other social and cultural features that their attention is never really drawn to matters of religion. Even here, however, Blake's observation is relevant. It may be safe to suggest that when religion does not appeal to an individual, it is because of deficiency in the specific religions known to the person, or because of a failure on the part of the individual to recognize the full breadth and depth of his or her own nature as a human being.

Genuine religion is an adventure that includes religare (return to Origin) and relegere (careful attention), both goal and method, both end and means. These roots stipulate the common goal and means of all genuine, transformative religion. In true religion, one moves toward Origin by following the signposts that inevitably appear when one is open and trusting, much as a bird migrates to its place of origin by simultaneously acting according to inner urge and navigating according to outer sign. Prior, then, to all forms of distorted or merely conventional religion is the inborn inclination to seek the Source of our humanness by following the way that unfolds as we attend to all that presents itself to us in the course of being human, from within and from without. This is the path of supreme happiness.

By conjoining the Latin roots, we have revealed the required human activity (awareness, attention) and identified the end result (reconnection, unity) that constitutes religion. As we attend carefully (and respond honestly) to whatever arises in the ordinary course of our lives, we are rejoining our Source, we are being generically religious, i.e., spiritual. These insights remain implied and determinative in all that is yet to be discussed about religion. But we still need a more formal definition, one that identifies more clearly what most people recognize as religion. Broadly defined, *religion is the human response to what is recognized as Ultimacy.** This definition implies that religion is a human construct, that humans have formulated religion in light of their sense of God and God's expectations of humans. Some believers reject this view by insisting that religion is given by God. This view is hard to maintain, however, in light of the many religions found in the world. One must ask why God would instill so many different, often conflicting, religions among humankind. An enormous amount of 'rationalizing' and 'justifying' of this mythic stance is required for a given religion to maintain that it is uniquely established by God and is the only true religion. Even a softening and liberalizing of this position is difficult to uphold in light of the increasing interaction, understanding, and appreciation that has occurred as a result of the practitioners of the world's religions coming together and conversing and worshipping with each other. Today, a far more defensible position is that of seeing religion as man-made.

Refinement of this initial definition will ensue but must wait investigation into the nature of consciousness and the ways humans have conceived Ultimacy. Before we can come to a deeper and more comprehensive understanding of religion, we must understand: (1) our own nature as consciousness and (2) how humans have conceived the central referent in all authentic religion, namely, Ultimacy.

---

* Use of the definite article, as in 'the Ultimate,' is avoided since 'the' implies that something is definite, distinct from other things. It will be shown subsequently that this way of envisioning Ultimacy, though common, is flawed.

Consciousness*

Consciousness is what we are. It constitutes our essential nature. Without consciousness we are not human as we know ourselves to be human. Consciousness is that field within which anything must appear if it is to have any recognizable contact with us or relevance for us. For anything to exist for us, it must arise in consciousness. In spite of the fact that we tend to identify ourselves first and foremost as a body with a mind (my body, my thoughts), consciousness rests prior to this identification; it is the field within which the identification occurs. A novice monk exclaimed: "Is there anything more marvelous than the wonders of nature?" His abbot replied: "Yes, your awareness of the wonders of nature."

The body and the thinking mind are inside consciousness, and not consciousness inside them, just as the brain is inside the mind and not vice versa (the mind can study the brain but not the reverse). A simple thought experiment will demonstrate the priority of consciousness to the body and the thinking mind. With imagination, a particular function of consciousness, we can envision ourselves without a body or thoughts. However, the sense of oneself as who one has always been will remain the same. In other words, it is quite possible to remain wide awake, and know oneself to be alive and existing, without identifying oneself as a body or a mind filled with memories, thoughts, feelings,

---

* Parts of the section on consciousness are simultaneously subjective and analytical, and may seem overly abstract and elusive to some readers. If preferred, one may proceed to the section on religion and continue reading the remainder of the book, returning to this section if and when desired. However, this section is not only important but vital because it helps resolve many of the problems and seeming contradictions we encounter in ordinary living and to understand the nature and role of nonduality in the higher forms of religion and consciousness.

intentions, expectations, etc. Accomplished meditators perform this feat repeatedly.

It is necessary to distinguish between consciousness itself or pure consciousness, on one hand, and the contents or objects of consciousness, on the other hand, that is, the sights, sounds, smells, emotions, intentions, thoughts, memories, etc., that arise in consciousness. Consciousness itself is analogous to empty space, while the contents of consciousness are analogous to mass and energy, the solid and energetic things that occur in space. More simply, consciousness itself is like the empty sky and its contents are like clouds, lightning, birds, etc. Or, to use a different metaphor, pure consciousness is like silence and its contents are like sounds. If we sense into consciousness itself, letting go of attention to specifics, we note that it has no apparent boundaries; no walls or demarcations are discernable anywhere. It is dimensionless; there is no way to measure it. It is nonlocal in the sense that it does not reside in any place; it cannot be located. Therefore, it seems to have the property usually denoted infinite; it is not finite.

We also discover that consciousness itself does not seem to be touched by time. We have the same consciousness today that we had as children. We know ourselves to be the same person even though we know also that every cell in our body, including our brain, has changed numerous times. The content of our mind has changed greatly—we have a larger vocabulary and perhaps additional languages, our sense of the world and human life are significantly different, yet we are the same person. While that which arises in consciousness is radically different over time, consciousness itself remains unaltered. It seems to have the property usually denoted eternal; that is, not marked by time. And, in consciousness itself there seems to be no sense of myself as a person; personhood and personality are absent. It is not a case of impersonalness but apersonalness, the simple absence of being qualified by personhood.

Thus, in pure consciousness—to the extent that we can disidentify with the contents of consciousness—we find a boundless, timeless, non-self-conscious awareness and simple presence (devoid of anything being present). Succinctly, if we have successfully engaged this 'experiential' experiment, we find that as humans, in consciousness without content, there is only the infinite and eternal.

Consciousness, as we ordinarily experience it in a typical twenty-four hour period, commonly takes two quite different forms, waking and sleeping. The sleeping state is further divided into dream and dreamless sleep, and will be investigated subsequently. The waking state, when observed in terms of its content, is found to comprise at any given moment innumerable thoughts, feelings, visual objects, sounds, tactical sensations, smells, etc., all perfectly obvious and well-defined, all co-existing in a more-or-less coherent whole. If we attend to vision alone, we find that at any given moment our consciousness registers a massive array of different and apparently discrete sights in foreground, mid-ground, and background. This brief consideration of moment-by-moment sensory awareness demonstrates that the contents of consciousness are always manifold and changing. Awareness of multiplicity, of an uncountable number of different 'things', then, is a universal characteristic of the waking state of consciousness.

Sheer multiplicity—multiplicity without an ordering principle— equals chaos outwardly in the environment and debilitating confusion inwardly in one's self sense, if not outright insanity. The eventual discovery of order, meaning, value, purpose, etc., in the human situation would be impossible in the face of sheer multiplicity. If we are to analyze further and systematize the overwhelming contents of the waking state of consciousness, thereby creating order and fostering sanity, we must simplify this vast and unordered array. This multiplicity, overwhelming in itself, must be made manageable to the mind by the mind. The simplest, most reduced form of multiplicity is two things or categories. Any further reduction would entail a qualitatively different state of awareness. Obviously, to reduce multiplicity to a single something is to do away with multiplicity. However, while the notion of 'one' is a common feature of our experience, it is so only by contrast with that which is other than 'one'. Therefore, 'one' as a number is one among many. It is 'one' as a thought and not 'one' as immediate awareness, as a mystical experience of oneness. Mysticism will be treated more fully later in this chapter and in the book. The important thing to note now is that ordinary experience and consciousness, when inspected, are seen to be made up of innumerable, single factors—always. Duality, awareness of two or more different factors, is the most fundamental and universal feature of our regular, common waking state of consciousness.

The thinking mind itself establishes order in itself and the cosmos by making distinctions between one thing and another. Without distinction, thinking cannot occur. Extrapolation, isolating one thing from other things, and thinking occur interdependently and simultaneously. Reason operates by means of binary division. It marks off apparent entities within an environment or milieu, attributes names, provides definitions and classifications, and creates/discovers principles of meaningful relationship, for example, big/small, before/after, above/below, cause/effect, energy/mass, etc.

By the time we become sufficiently mature to be aware of our mind and the multiple contents of awareness, we have already inherited an established order and set of meanings that govern these contents. This order and these meanings have been largely received from our family, community, religion, and state, in a word, from our culture. The world makes sense to us because the polarizing principle that operates in our mind is the same polarizing principle that operates in the minds of others. We have unwittingly employed the dichotomizing principle in tandem with that of our culture to produce a more-or-less coherent sense of self, a workable mode of relating to other humans, a reasonably accurate understanding of the natural world, and, perhaps, a religion and a conviction about the divine. We are not normally aware of the dichotomizing principle of the mind because it is an inherent and natural operation of the mind, and because our emerging worldview is largely inherited. The polarizing principle works so implicitly, essentially, and naturally that we are not conscious of its operation; it works behind and within the worldviews it constructs and communicates.

The dichotomizing principle of the mind constructs its worldview by splitting, and then splitting again each half of what has been split, continually splitting as long as each previously split unit affords still further splitting. To demonstrate the binary operation of the thinking mind, its automatic and unconscious dividing of reality initially into two-foldness and then into multifoldness, we can do no better than to begin where we are and as we are, right here, right now, awake and aware.

We will conduct another thought experiment in our immediate awareness, our inner experience this moment and each unfolding moment. Our present state, which is wakeful and aware, is clearly distinguishable from sleeping. So we have a first level, experientially incontestable, division between being awake and being asleep. And this is demonstrable to the extent that you, the reader, are participating in the thought experiment and presumably awake and alert, of sound mind, and cooperative. To continue the binary process, we will examine the sleep state briefly and then return to wakefulness.

The sleep state is divided into dreaming and non-dreaming or deep sleep. The dream state is an imaginary realm of endless possibilities. Duality operates here but in a more fluid and fantastic manner than in the waking state. Dreaming, because it is marked by distinctions and appears as images, colors, story lines, emotions, etc., can be analyzed further in terms of these categories and others. Deep sleep, since it is devoid of image and distinction, is non-dualizable and does not lend itself to further analysis.

Analysis of our immediate awareness in the waking state could proceed according to different applications of the dichotomizing principle, but the most natural and plausible (if we attend to our deepest assumptions) is that between me and not-me. This unconscious but nonetheless intended or projected division is assumed to be the case between oneself and everything else. This fundamental distinction characterizes every human and is the natural or inborn basis of the ego as the sense of being separate from everyone and everything.

To divide the 'me' half further we need to distinguish between 'I' and 'me' or between 'Self' and 'self'. 'Self', according to the distinction we are now making, is the unique and core feature of our humanness. Lower case 'self' represents our self as we know our self to be different from all other selves. If we label this primary division, 'I' and 'me', now distinguishing between 'I' and the rest of what constitutes me as a person, then 'I' represents the sense of Self that remains constant while everything else about me changes. It is the same 'I' that constituted me in infancy even though everything else, my body, thoughts, emotions, and aspirations, etc., have changed many times.

This 'I' is pure awareness, consciousness without content. 'I' is the unchanging background from which and within which all the operations of the ordinary mind occur, the naming, classifying, evaluating, etc. Nothing I can say about myself is 'I'. 'I' cannot be objectified. Anything I can say about myself is 'me'. Like all humans, I know myself to be a person. Yet, when I rest in and as 'I', my sense of personhood is absent; I seem to be apersonal.

When we investigate the nature of 'I' further we find that it seems to be without boundaries, inner demarcations or outer limits. It thus seems to be infinite. Nor does it seem to be marked by the passage of time. I am the same 'I' I was decades ago even though everything I can name about myself has changed considerably. While I know that my bodymind will die (having *learned,* as everyone does, that this will eventually happen), I nonetheless have a sense of immortality, of deathlessness. Though I know that I came into this world at a specific time, I also have a sense of never having not been, even though I may have no *personal* memory of events before my birth. As 'I', I seem to be untouched by the passage of time. Also, as 'I', I am non-local (not locatable or confined to any specific place) and dimensionless, neither divided nor divisible.

In summary, being untouched by time and space, 'I', *in the sense described,* i.e., as pure consciousness, may properly be characterized as eternal and infinite. This is certainly not true according to the way the singular personal pronoun 'I' is ordinarily used, or as we have defined 'me' in this discussion. For anyone to claim, "I am eternal and infinite," (i.e., to fail to make the distinctions made here between 'I' and 'me') is to engage in the most egregious form of ego inflation, to give telling evidence of psychosis, and, from the standpoint of religion, to fall victim to blasphemy. Clearly, in traditional religions, particularly those of the West, eternal and infinite are qualities reserved for God. To use Christian terminology, it is as 'I', as pure consciousness, that we are created in the image of God. A final point: this 'I' that we have distinguished from 'me' is the same 'I' that characterizes all humans. Here we have the ultimate basis for all forms of morality, all forms of justice and compassion between humans.

The other half of the first level duality is quite otherwise. The 'me' or 'self' half of the divide can be divided further, initially and most simply, into body and mind. Body can be further divided into organs, molecules, cells, atoms, or into various systems, skeletal, muscular, respiratory, circulatory, etc. Mind can be analyzed further as reason, intuition, volition, imagination, emotion, etc. Each of these units of the body and mind can be divided into still further parts. Even while acknowledging this useful division between body and mind, we remind ourselves that the body and the mind are an integral whole; so we speak of the bodymind.

Another common method of dividing ourselves is in terms of body, mind, soul, and spirit, with spirit now naming 'I' and soul serving as the link between bodymind and spirit or 'I'. Thus, the 'me' half of this division can be divided according to different categories and into ever decreasing units, each part becoming a whole comprised of still further parts. And, we know only too well from the experience of humanity that the bodymind will come to an end even as it once began; birth and death are inevitable. The remarkable features of 'I'—dimensionless, non-local, infinite, eternal—do not apply to 'me', to the bodymind, which occupies space, is marked by time, which begins and ends.

We must return now to the 'not me' half of the distinction we made between me, on one hand, and other people and the rest of the world, on the other hand. A workable and universally accepted first division of the 'not me' half, i.e., the entire objective or empirical world, is between time and space. Time we immediately polarize as now and not now. We will take up 'not now' in a moment, but first we must distinguish between two ways of understanding now, neither of which is divisible. The now that we ordinarily recognize identifies the present moment, the now between past and future. This now can never be nailed down, never precisely measured or even specified. The moment we designate it, it has passed. In fact, it has passed even before we can designate it because of the time lapse involved in the sensing and neural processing of what we declare to be now. In spite of this technical fact, we are aware experientially of now in so far as it designates that which is immediate rather than a past event or something in the future. Because our mind does not enable us to demark or divide now, it seems to be timeless. But it is actually in the flow of time as the link between past and future. It is at the same time, mysteriously, the link with the eternal Now.

The eternal Now is inherently and actually indivisible and unmarked by boundaries. It is not quantifiable since it is devoid of sequence or duration; it is truly timeless. Eternity is not a future state but an ever-present, apprehendable, and unchanging reality to the extent that we are able to disidentify with time. Time, from the viewpoint of eternity, is an illusion and a product of the human mind (in the customary sense of the thinking mind). To try to capture eternity or Now within the confines of time is a futile endeavor. One can think *about* eternity and Now but one cannot think eternity or Now. As we have seen, to designate any moment as now is already to have failed since the now so designated is no more. Now in either sense, Now (intemporal) or now (temporal), can be neither remembered nor anticipated.

Now is an immediate, lived reality, or missed entirely in either of two ways. One misses the sense of now if one is lost in thought, lost in objectification, lost in attention and attachment to what manifests as inner or outer. To state the matter somewhat differently, now is missed if one is thinking/feeling by means of memory or anticipation, i.e., in the past or future, or totally preoccupied with what is happening at any given time. Now in the absolute sense is missed to the extent that one is bound to time. The temporal sense, the sense of time, can be (1) transcended in the most profound states of meditation where the sense of the eternal prevails and (2) neutralized in the supreme realization of nonduality where eternity and time coalesce. Some saints and sages of the world attest that their awareness is without a distinction between time/space and Ultimacy. They see what the ordinary mind sees conjoined with a sense of the presence and reality of Ultimacy. This awareness is, of course, nondual and transcendent to the thinking mind.

To return to our discussion of the way the thinking mind splits time into parts, we must note that the second half or 'not now' portion divides further into past and future. Each of these represents a mental preoccupation accompanied by a corresponding loss of the sense of immediacy. Experientially, past and future lack reality since the past is no longer and the future is not yet. Past and future exist as mental constructs only. This is not to deny that there was a past or will be a future in the ordinary sense of the terms but to draw attention to the extraordinary difference between Now/now as immediate, lived awareness, on one hand, and past and future, as mental contents, on the other hand. Now is a qualitative experience; past and future are quantified mental constructs. Nor is this observation meant to minimize the importance of remembering the past or planning for the future. Each is crucial to our full humanness. There is a time to remember and a time to plan, but to be lost in an idle rehashing of the past or a redundant rehearsing of the future is to be distracted from the rich immediacy of the non-repeatable present.

To be fully present in each unfolding moment is the most expeditious way of utilizing past experience in service to future projects. This focus is very different from the repetitious rehashing and rehearsing just mentioned. Ideally, one's past becomes a reservoir of experience that, wholly present and accessible in each unfolding moment, contributes creatively to the unfolding future. In this way, past and future coalesce in the present and combine in the immediacy of full attentional presence.

Finally, to conclude our analysis of how the thinking mind continues to divide the not-now portion of time, we need simply note that past and future are each endlessly divisible in terms of calendar and clock, whether recording or remembering the past or thinking about the future.

In principle, space divides similarly to time; the dichotomizing mind sets up a first level division in space by distinguishing here from not-here. Here, like now, is not divisible. It is unlocatable and indefinable except by means of some additional designation, whether spoken or gestured. If we use the word 'here', we have to specify where here is, "here by this tree", "here in America", or trust that others will understand what we intend. When a department store indicates "you are here" on a floor plan designed to help customers negotiate the store, the here where one is standing is not the here of the diagram. Here is inherently ambiguous because it is without boundaries; it does not locate. Here as here is dimensionless, without internal or external boundaries. Here is marked by the features of infinitude. The other half of the division of space, not-here, is dimensioned by the thinking mind in numerous ways, principally by boundary making, naming, and mapping, thereby giving rise to cities, states, countries, continents, etc.

We have seen how the thinking mind creates a navigatable world by means of entitizing and dualizing that which seems to be given and apparent, both inwardly and outwardly, but which would be chaotic and meaningless without this active process of the mind. We have now investigated sufficiently this operation of the thinking mind to see quite readily how the human mind, when it identifies new areas of exploration, is able to analyze and order the data discovered in a meaningful way. The continuous application of the mind in this fashion gives rise to ever-expanding knowledge and understanding of the external and internal worlds.

This dividing operation of the thinking mind is natural, inevitable, and necessary. Without it we cannot discover or construct meaning, or communicate and connect thoughtfully with others. Without a sense of meaning, we become distraught and disfunctional; we become a burden to ourselves and to others. So we have no option but to define and divide, to categorize and classify, in a word, to create a mental net or model that we impose on reality—that is, on ourselves, others, and the world. Without this map of reality we would experience sheer chaos. But to live by means of this map alone results in real and frequently unsolvable problems. It gives rise to contradictions, paradoxes, and dilemmas that challenge the assumed rational order of reality. The map is crucial because it reveals order and meaningfulness; it is also distorting because it conceals the extraordinary principle of mutuality, interdependence, and wholeness. It is based on a fundamental but limiting operation in perception and understanding. Often times the conundrums created by the thinking, dualizing mind can be resolved only by accessing the larger mind, the mind that does not split reality into parts, the nondual mind.

That there is no such thing as a thing, an entity, an isolated and unrelated factor or element, becomes clear when we realize that everything that presently exists has come into existence by forces and factors other than itself. Therefore, the first existential split between me and not-me is a fabrication and distortion. Without the not-me there would be no me. I am because my parents are/were; and they are because their parents are/were. Who I am, to a significant degree, is determined by the culture in which I have been raised, the religion to which my parents belonged, the siblings with whom I spent so much time, the schools I attended, the books I read, the friends I had, the woman I married, the children born to this marriage, the work I do and all the uncountable influences that continue to impinge on my consciousness, day in and day out.

A first phase in the development of the human mind lies in the establishment of 'object permanence', i.e., becoming aware of solid shapes, surfaces, and colors. A significant further phase discovers relationships between these apparently permanent objects. Unfortunately, most minds stop here. But a further, monumental development that is crucial to truly mature thinking pertains to what is argued here, namely that relationships are so intricate and far reaching that literally nothing exists in isolation from its immediate environment, spatial and temporal, and that environment from its environment, *ad infinitum*. Arthur Koestler summarizes this perspective by means of his coined word, holon. Holons are wholes made of parts, each of which is simultaneously a whole comprised of parts, and each of these parts is also a whole made up of parts, on and on. Thus, in reverse, subatomic particles make up atoms, that make up molecules, that make up cells, that make up organs, that make up organisms. And these organisms, if they are human, make up families, communities, cities, states, nations, indeed, a species, that is itself one of many that make up the animal kingdom that, in turn, constitutes one part of the biosphere that is a dimension of earth that is part of the cosmos. In principle, holons extend all the way up, all the way down, and all the way out so that there is no beginning or end except where the human mind *arbitrarily* establishes one. Each holon is related to other holons in ever contracting/expanding complexes that are so intricately interconnected that, only by *arbitrarily* dividing reality into manageable units can the human mind begin to make sense out of it all, at all.

Everything that is, whether a part or a whole, depends on other things for its origin, its existence, and its eventual dissolution. Thich Nhat Hanh, a Vietnamese Buddhist monk, summarizes this view by giving the basic ontological term used in English a much needed prefix. Rather than simply affirming that things are, he insists— rightly—that things inter-are. Any thing that is, is what it is by right of its relationships to what it isn't. Therefore, it inter-is. Inter-being, rather than simply being, becomes a more accurate characterization of reality. Thich Nhat Hanh offers the illustration of a sheet of white paper and observes that it would not exist were it not for sunshine, clouds, rain, and trees, as well as the woodcutter, his parents, the bread he ate, the grain grown to make the bread, etc. He notes that we can say poetically that the sun and the clouds and the woodcutter are all *in* the paper.[3] Without them, and all that sustains them, the paper would not be; therefore, inter-being. That we do not immediately see these necessary and intricate relationships and dependencies is proof enough that the mind itself screens out this crucial information, which it distorts even as it reports.

The waking state of consciousness—where we try to figure out what is real and unreal, true and false, just and unjust, good and bad—this thinking mind is fundamentally and necessarily divisional. It divides, dichotomizes, bifurcates, polarizes, and splits reality up into apparently discrete units, ostensibly separate entities. This thinking mind actually 'entitizes' reality, creates so-called entities by projecting boundaries around selected features of reality, thereby treating them as if they were separate things. It produces illusory 'things', extrapolating objects from their milieu. Thinking only occurs by 'thinging', by throwing an imaginary net of 'thingness' on the interrelated and interacting whole of reality. The thinking mind does not allow us to *immediately see* relationships and interdependences, the mutuality of all that now is with all that was and all that will be. In other words, the thinking mind, with all its powers and enormous value, actually screens out more than it observes. It is an instrument of exceeding importance, but a limited instrument. Even as the thinking mind renders reality to us, it falsifies this reality through its dualizing function. It simultaneously reveals and conceals, discloses and distorts.

Thus, the ordinary waking state of consciousness, more specifically, the thinking mind, actually interferes with our immediate perception of life as a dynamic, interrelated, unfolding whole, as infinite and eternal. Even the fundamental split between time and space is arbitrary. Where do we ever encounter anything that isn't occurring at a specific time? When is there ever a time when we are not cognizant of specific things or thoughts? Where and when go hand in hand. Space and time are spacetime. And yet, as long as we are awake and our minds are active, we must continue to presume the divisions we have come now to see as relative and imposed on reality. Our humanness demands it. It would be foolhardy to demean the natural functioning of the thinking mind, crucial as it is to our full humanness. It is equally foolhardy to identify exclusively with the thinking mind as if it alone represents the fullness of our humanity.

We will return to the waking state of consciousness and discover that it need not be limited by its ingrained dualizing operation, but first we need to look somewhat more fully at the two common states of sleep, dream sleep and dreamless sleep. As we have seen, dream sleep continues to be marked by duality, but the laws and conditions that govern this state are considerably more fluid and flexible than in the waking state's condition of duality. There are far fewer images and they flow into and out of each other with great ease. The rigid, controlling factors of time and space do not apply. We can reside in the past or the future of the waking state and experience it as the present. We can reside in distant places and experience their immediacy. The law of gravity is suspended. We can perform feats with impunity that are unthinkable in the waking state. While awareness continues to be of something, the objects or forms that fill awareness are less distinct, and the physical laws of the natural world are in abeyance. Indeed, a radically different condition of reality prevails, though still marked fundamentally by duality.

An even greater difference from the waking state occurs in dreamless sleep. There are now no forms or images seemingly operative. Duality and distinction cease to apply. Awareness now is of absence, absence of form in any form. And yet consciousness continues. We can be awakened by sound, sight (bright light, for example), touch, smell, and perhaps even taste. Since many people can program themselves to wake up at a given time, somewhere in consciousness the passage of clock time is registered. None the less, the consciousness experienced in deep sleep is qualitatively different from that of both the waking state and dream sleep. It is one of nonduality; nothing is present in awareness that can be distinguished from anything else.

Some mystical traditions claim that enlightenment ensues (or at least is closely paralleled) by conjoining the non-duality of deep sleep with the bright awareness of the waking state. This conjunction occurs by means of a rigorous psychospiritual discipline usually centering in meditation. Some spiritual adepts contend that deep sleep is closer to our true state than any other that we ordinarily access. The primary reason we enter deep sleep, they say, is to escape the confusion and fatigue of the dualistic world by merging into our native condition, even though we are without our usual awareness when in this state. In some traditions, dream sleep is entered with the awareness of wakefulness, thus lucid dreaming.

A highly evolved mental/spiritual attainment is realized by some who are able to transition from the waking state through dreaming to deep sleep without losing continuity in awareness. The seemingly sharp boundaries that ordinarily separate the three common states of consciousness are seen to soften and finally disappear. This process contributes to increasing identity with consciousness itself rather than the states it assumes or the contents that fill it. With one's self-identity and consciousness becoming increasingly pure and undivided, the ego, or the separate self sense, falls away and one experiences all that arises without partiality. One knows oneself to be in total harmony with all that arises.

Meditation is the most commonly pursued means to this integral awareness. While meditation has been co-opted by religious traditions and centralized in their respective psychospiritual disciplines, it is essentially a human process that is religious only to the extent that it is incorporated into and conditioned by the forms of a particular religion. In itself, meditation is simply a process of self-exploration, a means of discovering through one's own immediate experience that one's essential nature is consciousness, even pure consciousness, consciousness devoid of the content that normally comprises it. Meditation begins with the thinking mind and proceeds by releasing attachment to the normal operations and contents of the mind, thereby coming gradually to rest in pure awareness. As one disidentifies with the contents of the mind, one comes to rest in and as pure consciousness. While the process is easy to describe, it is difficult to pursue and often requires many years of committed practice. Specific features of meditation will be explored in subsequent chapters.

We have now surveyed the three forms of consciousness that humans engage each day and night and seen how the principle of duality enables, determines, and limits the perception of what we experience. We will return to consciousness later and discover how it evolves in the normal course of life, particularly in the context of religious experience. We will also discover how, by expanding our understanding of what it means to be human and taking up specific transformational practices, this evolution can be accelerated. We will discover how consciousness can ascend to stages and states of awareness that provide views of self, others, and reality without the limitations inherent in the ordinary outlook of most humans. Those reaching these higher stages invariably experience and exhibit the values universally advocated by the world religions. In the meantime, however, we need to investigate what the world's religious, spiritual, and wisdom traditions mean by God. One's understanding of God either impedes or facilitates one's transformational process.

Ultimacy

Zoroastrianism has its Ahura Mazda; Judaism its Jehovah; Christianity its God; Islam its Allah; Hinduism its Brahman and Vishnu and Saraswati, et al.; Buddhism its Shunyata and Amitabha and Kannon, et al.; Jainism its Jiva; Sikhism its Ekankar; Taoism its Tao; Confucianism its Shang Ti; Shinto its Izanagi and Izanami. Less structured religions and those with little or no scriptures, such as Australian Aboriginal, Native American, and African tribal, also have their gods, spirits, ghosts, and demons, thereby acknowledging a region of power beyond the ordinary. Every religious tradition is founded on what we are calling Ultimacy, even though they expound a myriad of views, often conflicting, regarding just what this Ultimacy is. Ultimacy is the inclusive term we will use to designate whatever a religion founds itself on and centers itself in. Because the majority of the readers of this book are likely to share a Judeo-Christian heritage, either through commitment or culture, 'God' will occasionally be used in exchange for Ultimacy, in part to begin dislodging some of the more restrictive notions that have come to be imbedded in the traditional term.

As indicated, widely divergent views of Ultimacy are found within and outside the religions. A particular religion will be regarded as true or false depending on whether or not it propounds a view of God that conforms to the view of the questioner; does God exist and what is the nature of this God. At one level, the issue is argued interminably (and often banally) with the vigorous assertion of 'yes' or 'no' and the ready supply of so-called irrefutable evidence (some even claim proof). On the other hand, to hint at the subtlety that this discussion can attain, we may simply note that among some mystics, the issue is raised to a loftier level with the view that "if God is, nothing exists; if things exist, God does not." The meanings of the terms in this declaration are, of course, carefully explained by the mystics. We will leave open the question of God's existence since it is finally a personal view and conviction, devoid and incapable of any conclusive proof.

If one looks broadly at the world's religions, God is sometimes regarded as single or multiple, personal or impersonal, male or female, peaceful or wrathful, charitable or judgmental, tolerant or intolerant. Ultimacy may be thought of as God, as gods, a principle, a high, divine-like being, a power or force, or the highest level or sphere of reality. He, she, it, or they are conceived so differently throughout the religions, it might appear that other than as a central referent there is nothing held in common. Some might conclude that the differences and contradictions cause the so-called central referents, when viewed collectively, to be nullified right out of existence. But such is not the case.

The varied, even conflicting, views of Ultimacy may be understood to arise from the failure to distinguish between Ultimacy as It is in Itself and Ultimacy when appearing in time and space. This distinction, Ultimacy in Itself and Ultimacy in manifestation, provides a model by which the myriad differences and endless debates over the nature of God can be understood, even reconciled. An analogy to this distinction can be found in our human nature.

At the end of a busy day when we retire to the solitude and rest of our homes, when there is no one around to impress or interact with, when we are simply ourselves, this aloneness in and as ourselves is similar to Ultimacy in Itself. During the day when we are busy at work or school, constantly thinking, planning, and doing, we are in a state comparable to Ultimacy in manifestation or relationship. Psychology has convincingly shown that we humans typically project a persona when in public, portraying ourselves before others as we want to be seen and known, living out an ideal image, withholding those features of ourselves that we do not like or that we fear others will not like. In solitude, especially in our most honest moments, this natural and largely unconscious process is somewhat withdrawn. Thus, we seem to have at least two selves, a private self and a public self. And yet, we also know that in spite of these two selves, we are a single self that somehow mysteriously combines and includes both of these other selves. In a moment we will see that this integration is also characteristic of Ultimacy.

In the course of our exploration, we will modify and refine our understanding, but we can begin by noting that Ultimacy is, first and foremost, that beyond which there is nothing more. It is before, after, and around all that is. Nothing is equal to Ultimacy; if there was, Ultimacy would not be truly ultimate. Other than Ultimacy, there is nothing. To be ultimate, Ultimacy must be single and unrivaled. Ultimacy stands outside of time and space, the entire cosmos.

To unfold the nature of Ultimacy further, a number of additional terms must be introduced, terms commonly used in the religions to characterize God. For example, Ultimacy is generally regarded as Transcendent, a term virtually synonymous with Ultimacy, i.e., as just described, above and beyond time and space. If this is the case, we must wonder how we humans, who are confined to time and space, can possibly know or relate to Ultimacy. It would seem to be a case where we find ourselves inhabiting one region and Ultimacy an entirely different one. It is as if we are here, reading these words in a particular place, at a particular time and Ultimacy is, as it were, residing in a distant continent.

The apparent gulf is bridged when the religions affirm that Ultimacy is also immanent, here and now, everywhere present all the time, in theological terms, omnipresent. The thirteenth-century Christian mystic, Bonaventure, used a now-classic formulation to convey God's freedom from the constraints of space that ordinarily apply. For him, God is a "sphere whose center is everywhere and whose circumference is nowhere."[4] I once saw a church bulletin board imply much the same, but in a more homey fashion: "If God seems far away, who moved?"

While we have resolved one problem (how we, being confined to time and space, can know Ultimacy, which, as Transcendent is apart from time and space) we have created another difficulty since we are now asserting that Ultimacy is both *above and beyond* time and space and *within* time and space, in both realms simultaneously. It is the simultaneity that gives rise to the problem. Our position appears to be a logical impossibility, an outright contradiction; we are claiming the truth of two propositions that seem to be mutually exclusive. We are, in fact, affirming a paradox. In exercising our rationality, founded as it is in a binary approach to reality, we have fallen into the trap of intellection. Our thinking about our experience has led us to affirm two truths that are, according to the dictates of reason, incompatible. Thinking, as we have seen, requires distinction, and distinction often takes the form of opposition. So it is the actual nature of the thinking mind that has created the problem. The problem is not inherent in reality; it is inherent in our thinking about reality. Paradox is not a feature of reality but of thinking.

If understanding is to proceed beyond reason, important as reason is to our understanding, we must develop an appreciation for paradox. This we can readily do if we understand that a paradox is actually a product of the thinking mind recognizing its own limitation and pointing beyond itself to deeper or higher levels of knowing. Paradox is an admission of the intellect, bound as it is by divisionary analysis, that it has reached the end of its extraordinary and invaluable skills and must relinquish authority by passing it on to a more inclusive and integrative way of knowing. The seventeenth-century physicist and theologian, Blaise Pascal, offers the heart as a metaphor for resolving paradox: "The heart has its reasons which reason does not understand."

The heart rejoins what reason divides. Unless one learns to value paradox and even develop ease in the face of intellectual incompatibility, one can not hope to understand the deeper dimension of human nature and religious experience. Paradox, like doubt, is often an indication that one is on the threshold of great discovery. Insight occurs as one gains sight into the common ground beneath apparent opposites.

As we have seen, only by means of division can the thinking mind think; it is bound by this same limiting condition when it attempts to understand Ultimacy by means of reason. In our attempt to gain a fuller understanding of Ultimacy, we have been forced—because of the way the thinking mind operates—to postulate a distinction between Ultimacy in Itself (transcendent to time and space) and Ultimacy in manifestation (immanent throughout time and space). The mind then attempts to resolve the distinction/division by means of paradox as it declares, drawing on deeper resources of apprehension and understanding, the simultaneity of the seemingly contradictory states. The thinking mind creates the division and then suggests a healing of the split by pointing beyond itself to a transparadoxical or suprarational way of knowing. It imposes distinctions on Ultimacy that are not inherent in Ultimacy and then attempts to nullify the distinctions by asserting their simultaneous occurrence. Even as it creates the intellectual incompatibilities by right of the only way it can operate, the thinking mind intuits reconciliation between the postulated opposites by fashioning paradoxes, paradoxes that are embraced and resolved by our deeper, integrative ways of knowing.

As we have seen, the primary paradoxical distinction between Ultimacy in Itself and Ultimacy in manifestation unfolds into further paradoxical distinctions as the religions claim that Ultimacy is simultaneously Transcendent and immanent. Other apparently contradictory qualities are also ascribed to Ultimacy. For example, Ultimacy is Infinite in Itself and finite in manifestation, that is, without any limitation whatsoever in Its own right but taking on limitation in appearance as it manifests in time and space. Because Ultimacy cannot appear in time and space infinitely, since time and space are finite, It appears according to the conditions of finitude, the conditions represented by specific religious traditions and their respective names and attributes for Ultimacy. Thus, Ultimacy appears as God for Christians, Allah for Muslims, Vishnu or Shiva for Hindus, Shunyata or Amitabha for Buddhists. All religious traditions rightly declare their Ultimate to be Infinite but usually fail to realize that Its time and space manifestations are necessarily limited by the anthropomorphic, rational, and egocentric conditions imposed by the human mind. Over the years these *human* ways of seeing the divine become enshrined and codified in the historic and cultural expressions of the individual religions. To inflate the finite appearances of Ultimacy and extend them to Infinity is, strictly speaking, idolatrous, that is, treating that which is less than ultimate as if it were Ultimacy Itself.

In Itself, Ultimacy is Eternal while in manifestation It is temporal. It is crucial here to realize that eternal does not mean everlasting, time going on forever, but the total absence of time. The fact and features of time do not apply to Ultimacy in Itself. It is timeless, untouched by time. However, for Ultimacy to appear in time and space it accommodates Itself, so to speak, to the limitations of the human mind and to the temporal condition of the cosmos. As it appears in history—uniquely and momentously at certain times and places, and always everywhere when humans turn their full awareness to Ultimacy—it does so under the temporal conditions then and there prevailing. Ultimacy appeared to Christians early in this era as Jesus the Christ, to Muslims in the seventh century in the voice of Muhammad, to Hindus many millennia ago in the content of the Vedas, and to Buddhists in Gautama Siddhartha.

On those rare occasions when human awareness of Ultimacy is total, undistracted and unobstructed, Ultimacy appears as the Eternal and time gives way to timelessness. Serial time evaporates leaving pure consciousness 'qualified' by eternity. Sages and saints, mystics and theologians affirm that the most profound encounters with Ultimacy occur outside the normal flow of time; they occur in the timelessness of Now. The typical sense of passing time transforms into intense presence; time quantified becomes an enduring and endearing quality. Johann Scheffler, a seventh-century mystic who wrote under the pen name, Angelus Silesius, knew this: "Eternity is time, and time eternity; unless divided by one's mind."[5]

Similarly, if finitude is construed spatially to imply the limitations of boundary, mass, and number, then in such enduring timeless moments, space drops these features and becomes infinite. William Blake reminds us: "If the doors of perception were cleansed, every thing would appear to man as it is: infinite."[6] Now and here are limitless realities, the eternal and the infinite become lived, known realities, not just creedal assertions or mere beliefs, not simply theological or philosophical propositions.

In Itself, Ultimacy is Absolute and Unconditioned, fully self-subsistent and self-sustaining, independent of any reality or force beyond Itself, since there is none. But as It manifests in and relates to all that makes up time and space, it is as if It assumes the conditions of relativity. Ultimacy is Itself Formless, but when appearing under the conditions of time and space, Ultimacy takes on, or seems to take on, specific forms that are relative to and conditioned by the forms that commonly operate in a specific culture or religion. For example, when first-century Christians struggled to understand the extraordinary person whom they came to call Jesus the Christ, they made use of categories and forms of thought already present in their

Greco-Roman culture, namely, virgin birth, god-man, dying-rising god, etc. The history of religions has shown that newly emerging religions invariably borrow and incorporate into themselves features of the previous or prevailing religions.

To draw together what we have discovered so far about Ultimacy: in Itself, It is Transcendent, Eternal, Absolute, Unconditioned, and Formless; and, simultaneously, in manifestation, It is immanent, temporal, relative, conditioned, and formed.

Continuing our analysis, we find that in Itself, Ultimacy is One, All/Whole, and Undivided; in appearance, It is multiple (as seen in the many different notions humans have of Ultimacy), partial (as part of the whole that makes up human culture and the time-space continuum), and divided (not only distinguished as a specific form but frequently at odds with other specific forms). Other complementarities could be named, e.g., Undifferentiated/differentiated, but we will consider only one more, one that is unquestionably the most controversial of all: is Ultimacy personal or impersonal?

Most religious people believe deeply in the personal nature of God, particularly in the West but often in the East as well. At the same time, many in the Eastern traditions deny this and some in the Western religious world also uphold the ultimate impersonality of God, notably the 16th century German mystic, Meister Eckhart, who uses the term "Godhead" to designate Ultimacy in Itself. Because personhood is so central to human nature, it is only natural that humans would see Ultimacy—in whatever specific form it may appear to them—as personal. Personhood may be envisioned as a kind of filter in the processing structure of the mind that personalizes whatever is of profound significance, notably fellow humans, the Ultimate, and sometimes animals or other features of the natural world. On the other hand, experienced meditators frequently confess to meeting Ultimacy without any sense of personalness. If we adhere to the model postulated here, we can easily reconcile the two otherwise irreconcilable views by affirming that Ultimacy is impersonal—better apersonal—in Itself and simultaneously personal as It manifests and is experienced by most persons. Again we see how the thinking mind creates its own quandaries by dualistically assuming an either/or stance in reference to perplexities rather than resting more deeply in the integral mind, thereby seeing the underlying whole that is prior to the emergence of distinction and division.

In summary, we have characterized Ultimacy as It manifests in the world according to a set of lower case terms—immanent, finite, temporal, relative, etc.—complemented by a set of corresponding terms in upper case—Transcendent, Infinite, Eternal, Absolute, etc.—that are commonly ascribed to Ultimacy but usually without noting that these qualities pertain only to Ultimacy in Itself. Very few people realize that we are able to think only by dividing reality into segments; and people who are religious rarely make the particular distinction deemed essential here, namely between Ultimacy Itself and Ultimacy in manifestation. Consequently, traditionally religious people believe that God meets them in the history, rituals, and beliefs of their religion with the qualities of Ultimacy in Itself, and not the qualities of Ultimacy when revealing itself under the conditions of history, i.e., time and space.

This common position leads most religious people to believe that their religion is absolutely true and, therefore, either the only true religion or at least more true than other religions. This is an instance of the absolute/relative fallacy which inflates to absoluteness that which, from a more realistic, accurate, and inclusive standpoint, is actually relative. This common inflation fails to recognize that a religion can be simultaneously absolute and relative, absolute in relation to the Absolute and relative in relation to the realm of relativity, which includes all religions as they appear in time and space. Religions are necessarily relative to each other since everything making up time and space is relative to all the factors that cause and condition it. At the same time, every religion is absolute in so far as it derives from Ultimacy and orients toward Ultimacy. Every true religion, true in so far as it orients toward and opens to Ultimacy, constitutes an authentic appearance of Ultimacy in the world and thus an authentic path to Ultimacy. This does not mean, however, that other religions are false or inadequate. As we will see, some are more adequate because (1) they offer programs of personal transformation capable of leading to nondual awareness and (2) they are more inclusive of the many ways of being human and understanding the human adventure. Other religions may indeed be legitimate but less than entirely adequate because they emphasize ritual and doctrine to the neglect of on-going personal transformation, and tend to simply reject and condemn that which falls outside their often narrow and idealized discription of what constitutes the good life.

We have given the impression thus far that the capitalized terms accurately identify Ultimacy Itself and Its attributes. They do not. Ultimacy Itself cannot be described by the thinking mind or in any other way. At best, these terms point toward Ultimacy by way of negation. Each of the terms, from Ultimate to Apersonal, is an opposite of what is known by the thinking mind, conditioned as it is by its necessary dichotomizing operation and all the binaries that it has devised by way of making sense out of the time-space world. As embodied beings with intellect, we are located in and conditioned by the world of time and space, a world we implicitly regard as real rather than unreal, existing rather than nonexisting, positive rather than negative. In order to be true to the higher realizations of the world's spiritual and wisdom traditions, we have no option, given our total submersion as bodyminds in the conditions of time and space, other than to 'describe' (more properly, to indicate, allude to, nod or gesture toward) Ultimacy by way of denying of It what we know to be characteristic of the time-space continuum. If this realm is positive, then that of Ultimacy Itself must be negative. The dualizing, value-creating mind could just as well declare this realm negative and that one positive. In fact, as we will see, some religious people do. Convention, however, dictates otherwise.

A careful consideration of the capitalized terms that we have used in reference to Ultimacy Itself will reveal that each of them, in spite of appearing positive at first glance, is actually a negation of what we hold to prevail in the time-space world: Eternal is *not* touched by time, Infinite is *not* finite, Absolute is *not* relative, etc. Everything we know by means of the thinking mind is marked by time, location, limitation, relativity, conditionality, etc. At the same time that we infer and intuit Ultimacy by way of the thinking mind (and attempt to describe Ultimacy), we know in our better moments that Ultimacy cannot be qualified by the relative and conditioned factors of time and space, at least any Ultimate worthy of Ultimacy. Therefore, to be true to our deepest intuitions, we attempt to avoid anthropomorphism, i.e., projecting onto Ultimacy the limited features of ourselves and this world. Many who have plumbed the depths of spirituality restrain themselves, preferring to remain silent about the nature of Ultimacy, or perhaps employ, hesitantly, such symbols as space, emptiness, or void. As the Tao Te Ching, the classic religio-philosophical text of ancient China, observes: "Those who know don't talk, those who talk don't know."[7]

The religions espoused by most humans are religions crafted by the thinking mind, informed one would hope by revelation or at least profound inspiration, as well as intuition and clear thinking. As systems of belief, that is, of thought, some are more reasonable than others—less contradictory, less preposterous, less fantastic—but all are products of the thinking mind. Theology, reflection about God, is more of a Western development than Eastern, though even in the East one finds rational thought similar to it. Theologies that describe God as manifested, that characterize God in terms drawn from human experience (such as, just, righteous, powerful, loving, etc.), are properly known as kataphatic (or cataphatic) theology. Most people know only these kinds of theologies since they dominate the religious world.

Far less common is apophatic, negative, or mystical theology, which directs itself to Ultimacy in Itself. A spokesman for the latter is the pseudonymous mystic, Dionysius the Areopagite, a mystical theologian of early Greek Christianity, who noted that kataphatic theology, formed as it is within and from the stance of the material world of knowing, always points beyond itself to the Transcendent God, while apophatic theology, preferring negation in order to avoid attributing any hint of limitation to Ultimacy, rests in unknowing. Greatly influenced by Dionysius, the seventh-century Greek monk, Maximus the Confessor, declared: "The one who speaks of God in positive affirmations is making the Word flesh. The one who speaks of God negatively through negations is making the Word spirit. Using absolutely nothing which can be known, he knows in a better way the utterly Unknowable."[8]

Each of the world's major religious traditions has produced a vast collection of reflection based on thinking about Ultimacy. Each also contains a few voiceless voices, the silent speaking of those who, knowing what cannot be known, know also that this knowing cannot be spoken. And yet, even these who know Ultimacy can never be adequately described, speak and write. They speak and write out of an inner urgency to give expression to that which they have discovered to be most profound, most crucial, in hope that this verbal gesturing will tilt some toward this same crucial profundity. The common conviction of those who have opened to the depths of Ultimacy is that human life thereby becomes profoundly enriched.

Three Ways of Being Religious

Now that we have investigated the two poles of religion, consciousness (the human pole) and Ultimacy (the God pole), we can look more closely into religion as the relationship between these two poles, more specifically, religion as the human response (in, as, and by means of consciousness) to what is conceived as Ultimacy. The response takes three different but interrelated forms. Three distinguishable but interdependent views of and responses to Ultimacy give rise to three different ways of being religious. These three ways of being religious are found in virtually all religious traditions, definitely in the four largest religions of the world that form the focus of this book. Thus, there are three ways of being Christian, three corresponding ways of being Hindu, of being Buddhist, and of being Muslim. These three ways of being religious, regardless of one's specific religious tradition, may be named exoteric, esoteric, and metateric. Each is a distinctive way of being human in which religion is the major, or at least a significant, shaping force in how life is lived. Each will be described but first we need to consider briefly their relative value as comprehensive ways of being human, of sensing and manifesting the uniqueness of our humanity. Each way is a combination of view (beliefs, ideas held in the mind), disposition (character, personality, moral stance, emotional makeup), and behavior or action.

If truth and value are to be based on something other than mere familiarity and preference, a standard of evaluation is needed. The standard upheld here is comprehensiveness; a truth claim is most valid to the extent that it is most inclusive. Whole takes precedence over part, universal over parochial, unitive over fragmentive. That view is most valid that accounts for more of reality, which does not arbitrarily exclude actual features of the world and life as we know it because of some *a priori* claim. A particularly unsavory form of exclusivity lies in the dogmatic declarations of right and wrong or good and evil that are often met in discussions of religion. For example, one's own religion may be regarded as true and upright while others are deficient, some even condemned as full of myth, falsehood, and evil. That which is deemed true, right, and good is found in one's own religion, political party, or worldview, while others are regarded as false, wrong, evil and summarily dismissed. Prejudice is another instance where the norm of inclusivity is violated; a worldview that demeans or rejects a segment of humanity is thereby exclusive and less valid or true than one that affirms the equal worth of all humans. Similarly, a view that extends to humans the unrestrained right to subjugate, even destroy, other forms of life is less inclusive than one that honors all expressions of life. Clearly, environmentalism is more inclusive of life in the widest sense than blind adherence to the notion that humans have the right to subdue and dominate the natural world. Any view that reserves privilege for itself while denying it to others is limited and thus less valid than one that affirms equality and generosity.

It might be argued that any standard of evaluation is arbitrary, defendable only on the basis of personal preference, since no universally acclaimed standard exists that might judge all other values. Such a stance, however, is unworkable, falling as it does in what is sometimes called 'flatland' where 'anything goes'. The result is chaos and immorality. This view is also self-contradictory since it rejects all standards except its own position which is itself a standard, a standard that attempts to exclude all other standards. It exhibits the performative error; it performs or exemplifies what it denies to others. A hierarchy of truth and value based on increased concern, care, and compassion that widens to include all forms of life is inarguably more inclusive than one based on self-interest alone. A hierarchy that postulates views and behaviors that are restrictive and rejective, that excludes much of what is undeniably part of life, is foreign to the stance taken in this book. But one that opens upward and outward to affirm views and behaviors marked by wisdom and compassion, such a hierarchy is not only authentic but one that offers a framework for on-going and radical personal transformation. Such a hierarchy is perfectly matched for evaluating religious views and behaviors since the word ultimate means, as we have seen, that outside of which nothing can be found. Therefore, since Ultimacy is all-inclusive, that view, disposition, and activity that is most inclusive is most true, valid, and authentic. The world's sages and saints are known as such because their lives exhibited the wisdom and compassion that shows no partiality. Shankara and Ramana Maharshi, Padmasambhava and Bodhidharma, al-Ghazzali and Rumi, St. Francis and St. Catherine are revered because of their open embrace of all humans, regardless of who they were or what they stood for. More recently, Gandhi and Martin Luther King, Jr., each motivated by their respective religion, demonstrated an all-encompassing and unconditional love as they stood resolutely against artificial and demeaning barriers between humans. Their lives were so inclusive that they threatened the narrow positions of those who depended, apparently for their own sense of worth and safety, on denigrating others and denying them the rights and privileges they claimed for themselves.

The comprehensiveness of one's religion and worldview can be gauged by the ease with which one engages other religions and the world at large. A reciprocal relationship exists between inclusiveness and harmony: the more one increases, the more the other increases. If one feels unconnected and ill-at-ease, one is necessarily resisting and excluding, at the emotive level if not the ideational. And this, of course, is a sign of need for further personal integration, for incorporating into one's sense of self and world something that is still resisted or rejected. The building of a comprehensive, all-inclusive worldview, far from being only, or even mainly, an intellectual venture, is an on-going, whole person, transformational process.

To put the matter a little differently, because a worldview is a view of the world, both cosmic and human, it cannot dismiss anything that is found in the world; it must be a view of the whole, the whole that includes all aspects and ramifications of oneself, along with everything that constitutes the rest of reality. The cosmos operates harmoniously. A narrow perspective might reject cyclones, lightning fires, earthquakes, etc., as inharmonious, but these events in the natural order of things must be seen as a natural part of the larger cosmic process because, even though they are temporarily disruptive to human interests, the cosmos as a whole adjusts and continues to operate smoothly. Only a narrow human stance sees "natural catastrophes" as undesirable. Since the cosmos, certainly a sphere of reality on which human life depends, operates as a harmonious whole, one's life and outlook is undisturbed to the extent that one makes harmony an objective in one's transformational process. This, of course, means that such inevitable features of human life as fear, anger, hatred, loss, death, and war must be accommodated in one's personal life and outlook on life.

On the basis of this brief discursive on valuational norms, we can now move from simply identifying three different ways of being religious to understanding how these three ways are actually stages or levels of religious growth and development. A stage may be regarded as a stable structure in consciousness, a perspective that conditions how one perceives, processes, and responds to the events, persons, and other living beings that appear in one's life. As Ken Wilber, a major explorer of consciousness and its evolution, indicates, each ascending stage shows "greater consciousness, more embracing love, higher ethical callings, greater intelligence and awareness."[9] Each subsequent way of being religious marks an advance in experience and understanding because it is a worldview that accommodates more of what actually occurs in life (there is less denial) and, at the same time, results in a personal disposition that is more accepting and integrating of whatever occurs (there is less resistance). Each developing stage represents a wider view of reality and a more harmonious way of being in the world.

Exoteric/Conventional Religion

Exoteric religion is the religion we see all around us. It is conventional, institutional, historical, customary, traditional. This is the religion everyone recognizes as religion: the religion of synagogue, church, mosque, temple, and shrine; of rabbi, clergy, imam, and priest; of ritual, rite, ceremony, and sacrament; of symbol, icon, and image; of belief, doctrine, and dogma; of moral requirements, do's and don'ts, rules and regulations; of sacred text (particularly when read literally) and devotional literature. Exoteric religion is lived out as practitioners focus on the exteriors, the forms of religion, on those features that are apparent and obvious.

Within our broad characterization of religion as the human response to what is seen as Ultimacy, exoteric religion may be described more precisely as a system of beliefs and practices designed to change one's life to meet the expectations of the Ultimate, or more commonly, to abide by the law of God, to keep the commandments. Exoterically, to be religious means to believe and practice as one's religion enjoins. Exoteric religion is the dominant form of religion in any given society; most people who are religious are so in the exoteric sense. Exoteric religion is made up of a wide gamut of orientations that may be characterized as fanatical, fundamentalist, conservative, moderate, and liberal. In addition, there are those nominally associated with exoteric religion.

Exoteric religion provides enormous benefit to many, many people. Humans require a sense of meaningfulness in their personal lives and exoteric religion offers this. It enables practitioners to relate positively to God and feel that He is concerned about their lives. Exoteric religion assists in the development of a model of the cosmos and the world that helps individuals know how they fit into the larger physical universe. The creation stories found in all religions contribute to this end. Conventional religion offers needed social interaction, encouragement, and support during times of personal or family difficulty. It sets forth a code of behavior that contributes to harmonious interpersonal relations. It fosters a sense of personal wellbeing by giving guidance in the development of positive personal qualities and attitudes. In a word, exoteric religion meets the religious, cosmic, social, moral, and psychological needs of most people.

Along with the benefits bestowed by exoteric religion, there are some unwarranted features that are limited, untrue, or harmful. In fact, the form of religion most often criticized is exoteric. This is inevitable because most people, whether religious, indifferent, or opposed, are acquainted only with conventional forms of religion.

Limitations in Exoteric/Conventional Religion

It is doubtful if any topic is fraught with more muddled thinking than religion. Yet clear and consistent thinking is required if one hopes to accurately understand religion from the outside or to engage it beneficially from the inside. The faulty thinking that all too frequently occurs in exoteric religion is particularly egregious because it virtually condemns those victimized by it to a life of comparatively mediocre religiosity. Clear thinking is necessary in order to discern how one's opinions and beliefs hinder realization of the full richness of religion and spirituality. Jumbled thinking sets up a mental tangle that impedes growth and results in a closed system of distortions and disturbance. On the other hand, lucid thinking in a mind committed to truth no matter where it leads will lead that mind into ever expanding realms of realization and freedom.

If one form of exoteric religion critically judges another form of the exoteric, a monotonous back-and-forth is usually set in motion that rarely proves beneficial or results in the resolution of differences. This kind of criticism is rarely backed by little more than familiarity and preference. Evaluation is most constructive if it stems from a viewpoint that is higher in the sense of being more inclusive, that embraces a wider and more integrated outlook than the one being evaluated or criticized. Therefore, the only legitimate and constructive criticism of exoteric religion stems from the esoteric or metateric perspectives (these terms will be defined later in the chapter). This is the case because each of the subsequent ways of being religious is more inclusive and integral than the one or ones before it. This process can also be understood as one of transcending, i.e., moving beyond the former while including in the new outlook that which is of abiding value in the former. It is a matter of dropping what was faulty or limiting and keeping what is deepening and broadening. For example, metateric religion recognizes value in the earlier forms, along with error and limitation, but the earlier forms tend to see only error in the later. An undeniable evolution in breadth of acceptance and understanding operates from exoteric through esoteric to metateric. Each ensuing way of being religious is more comprehensive and integrative, and therefore more evolved, than the preceding ones.

Conflation Fallacy

Most of the limitations and shortcomings found in exoteric religion stem from the fallacy of conflation, an error in thought that produces confusion because it meshes ideas which, to be correct, must be kept separate. These notions must remain distinguished from each other in the thinking mind, otherwise muddled thinking results that readily leads to unfortunate opinions about religion and actions in the name of religion. There are two aspects to this conflation and resulting confusion. The first arises from the failure to distinguish between a contradiction and a paradox. Contradiction indicates that the rational mind has violated itself; paradox indicates that the rational mind has exhausted itself. Contradiction urges a more careful use of the rational mind; paradox points beyond the rational mind. Resolution of a contradiction results in a more logical and consistent outlook; resolution of a paradox results in a more transcendent and integral outlook. An example can be seen in exoteric Christianity and Hinduism where the differences are so vast and incongruent that they cannot be reconciled by the rational mind. The differences represent

41

a paradox requiring a higher view that includes each of them, that sees each of them as simultaneously absolute (as a manifestation of Ultimacy) and relative (in relation to other religions).

The second aspect of the conflation problem stems from attributing to religion the qualities of Ultimacy, of fusing—and thus confusing—the features of the Ultimate Itself with the religious tenets that affirm these qualities. This witting or unwitting meshing of Ultimacy with religion can not occur, of course, if one understands that religion is not God-given but the product of the human response to God or Ultimacy; i.e., a human construct. Many of the shortcomings found in religion arise from the failure to recognize Ultimacy as first and foremost what It is in Itself, and that the human response to Ultimacy is overwhelmingly conditioned by conceptualization. There is an unfortunate tendency among humans to reduce God to human proportions, a process that has enabled humans to believe they know who God is and are performing his will when they are more likely expressing their own egoist, limited, and often prejudicial views. Wars between religions erupt because of the failure to recognize these conflationary errors.

We will now look at three examples of the conflation fallacy. The first is the fallacy of fixity and finality. It confuses the changelessness of eternity/infinity with the changing conditions of time/space. This fallacy assumes that the forms of religion are permanently established once and for all, that what was true and effective at one time in one place must be true and effective for all times in all places, that earlier means better, that true religion does not—or should not—change. If there is any principle of life itself that is incontrovertible, it is change, impermanence. Life is always changing, developing, and evolving. Within religion, there may be no greater disservice than to oppose the new and the different simply because it is new and different. Religion thwarts its own essence and distinctiveness when it opposes change. While the tendency toward stasis enables exoteric religion to maintain itself, this reluctance, even resistance and refusal, to change may be conventional religion's greatest disservice to humanity.

A second form of conflation is the fallacy of absolutizing the relative, of attributing absoluteness to that which is relative. This fallacy fails to distinguish between the simultaneity which characterizes Ultimacy in Itself and the duality in human thinking. As we have seen, Ultimacy is simultaneously Absolute in Itself and relative in manifestation. But this does not mean that its manifestations are absolute. Reduction of the Absolute to the relative cuts religion off from its transcendent source and robs it of transforming power. A common instance of this fallacy occurs when scripture itself is treated as the final authority. A preacher in a radio sermon repeatedly proclaimed, "The Bible says," by way of authenticating his various points; not a single reference was made to God. In some fundamentalist households, the Bible must always be open with nothing ever placed on top of it. Far worse is treating the relative as if it were Absolute; this results in arrogance, religious imperialism, and war.

A third form of the conflation fallacy is that of materializing the spiritual, of treating that which is essentially spiritual as if it were material. Those who literalize scripture tend to fall victim to this fallacy. A clergyman once declared in a sermon that a sufficiently powerful rocket ship could carry one to heaven, that heaven is as "geographically real" as New York City or London. In its most extreme forms, exotericism even succumbs to idolatry. Idolatry can manifest in belief as much as in material figures. When fundamentalism rails against the idolatry of so-called paganism or exoteric forms of worship in Eastern religions, it may well be empowering itself subliminally by its own unacknowledged idolatry of belief, of unconsciously attributing absoluteness to the necessarily limited, intellectual formulations of who God is. Scripture can be subverted to idolatry as easily as stone, wood, or metal, as we just saw when the Bible's heaven is made a physical place.

Disjunctive Fallacy

At the same time that exoteric religion is succumbing to the conflation error, it may be falling victim to an opposite fallacy, the disjunctive or dissociative fallacy. This fallacy commonly takes two forms: (1) imposing distance where there is none and (2) radicalizing difference to the point of blindness to similarity and unity. An example of the first can be seen in the common stance found in most exoteric religions regarding the 'location' of God. In spite of formal pronouncements to the contrary, God tends to be seen as distant, as elsewhere, usually 'out there', sometimes 'up there'. In religious discourse—whether of the formally trained or of the religious masses—this will be denied since God is almost universally affirmed to be omnipresent. Nonetheless, in worship settings, God's presence is sometimes formally invoked, as if God is absent until invited to be present: "Come, O thou God of grace, dwell in this holy place, e'en now descend."[10]

Locating God spatially elsewhere is not so much a considered position as an uninvestigated presumption. Most religious people simply live their lives *as if* God is somewhere else, some place other than where they live their lives moment by moment. Ordinarily, only in the rarest of instances and for brief intervals is God sensed as here and now, as an immediate, realized presence.

A second case of the disjunctive fallacy may come into play as exoteric religion contributes to the formation of personal identity, i.e., as it helps shape the self-sense of its members. This role of exoteric religion builds on the need of every human being to feel part of a group and, at the same time, to be a distinct person, to have a personality and possess qualities that are unlike those of anyone else. We need to simultaneously belong and stand out. Especially during the first few decades of life, we incorporate into ourselves the qualities and features of those we admire. But we also need to be unique. So our emulation and incorporation of admired qualities is integrated into what we take to be our own individuality.

Even though the process is usually unconscious and unquestioned, everyone is driven by the need to be somebody special within the context of a group that shares common values. This process is sometimes called "somebody training". And religion, especially exoteric religion, plays a crucial role in forming and contributing to this personal identity based on both shared and distinctive features. To belong to a particular religion provides both acceptance within the group and distinctiveness in relation to other religions. One's personal identity takes on solidity and confidence by right of identification with a particular religion whose beliefs and practices are declared to be true and right.

Unfortunately, often added to this position is another that is assumed to follow, namely, that because one religion is true and right other religions must be false and wrong. Difference becomes divisive as it gets extended to an unbridgeable gulf between true and untrue, valid and invalid, even good and evil. The psychological need for personal distinctiveness oversteps its legitimacy when it declares other persons or religions, equally distinctive, to be in error. The dualizing function of the mind distorts to a simplistic, "I'm right; therefore, you're wrong." The need to be unique and somebody special succumbs to the temptation to fulfill that need by demeaning others. The rightful pursuit of a distinctive self-sense gets subverted into an ill-founded attack on that which is simply different. Unfortunately, exoteric religion, particularly in its fundamentalist forms, tends to play a major role in this process. The result of succumbing to the disjunctive fallacy is exclusivity and discord.

To summarize, the conflation fallacy errs by conjoining what must remain distinct and distinguishable within the ordinary setting of time and space. By blurring necessary distinctions, exoteric religion subverts Ultimacy and religion to narrow interests and ends up artificially separating itself from much of humanity and sometimes even the natural world, often with devastating effects. Some religious groups actually justify their existence with the rallying cry: "Come out from them, and be separate" (2 Cor. 6:17). In spite of overpopulation and ecological destruction, some continue to blindly and arrogantly justify their theological stance and self-interest with the so-called divine command: "Be fruitful and multiply, and fill the earth and subdue it" (Gen. 1:28).

We have seen similar and equally harmful effects resulting from the disjunctive fallacy, which imposes difference and division where none exists. Whether a variety of the conflation or disjunctive fallacy, or a combination of several fallacies in a single belief, these kinds of distortions cause some members and outsiders a great deal of consternation, frustration, and anxiety. They lead to views and actions that give rise to indifference to religion on the part of some and outright opposition on the part of others. They frequently contribute to views and practices that inhibit personal transformation. And worst of all, they sometimes so totally misrepresent the authentic nature of religion that war erupts and mass death results.

Most humans are born into exoteric forms of religion, and die in these same forms. But some few become aware of the limitations outlined above and adopt one of several courses of action. Following the exhortations of their religion, they may quell their doubt and continue to believe and practice. They may do this nominally, i.e., in a routine and perfunctory fashion, or they may muster enthusiasm and continue to be 'faithful' with great energy. Some may be motivated by a sense of obligation to their friends and the group to continue supporting the beliefs, practices, and programs.

Quite a different response to seeing the shortcomings in religion is to reject religion entirely, to espouse agnosticism or atheism. It would be interesting to know how many avowed agnostics and atheists hold their position because they have never come to know a religion founded on an adequate view of Ultimacy. Agnostics and atheists are to be respected who reject religion because the views of God advocated there are too small, are inadequate to their sense, unclear though it may be, of what an adequate God must be. Their courage and authenticity in refusing to affirm a god that is no God is commendable, even as it indicts the religion in question.

A third way of responding to the fallacies, limitations, and inadequacies is to look for an alternative way of being religious. In some cases, this may simply lead to a transfer of allegiance to another exoteric form of religion, thereby constituting a lateral shift. In other cases, however, rather than suppress doubt and 'pretend', or reject religion outright, the disaffected may go deeper into religion to explore beyond the common forms. This courageous and adventuresome undertaking typically leads to esoteric religion.

Some forms of exoteric religion open up to other religious expressions and acknowledge to varying degrees their authenticity. When this is the case, we may already be in the presence of persons who are beginning to move toward esoteric religion. As maturing humans desire a more harmonious and inclusive stance in relation to other humans and the world at large, they may well find themselves questioning the received traditions: political, social, moral, as well as religious. The doubt that arises in the context of exoteric religion is precisely the motivating force for reinterpreting, for going beyond, for reaching deeper—for opening to esoteric religion.

Esoteric/Mystical Religion

The term 'esoteric' refers to that which is hidden, not obvious. It also carries the connotation of secret. Esoteric religion is secret, however, not in the sense of something haughtily or selfishly withheld, but in the sense of something withheld until there is evidence that the potential recipient is ready to receive it, is mature enough to understand and assimilate what is to be transmitted. Esoteric also implies a quality of experience, realization, or awareness that cannot be conveyed by words, as words are customarily used. The words used to convey esoteric religion can never be taken literally. They always point beyond themselves toward that which must be intuited, sensed, felt into, even imagined without imagery. They point toward a realm of transcendence that concept and the thinking mind cannot enter, the same general realm toward which paradox points when the thinking mind reaches its limits.

Esoteric religion is discovered anew by each generation on the basis of self-investigation and careful consideration of the human condition, even while being guided by expressions of both exoteric and esoteric religion. Esoteric religion builds on and deepens what is presented in exoteric tradition, the principal difference lying in the more symbolic/less literal, more experiential/less formal interpretations applied in the esoteric orientation.

Esoteric tends toward the inward and the spiritual rather than the outward and the historical or institutional. Some regard it not as a form of religion but as a purely spiritual venture. But this is to limit religion unduly to institutional forms. Esoteric religion may also be characterized as acosmic, unbound by the conditions that prevail in the time-space continuum. Esoteric awareness penetrates deeply into consciousness, which, as we have seen, is essentially open and unlimited. Similarly, as exoteric religion is dynamically involved with the forms or outer expressions of religion as they exist in the objective world, esoteric religion is more subjectively involved with these forms, not content to simply identify with existing beliefs and practices but penetrating into their essence in order to discover their abiding or essential meaning and significance. To put it most concisely: exoteric religion is concerned with the outer existence of religion, esoteric with its inner essence. The former is historical, the latter ahistorical. Even though culturally conditioned words and practices may be used to foster esoteric realization, the realization itself is transverbal; it is devoid of words since the very act of conceptualization, of thinking by means of words and concepts, impedes the awareness represented by esoteric religion in its purest expression.

Esoteric religion is mystical religion. Neither term, esoteric or mystical, has anything to do with the bizarre, the occult, or the superstitious, though these terms are sometimes popularly used as if they mean the same thing. As employed here, mysticism refers to the very heart of religion, to that profound experience of Ultimacy that gives rise to the authentic forms of exoteric religion. Mysticism denotes an experience which extends over various degrees of oneness. Specifically, these experiences range from an awareness of presence (accompanied by a sense of connection or harmony), to an even stronger sense of union (intimate conjoining), to unity (absorption into something other than oneself), and, finally, to nonduality (awareness of all things as not different from oneself). Mystics are those who feel themselves drawn deeply into the presence, union, unity, or nonduality with that which is unquestionably real. In each case, the so-called 'object' of the mystical experience is different; the sense of presence is either with the world of nature or God, union is with God, unity is with the formlessness of Ultimacy, and nonduality is with Ultimacy and everything.

Union mysticism tends to be characteristic of theistic religions. As used here, union implies the coming together in intimate harmony of two distinguishable entities or forces, the worshipper and the worshiped, the lover and the beloved, the human and the divine. When in mystical union, mystics are typically aware only of themselves in devotional submission to God, all else vanishes from awareness, only they and God are. On returning to conventional waking consciousness, they know that everything has changed. They now feel more connected and harmonious with God and all that He represents than ever before. They feel more loving, more centered, and more confident in their relationship to Ultimacy. They may feel more connected and comfortable, at least in the days immediately following their experience, with that which arises in the ordinary course of daily activities. They live with a relaxed certitude based on knowing that God is at the heart of all things; God is in charge. In union mysticism, the mystic conjoins with Ultimacy in Its manifestation as a personal God. The mystic no longer simply believes that God is personal; he or she now knows it.

In unity mysticism, on the other hand, mystics cease to be aware of themselves as specific persons. All sense of personal separateness disappears as they are absorbed into the formlessness of Ultimacy. Only Ultimacy is. The subtle, ever-present sense of being distinct from everything else dissipates into the overwhelming presence of the One. The separate-self sense that characterizes ordinary awareness entirely vanishes. Self-identity becomes that of Ultimacy. Awareness is infinite and eternal. Pure consciousness prevails. To use a metaphor from India, the drop of water becomes absorbed into the ocean, becomes/is the ocean. Li Po, a Chinese mystic, wrote: "The birds have flown from the sky; the last cloud now fades away. We sit together, the mountain and me, until only the mountain remains."[11] In unity mysticism, the mystic disappears into Ultimacy Itself, as Li Po disappeared into the mountain. On returning to the consciousness marked by time and space, which can no longer be merely conventional, the mystic's sense of self in relation to others parallels that described above, but may also incline him or her toward a metateric outlook, to be treated shortly.

Esoteric religion suggests a modification of our working definition of religion as the human response to what is viewed as Ultimacy. The focus now is on personal transformation and the inward presence of Ultimacy. Religion now becomes an increasingly spiritual process of personal transformation. Transformation occurs by means of transcendence, of moving through and rising above. Moving through implies fully experiencing; rising above indicates releasing. One who transcends embraces life entirely but also detaches subjectively from all that is not one's deepest nature and objectively from all that is conditional and temporal. Transcendence takes place by disidentifying with one's usual sense of self, by dissolving the mind-made boundaries that cause fragmentation within oneself and separation or estrangement between oneself and the rest of reality. Ongoing commitment to a psychospiritual discipline is normally required to facilitate this degree of transcendence.

Conventional religion promotes personal change by urging practitioners to live according to the standards of God and one's particular religion. On the other hand, esoteric religion requires not just change but transformation. Change indicates a rearrangement of elements at the given level of awareness, the level of the ordinary mind; it is a horizontal movement. For example, to change a room one might paint the walls, rearrange or buy new furniture. To exchange one belief for another or to convert from one religion to another probably indicates exoteric change, a lateral shift. Personal transformation calls for movement to a new level of awareness; it is vertical movement. For example, the ceiling may be raised, walls moved out, doors and windows relocated and widened; a different use of the room may occur. To actually experience unity with Ultimacy, to discover an integrating principle and become more comfortably aligned with reality indicates esoteric/mystical transformation; this is raising/deepening consciousness.

We saw the need of all humans to develop a distinct identity, which we called the drive to become somebody special, and the role that religion plays in that process. Because of the emphasis on inwardness in esoteric religion and the requirement to disidentify with all that we normally take to be ourselves, the parallel drive might well be to become nobody, to become so thoroughly detached that no sense of self as separate exists at all. Certainly in profound states of meditation, nobody is to be found. The effect of this meditative awareness, especially when coupled with detachment in the waking state, undermines the gross and subtle forms of the assumed specialness and self-preference that prevail in the self-awareness of most people. As one detaches from one's own bodymind, one becomes nobody special. This process has been called "nobody training."

Limitations in Esoteric/Mystical Religion

While esoteric religion represents a developmental advance over exoteric religion, it too is susceptible to limitations and distortions. For example, a possible—but certainly not inevitable—distortion concerning self-identity would be to regard oneself as special because one is nobody special, that is, to assume superiority in reference to the masses who are seen to be driven by the narcissistic need to be somebody special. This, of course, is another version of the same spirit of elitism that may plague exoteric religion. Because of the extraordinarily pleasant tranquility and expansiveness realized in esoteric states of awareness, a second limitation occurs if one becomes so attached to these states that one begins to denigrate ordinary awareness and material reality. The conditions and events of the time-space continuum may be devalued and shunned. One may fall victim to withdrawal and quietism, a state commonly disparaged as navel-gazing. But these, of course, are erroneous and fallacious misinterpretations of the esoteric perspective. A third error pertains to a possible dualism. Because the esoteric orientation is inward, paralleling the exoteric outlook as outward, some who engage this second stage of religious evolution may believe that a real divide exists between the spiritual reality they have come to experience and physical or material reality. They may assume an implicit dualism as invidious as that found in the common forms of exoteric religion. The over-valuation of the material pole of a material-spiritual duality has simply been replaced by the over-valuation of the spiritual pole. In both cases, one dimension is acknowledged to the diminishment of the other. The either/or fallacy has imposed a split on reality that is not there, that seems to exist only because of the dualizing function of the mind.

The exoteric and esoteric persuasions are in competition with each other only when either succumbs to the distortions to which they are prone. Each becomes fallacious only in the absence of the other. Rightly understood, exoteric and esoteric are complementary and mutually supportive, in fact, are essential to each other—if authentic religion is to prevail. Exoteric without esoteric is shallow form; esoteric without exoteric is vacuous formlessness. Without the esoteric, the exoteric is pretense; without the exoteric, the esoteric is private indulgence. When either is absent to the other, distortion inevitably ensues. The proper relationship between the esoteric and exoteric is parallel to that between experience and expression.

As human beings we express who we are by means of action, gesture, sound, and word. As communal beings we create community by means of communication. What we try to communicate, or express, is our experience. Three factors must be considered in order to understand the relationship between experience and expression. First, the expression of an experience is not the experience. There is an immediacy in experience that is absent in the expression of the experience. Expression is based on recall, on reconstruction, and therefore is after the fact. To understand the deeper dimensions of human experience, it is crucial to be aware of the fundamental difference between an experience in itself and the expression of that experience.

Most of our experience is quite common and more-or-less readily communicated. But occasionally we experience something that is more difficult to share. Many have experienced nature in a particularly meaningful way: a striking sunset, a star-lit sky in the country, a fresh blanket of snow in the mountains, at sea surrounded by vastness, deep in a forest under majestic trees. If we have ever tried to share the experience with another person, we invariably will have come away feeling as if we failed to convey the meaningfulness and richness of the experience. The problem is not one of language; the problem is inherent in the very task we set ourselves. Even if we knew every word in every language, the problem would remain; words are not the experiences, they merely describe it.

A second feature of the experience-expression relationship is that the expression of an experience is always less than the experience itself. There is always reduction, a loss of immediacy, of quality, of sensation, of awareness—none of which can be accurately portrayed by means of words, much less captured by or contained in words. Everyone knows through personal experience what love is. But who can say what love is? All the songs, poetry, novels, dramas, choreography, statuary, scholarly treatises, even scriptural and commentarial literature, all of these expressions of love, even combined, fail to articulate what love is as an experience.

The third reason for loss when attempting to couch experience in words arises from the profundity of experience: the more profound the experience, the more inadequate the expression. At the top of the list of profound human experiences is the mystical experience. Therefore, it follows that mystical experience is one that least lends itself to description. Mystics are virtually of a single voice in admitting the inadequacy of their words. They are frequently misunderstood, even charged with heresy, because their words fail to do justice to the unique quality of their experience of oneness. In this sense, their words betray them, particularly when interpreted literally by those locked into an exoteric focus. Therefore, mystics are forced—if they are to give verbal expression to this most profound of experiences—to make use of symbol, metaphor, myth, paradox, and finally, silence. Mystics often use poetry to minimize the constraints of prose. The Tao (pronounced and frequently written 'Dao') is the term of choice for Ultimacy in Taoism. The Tao Te Ching begins: "The tao that can be told is not the eternal Tao. The name that can be named is not the eternal Name."[12]

How does this digression on experience and expression relate to our discussion of esoteric and exoteric religion? Experience and esoteric have to do with inwardness. Expression and exoteric have to do with outwardness. Esoteric has to do with profound experiences of Ultimacy; exoteric has to do with the expressions of those experiences. The expressions of esoteric experience give rise to exoteric formulations, to the forms—words, symbols, myths, beliefs, rituals, etc.,—that make up religion as conventionally understood and practiced. Thus, authentic exoteric religion, exoteric religion devoid of distortion and fallacy, is comprised of forms—formulations or expressions—inspired by the deep spiritual and mystical experiences of its founders, reformers, saints, prophets, and sages. What the founders, restorers, and revitalizers of a religious tradition express as their experience becomes the content making up the tradition.

Clearly, the authoritative voice in most religions is that of the ancients, the founders. Their expressions, typically few and enigmatic, are invariably interpreted again and again by the time they reach contemporary times. Many of these interpretations emerge from the same deep awareness that informed the founders, successors, and reformers. Others do not. Some represent a dilution, digression, and even mistaken departure from the insight and spirit of the earlier formulations. A wholly valid and enriching exposition of a profound encounter with Ultimacy can only ensue from those who have comparable encounters. Anything less will diminish and distort according to the egoistic, limited, and separative tendencies in the mind of the interpreter.

The exoteric forms of religion (having originated as more-or-less accurate expressions of mystical encounters with/in/as Ultimacy) constitute religion as it is commonly observed in all cultures. As we have seen, these forms constitute the religion of the vast majority of people. Consequently, they tend to become identified not only with religion but as religion; they are religion. This is where the fallacy of fixity and finality begins to take hold. If one fails to distinguish between symbol and its referent, myth and its meaning, belief and its intent—in a word, between expression and its originating experience—one is apt to equate the forms of public religion with the life-transforming encounters with/in/as Ultimacy that inspired those forms. Add to this the fact that the original expressions, after centuries of interpretation and re-interpretations, as well as translation into different languages, are undoubtedly altered and sometimes even reduced to mere form, formulation, formula, and formalism. Such is the ever-present danger in exoteric religion.

Those of esoteric sensibility may come to see that the forms of conventional religion are so far removed from the experience that initiated them that they cease to point to that experience; they no longer open to Ultimacy. Having become rigid and formalized, they may even have taken on the property of idolatry. Those who intuit the truth of mysticism tend to see more clearly than others that the forms of their religion are expressions of the ultimate experiences of those most highly revered in their tradition, experiences to which they may themselves aspire. They may be drawn to take up spiritual practice in order to come to full mystical awareness themselves. The authentic dimensions of their religion, if they can discern them among the merely exoteric forms, may become the motivation and the means to personally discover oneness with Ultimacy.

Others with esoteric propensities may find themselves attracted to alternative religions where deep personal experience seems more openly valued. When any religion becomes merely exoteric, some will turn to other religions for their spiritual succor. To be sure, there are esoteric expressions opening to infinitude in all the world religions. But if the mystical is not apparent in one's own religion, one may be inclined to look elsewhere.

Still others may be nurtured more by non-traditional formulations of spirituality, formulations that fall outside the framework of traditional religion, formulations in poetry and ritual that may be regarded as bizarre or heretical by the conventionally religious. Just as no form is adequate to Ultimacy, widely disparate forms may open to Ultimacy. Deep interest in spirituality and mystical experience indicates an esoteric yearning for direct, personal communion with Ultimacy. True to the spirit of mystical thirst, it may matter little in which historic religion, if any, the expressions occur.

Metateric/Nondual Religion

If one appreciates the carrying capacity and expressive richness of exoteric religion, the immediate and vital experience of esoteric religion, and couples this with awareness of the errors and limitations in each, one may be opening to the perspective here called metateric. The prefix 'meta' denotes both 'along with' and 'beyond'. To this extent, it conveys much the same sense as 'trans'. Thus, metateric religion incorporates and carries along with itself that which is of continuing validity in both the exoteric and esoteric perspectives, while moving beyond each to a continuing affirmation with new integration of these respective, valid insights.

More than either exoteric or esoteric, the metateric outlook (or 'outinlook') rests comfortably in paradox and ambiguity. It is radically inclusive; the both/and stance reigns supreme. 'Meta' also indicates 'occurring later or in succession' as well as 'more highly evolved or specialized'. Finally, it denotes a transformation in respect to earlier stages. Given these complementary significations, metateric is an apt term to designate the qualities of this third stage of spiritual realization. Because it is a new term, it is important to note that in other writings the term esoteric is commonly used to designate what is here termed metateric. We have already mentioned the shortcomings found among some esotericists: elitism, withdrawal, quietism, denigration of conventional religion, and an implicit dualism. For these reasons, it is desirable to designate a third stage where these limiting perspectives are not found.

We have seen that each way or stage of being religious emerges naturally out of the former—when growth is not impeded. Exoteric religion serves as the nurturing matrix from which esoteric religion emerges. Esoteric religion serves as the nurturing matrix from which metateric religion emerges. We have also seen that each subsequent way serves as a corrective and revitalizing force for the former stages. The esoteric and metateric perspectives serve to ameliorate the limitations that seem to inevitably find their way into exoteric religion. And the metateric serves the same purpose for the esoteric when there is a distortion that appears. Thus, the three stages are interconnected and vital to each other. Distortion occurs only when they become isolated from each other and communication breaks down between them. As mentioned earlier, only from the perspective of a subsequent stage can one see both the limitations and the lasting values in a former way. Because each subsequent stage is increasingly inclusive and integral, it can relate to the former out of greater understanding, acceptance, and charity.

In metateric religion, everything is seen as a manifestation of Ultimacy. Ultimacy is the only reality, simultaneously and indivisibly inside and outside everything, always already. This way of seeing/ being dissolves, integrates, and transcends all duality. All distinctions (sinful/holy, good/bad, inner/outer, subjective/objective, spiritual/ material, sacred/profane, esoteric/exoteric) cease to have final or ultimate significance, though they continue to have expedient or conventional meaning. Common distinctions allow the metatericist to continue to name, to categorize, and to see the order and meaning that most people recognize in conventional reality. In a word, they enable relationship and communication.

At the same time, the metatericist knows that those not at this third stage need a sense of identity and security as a base for their continuing growth and development. Therefore—and unlike some at the esoteric stage—a metatericist has an accepting, encouraging, and charitable attitude for those engaged in the other ways of being religious, and even for the irreligious. The metatericist knows that no one comes to this last stage without first passing through the earlier ones. The exoteric and esoteric ways of being religious are seen as learning and practice phases preparing for the metateric, but only when those in these stages continue to open to and engage authentic transformational perspectives and practices. Metatericists know that Spirit pervades all dimensions of life and that those open to Spirit continue to mature and evolve until they eventually see that Spirit, i.e., Ultimacy, is the only, truly Real.

The sage/saint of this stage identifies with and as everybody. Even as exotericists are driven to become somebody special and esotericists to be nobody in particular, metatericists have so thoroughly dropped all sense of self-preference, and feel so completely at one with others that they can be said to have become everybody. They know no fear because, as paraphrased from a Hindu text, where there is no other there is no fear.[13] Metatericists have rediscovered their original nature, their original mind, a nature/mind at one with Ultimacy and therefore without the distortions of conditioning and culture. Consequently, metatericists are content and supremely happy—in themselves, with others, and with whatever circumstances happen to prevail.

This extraordinary way of being prevails because metatericists see life as seamless, as an interactive whole with everything intermeshing harmoniously, and themselves as part of this whole (as a specific body/mind) as well as one with the whole. This awareness derives from knowing that the sacred is not different from the profane, that eternity is not different from time, that being is not different from becoming, indeed, that Ultimacy is not different from this ordinary world of time and space, in each case distinguishable but not different. Metatericists continue to be aware of the entitizing, dualizing, and thus distorting operations of the ordinary thinking mind. Their profound experience in the presence of non-dual Ultimacy, however, enables them to participate actively in the conventional world even as they rest easily in the acosmic world.

Because metateric religion is the culmination of religious experience and the focus of this book, it seems advisable in this introductory chapter to anticipate the fuller treatment yet to come by mentioning a few instances of its presence in the world religions, especially given its rarity among the religious and irreligious masses.

The central doctrine of Christianity, the incarnation, attests to the inseparability of the transcendent and the immanent, or the supernatural and the natural. Jesus the Christ is wholly man and wholly God. Henri Le Saux/Abhishiktananda, a Hindu/Christian monk who will be introduced more fully later, addresses Christ as the perfect integration of these seemingly different realms: "In the whole world there is no form which is not yours, which does not conceal you from the ignorant and reveal you to the one who knows."[14] Meister Eckhart, the thirteenth/fourteenth-century German mystic, writes: "We should accept all things equally from God, not ever looking and wondering which is greater, or higher, or better. We should just follow whatever God points out for us, that is, what we are inclined to and to which we are most often directed, and where our bent is. God is in all modes, and equal in all modes, for him who can take Him equally."[15] In similar vein, William Blake observes: "He who sees the Infinite in all things sees God."[16] Using metaphors informed by the Bible, the nineteenth-century British poet Elizabeth Barrett Browning is of similar mind when she declares: "Earth's crammed with heaven, and every common bush afire with God."[17]

Muslim mystics are fond of confessing: "I did not see anything without seeing God before it and after it and with and in it."[18] Shibli, a tenth-century Sufi of Baghdad, puts it even more succinctly: "I never saw anything except God."[19] A thirteenth-century Egyptian Sufi, Ibn ᶜAtā'illāh, exclaims: "He who knows God contemplates Him in everything."[20] Jilāl ad-Dīn ar-Rūmī, arguably the most revered mystic poet in Islam, sets forth a view identical to that quoted above from Abhishiktananda: "Every particle of the world, one by one, is a fetter for the fool and a means of deliverance for the wise."[21] Imam Malik, founder of one of the major Islamic schools of law, affirms the need to integrate the exoteric and esoteric: "Whoever has the outer Law without the inner Reality has left the right way; whoever has the inner reality without the outer Law is a heretic; whoever joins the two of them has realization."[22]

In Hinduism's most widely read sacred text, the Bhagavad Gita, Krishna, incarnation of the God Vishnu, lauds the one "who sees Me everywhere and sees all in Me." Elsewhere he proclaims: "He who sees the supreme Lord abiding equally in all being . . . , he (truly) sees."[23] India's Noble Prize winning poet, Rabindranath Tagore, contends: "When you know that whatever there is is filled by him [God] and whatever you have is his gift, then you realize the infinite in the finite, and the giver in the gifts." Confirming another metateric perspective, Tagore notes that "true spirituality . . . is calmly balanced . . . in the correlation of the within and the without."[24] Krishnamurti, one of India's chief philosopher saints of the twentieth-century, declares: "You will not understand the Beloved until you are able to see Him in every animal, in every blade of grass, in every person that is suffering, in every individual."[25] One of the central religio-cosmic principles of Hinduism, *maya*, maintains that every single thing making up reality both is and is not the Ultimate; everything simultaneously reveals and conceals Ultimacy.

The famous ox-herding pictures of Zen Buddhism depict the entire transformational path in ten stages. The early scenes represent the exoteric stage. The eighth scene consists of an empty circle, symbolizing mystic absorption in Ultimacy. The tenth and culminating scene shows the monk back in the market place living an ordinary life, thus attesting to his realization of the ultimate identity of *samsara* (bondage) and *nirvana* (liberation). The Heart Sutra proclaims: "Form does not differ from emptiness, emptiness does not differ from form. That which is form is emptiness, that which is emptiness form."[26] Fa-tsang, the Chinese proponent of Hua-yen Buddhism, draws on the Heart Sutra to show the essential integration of Buddhism's cardinal virtues, wisdom and compassion. He declares: "When one sees that form is empty, one achieves great wisdom and no longer dwells in samsara. When one sees that emptiness is form, one achieves great compassion and does not dwell in nirvana."[27]

Summary

In the foregoing survey of consciousness, Ultimacy, and religion, we have seen how the thinking mind projects disjunction, division, and discord onto integral reality and how that misperception typically conditions one's view of God or Ultimacy. We have also seen how one's view conditions one's involvement in religion, of which three different but interrelated forms exist. Two of these, exoteric and esoteric, are based on an assumed separation between outer and inner, material and spiritual, profane and sacred, and are thus dualistic, the first explicitly so, the second implicitly so to the extent that it minimizes ordinary reality. The third, metateric religion, recognizes the impossibility of either pole without the other, and is thus nondualistic. These three ways of being religious are found in all major religions of the world, in the smaller ones as well, and in the practice of many individuals who align with no specific tradition.

The following four chapters introduce the world's two largest Eastern and two largest Western religions. Exoteric forms are introduced to provide a context for understanding the esoteric and metateric forms, which, as we have seen, grow out of and advance the former. Only rarely will specific forms of the religions be identified as exoteric, esoteric, or metateric. Several reasons inform this reluctance to classify specific experiences or practices. First, in principle, the three ways are so mutually interrelated that fixed boundaries between them cannot be established. Each way represents different emphases, tendencies, orientations, dispositions; each is fluid and open in that individuals can move in and out; they can cross the distinguishing lines. Rather than sharply demarcated, the three stages/ways are best envisioned on a continuum, each flowing into and overlapping the next. Second, personal transformation is a fluid process involving advance and retreat. In other words, particularly as an individual approaches transition from one stage to the next, personal experience will oscillate between the stages, the person will be in one stage in some ways and in another in other ways. Third, because the ways of being religious pertain to inner experience, they are liable to misinterpretation by an outside observer. Delineating might prove inaccurate. Only the practitioner knows his or her experience, i.e., the disposition of the heart and the content of the mind.

So what is the value of this enterprise to delineate three ways of being religious, three stages of religious development? What is its justification? Why the exercise? There are three reasons. First, it enables us to survey the world's major religions by focusing on their experiential dimensions in contrast to most books in the field that focus on the history, the sacred texts, the beliefs and rituals, or the theology of the religions. These topics will be included here but only as background to the religion as a whole and to provide a context for understanding the transformational modes. Second, by drawing on the actual experience of those who make up religion, i.e., those at various levels of realization, a scale of advancement can be seen that demonstrates empirically that religio-spiritual experience can and does evolve. Third, seeing how religious experience evolves can be of value to a reader who may be drawn to a deeper exploration of her or his own religio-spiritual life. The interested reader can locate his or her present state of religious awareness and involvement on the continuum of human religiosity. The stages can serve as a scale for self-assessment that may motivate one to expand his or her sense of self, other, world, and Ultimacy. Finally, a caveat: to use the scale as a means of disparaging the religious views or practices of others would be an egregious act that benefits no one.

The term 'religion' has dominated our discussion so far with 'spiritual' appearing occasionally. We need to clarify the distinctions between the two. In common language, religion denotes an organization with religious specialists, authoritative scriptures, traditional beliefs, customary rituals, and prescribed standards of behavior. Religion, in the customary sense of the term, is institutionalized. Spirituality cannot be organized or institutionalized; it lacks the fixed demarcations required for such structuring. The term religion is usually applied to what we have called conventional or exoteric religion. While spiritual experiences certainly occur in traditional religion, the extent to which they entail fundamental personal transformation is limited compared to the depth and profundity of transformation at the esoteric and metateric levels. Religion at its best prepares the way for deep spiritual awareness and ultimate realization. As emphasized earlier, spirituality in the sense of mystical experience, or non-mediated awareness of the divine, is the very core of authentic religion.

The Evolution of Consciousness and Religion

As we have seen, religious experience evolves—or can evolve—through three unfolding, deepening, and expanding ways. These three ways represent religio-spiritual development that follows an inherent pattern in our nature as humans. That is, built into our constitution is a 'mechanism' that enables us to mature in ever deepening and expanding ways, providing we become exposed to the necessary external conditions, and practice according to proven methods. Familiarity with the developmental patterns enables us to see more clearly how the evolution of consciousness leads to religious experience that moves from exoteric through esoteric to metateric.

Investigation of the mind and its evolution has been pursued by philosophers and scholars since classical times. One may argue whether evolution has occurred between species, specifically whether humans have evolved from earlier primates, but the evidence is virtually incontestable that humans have developed, matured, evolved over time. A remarkable amount of empirical work has been done in recent decades to delineate and clarify the phases of consciousness unfoldment. This work has been undertaken by different scholars working in different cultural settings. Consistency in their findings attests to the reliability of their independently-reached conclusions. The pattern of consciousness evolution presented here is so solidly established by empirical evidence that only someone with a dogmatic belief to the contrary could possibly contest it. This schema is drawn mainly from the work of Ken Wilber and the Integral Institute, founded by Wilber, which promotes a wider understanding of consciousness evolution, and the principles and practices that facilitate ongoing personal transformation.[28]

Wilber builds on and expands the Great Chain of Being, which postulates an emanation of metaphysical and consciousness levels originating in what we have called Ultimacy and descending to the most elementary levels of matter. Wilber himself prefers the expression, the Great Nest of Being, because each higher dimension includes and embraces those lower, similar to a series of concentric circles or Chinese Boxes. The Great Nest consists of levels of being that apply to the natural order, and levels of knowing or consciousness which apply specifically to humans. In a descending scale, these levels range from Spirit to soul to mind to body to matter. Spirit manifests with increasing purity in each ascending level and is also present as the nondual ground or basis of all the levels. Wilber sometimes illustrates this view by referring to a ladder where each higher rung represents increased Spirit and where Spirit is also the material from which the entire ladder is made.

Two ways of studying consciousness, namely, the historical study of its evolution over time and the study of individual psychospiritual development, demonstrate salient parallels between the way humans have evolved throughout time and the way an individual evolves in a given lifetime. Ontogeny recapitulates phylogeny; evolution of an individual follows the same general stages as the evolution, in this case, of humanity. This means that the mental, moral, psychological, religio-spiritual unfolding of a single human will generally move through the same stages as those of the human race. Striking similarities exist, for example, between the mental and moral stages of childhood and adolescent development with the prevailing norm in early human societies, as well as today in some tribal societies and isolated groups of people.

Common ways of marking and labeling the stages of development include: (1) egocentric, ethnocentric, world centric (concern for all people), kosmos centric (concern for the entire biosphere and beyond); (2) prepersonal, personal, transpersonal; and (3) preconventional, conventional, postconventional. Stage development usually occurs at different rates in the different areas of life (developmental areas or lines include moral, intellectual, spiritual, social, etc.) in individuals, and in parallel areas or lines in the historical unfolding of societies. No matter his or her culture, every child begins life at a prepersonal/preconventional level, becomes personal/conventional, i.e., develops personal characteristics and interacts conventionally with other persons and, if growth continues, moves to a transpersonal/postconventional stage.

The fact that moral and other forms of development move through these stages opens the door to some common confusions and mistaken conclusions. For example, because prepersonal and transpersonal are each nonpersonal, it is easy for the undiscerning eye to interpret that which is highly developed as an instance of that which is undeveloped or poorly developed, or vice versa. Also, the postconventional may be misconstrued as preconventional, or vice versa, since each is nonconventional. Wilber calls this the pre/trans or pre/post fallacy, i.e., confusing the beginning and end stages because neither is the middle. A single example will suffice: some writers have argued that advanced mystical experiences are simply cases of infantile regression; others view some early childhood experiences as instances of advanced mystical awareness. Knowing how we develop as humans, including understanding the upper reaches of growth, avoids these kinds of flagrant error.

A pioneering investigator of the evolution of consciousness and culture was Jean Gebser who identified five stages: archaic, magical, mythical, rational, and integrated. Although Gebser's analysis is of immense importance, the last stage in his model does not adequately cover the transpersonal realms that have been more thoroughly investigated in contemporary times. Recent scholarship has refined and extended his fifth stage to include pluralistic, integral, and super-integral. Thus, by combining these transpersonal stages with Gebser's, we get a seven-fold pattern: archaic, magical, mythical, rational, pluralistic, integral, super-integral.

In terms of individual development, the archaic stage represents the generally undifferentiated awareness of infancy. Children, in the next stage, pass through a magical period where Santa Claus, for example, is a real person. Adolescents and adults enter a mythic stage where the conventional beliefs and rituals of religion are regarded as literally true and efficacious. Sacred literature, for example, is believed to be historically accurate and literally true as written. With the development of reasoning, some begin to interpret the myths in allegorical, metaphorical, and symbolic ways. Many others do not reinterpret and, therefore, remain at the mythic stage even though they may exercise their critical thinking in other areas of life. The pluralistic stage is reached when, for example, a person recognizes truth in other religions. Integral awareness is seen in the concern for inter-religious accord; one may become interested in inter-religious dialogue and cooperation. Super-integral is a transrational and transpersonal stage where, among other things, one sees clearly the interconnectedness of all things; nothing exists in isolation. From the rational stage on, impetus toward the higher stages emerges and intensifies. Reaching these stages impels one away from allegiance to an exoteric outlook; the door to the esoteric and metateric opens.

In order to further clarify how we advance from stage to stage we must distinguish stages of consciousness from states of consciousness.

While the former are permanent once they have been reached, the latter are transitory until they have evolved into a stable structure, i.e., until they become the dominant organizational pattern in one's awareness and way of being. The evolutionary process may be seen as one of transforming transient states into the permanent traits of stages. We see this happen in the esoteric stage where mystical experiences begin as occasional, passing states of realization that may transport one to the metateric stage.

These mystical experiences fall into four progressive kinds: nature, deity, formless, and nondual mysticism. Reference was made earlier to the extraordinary but indescribable experience one can have with nature, when in the mountains, at the seashore, under a starry sky. In these natural settings or others, if one feels a profound sense of connection and wholeness with one's surroundings, one is probably having a mystical experience in the ordinary or gross waking state of consciousness (called gross only to avoid confusing it with the still more subtle states). Deity mysticism occurs as a psychic state when one dreams of gods, goddesses, or spirit beings, as well as in mystical states when one has a vision of a divine being. This is the mystical experience designated earlier as one of union. Christian saints tend to have this type of experience. Formless mysticism relates to the causal state of consciousness and is the type we earlier called unity mysticism. In this state, there is no sense of oneself or a specific being; awareness is without any imagery whatever. This state is described by Hindus as *satchitananda*, literally, existence/consciousness/bliss. In this state, one is conscious only of blissful existence. Nondual may also describe formless mysticism but is better reserved for the unity of form and Ultimacy, for oneness with all that arises in the earlier stages and states. As we have seen, nondual best describes the metateric stage of development where one's personal sense is that of being profoundly united and harmonious with all that is, including the exoteric and esoteric stages of religio-spiritual development. The nondual or metateric stage constitutes the awareness of sages.

How do these transient states become permanent traits, i.e., how does one transform from one state to another so that an occasional state of awareness becomes a stable structure of consciousness? A more comprehensive answer to this question is presented in the last chapter of the book where we will discuss some of the main principles and practices of personal transformation. Here, however, as a precursor to that discussion, we may simply note that empirical evidence demonstrates that consistent meditation over time accelerates transition to higher stages. This solid, demonstrable evidence lends support in a scientific age to what the world's religions and wisdom traditions have consistently maintained, i.e., that working with the mind meditatively is the *sine qua non* of personal transformation. Buddhism, for example, describes meditation as the royal road to enlightenment.

Broadly considered, meditation may be thought of as self-exploration, a process of becoming acquainted with the inner workings of one's own mind/heart, a means of gaining personal, incontrovertible insight into the way things are, within oneself and in the world at large. Consistently pursued, this process uncovers new domains of one's own nature that correlate with new ways of seeing and being in the world. Over time and coupled with other transformative practices, meditation contributes to transient states becoming permanent traits.

Another way of understanding meditation in the transformational process is that of gaining new and ever-expanding perspectives. When meditative states, accompanied by expanded and deepened understanding, become structured stages, perspectives enlarge to include more and more of life in its totality. With this fundamental transformation in our perspective, perception changes. Little if anything changes in the external world, but because our way of perceiving changes, we see differently and act differently. For example, even though we may hold views that are markedly different from those of others, we understand how their views stem from their particular stage of evolutionary growth. As a consequence, we are at ease with those views even as we may point out, given an appropriate opportunity, how limiting to themselves or hurtful to others they may be.

Also, we perceive ourselves living a more easeful life than in earlier years, more in harmony with what is. What used to trouble us does so no longer. We feel a deep gratitude for the life we have been privileged to live, with a sense of not having deserved, not having 'earned' the life we now enjoy. At the same time, we perceive more clearly than ever the suffering and confusion that plague so many others. We become more caring and compassionate toward others in light of their suffering, regardless of their ideology or actions, regardless of whether they are victim or victimizer. Though it is a very different kind of suffering, we can see the suffering in those who inflict suffering on others. We feel concern and compassion for all sentient beings even though its expression will take different forms depending on the nature of the suffering. The transformational journey is difficult, but the result is incomparably worthwhile.

A Word about Words

All writers know how difficult it is to communicate accurately what they want to express. Since words are more like symbols (with multiple meanings) than signs (with single denotations), they often carry several connotations, and when linked with other words even more meanings and inferences may arise. Writing about matters of religion and spirituality compounds the problem since the realm of Spirit, though it penetrates the ordinary world, exceeds it as well. Since the unambiguous expression of profound human experience by means of words and concepts (such as love, transcendence, unity, union, nonduality, spirit, Ultimacy, and Spirit) is so difficult and problematic, as we have seen, a burden is placed also on the reader to be sensitive not only to meanings and nuances of meaning, to the author's attempts to clarify, but also to what words intend, to subtleties conveyed as much by context as text. This becomes an especially delicate process when one is endeavoring to understand matters that exceed one's present experience, that point toward perspectives not yet firmly established, and especially those that are inherently elusive because they relate to subjective, inner reality (spirit, consciousness) rather than objective, seemingly definitive matters (things and events).

Several words and expressions have been used rather straightforwardly so far, and will continue to be so used in order to avoid repetitive qualification. These need qualification now. First, even though such words as liberation, enlightenment, realization and achievement are used frequently, some spiritual adepts deny that there is anything to achieve or realize. They make this claim based on the view that this final/ultimate state is actually our present reality and we would know this to be the case if it were not for the contractions of the ego. More will be said about this issue, but in the meantime, given our position in time and space, we will continue to talk about progressing toward this higher realization. Because thinking occurs within the conditions of time, which is customarily believed to move forward, a linear or progressive assumption is ingrained in language.

A related consideration pertains to the perpetual change that marks the unfolding of reality. Given the fact of continual change, on one hand, and the testimony of the world's sages and saints that the eternal/infinite is both other than and integral to the time-space realm, on the other hand, is it ever appropriate to imply finality, conclusion, end (or beginning)? In spite of the first factor and because of the second, many adepts, after realizing what we are calling liberation, realization, etc., contend that nothing new was added, nothing that had not always already existed. The new state is more one of opening to and allowing what is everywhere present and available all the time. Ramana Maharshi, for example, declares: "There is . . . neither path nor achievement: this is the final truth."[29] *A Course in Miracles*, a purportedly channeled work of deep psychospiritual relevance, attests: "The journey to God is merely the reawakening of the knowledge of where you are always, and what you are forever. It is journey without distance."[30]

The way of being religious that we have been regarding the highest, the metateric stage, is one of seeing Ultimacy shine forth in, through, and as oneself, as well as in, through, and as everything that is. It represents a nondual, spiritual awareness that, rather than being just the highest stage, is discovered to be the foundational, all-encompassing, and integral 'Way' that is reality when the distortions of the (merely) thinking mind are removed. This was Blake's seeing when he declared that everything is infinite.

Rather than something one attains or discovers or does, the experience of realization is more akin to a fundamental shift in awareness, analogous to that of waking up from a dream. Some deny that it is an experience at all because of its qualitative difference from all ordinary experiences, invariably colored as they are by ego, personality, and character. So, speaking more precisely, the so-called experience of realization is more a way of being conscious with all aberrations and obstructions removed. Note that this last characterization is by means of negation, identifying that which is absent. As we previously saw, negation is frequently the most accurate way of 'indicating' what cannot be indicated.

Also in order is clarification about the use of prepositions, those little words in English that denote relationship. The notion of moving *toward* or *to* Ultimacy is appropriate in exoteric religion since it operates as if God is different and other than everything else that is known. When someone in exoteric religion claims that God is within, the idea is usually that God is present in addition to other dimensions of oneself. Often in esoteric and always in metateric religion, Ultimacy is deeply 'known', not simply believed, to be omnipresent. Therefore, 'with' and 'as' are appropriate prepositions to indicate the mystical experiences of union and unity. Since Ultimacy is all there is, it is also appropriate to speak of presence and movement *in* Ultimacy. 'To' sometimes functions as a term of interface between exoteric, esoteric, and metateric, thereby suggesting transition from moving toward Ultimacy to being *with* or *as* Ultimacy. When Ultimacy becomes one's entire awareness, the most appropriate prepositions are 'in/with/as'.

Since the approach of this work is phenomenological, an effort is made to use neutral, generic language when treating categories or topics that are common to all or many of the religions. For example, the term transformation is used in this chapter instead of salvation, liberation, or enlightenment because the latter terms name transformation in particular religious traditions, Christian, Hindu, and Buddhist. For the same reason, Ultimacy, Transcendent, etc., are used rather than Brahman or Allah. The language that a specific religion customarily uses is also used in the text when treating that religion. There are a few instances when a term common in Western religions is used when treating a comparable aspect of an Eastern religion. This is done to avoid tiresome repetition and when it aids more accurate understanding.

Finally, to read about religion is not the same as being religious, just as being religious is not the same as realizing Ultimacy. As sometimes stated, map is not territory, menu is not meal, words are not reality. Everything written here is map, in much the same way that religion, or even a rigorous spiritual discipline, is at best a map. Only the reader, in relationship to the Ultimate or in/with/as Ultimacy, can enable map to dissolve into territory.

Notes

1. Carl Woodring and James Shapiro, eds., *The Columbia Anthology of British Poetry*. (New York: Columbia University Press, 1995), 761f.

2. David V. Erdman, ed., *The Complete Poetry & Prose of William Blake*. rev. ed. (New York: Doubleday (Anchor Books), 1988, p. 38.

3. Thich Nhat Hanh, *The Heart of Understanding*. (Berkeley, CA: Parallax Press, 1988); See also his *Interbeing*. (Berkeley, CA: Parallax Press, 1987).

4. Ewert Cousins, trans., *Bonaventure, Classics of Western Spirituality*. (New York: Paulist Press, 1978), 100.

5. Frederick Franck, *The Book of Angelus Silesius*. (Santa Fe, NM: Bear & Company, 1985), 43. (The author has modified the text slightly as found in Franck.)

6. Erdman, *William Blake*. 39.

7. Stephen Mitchell, trans., Tao Te Ching. (New York: Harper & Row, 1988), 56.

8. George C. Berthold, trans., *Maximus Confessor: Selected Writings, Classics of Western Spirituality*. (Mahwah, NJ: Paulist Press, 1985), 156.

9. Ken Wilber, *Integral Spirituality: A Startling New Role for Religion in the Modern and Postmodern World*. (Boston: Integral Books, 2006), 5

10. *Hymnal of the Church of God*. (Anderson, IN: Warner Press, 1971), 31.

11. For a slightly different rendering, see "About a Poem: David Hinton on Li Po's 'Drinking Alone Beneath the Moon'," *Shambhala Sun*, May 2009, 104.

12. Mitchell, Tao Te Ching. 1.

13. Brhadaranyaka Upanisad. 1.4.2. In Patrick Olivelle, trans. and annotator, *The Early Upanisads.* (New York: Oxford University Press, 1998), 45f.

14. Abhishiktananda, *The Secret of Arunachala.* (Delhi: I.S.P.C.K., 1979), ix-x.

15. M. O'C. Walshe, trans. and ed., *Meister Eckhart: Sermons and Treatises.* vol. 3, (Longmead, Eng.: Element Books, 1987), 147.

16. Erdman, *William Blake.* 3.

17. Elizabeth Barrett Browning, Aurora Leigh, Kerry McSweeney, ed., *Oxford World Classics.* (Oxford: Oxford University Press, 1998), 246.

18. Annemarie Schimmel, *Mystical Dimensions of Islam.* (Chapel Hill: University of North Carolina, 1975), 147.

19. Ibid.

20. Victor Danner, trans., *Ibn 'Ata'illah's Sufi Aphorisms.* (Leiden: E.J. Brill, 1973), 47.

21. Reynold A. Nicholson, trans., *The Mathnawi of Jalaluddin Rumi.* vol. 6, (Cambridge: University Press, 1982), 495.

22. As quoted by al-Darqawi and reported in Fadhlalla Haeri, *The Elements of Sufism.* (Rockport, MA: Element, 1993), 113, cf. 49.

23. Eliot Deutsch, trans., The Bhagavad Gita. (New York: Holt, Rinehart and Winston, 1968), 69, 110.

24. Rabindranath Tagore, *Sadhana.* (London: Macmillan, 1957), 148, 127.

25. Mary Lutyens, *Krishnamurti: The Years of Fulfillment.* (New York: Farrar Straus Giroux, 1983), 14.

26. Mu Soeng Sunim, commentator, *Heart Sutra.* (Cumberland, RI: Primary Point Press, 1991), 34.

27. Fa-tsang, "A Brief Commentary on the 'Heart of the Sutra of the Perfection of Wisdom'", in Francis H. Cook, *Hua-yen Buddhism: The Jewel Net of Indra.* (University Park: Pennsylvania State University, 1991), 121.

28. The account given here is drawn from the work of Wilber and others cited in this note. Ken Wilber, *Integral Spirituality; The Spectrum of Consciousness.* (Wheaton, IL: The Theosophical Publishing House, 1977); *The Atman Project: A Transpersonal View of Human Development.* (Wheaton, IL: The Theosophical Publishing House, 1980); *Sex, Ecology, Spirituality: The Spirit of Evolution.* (Boston: Shambhala Publications, 1995); *Integral Psychology: Consciousness, Spirit, Psychology, Therapy.* (Boston: Shambhala, 2000), 5. Most of these books and many others, plus articles, are published in *The Collected Works of Ken Wilber.* 8 vols., (Boston: Shambhala Publications, 1999 to 2000). Two additional, especially significant books are: Jean Gebser, *The Ever-Present Origin.* trans. Noel Barstad and Algis Mickunas (Athens, OH: Ohio University Press, 1985); Don Beck and Christopher C. Cowan, *Spiral Dynamics: Mastering Values, Leadership, and Change, Exploring the New Science of Memetics.* (Malden, MA: Blackwell, 2006). The Integral Institute can be reached at www.integralinstitute.org.

29. Arthur Osborne, ed., *The Collected Works of Ramana Maharshi.* (London: Rider, 1969), 93.

30. Robert Skutch, *Journey Without Distance: The Story behind A Course in Miracles.* (Berkeley: Celestial Arts, 1984), following title page.

II Hinduism: The Mind of Liberation

The mind alone is man's cause of bondage or release: it leads to bondage when attached to the sense objects, and to release when freed from them."—Maitri Upanishad

"One may adopt that path which suits the maturity of one's mind."—Ramana Maharshi

India offers a greater variety of living religions than any other country in the world. In addition to Hinduism, which constitutes the faith of about eighty-five percent of the population, one finds Islam, Jainism, Buddhism, Sikhism, Zoroastrianism (Parsees), even Judaism and Christianity. Like all religions, each of these exhibits varied forms, but none more so than Hinduism, the third largest religion in the world. Here are expressions of religion ranging all the way from subtle spiritual experiences and elusive philosophical speculations to brightly colored pictures of multi-armed deities and popular street rituals accompanied by drums and dancing. In the massive collection of texts that make up Hindu scripture, one easily becomes lost in the vast array of gods and goddesses, myths and symbols, doctrines and practices. Hinduism is, in fact, so multiple and varied that agreement is lacking in what constitutes a Hindu. C.R. Das, when wrestling with this question, concluded—perhaps with a tinge of both exasperation and humor—that a Hindu is anyone who doesn't deny the name when it's applied to him or her. Underscoring the extraordinary inclusiveness of their religion, some Hindus claim that no one is outside of Hinduism.

Hindu Scripture

The Vedas (Sanskrit, knowledge), the earliest Hindu scriptures, which date back to 3000 BCE or earlier, provide the surest means of identifying a Hindu. Accordingly, a Hindu is one who acknowledges the authority of the Vedas. The four books constituting the Vedas serve as the basis for the subsequent development of Hinduism's many holy texts. The earliest and most important Veda is the Rig. Here we meet, in a little over one thousand hymns or poems, about seventy-five different gods and goddesses who reside in three realms: earth, sky, and heaven. Agni, God of Fire, and Soma, a god and an ecstasy-inducing drink made from the juice of a plant, are two prominent earth gods whose principal function is to entice other gods, such as Indra or Varuna, to the worship site. Indra, the most important sky god, is young and robust, fully capable of slaying the evil dragon that withholds the life-giving monsoon rains—if his favor can be won through generous offerings of fire, soma, and food. Varuna, the most righteous of all Vedic deities, a celestial resident, grants forgiveness of sin and freedom from guilt. The sacerdotal emphasis of Vedic religion continues to the present time through the lineage of priestly families, whose meticulous knowledge of proper ritual forms insures influence with the gods.

While ritual and polytheism were dominant in Vedic times, other modes of religious experience and expression also emerged. In the Rig Veda (1.164.46), we find a perspective that contributed powerfully to the formation of major strains in subsequent Hinduism: "To what is one, sages give many a title."[1] This profound insight provides a way of reconciling innumerable gods and a single Ultimate, a way of integrating multiplicity and unity. The religio-philosophical stance of monism begins here. From this and related notions, another, varied, and complex class of scripture arose, the Upanishads.

Upanishad ("to sit down near") refers to the practice of seekers finding a sage and sitting down near him to gain spiritual insight and learn methods that lead to realization. The Upanishads are a vast compendium of spiritual insight that contains much of Hinduism's deepest reflection on religion. They represent a crucial development out of the mainly exoteric religion of the Vedas and, at the same time, contain and anticipate the esoteric/metateric perspectives that mark the continuing unfoldment of Hinduism.

No overview of Hindu scripture, itself a veritable library of spirituality, would be adequate without reference to the Bhagavad Gita (Song of the Lord), the most widely read and influential sacred text in India. Composed prior to the Common Era and incorporated into the Mahabharata, one of India's national epics, the Bhagavad Gita consists of eighteen short chapters in verse form. The text recounts a dialogue between Arjuna, a warrior, and Krishna, his charioteer who is an incarnation of Vishnu, the God of Preservation, which takes place just prior to a battle between two armies made up of cousins. As a member of the warrior caste, Arjuna is beholden to fight, even against relatives, in order to fulfill his duty. Stricken by conscience, Arjuna balks. But Krishna, who employs a variety of arguments (thereby making the Gita a compendium and synthesis of much Hindu teaching), urges Arjuna to fulfill his role, to be true to his lot in life.

Those with pacifist leanings may be appalled that a sacred text would advocate fighting. To conclude that it does, however, follows only from a literal reading of the Gita's plot. If we interpret the Gita symbolically and metaphorically, we find that the battle scene provides a setting for issues of life and death, that is, of spiritual life and death and therefore of utmost significance. As an encounter between relatives within a larger family, the confrontation can be seen as one taking place within an individual, between one's higher, spiritual Self and one's lower, egoistic self. Krishna urges Arjuna to accept the circumstance of his life as an opportunity for transcendence. The given context of one's life, regardless of what it might be, is the place where transformation can occur. Thus, when read as scripture, the Bhagavad Gita is not an historical account of ancient warfare but timeless counsel setting forth perspectives and principles that facilitate liberation. Mohandas Gandhi confessed that during times of personal turmoil he often drew sustenance and guidance from the Gita. Since the twentieth century produced no pacifist more committed to non-violence than Gandhi, we can be confident that he did not understand his favorite sacred text to promote military conflict.

Worldview

Without a sense of meaning, human life fails to thrive. Crucial to a sense of meaning is a sense of belonging, of fitting in. Since the most obvious context of our lives is the natural world, we need to know how we fit into this world, and how this world in turn fits into a still larger reality. Nearly every religion provides an account of creation that enables humans to orient themselves meaningfully to the physical world and the power that produced it. Hinduism is no exception. The Rig Veda offers speculation on creation that is noteworthy, not only because of its antiquity but, more important, because of its profundity and poetic beauty.

> Non-being then existed not nor being:
> There was no air, nor sky that is beyond it.
> What was concealed? Wherein? In whose protection?
> And was there deep unfathomable water?

Death then existed not nor life immortal;
Of neither night nor day was any token.
By its inherent force the One breathed windless:
No other thing than that beyond existed.

But was the One above or was it under?
Creative force was there, and fertile power:
Below was energy, above was impulse.

Who knows for certain? Who shall here declare it?
Whence was it born, and whence came this creation?
The gods were born after this world's creation:
Then who can know from whence it has arisen?

None knoweth whence creation has arisen:
And whether he has or has not produced it:
He who surveys it in the highest heaven,
He only knows, or haply he may know not.
(Rig Veda 10:129.1-3, 6-7)

Most Hindus believe that the 'motive' for creation is play or sport (*lila*). Being self-sufficient, God has no need for anything outside Himself. His creative act is entirely spontaneous and autonomous, totally devoid of any purpose that might imply need or necessity. The view of the Bhagavad Gita, that God incarnates Himself to rectify wrong, does not contradict lila since in neither case is there any self-interest or compulsion. From the perspective of the divine, grace and lila are the same. Some Hindus envision the ultimate aim of human existence to be endless involvement in Krishna's celestial delights, to play forever in His company.

Gods, God, and Ultimacy

While Hindus themselves are not at all troubled by the vast number of gods recognized in the Hindu pantheon, those with a monotheistic heritage usually are. How can there possibly be 330 million gods, a number frequently cited? We have already seen that the Rig Veda regards these as but different names for the One Ultimate. A related but more reasoned synthesis is offered by Advaita Vedanta, one of Hinduism's most profound and comprehensive religious philosophies. Advaita (non-dual) Vedanta (end or aim of the Vedas) was formulated in the ninth century by Shankara (d. 820), one of India's most astute sage-saints. Though he died in his early thirties, his writings set forth what many believe to be Hinduism's most creative and integral system of religious thought and practice. While his thought has been modified by his followers, and contested by those who disagree with him, his system marks a watershed in Hinduism. It was one of the first systems to attempt a comprehensive integration of the great diversity of views found in Hinduism. It offered Hindus an attractive alternative to the growing appeal of Buddhism. And, finally, it set a compelling standard for subsequent religio-philosophical systems.

Advaita Vedanta, following the Upanishads, gives to Ultimacy the name Brahman. Brahman is the transcendental source of all that is, the Absolute beyond which there is nothing more. Brahman, in fact, wholly exceeds the human ability to conceive its nature. It is thus Brahman Nirguna (without attributes, qualities, limitation). Nothing can be postulated of it, "not this, not that" (*neti, neti*). Brahman Nirguna is neither existent nor non-existent. Since Brahman Nirguna is completely unknowable, no relation to it is possible. It cannot be thought about, surrendered to, worshipped, or even resisted.

Existence, as we ordinarily perceive it, is constituted by multiplicity and relationship. Reality is interconnected manyness. How can we account for the connection between the One and the many? What is the link between the Unmanifest Transcendent and the myriadness of immediate experience? According to Advaita Vedanta, and for reasons that are ultimately as unknowable as Ultimacy itself, Brahman Nirguna 'manifested', 'projected', 'displayed', 'extruded', 'expanded' itself in the 'form' of Brahman Saguna, (with attributes). It did this by means of its mysterious power known as *maya* (illusion, appearance), the ability to reveal and conceal at one and the same time. Thus, Brahman Saguna discloses Brahman Nirguna, but that disclosure is simultaneously a hiding, a disguising. The qualities that mark Brahman Saguna are three: *sat* (being, existence), *chit* (consciousness, awareness), and *ananda* (bliss, deep contentment). Because these qualities cannot be said to characterize Brahman Nirguna they act as veils in Brahman Saguna that occlude its ultimate, prior, and essential reality as Brahman Nirguna. Thus, Brahman Saguna is Brahman Nirguna but 'overlaid' with satchitananda, blissfully aware existence. Again by means of maya, Brahman Saguna manifests itself as Maheshvara, the Supreme or Eternal Lord who, out of itself, also by means of maya, produces innumerable *brahmandas* (cosmic eggs) and an equal number of Ishvaras (Created or Personal Lords), each of whom rules over a single cosmos. One of the early texts asserts that it may be possible to count the grains of sand along the banks of the Ganges, but one could never count all the brahmandas, or the gods controlling them.

Among this virtual infinitude of cosmoses is the one we now inhabit. The Ishvara of this cosmos projects himself in three forms: Brahma, the God of Creation, who actually materializes the cosmos, Vishnu, the God of Preservation, and Shiva, the God of Destruction. Brahma, even though appearing frequently in scripture, myth, and iconography, is the least important god in the life of Hindus; his work is completed. Vishnu and Shiva, directly or in one of their several forms, serve as the devotional and theological focus for most Hindus. The pattern of descent into increasingly manifest form continues as Vishnu incarnates in the form of an *avatar* (descent, incarnation). The Bhagavad Gita (4:7-8) declares: "Whenever there is a decay of righteousness and a rising up of unrighteousness, O Bharata, I send forth Myself. For the preservation of good, for the destruction of evil, for the establishment of righteousness, I come into being in age after age." Krishna is Vishnu's incarnation for this period of history. As the God of Destruction, Shiva destroys evil and all that impedes spiritual advance. He wipes out the old to make way for the new. At the end of time, when decay and degeneration are irreversible, he will obliterate the entire cosmos in order to prepare for the emergence of another round of existence. Shiva also assumes other forms; one of the most notable is Nataraj, King of the Dance. Many images and statues are found throughout India depicting Nataraj performing his cosmic dance. He is one of the most popular gods because he combines within himself the entire descent depicted above and provides a means by which his devotees can make the ascent to Ultimacy.

The symbols making up Nataraj's iconic form convey his all-inclusiveness and ultimacy. Three of his hands represent the cosmic processes of creation, preservation, and destruction. The remaining hand points to his suspended foot, which, surrounded by space and free to move in any direction, symbolizes liberation. Liberation is also symbolized by his face; the tranquility, seeming indifference, and non-involvement suggest the nonattachment that leads to liberation. The peacefulness and aloofness of his face, in spite of the vigorous, powerful dance, indicate that liberation can be realized in the midst of a chaotic, tumultuous, and distractive world. Nataraj's feet, as they pound out the thunderous dance, keep the dwarf-demon of forgetfulness under control, thereby undermining the forgetfulness that keeps us from knowing our true nature as not other than divine. The cosmic dance occurs within a circle of fire that supplies the energy that sustains the whole, and the grace that enables transformative alignment within the whole.

The dance of Nataraj reveals a cosmos filled with divine presence and grace, as well as the principles of transformation that attune one to this presence and grace. Devotion to him, coupled with detachment from the appearances and forces that dominate ordinary life, lead to the rediscovery of one's true nature as not different from Ultimacy.

One of the most important insights communicated by Nataraj is a paradox. As a single, specific form of Shiva, Nataraj is a distant deployment of Brahman Nirguna. He is simply one of 330 million gods in one cosmos among a countless number of other cosmoses. But at the same time, mysteriously, inexplicably, paradoxically, he is Brahman Nirguna. One of many is the One. A God is Ultimacy. Part is Whole; Whole is part. Thus, in principle, each of the deities in the Hindu pantheon contains within itself the power and grace to carry a devotee from itself as part to Itself as Whole. Or, to shift the focus to the human level, by moving from attachment to form itself to the essential reality hidden in and as form, an individual can come to the Whole.

Nataraj is not the only instance of one god among many who comes to be seen as the One that comprises the many. Krishna, too, for some who worship him, sustains a similar transfiguration from a single incarnation of Vishnu to become the originating and sustaining principle of all that is. The same is true of Vitthoba, a relatively unknown, rural deity, who was the devotional focus of Tukaram, a 17th century poet-saint whose life we will investigate toward the end of the chapter.

Though rare, notions of interconnection and equivalency of part and whole are not unknown in Western culture. For example, Alfred Lord Tennyson may have had something of this outlook in mind when he wrote:

Flower in the crannied wall,
I pluck you out of the crannies;
Hold you here, root and all, in my hand,
Little flower, but if I could understand
What you are, root and all, and all in all,
I should know what God and man is.

85

William Blake was similarly aware: "Pick a flower and trouble a star." Not only poets but scientists as well have come to similar conclusions. Biologists have shown that a single cell, in the earliest stages of its formation, contains within itself the information that constitutes the entire organism of which it is part. Another instance of part containing whole is demonstrated by a hologram, a three-dimensional image. A holographic plate is produced by sending half of a split laser beam directly from its source to the object being copied and then to the recording plate. The other half reaches the plate after being reflected off a mirror, bypassing the object. As expected, when the plate is projected the entire object is seen. So far there is nothing really different from ordinary photography. However, if a holographic plate is broken into pieces, each piece when projected reveals the entire object photographed, a single piece contains the entire image. Part contains whole. Inconceivable but demonstrable.

Hinduism has long recognized the interconnection and ultimate identity of all things, the deep, essential, single nature that is revealed when reality is read accurately, beyond appearance. Based on an analysis of the empirical world and the bondage that accompanies attachment to it, Hinduism provides clarifying insight into the human predicament. Given its discovery of the essential nonduality of reality, Hinduism also provides ways of overcoming bondage, ways that facilitate transformation from imprisonment as part to liberation as Whole.

The Human Predicament—Bondage

According to Hinduism, the most fundamental problem we humans face is the bondage arising from *samsara,* the endless wheel of becoming, of birth and death. Since Hindus believe in reincarnation, they do not expect death to end the perpetual process of becoming. Death is simply a pause in the endless cycle. Death is followed by birth which begins a new life which in turn passes through death to form still another birth and life. And thus the process continues. *Karma*, the law of cause and effect, sustains the ongoing, cyclical process. The uninterrupted and binding circularity inherent in the law of cause and effect is not immediately apparent, but becomes so on realizing that every effect is simultaneously a cause. At the same time that an effect is derived from a cause, it is a cause for a subsequent effect, which is also a cause for still another effect. Causes cause effects and effects effect causes. There is no end, just perpetual process. Hindus feel trapped in the endlessness of again followed by again followed by many more agains.

Both macrocosm and microcosm are governed by samsara and karma. Universes appear, disappear, and reappear. Individuals arise, pass away, and arise again. As the fundamental structure of the universe, samsara works its effects on many levels. In addition to its cosmic and individual manifestations, samsara applies to the typical workings of the ego. In fact, the bondage and suffering that are implicit in samsara is easily seen in its egoic form. Repeated patterns of thoughtless behavior, as opposed to spontaneous and creative action, are its most obvious expressions. The feeling that accompanies routine activities is usually boredom and discontent. If the patterns become addictive and self-destructive, the ennui may deepen into melancholy and despondency. Samsara names the compulsive behavior over which many feel entirely helpless. In the mind, samsara takes the form of compulsive thinking and fantasizing, rehashing the same old thoughts and images. Emotionally, it appears as the frequent, sudden return, against intention and attempts at control, of such feelings as guilt, fear, anger, sadness. Samsara is experientially undeniable if we admit our repeated failure to be as we would like to be, our bondage to patterns that are disconcerting and unproductive.

Though samsara is the central human problem in Hinduism (and Buddhism), it has not gone unacknowledged in the West. In fact, even in the literature of India one is not apt to find a clearer description of samsara than that of Koheleth, the royal philosopher, as set forth in the opening lines of Ecclesiastes (1:2-9):

Vanity of vanities, says the Teacher,
vanity of vanities! All is vanity.
What do people gain from all the toil
at which they toil under the sun?
A generation goes, and a generation comes,

....

All things are wearisome;
more than one can express;
the eye is not satisfied with seeing,
or the ear filled with hearing.
What has been is what will be,
And what has been done is what will be done;
There is nothing new under the sun.

Though he gave it a different interpretation, Paul, in his letter to the church in Rome (Romans 7:19), confessed to the helplessness felt when one is in the grip of samsara: "I do not do the good I want, but the evil I do not want is what I do." Even some of our common Western aphorisms set forth the samsaric perspective: "What goes around, comes around"; "Like father, like son"; and "The more things change, the more they remain the same."

As we have seen, this perpetual cycle is powered by karma, endless cause and effect. Samsara is also sustained by maya. From the perspective of Ultimacy, as we have seen, maya is the power to simultaneously manifest and hide, the power of the gods and goddesses to disguise themselves in the very showing of themselves. From the human side, maya operates as illusion, the mistaken attribution of reality to that which is unreal. Because of ignorance, the mind is fundamentally deluded. This causes a seeing of what is not, and a failure to see what is. We see through veils and not clearly or directly. Our entire psycho-physical, often even spiritual, experience of the world is occluded by the erroneous assumptions, defenses, projections, repressions, rationalizations, etc., that characterize the mind and filter all experience, whether inner or outer. This is by no means true only of the psychotic or neurotic. Even when we are considered 'normal', our minds are fundamentally qualified by maya.

Hindus illustrate maya by drawing attention to our typical reaction to seeing a snake. Let's suppose we're walking along a narrow jungle path at dusk and come upon a snake. We immediately experience a fright-flight reaction. Breathing may halt momentarily with a gasp, then speed up, our heart beats faster, prickles flush over our skin, our mind shuts down except for the impulse to strike or run. And then we suddenly see that the snake is actually a piece of rope. Our entire reaction was based on a misreading of the actual situation. Similarly, Hindus say, our entire perception of self and world is distorted and colored by the mind's delusionary precondition, by its inherent inability to see reality as it is, therefore, its ignorance.

So far we have understood maya to designate a perceived split between the Real and the unreal, between Ultimacy Itself and Ultimacy in Its manifestations. We can refine our understanding by seeing maya as indicative of both reality and nonreality. Any given thing, event, perception, or experience is both real and not real, real in so far as it is seen as 'sourced' in Ultimacy, unreal in so far as it appears to be other than Ultimacy. A thing is unreal in comparison to its Source, unreal as an appearance in reference to its essential, hidden nature. At the same time, it is real in terms of its manifest form and qualities, real in relationship to other things, entities, factors that constitute its context. Maya means that experiences, perceptions, events, and things are relatively real; their reality is relational, contingent, derived. Since nothing in the phenomenal world is self-sufficient or changeless, since everything is dependent on a prior reality *ad regressus* and on a supportive milieu *ad infinitum*, maya aptly characterizes our everyday experience. Everything appears to be real but is devoid of reality vis-à-vis the larger or final reality, i.e., Ultimacy. Everything that appears is merely an appearance. A drama is real on stage but unreal, at best, relatively real, in reference to the larger world. The make-believe of children is quite real to them but unreal, at best, partially real, in reference to the adult world. Our dreams are very real when dreamed but unreal, at best, somewhat real when interpreted from the vantage point of the waking state.

The illusory nature, at best relative reality, of our experience in and of the world would seem to lock us into a hopeless situation. Endless repetition, bondage, ignorance, and illusion paint a grim picture of the human situation. It is no wonder that Hinduism has sometimes been labeled pessimistic. Pessimistic it would be if it only identified the problem. But Hinduism is an authentic religion and as such it offers a resolution to humankind's predicament of ignorance and entrapment.

Resolution of the Predicament—Liberation

When not thwarted by debilitating karmic accumulations, a Hindu's life is seen to progress through four stages. This classical pattern applies only to males among the three highest castes; though rarely completed, it remains an ideal. Women engage the stages in modified form. The first stage, that of chastity or continence, begins when a boy of eight to twelve is formally initiated. If he is a member of the Brahmin caste, the sacred thread will be given. He is expected to study the ancient traditions, serve his teacher, remain chaste, and practice poverty and simplicity. The second stage is that of the householder and begins with marriage. He carries such obligations as maintaining certain rituals, fathering children, earning a livelihood, and supporting the community. When a man sees his own children reach maturity, he may enter the third stage, that of the forest dweller. He is expected to continue performing the rituals, extend his study of the Vedas, deepen his practice of meditation, and increasingly simplify his life through nonattachment. His wife may accompany him, but they must remain chaste. The final stage, entered by only the stalwart few, is *sannyasa* (renunciation). The practitioner must now wander alone; give up his name, caste, and family; tend no rituals; own nothing; observe *ahimsa* (non-injury) or non-violence; become desireless; and seek only liberation. The *sannyasi* (renunciant) adopts an unencumbered outer life in order to realize a totally free inner life. A sannyasi will usually change his name to indicate that a totally new life is underway. All prior roles and relationships—husband, father, uncle, wage earner, etc.—are dropped. Reminiscing about the past is avoided. The attempt is to be wholly and only aware of the immediate here/now. I was once waiting outside a temple for the evening worship to begin. Hoping to strike up a conversation, I asked a nearby sannyasi where he was from. After a long and for me embarrassing pause, he said, with a chuckle, "I'm a sannyasi," thereby reminding me that a sannyasi has no past, is from nowhere. Here and now is the only reality.

That Hinduism is not a life-denying religion is seen in the four values or goals the tradition upholds as worthy and desirable. The first, *kama*, specifically denotes sexual love. When properly regulated, sexual activity is an authentic value. The Kama Sutra, a collection of aphorisms on love-making, treats sexual pleasure in an objective and reverential fashion, extolling it as an entirely valuable part of human life. The meaning of kama is commonly extended to include all forms of sensual pleasure and, even further, to affirm the general enjoyment of life. The second goal is *artha*, which designates material wealth. To make money in Hinduism is commendable. The concept and the practice refer not only to financial well-being, however. Artha also includes the exercise of whatever power and authority is necessary to insure the harmony of family life and the governance of society.

Dharma, the third value/aim, covers a range of overlapping activities and objectives, i.e., religion, righteousness, ritual performance, moral obligation, and social duty. The fourth goal, *moksha* (release, liberation), is sought by very few Hindus, and realized by even fewer. While a natural progression links the four values, the fourth is in a different category since it requires a total transcendence of the prior three. Pleasure, wealth, and conventional religion are among the conditions from which liberation is sought.

A correspondence exists between the stages and goals of life. Pleasure and enjoyment are most appropriate during the earliest stage, though the one who practices chastity must eschew sexual involvement. A householder is expected to earn a livelihood and, according to his particular social role, contribute to the welfare of the community. On relinquishing family and social duties, a man naturally gives himself increasingly to matters of religion and righteousness. And finally, the renunciant orients himself toward nothing but Ultimacy, seeking liberation from even the most subtle forms of bondage.

Hinduism offers a number of ways to become liberated. These approaches to liberation are called *margas* (paths) or yogas (union, i.e., with the divine or Ultimacy), thereby connoting the disciplines or practices that lead to liberation. The Bhagavad Gita speaks of three paths to liberation: karma yoga, bhakti yoga, and jnana yoga, each of which will be developed below. We will then consider raja yoga, another widely followed path, as well as a few others.

Karma Yoga

In addition to designating the law of cause and effect, karma in some contexts means deed or action. The term refers not only to overt, physical action but also to mental and emotional action. Thoughts and feelings are karma. Even an intention or inclination is karma. Thus, any instance of movement or change is an instance of karma. The two meanings of karma combine in the view that every action is the result of a prior action and leads to a following action. Karma as the cosmic law of cause and effect is substantiated in karma as action. Karma as action 'materializes' karma as cause and effect. There are not, of course, two karmas; neither exists without the other. The distinction is solely conceptual. All action manifests as and by the law of cause/effect.

Karma yoga takes two forms, the first of which centers in the fulfillment of duty. Duty in Hinduism has been construed traditionally in terms of caste duty. The caste structure was legitimized as early as the Rig Veda and has enabled Indian civilization to maintain continuity and stability that is unrivaled, except perhaps by China. Essentially, caste is a way of organizing the labor force. The brahmin caste carries the greatest prestige and privilege; its members traditionally serve as priests and educators. The kshatriya caste consists of those with governing and military responsibilities. The vaishyas represent commercial, industrial, and agricultural operations. They are the white-collar workers. Shudras, occupying the lowest position in the caste structure, are the blue-collar workers, artisans, laborers, and servants. Outside the formal caste system, and historically known as the untouchables, are the harijans, (children of god), so named by Gandhi when he campaigned on their behalf early in the twentieth century. Harijans perform those tasks considered unclean, such as tanning leather, removing human waste, etc. Each caste is divided further into subcastes.

The social stability of the caste structure has become also, in effect, social rigidity since it is impossible to change one's caste during one's lifetime. Caste status is no more changeable within a lifetime than is one's ethnicity. If one is born a shudra, one dies a shudra, no matter how much educational, cultural, or economic change may occur. Individual social change does occur today— though rarely and with difficulty—in light of policies established by the Indian government since independence in 1947. However, even though one's overt social position may improve, one continues to carry the caste identity of birth, with the inherent limitations and privileges that derive from longstanding religio-social practices.

The only way to effect beneficial caste change is by fulfilling one's caste duties, whatever these are, to the best of one's ability. By means of reincarnation, one moves up or down the caste scale depending on success or failure in meeting caste obligations. Krishna says to Arjuna in the Bhagavad Gita (3:35): "Better one's own dharma [duty], though imperfect, than another's well performed."[2] Thus, one moves up the caste scale and closer to liberation by faithfully executing one's own caste responsibility, and down the scale and farther from liberation by failing to do so. By ascending in the hierarchy, one naturally enjoys more opportunity for religious pursuits, as well as perhaps more talent and inclination. By descending in the hierarchy, one's life situation not only becomes more difficult but probably will also offer less opportunity, support, and motivation for religious practices and ideals.

Non-Hindus have tended to fix on what they see as liabilities in the caste structure, particularly the tendency to maintain the status quo and the failure thereby to rectify apparent inequities. Hindus themselves, however, understand the so-called injustices to be in fact the very working of justice. One is born into precisely the caste one deserves; one's present position is the just effect of the quality of one's life during one's previous existence. The laws of karma and rebirth provide the most reasonable explanation for the exigencies of birth, fortuitous or otherwise, claim Hindus. Non-Hindus also tend to recoil from the notion of duty, seeing it as an imposition on personal freedom, and indeed it has often taken this form. However, the universal principle (of which caste duty is a specific, religio-social form) is hardly arguable, namely, the principle of developing one's natural abilities to the fullest extent possible within the context of one's life. Few would deny that one's life circumstance is more apt to improve through diligent application than through irresponsibility and laziness.

Karma yoga as fulfillment of duty is a slow process, usually requiring many lifetimes of gradual ascent (and perhaps descent). In this respect, some Hindus note that God is not in a hurry. While this may be consoling to some, it provides little inspiration to those who feel as constrained in the path of karma yoga as by samsara itself. A second form of karma yoga speeds up the process by offering liberation within a given lifetime. A crucial modification requires that all action be performed with a particular attitude or disposition. This unique path is described in the Bhagavad Gita (3:19) when Krishna says to Arjuna: "Always perform the work that has to be done without attachment." Krishna declares that actions did not stain the wise ones of old because they had no longing for the effects of their action. Nor do actions burden him as God because he too is unattached to their results. The cause/effect cycle is broken by the attitude of indifference to effects. In other words, unconcern about the outcome of one's action avoids the accrual of debilitating karma, and the necessity of rebirth. One does what one does simply because it is the appropriate thing to do. No consideration is given to personal gain or loss. In the absence of vested interest, only appropriate action can ensue. Devoid of self-interest, one can do only what is right.

This totally selfless way of acting is also called actionless action, or inaction in action, by the Bhagavad Gita (4:18, 20): "He who sees inaction in action and action in inaction, he is wise among men; he does all actions harmoniously . . . . Having abandoned attachment to the fruits of action, always content and independent, he does nothing even though he is engaged in action." How is one to understand this seemingly contradictory way of action, of acting without acting? A story (sometimes also told about Buddhist monks) discloses the needed disposition or proper inner orientation. A young man who had tried for months to become the disciple of a certain revered spiritual teacher was finally accepted. The two men were walking together along a path during the monsoon season. The young disciple, excited and animated by the prospect of guidance from his newly-won teacher, was bubbling with question after question. They came to a river, swollen and surging because of the heavy rains. Waiting by the side of the river, unable to cross because of the deep and rushing water, was a prostitute. Without a word, the sage picked her up, carried her across the river, and put her down on the opposite side. The woman went her way and the two men continued their journey. But now in complete silence. The young man, formerly buoyant and talkative, was now sullen and withdrawn. After several minutes, he blurted out, "Why did you, a saintly man, touch that unclean, sinful woman?" The sage calmly replied, "I put her down back by the river's edge; why have you been carrying her all this distance?"

Here we see the sage exhibiting inaction in action, inner inactivity or nonattachment while outwardly acting. At the same time, the novice demonstrated action in inaction, inner activity or attachment while doing nothing overtly. The young man was so caught up in the assumptions of his society—that prostitutes are unclean and sinful, and that saints must maintain their purity by avoiding unclean, immoral persons—that he was rendered immobile at the river's edge. The sage, on the other hand, had completely transcended such religio-social notions and proscriptions and was able to act freely and appropriately. The young man saw a contaminated and contaminating prostitute and reacted out of prejudice. The wise man saw a fellow human in need and acted out of compassion. In the one case, inner activity centering in attachment to emotional, prejudicial notions forestalled a genuine response. In the other case, inner freedom from limiting notions allowed an authentic response. The young man, undoubtedly a devout exoteric Hindu, had received his first lesson in metateric religion.

The difference between the two positions may also be seen in terms of the role played by time—past, present, and future. The disciple brought with him to the present—the situation at the river—a great deal of conditioning from his past that immobilized and deeply troubled him. He was unable to see the immediate situation clearly because of mental, emotional clutter held over from the past. The sage, however, was free of such conditioning, free of such karmic accretions. His action at the river was as unhampered by vestiges from the past as by anticipations of the future (for example, what his new disciple or an on-looker might think if he touched a prostitute). A sage/saint, unaffected by sorrow, fear, anger, prejudice (states rooted in past experience) and by apprehension, dread, or expectation (states oriented to the future), is free (i.e., liberated) to respond appropriately to situations as they arise. Wise and compassionate action ensues.

Action without attachment to results may seem to undermine goal setting, commitment to working toward a worthy objective. How can one do anything without an end in view? What happens to motivation? Why would anyone do anything if no benefit was expected? To be sure, actionless action does imply a radically different way of being in the world. It sets up conditions for finding contentment within oneself, in one's inner self, not in prizes won or goals achieved. One finds meaning, satisfaction, and joy in the very process of life, in what one does moment by moment, without projecting these most-important values into a fantasized future.

Happiness as a deep and permanent condition can only be realized in the present. As long as it is hoped for as a future reality, it can never become an immediate, lived reality. Action without attachment means that one does not stake happiness on personal gain or achievement; instead, one focuses entirely on the task at hand without dissipating attention or energy by longing for better circumstances or a better time. To be only partially present in the unfolding moment because of longing, whether for an idealized past or an imagined future, is tragic. Action without attachment means that one avoids basing one's self-sense, or sense of worth, on factors outside one's own nature, i.e., in pride of past achievement or hope of future gain.

As a psychospiritual discipline, karma yoga fosters freedom in each unfolding moment by nullifying bondage from the limiting past and an imagined future. The transformative principle is to do what one does because it is the appropriate thing to do, given the circumstances of the moment. When studying, study (and not just to pass a test). When walking, walk (and not just to get somewhere). When laughing, laugh (and not to make an impression). When working, work (and not just to get a paycheck). The quality of every situation shifts remarkably when fully accepted as the reality of the moment.

Bhakti Yoga

Bhakti yoga is the path to liberation by means of loving devotion (*bhakti*) directed to one's chosen deity (*ishta devata*). While any god or goddess in the pantheon may become the deity receiving devotion, most *bhaktas* (those practicing bhakti yoga) worship Vishnu or Shiva, one of their forms, or a deity associated with them. As the principal incarnation of Vishnu, for example, Krishna is the devotional focus for large numbers of Hindus. Krishna assures Arjuna in the Bhagavad Gita (9:26-31):

> Whoever offers Me a leaf, a flower, a fruit, or water with devotion,
> I accept that offering of devotion from the pure in heart.
>
> Whatever thou doest, whatever thou eatest, whatever thou offerest, whatever thou givest, whatever austerities thou performest, do that . . . as an offering to Me.
>
> Thus thou shalt be freed from the bonds of action which produce good and evil fruits; disciplined by the yoga of renunciation, thou shalt be liberated and come to Me . . . .

98

Those who worship Me with devotion, they are in Me and I am in them.

Even if a man of very evil conduct worships Me with undivided devotion, he too must be considered righteous, for he has resolved rightly.

Quickly he becomes a righteous self and obtains eternal peace; . . . know thou that My devotee never perishes.

Ramanuja (d. 1137) provided the theological-philosophical system for the bhakti approach. In his system, known as Qualified Nondualism, Ultimacy is threefold; Brahman, the world, and individual souls or selves. Brahman is the Spirit of which the physical world and individual souls are embodied forms. The three are eternal, different, distinct, and interrelated. Liberation for the bhakta does not mean dissolution in the whole, with consequent loss of individuality, but instead eternal, intimate, loving harmony with Brahman in one or another of His forms. Bhakti, therefore, is a form of what we have called union mysticism.

All Bhaktas recognize the divine as gracious but differ on the role of work, or personal effort. Those in the cat school (mother cats carry their kittens by the nape of the neck) believe that liberation comes entirely through God's grace; no work is required. Followers of the monkey school (baby monkeys must hang on to their mothers while being transported) believe that God's grace becomes available through devotional acts, i.e., work. Bhakti yoga is often guru-centered. In fact, guru devotion sometimes takes the place of devotion to the divine since the guru is seen as an embodiment of the divine. Bhakti yoga has had mass appeal in India, employing vernacular languages instead of the traditional Sanskrit, as well as relaxing and sometimes ignoring caste lines.

Ramanuja outlined a number of practices for those who pursue the devotional route: eat only foods that contribute to clarity and lightness (in this respect a vegetarian diet is helpful); restrain the spirit of ownership and possessiveness; practice selflessness by doing good to others; develop inner purity by being truthful, compassionate, fair, honest, and charitable; avoid giving injury; live according to the mean between despondency and frivolity; and, finally, practice loving devotion steadily, refusing to be thrown off course by fluctuating whims. Bhaktas believe that self-surrender is the quickest way to the divine, though this does not mean it is necessarily the easiest. Unreserved commitment to the divine, the withholding of absolutely nothing, requires dissolution of all self-interest, of the ego, and that, as we have seen, is exceedingly difficult. By releasing all that impedes full submission to the divine, however, one comes to a transcendence of the separate self-sense and experiences harmonious union with the Ultimate.

Jnana Yoga

Jnana yoga is liberation by means of knowledge (*jnana*). Jnana is not knowledge in the sense of information, or even intellectual understanding, but profound intuitive insight. It is a knowing beyond the rational mind, a knowing beyond knowing, even a knowing of unknowing. This knowing in the core of one's being is a re-cognition of one's identity with Brahman, Ultimacy. A central formula in jnana yoga is "That art Thou" (*tat tvam asi*). 'That' refers to Brahman and 'Thou' to Self. But what or who is this Self that is one with Brahman—certainly not the body, or thinking mind, or emotions, or ego? The Self that is one with Brahman is known in Sanskrit as *atman*. Atman is the essential Self, pure consciousness, beyond anything one can say about oneself. Atman and Brahman are two words for Ultimacy.

When living in India some years ago, I met a man who had been born into an Orthodox Christian family and who later converted to Islam. What he said to me on one occasion demonstrates the extent to which Hinduism pervades the religious outlook in India. Outside of India, no Christian or Muslim is apt to announce that "the self is like the skin of an onion," a view entirely appropriate in the Hindu liberational path. When we peel away a layer of onion skin, under it we find another layer. Remove this layer and still another is found. This process continues until reaching the central core, the very heart of the onion, beyond which there is nothing more. A similar process is followed to discover the true Self, namely, one of progressively disidentifying with each of our self-images and the various social and family roles we play. A chorus sung in some Hindu ashrams (monasteries, spiritual retreat centers) affirms: "I'm not this body, not this mind; immortal Self am I."

The first step is to realize that 'I' am not an employee, parent, son or daughter, athlete, student, teacher, craftsman, singer, etc. It is relatively easy to image ourselves as other than these social roles. The next, more difficult step is to see ourselves as other than our emotions and our bodies. Even more difficult—and this requires a meditational approach—is to disidentify with the contents and processes of our minds, our thoughts, images, intuitions, etc. When this arduous process is successfully completed, we 'see' that there is no difference between our essential Self and Ultimacy, Atman equals Brahman.

This discovery of nondifference between Self and Supreme is, as we have seen so far, by way of subtraction. It is a *via negativa*. No new knowledge is added; rather, ignorance is removed. Because of ignorance we do not realize our true identity. Ignorance causes us to 'ignore' our true nature, and consequently to identify with that which we are not, with the transitory and derivative. By taking away the false, or the relatively real, the true and absolutely Real shines forth. By removing what we take for granted, i.e., the unquestioned assumptions that make up ordinary knowing, we come, by way of unknowing, to true knowing, the *gnosis* (Greek, knowledge) that liberates. Maya as concealment opens to maya as revelation. What has always been the case is now known to be the case.

The religio-philosophical framework for jnana yoga, called advaita (nondual) vedanta, was produced by Shankara, the ninth-century sage. Philosophy in Hinduism is not simply a way to think; it is also a way to be. Hindus strive not simply to know the truth but to be the truth. And Shankara, besides arguing at great length to establish a comprehensive view of how things are, set down specific guidelines for becoming the truth. Four steps make up his transformational path. The first requirement is to discriminate between the real and the unreal. Here Shankara is undoubtedly drawing from one of the best known prayers of the Upanishads: "From the unreal lead me to the Real! From darkness lead me to Light! From death lead me to Immortality!" Discrimination, discernment (*viveka*) was so important to Shankara that he wrote an entire tract devoted to it. The ability to distinguish between appearance and reality improves through exercise. By identifying and then disvaluing the obviously unreal, one's skill is improved for distinguishing between more subtle forms of the real and the unreal. A mere identification of the unreal is insufficient; the unreal must also be renounced. Shankara's second principle calls for a renouncing of all that might impede realization of the real. Pleasures that are acceptable for a householder, for example, are not for one wholly committed to this path. The third discipline includes several practices and virtues: inner tranquility; control of the body, senses, and mind, including the practice of restraining the mind from its habitual preoccupation with sense objects; patience, including the ability to endure hardship; concentration of one's mental powers on the goal of liberation; and finally, faith, that is, an open and positive attitude toward one's teacher and the scriptures. Shankara's fourth transformative principle underlies and informs all the others, namely, a deep longing for freedom. This deep and pervasive yearning for liberation provides both the orientation and motivation for ultimate realization.

Raja Yoga

The fourth and final yoga to be considered carries a number of names: raja yoga (the royal path), ashtanga yoga (the eightfold path), kriya yoga (the path of action), and classical yoga. This is the system formulated by Patanjali in his Yoga Sutra, perhaps in the second century CE. The ideas had been in circulation for centuries, but Patanjali systematized them in 195 aphorisms, terse statements requiring commentaries, of which many have been written over the centuries. The metaphysical framework of raja yoga is supplied by samkhya, another of the orthodox religio-philosophical systems of Hinduism. Here we find two fundamental realities, Spirit (*Purusha),* and Nature or Matter (*Prakriti).* The two are sometimes rendered Subject and Object. The interaction and mixing of the knowing subject, Spirit, and the known object, Nature, constitutes all experience. As a metaphysical principle, Nature is not actual matter but a force that materializes through the interaction of three qualities (*gunas*): consciousness, activity, and inactivity or dullness. Hindu literature gives many additional characterizations of the gunas; in principle, they are, in order, positive, neutral, and negative. Creation in all its variety is the result of different combinations of the three gunas. Nature in itself is unconscious and pure potentiality. When impinged upon by Spirit, the equilibrium of the three gunas making up Nature is disrupted and creation occurs. As the practical arm of samkhya philosophy, raja yoga provides a means of releasing Spirit from entanglement in Nature. Embodied and occluded consciousness is thus restored to its true and eternal state as Pure Spirit.

In the second aphorism of the Yoga Sutra, Patanjali gives the essence and aim of the approach he is about to outline: "Yoga is the restriction of the fluctuations of consciousness."[3] Classical yoga, thus, is a discipline that holds in check the characteristics of Matter that adulterate and becloud human consciousness, thereby permitting Purusha, or Pure Consciousness, to shine forth in full resplendence.

To say the same thing a little differently, Classical yoga is a method of eradicating the distorting effects of the mind so that one can see reality with total clarity and accuracy. Distortion occurs, Patanjali says, whether experienced as distressful or not. He goes on to identify five modifications of consciousness that distort true seeing. These are (1) valid cognition, whether the result of perception, inference, or testimony; (2) conceptualization, ranging from abstract thinking through fantasizing; (3) misconception; (4) memory, an inevitable realm of attachment whether the remembering is pleasant (clinging), unpleasant (resisting), or neutral (connected even in this form to a sense of personal self—why else would one argue the correctness of one's recall when challenged?); and finally, (5) dreamless sleep (containing subtle forms of conditioned awareness—how else, for example, would it be possible to program oneself to awaken at a precise time?). These five deluding agents of the ordinary mind, Patanjali says in summary fashion, are neutralized through practice and dispassion.

Patanjali gives a more elaborate description of the transformational program of raja yoga in terms of eight specific requirements, from whence comes the name, ashtanga yoga, eightfold or eight-limbed yoga. These eight are the means to realizing total lucidity and faultless discernment. The first is called restraint and consists of five moral requirements: non-injury (ahimsa), truthfulness, non-stealing, chastity, and greedlessness. The second entails five observances: purity, contentment, austerity, self-study, and devotion. The third limb is *asana,* or bodily posture. For Patanjali, the body must be brought under control, made stable and comfortable, as preparation for non-distracted meditation. Countless postures have been added to Patanjali's repertoire, with the consequence that hatha yoga has developed as a yoga in its own right.

The fourth dimension of raja yoga proper calls for breath control. When the yogi (practitioner of yoga) has learned to relax while sitting in a fixed but comfortable posture, attention can be shifted to breathing rhythmically and freely while giving special focus to the pause between inhalation and exhalation. Hindus have discovered intimate connections between patterns of breathing and states of consciousness. The pattern employed in raja yoga is designed to lead to mental calmness and control. Sense-withdrawal is the fifth limb and the last in what are regarded as the outer dimensions of raja yoga. The Bhagavad Gita (2:58) observes: "When he completely withdraws his senses from the objects of sense, as a tortoise draws in his limbs, his mind is firmly established." With a firmly established mind, the yogi is ready to begin the descent into deeper levels of consciousness.

The inner dimensions of raja yoga begin with concentration, the fixing of attention on a single object. This one-pointedness may be directed to a spot on or in the body, to a sound, to the image of a deity, in a word, to anything that will foster the narrowing of attention. Meditation (*dhyana*) is the seventh limb. In texts after Patanjali, a distinction is made between meditation with a form or qualities and meditation without a form or qualities. The former amounts to an extension and deepening of concentration. The latter calls for one to open and expand consciousness in order to identify with the Absolute, totally devoid of objectification.

Sense-withdrawal, concentration, and meditative absorption are progressively flowing and overlapping phases in the process of ever-deepening interiorization and unification. Ideally they lead to *samadhi*, the eighth and final limb of raja yoga. Literally rendered as 'putting together' or 'making firm', samadhi is sometimes translated, though misleadingly, as 'trance'. Somewhat better is 'ecstasy', though this is still inadequate since it implies being 'outside' oneself (indeed, one is outside the ego, or limited self-sense). Perhaps the best translation is 'enstasy', carrying the sense of standing deeply and undistractedly within one's true nature, and consequently, as the Transcendental Self, as Ultimacy. Rather than being experientially sensed as a state of absence, samadhi is marked by a profound sense of presence (here/now) and extraordinary clarity. All of the taints and fluctuations of one's ordinary self have disappeared and one stands as pure subjectivity or, which is the same, pure objectivity. The subject-object dichotomy that qualifies conventional consciousness has dissolved.

Hindu literature provides numerous descriptions of samadhi, often with different characterizations. Broadly speaking, however, two major types are found. *Savikalpa* samadhi entails identification with an 'object' of consciousness and includes thought processes of a higher or gnostic quality. In this form of samadhi, totally accurate insight into the inherent nature of the 'object' is gained; it is seen wholly and only as it presents itself, without any adulteration by the mind, now stripped of all taints. *Nirvikalpa* samadhi consists in one's complete identification with the Transcendental Self. There is now no separative content in consciousness whatsoever, no relationship, no other, no self-sense. The self merges in the Self so that there is no longer a knower, a means of knowing, and something known. All distinction dissipates and one becomes what one experiences. This second type of samadhi constitutes liberation or Self-realization, but only after becoming the permanent condition of one's consciousness. Some Hindu schools call this final form of samadhi *sahaja*, natural or spontaneous enstasy. This state marks a thorough integration of one's inner sense of selflessness and liberation with active involvement in the outer world. This is metateric realization. Such a person is known as a *jivan mukta*, one liberated while still alive. Ramana Maharshi is widely acknowledged as a twentieth—century jivan mukta.

Other Yogas

The four liberational paths outlined above by no means exhaust those available in Hinduism. *Laya* yoga attempts to dissolve the ordinary mind by such means as breath control or intense veneration of a deity and thereby cause it to become absorbed in the Absolute. Mantra yoga involves the recitation of a *mantra*, a sacred sound or formula, imparted to a disciple by a teacher in a formal initiation ritual. Because of the numinous power believed to be inherent in the mantra, the concentrated chanting and eventual meditative focus and identification with the mantra leads to a transcendence of the ego and merging into the Ultimate. In addition to the psychospiritual power inherent in its vibrational quality, a mantra such as *om* carries profound symbolic meaning for Hindus. The three components making up the Sanskrit word (sometimes rendered *aum*) represent the three common states of consciousness, waking, dreaming, and dreamless sleep, with the silence surrounding the pronunciation symbolizing the fourth state, *turiya*, the state of complete absorption in Brahman. A mantra such as *aham brahman asmi*, "I am the Absolute," affirms cognitively what the practitioner intends to realize fully through meditation on the mantra.

Kundalini yoga sets out to arouse the *kundalini* (snake) that lies coiled and dormant at the base of the spine, thus releasing energy to rise along the spine through the seven *chakras*, or psychospiritual centers. The final objective is to reach the seventh chakra at the crown of the head where the active energy as the Goddess Shakti (a consort of Shiva) unites with the passive energy of Shiva, a union which culminates in enlightenment. Various physical, emotional, mental, and spiritual properties are activated and integrated as the divine energy rises through the centers. The ascent begins at the base of the spine, moves through the genital region to the navel, then to the heart, the throat, the forehead, until reaching the final chakra. The ascent may be gradual and mild, or rapid and dramatic. Various occult powers may be experienced along the way. Wise teachers warn of the distractive and corrupting potential of these powers and point out that none of them constitutes enlightenment. Of all the paths leading to liberation, kundalini yoga, because of the enormous psychospiritual energies activated, requires the constant and careful oversight of an experienced adept.

How do these various paths to liberation relate to each other? Are some superior to others? Hindus generally assert that the different paths are designed to appeal to different temperaments. A person who tends toward activism, for example, is probably going to feel drawn to karma yoga. One who likes to ponder abstractions may incline toward jnana yoga. The emotionally vital person will probably find bhakti yoga most appealing. Some Hindus combine these three paths into a single discipline they find identified in the Bhagavad Gita as *buddhi* (awakened) yoga. Though some Hindus may debate the pros and cons of the various paths, most believe that one is as free to choose a path as to choose one's preferred deity. That path is best to which one feels the greatest attraction. And, of course, one may draw from the various approaches to tailor a distinctive practice that will best serve one's particular needs and circumstances.

The proponents of all paths agree that a guru is either advisable or essential, though differences exist on the precise role of the guru. Carrying the sense of 'weighty one', one whose words are weighty, the guru is one who is enlightened and therefore able to guide others. The teacher-disciple relationship in India reaches back to ancient times and has become virtually institutionalized as a crucial dimension in the transformational process. The guru not only formally instructs his disciple in the general principles of transformation but, even more important, introduces and adapts these principles to the particular needs of the disciple. With an intimate knowledge of both the spiritual process and the distinctive personality of his student, the guru is able to fit the program to the disciple and his or her particular level and rate of progress. Most important of all, the fully realized guru is able to transmit his inner state of liberation to his disciple, to the extent that the disciple is open and ready for it, thus greatly accelerating the process of enlightenment. Some Hindus deny that the guru must invariably be a living person. Some even broaden the concept so that a guru becomes anything that teaches. Thus, anyone or anything—an animal, a child, a book, a life circumstance—can serve as a guru.

And some believe that the guru is within oneself. Ramana Maharshi taught that God, guru, and Self are One.

The disciple's role in the traditional teacher-student relationship is to unreservedly obey and serve the spiritual master. This submissive trust itself greatly facilitates the dissolution of the ego. Unfortunately, it also opens the way for the unscrupulous pretender to work havoc on the unwary seeker. Both as a precaution against violation by an unqualified teacher or charlatan, and as a crucial factor in the process of psychospiritual assimilation and integration, anyone involved in a teacher-student relationship must never relinquish discernment, the power to decide what is authentic and appropriate for oneself. To relinquish discernment is to relinquish one's core, one's authenticity and dignity as a human being. To give up sound judgment and responsibility for oneself is to jeopardize the entire transformational journey since these are qualities, when purified, that mark the realized person. If they are not active throughout the journey, they are not likely to have any tainting features removed. Only by drawing on the depth of one's commitment, the purity of one's integrity, and the breadth of one's experience can the student distinguish discernment from egoity—and even then only with great difficulty, given the subtlety of egoistic maneuvers. If one makes an error in judgment, as may well happen in spite of one's best intentions, the error itself can become part of the transformational process if it is accepted and pondered in a discerning and integral fashion.

The Jivan Mukta

Before introducing the biographies and transformational principles of two Hindu sages, it may be well to draw from Hindu scripture and expository writings to describe the liberated person. In this literature, we find succinctly outlined portrayals of the inner self-sense and outer behavior of the spiritual adept. In the Bhagavad Gita, Krishna says:

> He whose mind is not troubled in sorrow, and has no desire in pleasure, his passion, fear and anger departed, he is called a steady-minded sage.

> He who is not attached to anything, who neither delights nor is upset when he obtains good or evil, his mind is firmly established (in wisdom). (Bhagavad Gita 2:56-57)

> He who has no ill feeling to any being, who is friendly and compassionate, without selfishness and egoism, who is the same in pain and pleasure and is patient,

> He before whom the world is not afraid and who is not afraid before the world, and who is free from joy and impatience, fear and agitation, he is dear to Me.

> He who neither rejoices nor hates, neither grieves nor desires, who has renounced good and evil and who is devoted, he is dear to Me.

> He who is alike to enemy and friend, also to honor and disgrace, who is alike to cold and heat, pleasure and pain, and is freed from attachment,

> He who is thus indifferent to blame and praise, who is silent and is content with anything, who is homeless, of steady mind and is devoted—that man is dear to Me. (Bhagavad Gita 12:13, 15, 17-19)

Some of the qualities indicated above may appear unnatural and dehumanizing, even contrary to religion as commonly understood. The standard of human realization espoused in the Bhagavad Gita extends far beyond that of conventional religion, and even further beyond that of ordinary social expectation. In denying joy, the Gita is only affirming that the pervasive happiness, contentment, and bliss of the realized person is uninterrupted and not dependent on external circumstances. In proclaiming disinterest and unconcern, the Gita is not implying that the enlightened adept is cold and heartless but impartial, with compassion extended equally to all, without prior conditions. Renunciation of good and evil is possible for the sage because he is rooted in the Absolute Good and thus able to recognize the relativity and conventionality of what is ordinarily regarded as good and evil. In saying that adepts do not grieve, the Gita is not asserting that they remain heartlessly stoic, for example, at their mother's funeral. Instead, they remain calm and peaceful in their deepest center as the Self, even while feeling sadness and expressing it.

The Avadhuta Gita, a late Advaita Vedanta work, extols the life-style and inner perspective of the *avadhuta* (cast off, sometimes rendered, the naked one), one who feels no compunction to proclaim or practice anything, who feels bound by absolutely nothing. Following are select verses that begin the treatise.

All is verily the absolute Self. Distinction and nondistinction do not exist. How can I say, "It exists; it does not exist!" I am filled with wonder!

The essence and whole of Vedanta is this Knowledge, this supreme Knowledge: that I am by nature the formless, all pervasive Self.

There is no doubt that I am that God who is the Self of all, pure, indivisible, like the sky, naturally stainless.

I indeed am immutable and infinite and of the form of pure Intelligence. I do not know how or in relation to whom joy and sorrow exist.

I have no mental activity, good or bad; I have no bodily function, good or bad; I have no verbal action, good or bad. I am the nectar of Knowledge, beyond the senses, pure.

The mind indeed is of the form of space. The mind is all. But in reality there is no mind.

The scripture declares in many different ways the well-known dictum: "All is Brahman." (Avadhuta Gita 1:1-13)[4]

Tukaram (ca. 1598-1650)

The life of Tukaram, one of the most highly revered and widely read mystical poets of the bhakti tradition, exhibits the profound transformational power inherent in devotional religion. Tukaram was born into the shudra caste of farmers, though his father operated a small cloth shop. He inherited this shop from his father but later lost it due to neglect. Following the custom of the time, he married at an early age. His wife and son died during a famine. By the time of his initiation into bhakti at the age of twenty-one, both his parents had also died.

Tukaram was initiated in a dream by Guru Babaji, who gave him the mantra, "Rama, Krishna, Hari". Tukaram wrote: "Verily my teacher, being cognizant of the aspirations of my heart, bestowed on me a mantra I loved so well."[5] Tukaram memorized lengthy passages from the poetry of earlier saints, especially those who, like himself, were devotees of Vitthoba, a form of Vishnu enshrined in a temple in Pandharpur, a town not far from the city of Poona in Maharashtra State.

One of these saints, Namadeva, appeared to Tukaram in a dream, calling him to the vocation of mystical poet. Namadeva, who preceded Tukaram in the Varkari tradition by about three hundred years, had set himself the task of composing one billion mystical poems. Unable to realize this goal, he charged Tukaram in the dream to complete the number. Tukaram was unable to write such a fabulous number of poems, though he did compose several thousand.

As a result of his mystical life and teaching, Tukaram encountered a great deal of opposition, even persecution. His second wife resented the many hours he devoted to God and also the great number of visitors who came to him for inspiration and direction. A learned Brahmin, jealous of Tukaram's influence, arranged for boiling water to be thrown on the saint. After much suffering, Tukaram recovered. The Brahmin then began to experience bodily pain similar to Tukaram's. He was told in a dream that he had brought his pain on himself through his opposition to Tukaram. The Brahmin went to Tukaram, repented of his evil actions, and received from Tukaram a poem that effected his cure. This poem included the line, "If the mind is pure, then verily even enemies become friends" (275).

The dominant principle of Tukaram's religious life was, of course, devotion. Devotion for a bhakta is the *sine qua non* leading to liberation. Worshipping stone, brass, or any material form will not lead to salvation, nor will finguring beads, singing with a beautiful voice, or even great learning. Devotion requires an intense, overwhelming longing for God. All else is of no avail. A poem from Tukaram highlights the degree of yearning required.

As a fish that is dragged from the water gaspeth, so gaspeth my soul. As one who hath buried his treasure, and now cannot find the place, so is my mind distraught. As a child that hath lost his mother, so am I troubled; my heart is seared with sore anguish. O merciful God, Thou knowest my need. Come, save me, and show me Thy love.[6]

Tukaram underscores the experiential nature of true devotion by noting that tears flowing out of one's eyes because of longing for God are a good sign.

The measure of a bhakta's devotion is also indicated by the extent of his desirelessness. When the heart is empty of all desire except for God, God will fill it with Himself. Desirelessness is essentially a condition of the heart and does not necessarily require abstention, poverty, or asceticism. In fact, the latter, in themselves, are no indication of one's inner state. One may be outwardly without possessions but inwardly dominated by covetousness. To be desireless, one need not necessarily fast or retire to a forest. Tukaram believed that if one is truly devoted to God, one may then enjoy all things. This enjoyment is possible, however, only when commitment to God is prior and absolute. It is not possible to be attached to earthly values and live a truly spiritual life. One's ordinary life in the world becomes sanctified by the force of one's resolute commitment to the divine. "I am walking my worldly way, as a man must . . . but my mind is ever set on Thee" (285). From the standpoint of conventional religion, Tukaram came close to heresy in believing that devotion could actually control God. By this he surely meant, however, that by means of love one comes so totally into harmony with God that no difference in will or action exists between oneself and God.

The devotional path that Tukaram followed requires a deep sense of humility, combined with full awareness of personal limitations and unworthiness.

No deeds I've done nor thoughts I've thought; save as Thy servant, I am nought. Ah, do not, do not cast on me the guilt of mine iniquity. My countless sins, I, Tuka, say, upon Thy loving heart I lay . . . . A beggar at thy door, pleading I stand. Give me alms, O God, love from thy loving hand.[7]

Tukaram's sense of himself in relation to his fellow humans and to the divine is clearly set forth in his confession:

Lowly am I, a man of no repute, no ground have I for pride. And when men honor me, this know I well—'tis Thou in me they honor, Lord, and not myself. I am a clout which men bear reverently because within is gold. Men may honor me, but in that honor comes to me no pleasure, and no pain. For what they honor is not I myself, but, Lord, Another.[8]

In light of the required humility, Tukaram's self-effacing honesty is all the more evident in his confession that he sometimes felt proud when other saints praised him. Continual vigilance toward every hint of arrogance may itself be a manifestation of humility, a humility that is prior to any prideful claim of the ego.

Two common bhakti practices are recitation of the name of God and singing to God, the latter often accompanied by music and dancing. Devotional practices of this sort have the effect of bringing Hindus together, even overcoming traditional caste distinctions. Tukaram gave caste a spiritual significance rather than the traditional religio-cultural import in his claim that a Brahmin who does not praise the name of God is not a Brahman while an outcaste who does is a true Brahmin. In these spiritual gatherings, Tukaram found solace and strength through the repetition of God's name. He felt God's nearness when His name was lovingly uttered. Tukaram gave specific directions for reciting God's name. One need not retire to a remote place but sit silently in one's own house, focus the mind on God, and utter His name lovingly, longingly, and repeatedly.

Reciting God's name in an attitude of complete reliance on Him has the power to nullify sin. Sincere meditation on the divine name leads to realization: "By the power of the Name of God, one shall come to know what one does not know. One shall see what cannot be seen. One will be able to speak what cannot be spoken. One shall meet what cannot be ordinarily met. Incalculable will be the gain of uttering the Name" (320). Heartfelt recitation of the name of God cancels karma and puts an end to reincarnation. Uttering God's name in an attitude of complete submission and reliance enables one to become liberated while still in the body, to become a jivan mukta.

So far we have seen Tukaram advocating attitudes to be cultivated and practices to be performed. He believed, however, that nothing a person does by way of personal development or ritual performance will ensure liberation, even though all that can be done, must be done. He feared that his own effort might be insufficient, but also knew that even perfect effort would not itself effect liberation. He knew well that human activity is powerless to eradicate sin and comes to naught apart from the intervening grace of God. "All my personal endeavor has been at an end; I am only waiting to have Thy grace." His conscience kept him vividly aware of his own sin. He confessed to picturing the faults of others in order to feel better about himself. He believed that he slept too much and tended to be lazy, and sometimes put on the airs of a saint. He summarized his inadequacy: "I have done things which I should never have done." Over against the disappointing awareness of his own inner life, Tukaram can rely only on God: "Thou art a mine of mercy and a sea of compassion."[9] Recognizing the deep contradictions in his own nature, he resigned himself to God's mercy: "I am my own destroyer. I am my own enemy, my own bitter foe. But Thou art an Ocean of Mercy. Save me in the way that seems wise to Thee."[10] Tukaram's confessions evince his utter self-honesty and full reliance on the grace of God. His total dependence on God demonstrates his adherence to the cat school of bhakti.

Before coming to a final and abiding awareness of God, Tukaram experienced not only his own inadequacy but a disturbing sense of God's absence, a state that is frequently described in Western literature as the Dark Night of the Soul. He longed for a vision of God, bewailing the fact that God did not appear to him, not even in his dreams. Familiar with the divine visions of earlier saints, he hungered to see the divine form himself. When his humility and repentance did not provide the vision he sought, he actually became insolent and abusive toward God. "God's impotence is now proved, says Tuka. His Name has no power." He continued: "I am ashamed to call myself Thy servant." And, finally, in utter despair: "In my opinion, God does not exist. My words have fallen short of reality. I have grown hopeless. I have lost both the life of the world and the life of the spirit . . . . To me, God is dead" (297-299). These assertions of despair only highlight the utter sincerety of the saint.

Three things can be noted about Tukaram's relationship to God. First is his reliance on his own immediate, direct, personal experience. No secondhand or hearsay religion would suffice for him. Second is his total honesty, even to the point of reviling God. Tukaram harbored no pretense but openly confessed his inner feeling, even at the risk of losing face before his peers. He was not concerned about reputation, just his own integrity. Third, after doing all he knew to do, he gave up. He realized with an intensity equal to death that nothing, absolutely nothing, he could do would avail him of God's abiding presence. Even his ardent desire for God proved ineffective. Having exhausted every possible approach, Tukaram, finally, could only resign himself totally to whatever might happen.

And then, mysteriously, inexplicably, God appeared. "I see God's face, and the vision gives me infinite bliss. My mind is riveted on it, and my hands cling to His feet . . . . Bliss is now leading me to an ever higher bliss." In ecstatic paeans, he exuded:

Evil has itself been transformed into the highest good . . . . I now see goodness in all created things . . . . Blessedness beyond compare! We, who are mad after God, are sunk in blessedness. We shall sing and dance and clap our hands, and please God. Every day to me is now a holiday . . . . All my emotions have been unified in God, as the rivers in an ocean . . . . My very body becomes

117

divine when I sing the praise of God . . . . My doubts and delirium are at an end . . . . Both my exterior and interior are filled with divine bliss, says Tuka. (300-302)

Early in his transformational journey, Tukaram was a vigorous opponent of Advaita Vedanta and all forms of nondualism. An Advaitin once challenged him to an exchange of views. He agreed provided he could go first and be covered by a blanket when the advaitin expounded his nondualism. Tukaram set forth his argument and then covered himself with a blanket while the advaitin advocated his doctrine and practice. When the blanket was removed, Tukaram was found with his fingers in his ears. In spite of this early opposition, it is a mark of his utter sincerity that his personal experience led him eventually to embrace advaita, and to actually synthesize it and bhakti in his own spiritual depth. This synthesis brought him the extraordinary insights we are about to witness.

As is the case with many mystics, Tukaram's inspired expressions take on an unconventional, paradoxical quality as he labored to articulate what he had come to realize. The ordinary demarcations and distinctions that usually prevail dissolved into a vast unity. His sense of himself as a doer, as one who acts, had altered fundamentally. Employing a classical mystical formulation, he asserts: "I am as I am. There is neither name nor form for me, and I am beyond action and inaction" (305). Tukaram was unable to worship God as he once had because now everything became God for him. God became the very worship he offered, the water used in abulution, the food offered, the songs sung, the musical instruments played. Houses and palaces became temples. He confessed to living in a state of uninterrupted bliss, that God is indeed everywhere. Tukaram's usual sense of 'me' and 'mine' no longer existed. He lived in the state of nirvikalpa samadhi. He was fully aware of the unorthodoxy of his inner awareness and the heretical tone of his pronouncements. He confessed that the words he spoke were not his words but those of

Panduranga, even that they surpassed the pronouncements of the Vedas.

One of the differences between bhaktas and advaitins concerns the personal-impersonal nature of God. Early in his life, contending that God is personal, Tukaram had decried advaitins for their depiction of the Ultimate as impersonal, for their hope of absorption into Brahman Nirguna. He denied Self-indentity and the absorbtion of the worshipper into the worshiped. He cherished the distinction between himself and God. And yet, as we have seen, Tukaram's own experience of identity with God inspired him to eventually claim formlessness, i.e., impersonality, for the divine. He came to deny the applicability of the usual categories for understanding the nature of God. God has no form, nor any name, nor any place where He can be seen; but wherever you go, you see God . . . . He fills the whole world. He is neither impersonal nor personal, but is beyond all knowledge. (324-325)

Tukaram identified the personal with the impersonal and revealed how the personal comes to be seen by the devotee who also knows God beyond the distinctions of concept and language. Concrete images of God are not different from the impersonal Ultimate. The power of devotion enables one to see the Impersonal in form. On many occasions, Tukaram repeated his view that devotion causes Ultimacy to be God, the Impersonal to be the Personal.

Another contention between bhaktas and advaitins centers in the possibility of humans becoming divine. Advaitins, as we have seen, believe that Atman and Brahman are essentially one, that the deepest nature of humans and God is identical. Bhaktas, on the other hand, tend to argue for a fundamental distinction between the human and the divine, typically claiming that no degree of closeness can dissolve the qualitative difference between the two. Earlier on, Tukaram taught that to call oneself God is the most extreme form of foolishness. And yet we have seen, he came eventually to identify himself with God. He believed that if one meditates on a specific God, one becomes that God, dissolving the customary distinctions. He believed that a true saint becomes God and God the saint. Describing further this unitive awareness, Tukaram noted: "The vagaries of the mind stop automatically. Space and time cease to have any existence. The Self illumines the whole Universe . . . . The identity of God and Self takes place. 'I am Thou' is the spiritual experience which emerges in a state of beatification" (348).

Tukaram's contradictory professions cannot be reconciled at the level of discursive analysis. They reflect different but equally authentic experiences that resist logical or consistent formulation. Tukaram's willingness to confess his experience in spite of seeming contradictions is further evidence of his integrity. Speaking from a standpoint of consciousness that is unbound by the dictates of reason, Tukaram proclaimed: "God indeed is an illusion. The devotee is an illusion. Everything is an illusion. Only those who have . . . this experience, says Tuka, will come to know the truth of my remark." Finally, he said: "The unreal Tuka, with an unreal devotion, speaks unreal things with unreal men" (344). With these pronouncements, he drew on the nondualistic view of maya and pointed to experience beyond experience, knowing beyond knowing.

Tukaram unquestionably remains one of the most beloved and quoted saints in the bhakti tradition. Gadge Baba, a renowned twentieth-century bhakta, opened his address to an assembly of over 10,000 people by drawing on the teaching of Tukaram. "Tukaram Maharaj, that saintly man, gives advice to the world . . . . Tukobaraya says [that] he who is born as a man and does *bhajan* [singing] to God, he will become God—*God*! He gives his own example. He says, 'I went looking for God, and I became God.'"[11] In spite of centuries of debate, of affirmation and denial, of explanation and analysis, the mystery of this claim remains rationally undecipherable. That it attests to fundamental transformation in one's sense of self, other, world, and Ultimacy is hardly arguable.

Ramana Maharshi (1879-1950)

Bhagavan Shri Ramana Maharshi is the name, with honorific titles, given many years after his birth to Venkataramana, who was born into a relatively poor and unexceptional Brahmin family in South India. His father worked in the law courts. When Venkataramana was just twelve years old, his father died and he was sent to live with an uncle in Madurai, a city famous for its temples. Though a bright student, he was more interested in sports than books. He showed no particular interest in religion until he was sixteen, when be began reading stories about the lives of poet saints. This created in him a love for Shiva and caused him to spend time in the Shaivite temples of Madurai, particularly the Minakshi Temple where worship centered in one of Shiva's consorts.

At the age of sixteen, in July 1896, Venkataramana experienced his spiritual awakening. He has carefully described what occurred.

It was about six weeks before I left Madurai for good that the great change in my life took place. It was quite sudden. I was sitting alone in a room on the first floor of my uncle's house. I seldom had any sickness, and on that day there was nothing wrong with my health, but a sudden violent fear of death overtook me. There was nothing in my state of health to account for it, and I did not try to account for it or to find out whether there was any reason for the fear. I just felt 'I am going to die' and began thinking what to do about it. It did not occur to me to consult a doctor, or my elders or friends; I felt that I had to solve the problem myself, there and then.

The shock of the fear of death drove my mind inwards and I said to myself mentally, without actually framing the words: 'Now death has come; what does it mean? What is it that is dying? The body dies.' And I at once dramatized the occurrence of death. I lay with my limbs stretched out stiff as though *rigor mortis* had set in and imitated a corpse so as to give greater reality to the enquiry. I held my breath and kept my lips tightly closed so that no sound could escape, so that neither the word 'I' nor any other word could be uttered. 'Well then,' I said to myself, 'this body is dead. It will be carried stiff to the burning ground and there burnt and reduced to ashes. But with the death of this body am I dead? Is the body I? It is silent and inert, but I feel the full force of my personality and even the voice of the 'I' within me, apart from it. So I am Spirit transcending the body. The body dies but the Spirit that transcends it cannot be touched by death. That means I am the deathless Spirit.' All this was not dull thought; it flashed through me vividly as living truth which I perceived directly, almost without thought process. 'I' was something very real, the only real thing about my present state, and all the conscious activity connected with my body was centered on that 'I'. From that moment onwards the 'I' or Self focused attention on itself by a powerful fascination. Fear of death had vanished once and for all. Absorption in the Self continued unbroken from that time on.[12]

Ramana's interest in school now waned even further. When his older brother chastised him for his perfunctory, mindless involvement in school, he decided to quit. From a visiting family member, he had learned just a few days earlier that there is a place known as Arunachala, a name that he associated with a mysterious inner force that had arisen spontaneously in his mind and that held great attraction for him. With scant directions and little money, Ramana set out for Tiruvannamalai, a small town at the base of Arunachala, South India's most famous mountain, the home of Shiva. After three days of walking and traveling by train, he arrived. He went immediately to the great temple of Arunachaleshwara and prostrated before the sacred image of Shiva. After having his head shaved, he tossed away the few coins he had left, as well as his clothes, keeping only enough to make a loincloth. He was now a sannyasi, an avadhuta, one whose ruling passion is dispassion toward everything except Ultimacy Itself. For more than a half century, until the end of his life, Ramana lived as a renunciant.

For the next several months, Ramana was in an almost continual state of samadhi, his consciousness merged in Universal Consciousness. In this state, he was unaware of his body and his surroundings. He was given food by benefactors, sometimes even fed. Months passed without bathing. His hair grew long and matted. His nails became so long that he could not properly close his hands. Ruffians frequently tormented him, dousing him with buckets of dirty water or throwing sticks and stones at him. To escape such attacks, he occasionally moved his place of meditation. In spite of its dampness, darkness, and absence of ventilation, he took refuge for several weeks in an underground cell. The depth of his ascetic practice attracted numerous devotees to him. A woman who brought him food each day discovered the sores that formed on his body due to unattended insect bites. Finally, a group of saintly men carried him, still in samadhi, to a safe and more healthful place. There was no want for patrons. Many found solace, inspiration, and spiritual power just sitting in his presence.

About two and a half years after coming to Tiruvannamalai, Ramana moved to Arunachala itself where he stayed in various caves on the mountain. He went down to the town only infrequently to receive food. Increasing numbers of people came to know about him and sought him out in order to sit with him. As question began to be posed about spiritual life and practice, Ramana answered from his own experience. In time, visitors began to ask him to clarify difficult passages of scripture. He often read the scripture himself, thereby becoming acquainted with the classical texts of Hinduism. Through his study of these texts, and especially the works of Shankara, he found confirmation of his own spontaneous awakening.

Ramana lived for fifteen years in one of the most important caves of Arunachala, one that had harbored countless sages before his time. Here he gave counsel and blessing to thousands of visitors. In 1916, he moved to a small hermitage that had been built for him further up the mountain. His fame continued to spread. In addition to the thousands of Hindus who came to him, there were many Westerners with Jewish or Christian backgrounds. Among these was Paul Brunton, one of the first to write about Ramana for the West.

> There is something in this man which holds my attention as steel filings are held by a magnet. I cannot turn my gaze away from him. My initial bewilderment, my perplexity at being totally ignored, slowly fade away as this strange fascination begins to grip me more firmly. But it is not till the second hour of the uncommon scene that I become aware of a silent, resistless change which is taking place within my mind. One by one, the questions which I have prepared in the train with such meticulous accuracy drop away. For it does not now seem to matter whether they are asked or not, and it does not seem to matter whether I solve the problems which have hitherto troubled me. I know only that a steady river of quietness seems to be flowing near me, that a great peace is penetrating the inner reaches of my being, and that my thought-tortured brain is beginning to arrive at some rest.[13]

Ramana's final move was to the foot of the mountain in 1922. What began as temporary thatched huts grew over the year to become Ramanashramam, today one of India's major ashrams. During the nearly three decades that Ramana Maharshi lived at the ashram, tens of thousands of visitors came to receive his *darshan* (viewing, audience), most in hope of receiving spiritual teaching, some to simply sit in his presence. During these years, he wrote a few short treatises, a few hymns, and a little poetry. He also translated and commented on certain scriptural texts, as well as some of the writings of Shankara. Most of what is known regarding his teaching, however, comes from notes recorded by devotees, notes containing his answers to questions raised by ashram residents and visitors.

Ramana Maharshi's teaching and practice is a modern version of Advaita Vedanta. His genius was to condense the complex nondualism of Shankara to the experiential pursuit of the question, "Who am I?" This query leads to Atman, the Self, pure consciousness devoid of duality. In the Self, one dwells simply as 'I' rather than "I am this" or "I am that." Every 'this' or 'that' is a formed and temporal limitation imposed on the Infinite. When transcending all objects, all duality, the ego, the separate self sense, dissolves into pure being or satchitananda, the state of conscious, blissful existence. The Maharshi's own experience was that of perpetual awareness of the Self even while engaged in so-called objective reality or, for that matter, his own conditional, subjective reality. Even while involved in everyday activities of life, eating, walking, listening, speaking, reading, he was uninterruptedly conscious of his essential nature as Ultimacy. He lived in the state of nirvikalpa samadhi.

Human nature is such that the ego or 'I'-thought, the sense of oneself as distinct and separate from other human beings and the outer world, inevitably arises sometime around the end of infancy or earlier childhood. As psychospiritual development continues, the 'I'-thought identifies with the body, the senses, the mind. Still further identifications occur as the natural developmental process continues, identifications with specific emotional states ("I get angry easily"), with gender ("I am a man"), with vocation ("I am a lawyer"), with political ideology ("I am a Democrat") and on and on without end. Each of these identifications is a particular something that not only limits and separates from the total life process but, even more important, occludes one's true nature as the Self. This is an instance where the sum of the parts does not equal the whole. The combining of all the parts that make up one's self is no closer to the Whole, that is, the Self, than any one of the parts. The distinction between self and Self is qualitative, not quantitative. Throughout this long developmental process, typically extending over decades if not a lifetime, the temporal self assumes itself to be that with which it consciously and unconsciously identifies. Ramana summarized: "Your duty is to *be* and not to be this or that. 'I AM that I AM' sums up the whole truth."[14]

The source of this continuous and pervasive process of identification—which keeps one bound, limited, separate—is the 'I'-thought, the ego. Ramana Maharshi believed that by tracing the 'I'-thought to its source, one will merge into the Self, the Atman, and discover one's true identity as the Absolute. The limiting identifications of one's life will be seen for what they are. One will become free to invoke specific positions, actions, roles, etc., as they are appropriate and not be compelled to habitual and restrictive ways of being because of blind identification. Of far greater significance, however, is the realization that one's true nature is the Self, infinite, eternal, perfect. Pure Consciousness is seen to be the only Reality; all supposed realities are discovered to be interdependent and changing. Everything arises and disappears except the Self. All subjects and objects arise from the Absolute Subject, Pure Consciousness, the only 'I,' and return to this same Unfathomable.

The Pure Consciousness of which Ramana Maharshi spoke is not private to each individual but an infinite and eternal reality that we experience as individual and private to the extent that we identify with our body-mind. There is only one Consciousness. All specific states of consciousness—waking, with all its varied contents and qualities; dream, with its unpredictability and myriad forms; and dreamless sleep, with its steady calmness—all of these are relative forms of the one Absolute Consciousness. Ramana Maharshi argued that without consciousness, time and space do not exist. They and all their dimensions and modifications appear only in consciousness. This may sound like extreme idealism but is not. Ramana does not deny the relative reality of everyday experience; he only denies its absoluteness, and that because it is ever-changing and far from self-sufficient. In contending that the world is a thought, he does not claim that it is only a thought; rather that as a thought it serves to occlude Pure Consciousness. All thoughts, all contents of consciousness, are blips on the ever-present screen of Pure Consciousness. The world is unreal only if seen as other than the Self. It is real when seen as the Self. Realization is realizing that the body, the mind, and everything else are not different from the Self. Using a metaphor from Western religions, Ramana noted that the Kingdom of Heaven and the world are not different. Their apparent difference lies only in the difference of viewpoint.

Ramana believed that thoughts are obstacles to true seeing, to realization of our inherent nature as the Self. Thoughts are screens that veil us from Reality. To be free from thought is to experience bliss. As the source thought of all thinking, the 'I'-thought must be traced to its source, the Self. If the source of the 'I'-thought is sought, the 'I' does not arise and one stands as the Real, one with all that is. And, being one with all that is, there is no fear since fear arises only where there is another. Ramana argued that our real nature is perfection, even though we usually feel imperfect. The true 'I' is experienced in deep sleep, where there are no thoughts, no change, only perfect peace. The sense of imperfection arises from the sense of separation from the All, and all because of identifying with a thought, the 'I'-thought.

Ramana often pointed out that if the source of the 'I'-thought is found, the ego 'I' does not arise. Why? Because it does not exist; it is unreal, an illusion (maya). It appears to exist only because of misidentification, because of ignorance, because of thinking oneself separate from the Whole. For Ramana, ignorance and the 'I'-thought are identical. That one's customary sense of self is not real is seen in the fact that it continually changes (over time and from circumstance to circumstance) as well as in its intermittent nature (it disappears in sleep even though one continues to be). By searching for the source of the 'I'-thought, one comes to Pure Consciousness (without an object) and realizes one's inherent nature. The ego vanishes into the Self.

Enquiry into the source of the 'I' is the single method that Ramana Maharshi continually recommended. He recognized the value, though limited, of other practices, pilgrimage, scriptural study, meditation, devotion, repeating God's name, etc., but believed self-enquiry to be superior because it is the direct route to the source of the 'I'. The other methods are for those who are unable to undertake the direct course. He also believed that the other methods would eventually lead practitioners to self-investigation. Following a classical threefold pattern of practice, he sometimes urged those seeking guidance to: (1) hear the truth and thereby dispel ignorance, (2) reflect on the truth and thereby dispel doubt, and (3) practice meditation and thereby dispel mistaken identification. He acknowledged the (limited) value of various kinds of breath control, as well as meditation on specific objects (an image or a mantra) but persistently and finally called seekers to self-enquiry. He sometimes distinguished between meditation, which entails an object (whether external to the body or in the mind), and self-inquiry, which is entirely subjective, i.e., with any object whatsoever. The inner-outer distinction, he pointed out, is ultimately arbitrary. Self is neither within nor without. The admonition to look within is only for those who presume a without. One's orientation in self-inquiry is not to see something but to rest in That Which Sees. Ramana sometimes equated self-inquiry and realization, in which case the former is not simply searching for the source of the 'I'-thought but remaining merged in the Source. Self-inquiry is holding to the Self, the source of the 'I'-thought, with effort. Realization is abiding in the Self without effort.

Ramana continually pointed out that realization is not about adding to awareness something that is absent, or to oneself something that is missing. What can be gained can also be lost. What comes and goes cannot be the Absolute. The Eternal, Pure Consciousness, Absolute Being, Infinitude, Self—all synonymous terms—can never be other than 'always already'. To regard the Absolute as absent or 'other than' is inconceivable. Realization is a process of subtraction—illusion, ignorance, mistaken identity—rather than addition. Ramana consistently taught: "Realization is only the removal of obstacles to the recognition of the eternal, immanent Reality."[15] "The feeling that I have not realized," he also claimed, "is the obstruction to realization" (163). The Maharshi expressed reservation about the very notion of realization since it implies the recognition of something previously unknown. How can we be *un*aware of our essential nature, since our essential nature is awareness? Such notions as realization, ignorance, and illusion are concessions made to the so-called unenlightened by the so-called enlightened. They are terms used by those on the 'other side' to communicate with those on 'this side'. Ramana taught: "To know that there never was ignorance is the goal of all the spiritual teachings" (248). The non-self (ego or 'I'-thought) is actually the Self forgotten. Forgetting implies knowing. One cannot forget what is not known. Therefore realization is the *re*membering of what was forgotten, the *re*discovery of what was known.

Some disciples misunderstood Ramana's teaching about the elimination of the non-self and took it to mean that if they progressively disidentified with who they are not, they would thereby discover who they are. Self-enquiry came to be misconstrued as simply the process of gradually disassociating from the many self-conceptions that everyone holds: "I am not the body," "I am not the senses," "I am not the mind," etc. The equating of self-enquiry with self-negation is relatively common. There is some value in the process of negation—"I am not this, not that"—because with each disassociation there is less attachment and more freedom and expansion. But such an approach cannot in itself lead to the Atman. Ramana cautioned: "The one who eliminates all the *not I* cannot eliminate the 'I'. To say 'I am not this' or 'I am not that' there must be the 'I'. This 'I' is only the ego or the 'I'-thought" (162). So the negative approach of gradual disidentification can at best lead only to the 'I'-thought because it is, as a process, the work of the ego itself. The thinking 'I' must itself become disidentified with the Self. This occurs when the Self is 'discovered' as the Source of the 'I'-thought and, simultaneously, of all that is.

Ramana Maharshi was able to see the interrelationships and ultimate oneness of human existence, cosmic processes, and Ultimacy, a seeing that eludes those of conventual outlook. Therefore, he could equate factors that ordinarily seem distinct. For example, he often pointed out that God, Guru, and Grace are not different. "The Guru is both exterior and interior. From the exterior he gives a push to the mind to turn inward; from the interior he pulls the mind towards the Self. That is Grace. Hence there is no difference between God, Guru and Self" (165). Though devotees longed to be in his physical presence, he firmly believed that physical proximity was unnecessary. "Grace is within you. Grace is the Self. You are never out of its operation" (208).

The negative approach to the Self through disidentification with the non-self and the positive approach by means of self-enquiry, "Who am I?", coalesce in silence. "Stillness is the sole requisite for the realization of the Self as God" (307). Ramana was especially fond of quoting the biblical injunction: "Be still and know that I am God" (Psalms 46:10). He believed that "silence is the most potent form of work" (370), and even attributed greater value to the silence purveyed by the guru than the information conveyed by scripture. "Stillness is total surrender," he claimed, "without a vestige of individuality" (322). This stillness prevails when mental agitation ceases—when all desire, all sense of independent doership, all assumption of distinct personhood vanishes. By following "Who am I?" to its Source, one finds absolute silence. "The mind . . . eventually remains still without the least ripple. That stillness is the Self" (165).

The Jews and Christians who visited Arunachala often asked Ramana questions from the perspective of their own religious backgrounds. As a consequence, Ramana gained familiarity with the main features of these Western religions. He developed an interpretation of the crucifixion and resurrection that, though clearly nontraditional in terms of Christian theology, accords with Advaita Vedanta and its understanding of psychospiritual transformation. "Christ is the ego. The cross is the body. When the ego is crucified, and it perishes, what survives is the Absolute Being, and this glorious survival is called Resurrection."[16] The Maharshi's interpretation universalizes the distinct Christian understanding thereby allowing those outside Christianity to sense the transformative power in the essential Christian event and message. Besides this, it provides a sterling example of the manner in which Hinduism is able to assimilate other religions into its own unique way of resolving the universal human predicament.

During the final days of his life, when it became apparent that he was soon to "drop his body," Ramana was approached by one of his distraught devotees who began to cry out, "Ramana, Ramana, don't leave us." The Maharshi calmly replied, "Where could I possibly go?" Only one who is not identified with the body-mind, who is grounded in Absolute Being, could make such a statement. True to his own experience and to his teaching, Ramana believed that "death is only a thought and nothing more" (203). He explained that the 'I' of a realized person includes the body. "There cannot be anything apart from the 'I' for him. If the body falls away, there is no loss for the 'I'. 'I' remains the same" (202-203).

On April 14, 1950, Ramana Maharshi, the Sage of Arunachala, dropped his body and merged into the Eternal and Infinite, the Only All.

NOTES

1. Unless otherwise indicated Vedic and Upanishadic quotations are from Sarvepalli Radhakrishnan and Charles A. Moore, eds., *A Sourcebook in Indian Philosophy.* (Princeton, N.J.: Princeton University Press, 1957).

2. Quotations from the Bhagavad Gita are from Eliot Deutsch, trans., *The Bhagavad Gita.* (New York: Holt, Rinehart and Winston, 1968).

3. Quotations from the Yoga Sutra are from Georg Feuerstein, trans., *The Yoga-Sutra of Patanjali: A New Translation and Commentary.* (Rochester, Vermont: Inner Traditions International, 1989).

4. Swami Ashokananda, trans., *Avadhuta Gita.* (Madras, India: Sri Ramakrishna Math, 1981).

5. Subsequent quotations followed by page numbers are from R.D. Ranade, *Mysticism in India: The Poet-Saints of Maharashtra.* (Albany, N.Y.: State University of New York Press, 1933, 1983), 270-271.

6. John S. Hoyland, *An Indian Peasant Mystic.* (London: H. R. Allenson, Ltd., 1932), 13.

7. Nicol Macnicol, *Psalms of Maratha Saints.* (Calcutta, India: Association Press, 1919), 76, 57.

8. Hoyland, *Indian Peasant Mystic.* 65.

9. Wilbur S. Deming, *Selections from Tukaram.* (Madras, India: Christian Literature Society for India, 1932), 140.

10. Justin E. Abbott, *Stotramala.* (Poona, India: Scottish Mission Industries, 1929), 35, 39.

11. Eleanor Zelliot and Maxine Berntsen, eds., *The Experience of Hinduism: Essays on Religion in Maharashtra.* (Albany, N.Y.: State University of New York Press, 1988), 227.

12. n.a., *Bhagavan Sri Ramana: A Pictorial Biography.* (Tiruvannamalai, India: Sri Ramanasramam), 1981), 10a.

13. Paul Brunton, *A Search in Secret India*. (New Delhi: B.I. Publications, 1934, 1970), 141.

14. Bharati Mirchandani, ed., *Heart is Thy Name, O Lord: Moments of Silence with Sri Ramana Maharshi*. (Tiruvannamala, India: Sri Ramanasaramam, 2006) 25. The quotation "I am that I am" is a title for God in Exodus 3:14 and is linked by biblical scholars with Isaiah 46:10 and elsewhere; Jesus' declaration in John 8:58, ". . . before Abraham was, I am" is thought to indicate his self-identity with God.

15. Munagala S. Venkataramiah (Ramanananda Saraswati), comp., *Talks with Sri Ramana Maharshi*. (Tiruvannamalai, India: Sri Ramanasramam, 1978), 168. All remaining quotations from Ramana Maharshi are from *Talks* unless indicated otherwise. The page number from which the quote is taken is given in parentheses immediately after the quote.

16. Mirchandani, *Heart is Thy Name*, 49.

**Buddhism:
The Mind of Enlightenment**

"The mind is the Buddha, and the buddha is the mind. Beyond the mind there's no buddha, and beyond the buddha, there's no mind."
—Bodhidharma

"Know the one thing that liberates everything— awareness itself, your true nature."
—Dudjom Rinpoche

"Our life is shaped by our mind; we become what we think."[1] So begins the Dhammapada (Pali, the path/way of truth and practice).* The most widely read text in Theravada Buddhism, the Dhammapada is believed by all Buddhists to contain the basic teachings of the Buddha. Another translation renders this first verse of the book: "Mind is the forerunner of all actions. All deeds are led by mind, created by mind." It continues: "If one speaks or acts with a corrupt mind, suffering follows . . . . If one speaks or acts with a serene mind, happiness follows . . . ." The second chapter of the Dhammapada, entitled "Mindfulness," opens: "Mindfulness is the path to immortality."[2] Another version, emphasizing the purity of mind that marks the Buddhist goal, reads: "Clear thinking leads to Nirvana."[3] While

---

* Pali is a dialect of Sanskrit and the principal language in Theravada Buddhism. Dhammapada in Sanskrit is Dharmapada.

each of the great religions recognizes the crucial importance of the mind, in Buddhism the mind is pivotal. Mind is the arena of transformation—the human predicament centers in the mind, and is resolved in the mind. Buddhism is designed to clear the mind of all distorting features so reality can be seen as it is.

Buddhism organizes its approach to transforming the mind by means of the three refuges: Buddha, dharma, sangha. When Buddhists confess, "I take refuge in the Buddha," they acknowledge the Buddha as their foremost teacher and exemplar. When they assert, "I take refuge in the dharma," they commit to his teaching and the practices he enjoined. When they affirm, "I take refuge in the sangha," they open themselves to the guidance and support of the Buddhist community, especially the monks and nuns. Also known as the three jewels, this tripartite division provides an outline of all that is Buddhist. After an overview of the sangha, giving special attention to specific forms that personal realization takes in each of the major branches of Buddhism, we will return to take up the life of the Buddha, followed by his teaching and recommended practices as found in the dharma. We will also see how the latter has been expanded and supplemented throughout history by the sangha.

The Sangha and the Enlightenment Ideal

Depending on context, sangha may refer to the entire community of Buddhists, lay and monastic, or, more narrowly, to the monastic community of monks and nuns only. The Buddhist sangha is divided into two major branches, Theravada and Mahayana or, with increasing frequency, three branches, Theravada, Mahayana, and Vajrayana, with the latter subsumed under Mahayana in the twofold classification.

Theravada, the Way (*vada*) of the Elders (*thera*), is the oldest form of Buddhism.[4] It purports to transmit a relatively unchanged tradition extending back more than 2500 years. While undoubtedly reflecting some change from the Buddhism of the Buddha's day, this is today the form of Buddhism that comes closest to that practiced by the Buddha and his disciples. It is also known as Southern Buddhism since it is the predominant form in South and Southeast Asia from Sri Lanka through Burma and Thailand to Vietnam. Monasticism plays a particularly crucial role in Theravada.

Mahayana, the Great (*maha*) Wheel or Vehicle (*yana*), is considerably more flexible and adaptive than Theravada Buddhism and consequently is much larger, having spread from India to Tibet, neighboring Himalayan countries, China, Korea, and Japan. Sweeping north on its move eastward, it is known also as Northern Buddhism. Willingly, sometimes eagerly, incorporating into itself features of the indigenous religions that did not conflict with its essential nature, Mahayana came to be significantly altered over the centuries. As one would expect, today Mahayana Buddhism offers the greatest array of teachings and practices.

Vajrayana, the Diamond (*vajra*) Vehicle, is the Buddhism of Tibet. It is also known as Mantrayana, the Vehicle of Power Sounds (*mantra*), because chanting, incantation, and meditation involving sacred syllables is a common transformative practice. Tantric Buddhism, after *tantra* (thread), a term designating the sacred texts of Tibetan Buddhism, also names the Buddhism of Tibet. Among other meanings, thread refers to the continuum of inner and outer practices that lead to enlightenment. Vajrayana Buddhists tend to think of their interpretation and application of the dharma as the culmination of the Buddha's teaching.

The Arahant in Theravada Buddhism

Supreme realization is represented in Theravada Buddhism by the *arahant* (Pali, the worthy one; *arhat*, Skt.), the one who has attained enlightenment. Arahants pass through three stages before culminating their spiritual journey in the final stage, full buddhahood. In the first stage, which is reached only after passing through countless prior lives, they are known as 'stream-winners', those who have finally and decisively entered the stream leading to full enlightenment. Behind them is the wavering and half-heartedness that characterize most. They are now resolutely committed to full realization. In order to become a stream-winner, they must remove the first three of the ten fetters that keep the mind bound to samsaric existence, the continuous round of rebirth also found in Hinduism. These fetters or impediments include the belief that one is an individual, separate from others and the world, doubt, and reliance on good works and ceremonies as means to liberation.

After a great deal of continuing effort, again typically over the course of numerous lives, aspirants to arahantship enter the second stage and become 'once-returners' to the samsaric cycle. Their essential endeavor now is to reduce desire and hatred to the fullest extent possible, to decrease clinging and aversion so that they are not pulled off-center by these distorting emotions. As they make headway in the reduction of lust and ill will, they gain a clearer sense of what enlightenment entails, but it is not yet their own uninterrupted experience. Their next lifetime will be their last, however, since they will then reach the third stage and become a 'non-returner'.

As non-returners, the arahant-in-the-making will completely remove all clinging and aversion as well as any remaining vestiges of the first three binding factors of the ordinary mind. In addition, they will undertake the elimination of the five remaining fetters, known as the higher fetters. These include desire for material life, desire for immaterial existence, conceit, restlessness, and ignorance. When all ten fetters have been entirely eliminated, the non-returner fully awakens to enlightenment and reaches the fourth and final state, that of the arahant, one who will enter nirvana (extinction) at death and never again be caught up in the samsaric cycle.

The fourfold path culminating in enlightenment is also depicted in terms of eliminating the *asavas,* variously translated cankers, intoxicants, inflows/outflows. A common epithet for the arahant is 'destroyer of the asavas'. The asavas are mental-emotional defilements that occlude the mind, thereby distorting perception and impeding appropriate response to whatever conditions prevail. A result of the limiting effects of karma during past lives and one's current life, the asavas are misperceptions (influxes) and projections (outflows) that make appropriate interaction in the natural flow of life impossible. The most entrenched asavas are craving and ignorance. Sometimes two more are added: becoming or being, i.e., attachment to existence itself; and, finally, attachment to views, i.e., believing that intellectual propositions are adequate explanations of reality.

Another analysis of the human condition and the path to enlightenment begins by identifying five hindrances that must be eliminated: desire, ill will, sloth and torpor, restlessness and compulsion, and doubt. When these psychological obstructions cease to be operative, the aspiring arahant is ready to enter *samadhi,* concentration or absorption. By entering successive meditative states and attaining the mental factors associated with each, the arahant comes finally to pure mindfulness and equanimity.

The common feature in these different ways of understanding the discipline and benefits of the arahant's path is the destruction of all the factors in the mind that obstruct its natural or inborn lucidity. This eradication of the distorting mental factors is recognized universally in Buddhism as the essential means to enlightenment. The fruit of the arahant's arduous discipline is personal awareness of the absence of the mental distortions that used to be so troublesome. Now he or she is able to live happily, appropriately, and harmoniously with whatever arises in the ordinary course of daily activities. The arahant is, of course, a capable and appropriate guide for other Buddhists.[5]

In addition to numerous references throughout the Dhammapada, the seventh chapter is devoted entirely to the arahant, attesting that "he has completed his voyage; he has gone beyond sorrow. The fetters of life have fallen from him, and he lives in full freedom." Summarizing further the inner state of arahants, the Dhammapada avers: "Wisdom has stilled their minds, and their thoughts, words, and deeds are filled with peace. Freed from illusion and from personal ties, they have renounced the world of appearance to find reality. Thus have they reached the highest." One of the effects of this inner purity is to "make holy wherever they dwell . . . . With their senses at peace and minds full of joy, they make the forests holy." Because the actions of an arahant are without desire or clinging, they do not create effects that bind them to the samsaric world, as do the actions of ordinary persons; thus, they live in perfect accord with reality. Accumulating no karma, the arahant lives a life that "leaves no trace, like the path of birds in the sky."[6] And, leaving no trace, at death they enter nirvana, never to return to the round of existence.

The Bodhisattva in Mahayana Buddhism

In Mahayana Buddhism, the ideal corresponding to the arahant is the bodhisattva. The bodhisattva, a being (*sattva*) of enlightenment (*bodhi*), is one in whom *bodhichitta*, the mind of enlightenment, has arisen. This is the mind that aspires to enlightenment, the mind that recognizes no other objective in life equal to buddhahood. The arising of the thought of enlightenment is actually a conversion, a fundamental psychospiritual shift based on the recognition that one's awareness and life heretofore have been based on ignorance, i.e., on misinformation, misperception, and misunderstanding. Accompanying this self-recognition is the knowledge that other human beings are similarly deluded. Realizing the interdependence of all life, the bodhisattva not only begins a discipline that will lead to his own liberation but also works for the liberation of all others.

The driving force of this aspiration is compassion (*karuna*) for all sentient beings. Every bodhisattva begins his explicit commitment to the path of enlightenment by taking a vow to become a buddha and to postpone final entry into nirvana until every living being has also become liberated.

Bodhichitta is considerably more than just the thought of enlightenment; it is an intention and commitment entailing an all-encompassing discipline directed simultaneously to one's own enlightenment and that of all others. Possibly the most important training manual for bodhichitta is the Bodhicharyavatara (Undertaking the Way to Awakening), described by some scholars as "one of the greatest works of world spirituality."[7] Shantideva, the eighth-century Indian Buddhist poet, philosopher, and author of the Bodhicharyavatara, declared that he became a son of the Buddha on the day he committed to the bodhisattva path, having felt bodhicitta arising within himself. With the awakening of bodhicitta the bodhisattva path begins. Open to all Buddhists, but engaged mainly by monks and nuns, or those who have abandoned lay life in order to give themselves more fully to spiritual ends, the bodhisattva path represents a commitment to move from ego entrapment to limitless being, for self and all others.

A bodhisattva, like a buddha, exhibits limitless compassion and infinite wisdom (*prajna*), the two qualities most highly valued by Buddhists. Strictly speaking, wisdom and compassion are not two qualities but two ways of talking about a single quality, a single way of being in the world. From the Buddhist perspective, wisdom without compassion is not wisdom, and compassion without wisdom is not compassion. Each is an integral dimension of the other, no more separable than the two sides of a coin. Because of compassion one cultivates wisdom; because of wisdom one practices compassion. Or, being wise is to be compassionate; being compassionate is to be wise. This is true, of course, only when each is thoroughly integrated into the other as a result of the perfection of each.

Buddhists arouse and foster a sense of compassion by drawing on their understanding of reincarnation. For example, the eighth-century scholar and meditation teacher, Kamalashila, points out that everyone in the universe has been one's friend hundreds of times in the past. Atisha, a tenth to eleventh-century Indian scholar who promoted Buddhism in Tibet, avers that all sentient beings have been one's mother in prior lifetimes. How can one not be loving toward one's former friend or mother? Vimalakirti, a layman and a bodhisattva, says, "the bodhisattva loves all living beings as if each were his only child." He notes further that the bodhisattva, recognizing in his own suffering the infinite suffering of other living beings, resolves to remove all suffering.[8]

In the Bodhicharyavatara, Shantideva offers a three-fold method for developing compassion: equality of self and other, exchange of self with other, and identity of self and other. Concerning equality of self and other, he writes (8:95f):[9]

> When both myself and others
> Are alike in wishing for happiness,
> What is special about me?
> Why do I strive for happiness for myself alone?

> When both myself and others
> Are alike in not wishing suffering,
> What is special about me?
> Why do I protect myself and not others?

In the stanza prior to the above, Shantideva actually goes beyond equalizing by giving preference to the other. "Others . . . are to be favored by me because their creaturehood is like my own creaturehood." He extends the bodhisattva's altruistic spirit even further by means of exchanging oneself for others. He writes (8:120): "Whoever wishes to quickly rescue himself and another should practice the supreme mystery: the exchanging of himself and the other."[10] This occurs by intentionally taking on the suffering of others and extending to them one's own happiness.[11]

In order to ease the suffering of others as well as himself, Shantideva confesses that he gives himself to others and accepts others as himself. He also affirms the identity of himself and others. He makes it clear that working for the liberation of another is indistinguishable from working for one's own liberation. Also, working for one's own liberation is indistinguishable from working for the liberation of another. If I and you are identical in our essential nature, how is there room for preference? Compassion flows when I and you are seen to be identical, a seeing that comes with wisdom.

When the six perfections (*paramitas*) of bodhisattvas are named, wisdom is the culminating one. The paramitas are the qualities that must be acquired if one is to become a buddha. Paramita also carries the meaning of 'gone to the beyond', suggesting both the increase of each quality to its absolute limit, thus perfectly, and reaching the absolute limit of human realization, namely, buddhahood, by developing all of the qualities perfectly. Hui-neng, the sixth Zen Patriarch of China, in his Platform Sutra, interprets paramita to mean 'to the opposite shore', an expression often used to designate buddhahood, and one that for Hui-neng implies a state beyond existence and non-existence.[12] When fully developed, the qualities are said to be transcendent. While constituting the express path of the bodhisattva, the paramitas outline a discipline that is accessible to all serious Buddhists.

The first of the perfections is generosity or giving (*dana*). The spirit of one's giving must be the same as if one were making an offering to the Buddha. In every act of giving, there must be no discrimination, no sense of one gift being greater or more important than another because of greater economic value, greater importance of the recipient, or any other consideration. Vimalakirti taught: "the giver who makes gifts to the lowliest poor of the city, considering them as worthy of offering as the Tathagata [Buddha] himself, the giver who gives without any discrimination, impartially, with no expectation of reward, and with great love;" this giver gives perfectly.[13] In addition to material gifts, one can give by offering guidance, encouragement, and instruction in living a worthy life. In the self-immolation of Vietnamese Buddhist monks protesting the war in their country, one sees an extraordinary application of dana. While such an extreme act is rare, it attests to the total commitment to the principle of giving that marks some practitioners of Buddhism.

In the course of following the bodhisattva path, particularly in practicing dana, a great deal of merit is accumulated. But instead of allowing this merit to insure future bliss, the bodhisattva transfers it to others so that it may accelerate their progress toward buddhahood. The merit gained through giving is itself given away, thus earning still further merit that in turn can be given away. Every act of giving amounts to a purifying that eventually results in an emptying that is itself an instance of nirvana. But how can there be an eventual emptying if every act of giving results in the formation of additional merit? The rational mind is perplexed at such a prospect. In the giving-merit-giving-merit cycle, we see a particular application of the law of karma (cause-effect) as it propels the samsaric cycle (the continual round of becoming). But we also see here an instance of the Mahayana insistence on the ultimate identity of samsara and nirvana, a position that will be discussed subsequently. In a word, beyond the rational mind there lies a wisdom that sees the final indistinguishability, the nonduality of samsara and nirvana. As pointed out in an introduction to the Bodhicharyavatara: "In the course of countless time cycles, [bodhisattvas] give and give and give until there is nothing left to give, and that state is *nirvrita*, the condition of being satisfied, happy, content, emancipated, extinguished."[14]

The second paramita is morality (*shila*). Shantideva calls attention to the profound significance of the bodhisattva's ethical behavior by noting that any wrongdoing on his part jeopardizes the welfare of others. The bodhisattva is expected to abstain from the ten non-virtuous acts: killing, stealing, sexual misconduct, lying, slander, harsh speech, frivolous chatter, covetousness, harmful intent, and false views. Several texts go beyond these prohibitions to spell out in greater detail the ethical requirements of the bodhisattva path. The perfected morality of the bodhisattva does not consist only in the avoidance of non-virtuous acts. He is charged also with the performance of virtuous acts, acts which show the bodhisattva to be, in fact, an adept social worker. Asanga offers a description of the bodhisattva's specific acts of giving to the needy and the sick.

> The bodhisattva attends the suffering. He nurses sentient beings beset by sickness. He leads the blind and shows them the way. He causes the deaf to understand using sign language by teaching them symbols for words. Those without arms or legs he carries himself or transports them by conveyance . . . . Furthermore, the bodhisattva protects fearful sentient beings from fear . . . . Furthermore, the bodhisattva takes away the grief of sentient beings who have suffered misfortune . . . . Furthermore, the bodhisattva provides necessities for those who want necessities. He gives food to those who want food . . . , drink to those who want drink, transportation to those who want transportation, clothing to those who want clothing . . . , a place to stay for those who need a place to stay, and light for those who need light.[15]

This commitment of the bodhisattva to alleviate suffering is clear evidence that Buddhism is not an other-worldly tradition that ignores the reality and importance of common human needs.

Buddhist morality defines the relationship between people and other sentient beings. If a person is moral in relation to another, harmony and happiness prevail between them. If one is immoral toward another, estrangement and unhappiness prevail. Because morality defines relationship, it affects the inner state of those in the relationship. To be violated or to violate another is to set up inner disturbance in both. Morality, on the other hand, contributes to inner contentment for both parties. This is particularly important for a bodhisattva since contentment is a prerequisite for inner tranquility, a state that must be cultivated by the bodhisattva. If a bodhisattva wronged others, he would not only violate the paramita of morality, he would also create a condition within himself that would make meditation, the fifth paramita, impossible.

This does not mean, however, that the bodhisattva is bound under all circumstances to abide by the requirements of conventional morality. Morality as a transcendent quality sometimes calls for action that may appear immoral from a customary standpoint. Ultimately, the bodhisattva is bound only by wisdom and compassion. While such a circumstance may be rare, if wisdom and compassion dictate a course of action in disregard of common morality, the bodhisattva will act in the best interests of those whose enlightenment he is serving, regardless of critical reactions from onlookers. The annals of Buddhism, as well as other religious traditions, are replete with instances where morality is subjected to transcendent values.[16] Shantideva declares that it is actually advisable to abandon customary morality rather than forfeit an opportunity to practice charity. Under certain circumstances the exercise of one virtue may require the exception of another. But only the perfect or transcendent wisdom of a bodhisattva will know when this is the case. Vimalakirti affirms that "when the bodhisattva follows the [so-called] wrong way, he follows the way to attain the qualities of the Buddha," and hints at how this is possible by observing that "even should he enact the five deadly sins, he feels no malice, violence, or hate."[17] It is, admittedly, difficult to understand how this could be. By loosening one's grasp on conventional ways, however, one may begin to glimpse the superior value of transcendent ways in exceptional circumstances.

The third paramita, *kshanti,* is usually translated 'patience' but sometimes as 'tolerance'. The integral nature of the two becomes apparent on reflection: without patience one is not apt to be tolerant; without tolerance one is not apt to be patient. The bodhisattva is expected to remain tolerant even in situations that would instill anger and hatred in ordinary persons. The reasons for this patience/ tolerance in the face of adversity are twofold: to extend compassion to all, even those who are hostile, and to preserve one's inner tranquility, an essential feature of bodhichitta, the mind and heart of enlightenment.[18] To react to hostility with hostility (virtually instinctual in most humans) undermines, perhaps even destroys, the virtue that has been manifested and the good achieved over time. Later in the same chapter (6:102), Shantideva underscores the difficulty and importance of practicing this virtue by claiming that "there is no austerity equal to patience." Signs of perfect patience are seen in the ability to remain without anger or agitation when undergoing hardship and pain, and to be forgiving of those who injure and abuse oneself.[19]

That humanity benefits from bodhisattvas is obvious. That bodhisattvas benefit from those they serve is perhaps less obvious. But Vimalakirti exclaims, "the more you teach and demonstrate virtuous qualities to others, the more you grow with respect to these virtuous qualities."[20] Shantideva extolled the symbiotic relationship between bodhisattvas and those who opposed them by declaring that the latter are in fact aids on the path to enlightenment. So-called enemies are actually friends because they provide opportunities to practice generosity, morality, and patience. Bodhisattvas cannot attain buddhahood for themselves or others without the ignorance and unvirtuous qualities of others. They depend on them for their own development of the compassion and wisdom that will enable them to win liberation for themselves and others. Shantideva observes that since the qualities of buddhahood are occasioned as much by ordinary persons as the instructions of the Buddha, a bodhisattva cannot justify any greater respect for enlightened beings than for ordinary beings.

The fourth quality to perfect is *virya*, or vigor. This is the great energy and effort that must be relentlessly directed toward the eradication of personal faults and the cultivation of noble qualities, the elimination of ignorance and the development of wisdom, and the performance of good deeds for the benefit of others. Virya connotes heroic effort and characterizes the bodhisattva as a hero who pushes through to buddhahood against virtually insurmountable difficulties. Shantideva underscores the incomparable value of human existence by drawing on an analogy from the Buddha which indicates that being born a human is as rare an event as a turtle poking its head through the opening of a yoke floating in the ocean. Given the immeasurable rarity of birth as a human, the Bodhicharyavatara concludes that failure to practice bodhicitta is the height of stupidity and self-trickery. Acknowledging the pain and sacrifice necessitated by the bodhisattva path, Shantideva notes that even as pain and discomfort often accompany healing remedies, disconcerting practices may sometimes be required in the pursuit of the good and worthy. The gains are well worth the effort and discipline expended in pursuit of the perfections.

The fifth paramita is *dhyana*, 'concentration', 'contemplation', or 'meditation'. By means of this discipline, the bodhisattva investigates the nature of his own mind, an absolute prerequisite to the attainment of wisdom, the next paramita. Shantideva (7:1, 4), knowing that effort has as much relevance for the interior life as the exterior, opens his chapter on contemplation by linking the two paramitas: "Having thus increased one's energy, the mind should be established in meditation." He continues, perceptively: "By means of tranquility (*shamatha*) one achieves clarity of vision (*vipashyana*). The tranquil person destroys passion . . . , and this comes through indifference to the world."

There are many ways of meditating in Buddhism, and many descriptions of the meditative experience. Two common elements are identified by Shantideva as 'perfect quiescence of the mind' (shamatha) and 'transcendental analysis' (vipashyana). Shantideva (8:39) describes the concentrative dimension of meditation: "Liberated from the thought of anything else, the mind centered one-pointedly upon its own thought, I shall strive for the composing of thought and its control." Shamatha may be further understood as the simultaneous practice of concentration and letting go. The mind is focused on a single object, usually mental, while letting go of everything else. When thoughts intrude and the mind is found to wander, it is brought calmly, without judgment, back to the point of focus. This process entails and deepens a physical, emotional, and mental quietness that is in itself clarity and that fosters a further clarity that prepares for and becomes insight (vipashyana). While many meditative states are without cognitive content (and thus characterized as ineffable), vipashyana is not. The Russian Buddologist, Obermiller, describes the meditator involved in transcendental analysis as follows: "He investigates the object as an empirical reality, perfectly examines its absolute nature, reflects on it, steadfastly pursues his analysis, experiences satisfaction in the process of it, distinguishes the particularities, and makes his thought-constructions."[21] Thus, Buddhists claim that meditation leads to insight into the real nature of the real. Later in the chapter we will discover the insights and consequent teachings that came to the Buddha during the meditative session that constituted his enlightenment.

The sixth-century Chinese Buddhist master, T'ien T'ai, clarifies still further this Buddhist approach to meditation.

There are many paths for entering the reality of nirvana, but in essence they are all contained within two practices: stopping and seeing. Stopping is the primary gate for overcoming the bonds of compulsiveness. Seeing is the essential requisite for ending confusion. Stopping is the wholesome resource that nurtures the mind. Seeing is the marvelous art which fosters intuitive understanding. Stopping is the effective cause of attaining concentrative repose. Seeing is the very basis of enlightened wisdom.

A person who attains both concentration and wisdom has all the requisites for self-help and for helping others . . . . It should be known, then, that these two techniques are like the two wheels of a chariot, the two wings of a bird. If their practice is lopsided, you will fall from the path. Therefore, the Sutra says: To cultivate one-sidedly the merits of concentrative repose without practicing understanding is called dullness. To cultivate one-sidedly knowledge without practicing repose is called being crazed. Dullness and craziness, although they are somewhat different, are the same in that they both perpetuate an unwholesome perspective.[22]

The link between the tranquility of concentration and the insight of analysis is crucial. In terms of the paramitas, meditation prepares for wisdom.

The sixth perfection, wisdom or prajna, is the culmination of all the others. The bodhisattva's wisdom is perfect when he thoroughly understands through direct seeing that all persons and all phenomena are without substance, without essence, without self, without inherent being, in a word; all things are empty (shunya). Vimalakirti summarizes: "All living beings are without intrinsic identity."[23] Shantideva advises practitioners to see everything as resembling space. The virtues other than wisdom assure the bodhisattva of better rebirths and enable him to teach and inspire other sentient beings, but not to liberate them or himself. Only wisdom allows him to cut through suffering and ignorance. Without wisdom, liberation is impossible. Seeing into the emptiness of all things, the central perspective in Mahayana Buddhism, will be explored more fully later in the chapter.

Skill-in-means (*upaya*) is sometimes added as an additional perfection. For example, Vimalakirti was "endowed with an infinite knowledge of skill in liberative technique" and employed each of the transcendent virtues as skill-in-means. He declares that the purpose of the paramitas is "to win the poor by generosity, to win the immoral by morality, to win the hateful by means of tolerance, to win the lazy by means of effort, to win the mentally troubled by means of concentration, [and] to win the falsely wise by means of true wisdom."[24] Kamalashila regards wisdom and method, i.e., skill-in-means, as essential to each other. "Method without wisdom and wisdom without method are the bodhisattva's bondage. Wisdom with method and method with wisdom are freedom."[25]

While the perfection of wisdom is the culmination of all the perfections, wisdom itself informs the practice of all the virtues, otherwise the others could not become perfected. It is only the wise exercise of the virtues that allows them to become truly perfected. A proper understanding of the paramitas indicates that "a virtue is practiced to perfection [only] when the most difficult acts are executed with a mind free from discriminatory ideas, without self-consciousness, ulterior motives, or self-congratulation."[26] Chandrakirti, an eighth-century philosopher, writes: "Giving void of giver, gift, and recipient is called a supramundane perfection. When attachment to these three is produced, it is called a mundane perfection."[27] If the giver has any sense of himself as one who is giving something of value to a needy person, the act of giving is simply ordinary and not transcendent or perfect. For a bodhisattva to give with perfect generosity, there must be no sense of a real gift being given by a real individual to a real person. His understanding of emptiness must permeate every action.

Somewhere along the path, a bodhisattva ceases to be an ordinary human being engaged in an extraordinary discipline and takes on supramundane qualities and powers. He is no longer imprisoned in the transient world of cyclical becoming, nor is he eternally absorbed in the infinite void. Because he resides in a realm that is simultaneously samsara and nirvana, he links the mundane and supramundane worlds. Having reached the end of the immeasurably long path to full realization, he is now able to assume any desired form, human or otherwise, in order to assist sentient beings on their respective spiritual journeys. As an infinite reservoir of wisdom, compassion, virtue, merit, skill, the bodhisattva is now available to all who call on him for aid. Sometimes called a buddha since his qualities are indistinguishable from those of a buddha, a bodhisattva dwelling in the Tushita heaven (Abode of the Contented Ones), through his omniscience, omnipotence, and omnipresence, responds with liberating appropriateness to those who direct their needs and aspirations to him. In Buddhism, the bodhisattva personifies the grace that permeates the universe.

Buddhism has a rich pantheon of bodhisattvas and celestial buddhas. Vimalakirti names about fifty bodhisattvas. Maitreya, whose name comes from a root meaning benevolent, is the Future Buddha; he will come, some say in thirty thousand years, to liberate countless thousands. Depicted as eternally youthful, Manjushri, the Bodhisattva of Wisdom, holds an infinite store of merit that aids those who call on him. Perhaps the most popular is Avalokiteshvara, the Bodhisattva of Infinite Compassion, who is known in Tibet as Chenrezi, in China as Kuan Yin, and in Japan as Kannon. Of male gender in India and Tibet and female in China and Japan, Avalokiteshvara is so vital in the consciousness of Buddhists that even in the otherwise image stark monasteries of Zen Buddhism, statues and paintings of Kannon are found. Followers of the Dalai Lama, the spiritual and political leader of the Tibetan people, regard him as an incarnation of Avalokiteshvara.

Amitabha, also known as Amitayus, is the Buddha of Infinite Light and Life, and one of the most important and popular celestial buddhas. He reigns in the Western Paradise, or Pure Land, which is conceived exoterically as a location but spiritually as a realm of being or state of consciousness. Amida (Japanese form of Amitabha) is the center of faith and devotion in the most popular forms of Buddhism in Japan, Jodo Shu and Jodo Shin Shu. Another important celestial buddha is Vairochana (Shining Out), also known as the Sun Buddha. He is both source and symbol of the highest wisdom. In Japan, Vairochana is known as Dainichi (Great Sun); his body, speech, and mind are believed to constitute the entire operation of the universe. In some Tibetan and Japanese forms of Buddhism, Vairochana personifies the Dharmakaya and is the Adibuddha, the first or primordial Buddha from whom all other buddhas emanate. While Buddhism officially denies the existence of gods and goddesses, the celestial buddhas and bodhisattvas function in god-like fashion for many Buddhists, and serve also as a means of relating individuals to larger or metaphysical realities.

Another way of understanding the metaphysical realm is by means of the *trikaya* (three bodies) doctrine, which envisions three forms or realms of Buddhist manifestation. Nirmanakaya (transformation body) represents the earthly body assumed by buddhas in their appearance among humans. Sambhogakaya (glorious or bliss body) identifies the celestial sphere where buddhas reside in an intermediate realm of great power and glory. This is also the realm of cosmic law prior to manifestation. The ultimate realm, the Dharmakaya (body of truth), is transcendent reality. Here buddha nature is the nameless source and unity of all that is. In reverse order, Sambhogakaya and Nirmanakaya are increasingly apparitional forms of Ultimacy, the Dharmakaya.

The Mahasiddha in Vajrayana Buddhism

In Tibet, Vajrayana Buddhism offers the *mahasiddha* as the enlightenment ideal. Mahasiddha denotes one who is a 'great master of magical powers'. The bodhisattva tradition carries over into Tibetan Buddhism but takes on distinctive features in its adaptation to the Tibetan milieu. Corresponding to prajna and karuna in Mahayana Buddhism are prajna and upaya in Vajrayana. The substitution of skill-in-means for compassion means that the methods used to effect liberation are all expressions of compassion, no matter what specific form they may take. Compassionate method is, of course, always directed by wisdom.

In search of a faster route to nirvana than the aeons of purification required in Indian Mahayana, Tibetan Buddhists undertake what they regard as a more intense outer and inner discipline involving, among other things, extraordinary rituals and complex meditative approaches, including intricate visualization processes. If the ordinary world of experience is not different from nirvana, then any object, circumstance, or action can be used as an aid to ultimate realization. Even negative emotions can be ritualistically transmuted in order to effect release from their binding power. If all is mind, as some Buddhist systems contend, then thought and consciousness can be controlled to create an inner seeing that becomes wisdom and release.

By means of their discipline, mahasiddhas gain *siddhis*, magical powers that manifest their liberated status and also serve to instruct and liberate others. The mahasiddhas are liberated humans, usually lay men and women, who often travel about with minimal if any regard for conventional norms. Since all social conditions are without any particular spiritual significance, in fact, are without inherent reality, enlightenment can occur as readily in one conditioned situation as another. A socially low ranking person is as capable of full realization as someone of high status.

Eighty-four mahasiddhas are recognized in Tibetan classical literature, though innumerably more have roamed the mountains and valleys. They are often long-haired iconoclasts who exhibit radical freedom in their teaching and lifestyle. A glimpse of the mahasiddha's depth of understanding and corresponding way of life is suggested by Saraha. Known as the Great Brahmin, he seems to have experienced a fundamental breakthrough to wisdom as a result of his involvement—deemed scandalous by the traditionalists of his time—with a low caste woman.

There is nothing to be negated, nothing to be affirmed or grasped;
For It can never be conceived.

153

By the fragmentations of the intellect are the deluded fettered;
Undivided and pure remains spontaneity.[28]

Spontaneity (*sahaja*, also coemergence) denotes an experience of wholeness and naturalness in which all opposites—subject/object, transcendent/immanent, good/evil, sacred/profane—merge into a single seeing. Sahaja signifies the life force unobstructively and unselfconsciously manifesting.

In addition to breaking social and religious taboos in order to demonstrate the impropriety of identifying any external form with genuine spirituality, the mahasiddha exercises magical powers in order to demonstrate that the perceived world is not as definite and firmly fixed as it appears. Just as the rigidity of social convention can be softened and opened by the mahasiddha, so the apparent laws of nature can be disrupted or transcended. Common sense perception of both the social and natural worlds is far removed from the transparent perception of the mahasiddha, who sees through the conditions that are accepted as absolute and inviolable by the untutored.

Mahasiddhas are credited with the power to turn people into stone, the ability to transmute base materials into diamonds, run at incredible speeds and not touch the ground, and walk on water. Whether these or other miracles actually occur is of less consequence to those who grant primacy to spiritual reality than to modern Westerners with their unquestioning acceptance of common sense perception and modern science. In final analysis, the truth may be one of both/and rather than either/or. Perhaps we live in a world where the material and spiritual are not in fundamental combat but where each is intertwined with the other. Such at least is the world declared by the wisdom and methods of the mahasiddhas.[29] Lama Anagarika Govinda, a European with a lifetime of Buddhist study and practice, mostly in Tibet, concludes that "the bodhisattva ideal . . . needs no justification through scholasticism, dogmatism, or religious history [we might add, secular history or scientific materialism], for it is the expression of an inner attitude that has repeatedly demonstrated its power of transformation."[30] The bodhisattva ideal validates itself through the countless lives it effectively and fundamentally transforms.

Our survey of the enlightenment ideal in Buddhism has shown a great deal of uniformity in the three branches, but some differences as well. One such difference is valuational. Vajrayana considers itself more advanced than Mahayana, and Mahayana thinks of itself as more advanced than Theravada. Vajrayana believes that it teaches a streamlined Buddhism, one that is entirely faithful to the bodhisattva ideal but which shortens the liberational path by intensifying the discipline. Mahayana, with Vajrayana, believes that Theravada arahants represent a selfish ideal since they aim only for their own liberation and do not postpone nirvana in order to help other suffering beings. Tibetan Buddhists occasionally claim that Theravada sets forth beginning practices, Mahayana intermediate methods, and Vajrayana advanced discipline.

In spite of these and other differences, an inclusive spirit of tolerance and conciliation exists throughout Buddhism. Vimalakirti quotes the Buddha himself as saying that "the nectar which nourishes each one differs according to the differences of the merits each has accumulated." The bodhisattva Ratnakara clarifies: "Although the Lord speaks with but one voice, those present perceive that same voice differently, and each understands in his own language according to his own needs."[31] The Chinese patriarch Hui-neng notes that differences do not exist in the vehicles that convey Buddhism but "in the differentiation of people's minds."[32] Finally, Tsong Khapa, a renowned scholar and reformer of Tibetan Buddhism in the fourteenth and fifteenth centuries, asserts that differences found in Buddhism are not "on account of the wisdom cognizing the profound emptiness, but on account of method."[33] By its very nature, skill-in-means is adapted to the different temperaments, levels of understanding, and situations of those to whom it is directed. Because the needs of people differ, the methods of Buddhism vary. But the supreme realization, the wisdom and compassion that flow from the awareness of emptiness, does not vary.

The Buddha

Buddha is a title, not a proper name; the word means 'One Who Has Awakened', i.e., to Reality as it is. Various dates have been given for the life of the Buddha; widely accepted by scholars is 566-486 BCE. He therefore lived to be eighty years old. His family name is Gautama and his personal name Siddhartha, meaning 'He Whose Aims Are Fulfilled'. He is also known as Shakyamuni, 'Sage of the Shakya Clan'. An epithet often given him is Tathagatha, 'He Who Has Thus Come' or 'He Who Has Thus Gone'. From an exoteric and dualistic perspective, Tathagata indicates that the Buddha has gone from ignorance, bondage, and unreality to wisdom, liberation, and Reality. From a metateric perspective, the come/gone ambiguity suggests that the notion of movement, of journeying, of becoming what one formerly was not, is itself untenable. The Tathagata knows that the Real is changeless, that coming and going are illusions, and that time is intemporal. Absolute Truth in Buddhism is often called *tathata*, 'thusness', 'suchness'. Reality is *thus, such* as it is, i.e., it simply is what is. Tathata indicates; it does not represent. The Tathagata knows the tathata of Reality. The Buddha, the Tathagata, was often characterized by the standard formula: "worthy, fully enlightened, endowed with wisdom and virtuous conduct, well gone, the knower of worlds, unsurpassed charioteer of men to be tamed, teacher of gods and men, an enlightened one, an exalted one."[34]

Traditional biographies of the Buddha declare that after countless lives dedicated to realizing the perfections and serving others, lives spanning a hundred thousand aeons and taking place in different worlds and celestial realms, he took birth in Lumbini, now a part of Nepal near the Indian border. His mother, Queen Maya, wife of King Suddhodana, had dreamed earlier that a white elephant entered her right side. Brahmins interpreted the dream to mean that her son would become either a universal monarch or a great religious teacher. Emerging from his mother's side as she stood beneath a tree in the Lumbini Grove, the infant Buddha-to-be surveyed all directions and announced that this would be his final birth.

Wanting his son to succeed him on the throne, Suddhodana determined to keep his son so preoccupied with the pleasures of life that he would have no occasion or inclination to reflect on the human situation. Siddhartha was thus surrounded with every imaginable luxury and pleasure. At sixteen he was married to his cousin; by the time he turned twenty-nine, his wife had given birth to a son who was named Rahula (fetter), perhaps an indication of Siddhartha's growing frustration and discontent. Suddhodana, observing restlessness in his son, arranged for Siddhartha to take a journey outside the palace grounds. However, to ensure that the excursion would boost his son's spirit, Suddhodana had his servants carefully prepare the route to be traveled so that no disturbing events or sights might be encountered. In spite of extensive preparations, however, Siddhartha came upon an aged person, stooped, wrinkled, and decrepit, on his first outing. His charioteer explained aging to him. On his second trip, Siddhartha saw a sick person, perhaps a leper with open sores and missing toes and fingers. He was now particularly distraught. On his third venture, he witnessed a funeral procession, seeing a corpse and meeting death for the first time. He was now more troubled than ever, seemingly beyond any possibility of consolation. On his final outing, he saw a monk, and his charioteer explained the religious quest. A glimmer of hope now arose within him. Perhaps a resolution to the problem of aging, sickness, and death could be found. Returning to the palace, he bade farewell to his family, including his wife and newborn son, and set out to solve the puzzle of human existence.

He sought out sages and holy men, and carefully pondered their teachings and practiced their disciplines. He quickly achieved the meditative states taught by two different teachers but, realizing that these states, though calm and pleasant, did not enable him to see into the cause of suffering, he left his teachers to continue his search. He adopted a rigorous ascetic regimen, according to some accounts, subsisting on one grain of rice a day. It is said that he became so thin that his belly button touched his backbone. So thorough was his commitment that five other ascetics took him as their teacher and guide. After six years of extreme discipline, he finally realized that he was no closer to solving the human predicament than he had been while living in his father's palace. Luxury and indulgence had only deluded him. Severe self-denial had nearly destroyed him. He decided to adopt a more moderate course, to avoid extremes and to search inwardly for answers to the problems that plagued him. When he took food and water, his disciples lost confidence and abandoned him.

After regaining strength and health, Siddhartha sat down under what has come to be known as the Bodhi Tree, the Tree of Enlightenment, an offshoot of which grows even today in Bodh Gaya, India. Exercising heroic determination, coupled with a calm and sensitive awareness, Siddhartha turned his attention inward. He was met by Mara, a demonic force bent on keeping humans trapped in sensuality and other attachments. Mara urged Siddhartha to give up his quest and settle for the accumulation of merit. When Siddhartha refused, Mara shifted his tactic and challenged Siddhartha to produce a witness who would affirm his worth. Siddhartha attested to his authenticity and his resolute, sincere pursuit of truth by touching the earth. It seemed that the earth, representing the entire cosmos, in turn attested to the accord existing between Siddhartha and cosmic law. Finally, Mara's daughters, representing the passions of craving, hatred, and folly, worked their wiles against him. But Siddhartha, protected by the virtues he had perfected during his long practice of the bodhisattva path, successfully resisted their temptations. Mara and his forces admitted defeat and fled.

Siddhartha continued to meditate throughout the night. By morning he had won through to enlightenment. In order to permeate his entire being with his new found state, to reflect on the import and implications of his enlightenment, and to decide whether or not to present it to others, he continued to sit in meditation for forty-nine days. He was thirty-five years old at the time. His breakthrough is reported in the Dhammapada: "I have gone through many rounds of birth and death, looking in vain for the builder of this body. Heavy indeed is birth and death again and again! But now I have seen you, house-builder; you shall not build this house again. Its beams are broken; its dome is shattered: self-will is extinguished; nirvana is attained."[35] The last two phrases are rendered quite differently in another translation: "My mind has gone beyond the transitory, the conditioned, and has achieved the extinction of craving."[36]

In his exploration of consciousness, the Buddha entered various meditative states and discovered the fundamental truths governing human existence. He witnessed his own prior lives. He saw exactly how karma works, how it keeps people bound to samsaric existence and gives rise to each succeeding round of birth and death. Some accounts claim that he gained extraordinary psychic abilities (clairvoyance, telepathy) and magical powers (levitation, walking on water). He realized the impossibility of conveying the truth of his discovery by means of words and decided to remain silent. He was informed by a compassionate god, however, that there are people "with little dust in their eyes," that is, whose vision is minimally distorted, and who would benefit from his teaching. When he met the five monks who had previously deserted him, they saw his extraordinary transformation, became his followers again, and soon gained enlightenment themselves.

Tradition indicates that the five monks became the first members of the sangha. Along with others who had begun to follow the Buddha, they were sent out and told to preach and teach "for the blessing of the many, for the happiness of the many, out of compassion for the world."[37] Among the Buddha's most renowned disciples was Ananda, his cousin and personal attendant, who possessed an uncommon ability to remember with precision the Buddha's talks. Ananda interceded on behalf of women to convince the Buddha to establish an order of nuns. Shariputra, another famous disciple, was revered for his exceptional wisdom and teaching skills. Kashyapa is prized by Buddhists for his exemplary self-discipline and moral rectitude. He assumed leadership of the sangha following the Buddha's death. Kashyapa is widely known for his spontaneous enlightenment when the Buddha, with no comment or explanation, held up a lotus blossom. Kashyapa smiled, thereby indicating his understanding. In reference to this event, the Buddha said: "The marvelous mind of nirvana . . . does not rest on words or letters but is a special transmission outside of the scriptures."[38] The view that enlightenment comes through a special transmission is particularly important in Zen Buddhism.

The Buddha and his entourage were sustained in their wandering by hospitality from those they served. In spite of illness, he continued to move about on foot during the last three months of his life. After unwittingly eating some spoiled food, he lay down between two trees, which miraculously sprung into bloom. Tradition says that gods from ten regions of the universe came to see the Buddha pass from samsara to nirvana. While meditating, he calmly and fearlessly passed into nirvana. Buddhists view the Tathagata's departure not so much as death as the attainment of deathlessness.

The Four Noble Truths

The Buddha began to expound publicly the profundities of his realization—in so far as words would permit—in what has come to be known as the Sermon in the Deer Park, a park near Benares. In this first "turning of the wheel of the teaching" he set forth the Four Noble Truths: the fact of suffering, its origin, its cessation, and the discipline leading to its cessation. The First Noble Truth diagnoses the human situation as one of universal suffering. All of life involves *duhkha*, usually translated as 'suffering' but designating a condition more comprehensive and more subtle than that denoted by the English term. The Buddha declared that birth, decay, sickness, death, sorrow, grief, woe, despair, contact with what is disliked, separation from what is liked—all of this is suffering. The drive behind greed, whether for material goods or sensual experience, is suffering. But duhkha is also the subtle yet pervasive sense that something is amiss, life is not what it should—or could—be. It is the gnawing sense of dissatisfaction that is almost always present if one but tunes into it. Even when we think we are happy, duhkha is present since we know our joy will end. Life will return to discontent when the temporary distraction has passed.

The very process of socialization tends to desensitize us to our suffering. When a child cries because of a fall, he is often met with the well-intentioned but discounting words, "Oh, that really doesn't hurt so badly." We become calloused to our suffering and typically grow up denying a great deal of our pain by repressing it, ignoring it, or convincing ourselves that it's just part of life. Finally, any time we wish the present circumstances of our life were otherwise than they are, we are suffering. To the extent that we assume the future will be better than the present, we are suffering. The assumption would not arise if we were not dissatisfied with the present. The Buddha's analysis sounds pessimistic, and it would be if it were not for the remaining Truths.

The Second Noble Truth identifies the cause of suffering as *trishna*, usually translated 'desire', but again more subtle and pervasive than the common English sense of the term. Trishna in its gross form is experienced as 'longing', 'thirst', 'craving'. Buddhism requires that every form of craving be relinquished, whether gross selfishness or longing for better weather, since in all cases there is some dissatisfaction with the reality of the moment. Desire in all of its forms arises in the contact between the senses and their respective objects, and leads to attachment, which is bondage and therefore suffering. Buddhism regards the mind as a sixth sense, where thoughts become the objects of thinking. Therefore, even ideas bind and cause suffering to the extent that one holds fast to them, either through cherishing or rejecting.

To desire an object that appeals to the senses is to become the prisoner of that object. To hate an object that repels the senses is equally to become the prisoner of that object. Hate is essentially the same as desire, only directionality changes. Desire attracts; hate repels. In both cases, there is attachment. In its universality and subtlety, trishna—as the psychic force of attraction/repulsion— ranges all the way from the overwhelming passion that results in ecstasy or violence, through the liking and disliking that lead to joy and sadness, to the hidden preferences that influence satisfaction or dissatisfaction. The centrality of desirelessness in the resolution of the human predicament was clearly recognized by the Third Zen Patriarch in China. He opened his brief tract, "Verses on the Faith Mind," with the assertion: "The Great Way is not difficult for those who have no preferences."[39]

The inherent link between duhkha and trishna is seen in the fact that every instance of suffering, obvious or subtle, is marked by a wanting of what is not (or, which is to say the same thing, a not wanting of what is). Suffering and desire inhere in each other so implicitly that they are experientially indistinguishable. If suffering is found, desire is present; if desire is present, suffering is found. They are no more separable then are concave and convex. The Buddha's brilliance lies in the articulation of the obvious.

The Third Noble Truth (named, *nirodha*, 'cessation', 'destruction') offers a promising prognosis; suffering ceases as desire ceases. Since the two are in fact one, a diminution of one is a diminution of the other, the dissolution of one is the dissolution of the other. The Fourth Noble Truth names the path (*marga*) by which desire and its accompanying suffering are overcome, even destroyed. This discipline is known as the Eightfold Path.

The Eightfold Path

The Eightfold Path is made up of eight dimensions in a single discipline. Each of the eight requirements begins with the word 'right' or 'correct'. This has nothing to do with orthodoxy, however, since there is no dogmatism in the Eightfold Path. Lama Govinda describes right as "the unconditional and unlimited engagement of the totality of our mental and spiritual properties and powers."[40] As the aspirant applies his whole person—thinking, speaking, acting—to each of the disciplinary steps, there results a deepening and purifying of personality and character that facilitates further balance, wholeness, and insight.

The Eightfold Path begins with Right Views, that is, right ideas, right mental contents, right understanding. If the mind holds ideas that are not in accord with reality, enlightenment will prove elusive. The mind in its natural or original state is pure and undefiled; false views occlude this natural purity and cause confusion. Mental confusion or ignorance in turn gives rise to all additional forms of suffering, whether fear, anger, hatred, jealousy, avarice, selfishness, etc. Hui-neng argues the point: "Enlightened by right views, we call forth the buddha within us. When our nature is dominated by the three poisonous elements [ignorance, greed, hatred] we are said to be possessed by Mara; but when right views eliminate from our mind these poisonous elements, Mara will be transformed into a real buddha."[41]

The first view that must be held rightly is that of the Four Noble Truths. Just as the fourth Noble Truth points ahead to the Eightfold Path so the first step in the Eightfold Path points back to include the Four Noble Truths. The Four and the Eight form an integral whole. Theravada Buddhists locate liberation in the full knowledge of the Fourfold Truth since that includes the practices outlined in the Eightfold Path. Buddhists ascribe to the Four Noble Truths not by dogmatically believing them but by experientially testing them. Buddhism is a tradition without dogma; it offers truths to be tried, not creeds to be affirmed. The truth of suffering, desire, and their cessation by means of a particular discipline is to be tried, tested, acted upon. Right views in Buddhism, then, does not imply mere assent; it implies views that have transformational import, views that impel from bondage to liberation, from ignorance to wisdom.

The second step in the Eightfold Path is Right Aspiration, or right intention, purpose, resolve. Right aspiration must be distinguished from the desire or craving that constitutes the Second Noble Truth. The destructive and limiting element in the kind of desire referred to in the Second Noble Truth is the inner sense that there is something wrong or deficient in the present circumstance, that it could and should be different than it is. There is also a 'stickiness' present by way of attachment to some imagined condition that is believed to be better. There is nothing of this in right aspiration since it is based on the full acceptance of existing conditions as the inevitable result of prior causes. Right aspiration recognizes the law of cause and effect and knows that every unfolding event or situation could not be different than it is, given the prior conditions and the decisions made by those involved in those conditions. In summary, desire implies some degree of resistance; right aspiration implies full acceptance.

The second step in the Eightfold Path underscores the interior dimension of Buddhist practice. To merely exhibit correct behavior is insufficient; one's heart, one's deepest intention, must accompany the manifest action. To mindlessly perform an act of charity—or worse yet, to act with a hidden intention of ill will—neither benefits the other nor aids in the purification of one's own mind. The conscientious Buddhist will resolve to renounce all that is not conducive to realization, to not only eschew all action that might harm others but to will only the best for them. Right intention is simultaneously karmically purifying and beneficial to others.

Right Speech entails not only abstention from lying, slander, malicious criticism, gossip, and idle chatter, but any speech that fails to facilitate positive states of mind in oneself and others. Addressing himself to the effects of speech on the speaker, the Buddha said: "Those things . . . by which the speaker's unwholesome mental phenomena increase and wholesome mental phenomena decrease, those things should not be spoken of, so I say. Those things . . . by which the speaker's unwholesome mental phenomena dwindle and wholesome mental phenomena increase, those things should be spoken of, so I say."[42]

Right Conduct includes the prescriptions and proscriptions of a general or universal morality. In its emphasis on purity of motive, Buddhism in no way minimizes the importance of right behavior. All Buddhists are expected to observe five prohibitions: to refrain from killing, from taking what is not given (which includes but is not the same as abstention from stealing), from illicit sexual relations, from lying, and from intoxicants. Monks and nuns observe additional rules designed not only to create harmonious interpersonal relationships but also to free attention from matters extraneous to the liberational process.

Right Livelihood, or vocation, requires Buddhists to earn their living by means that do not violate Buddhist precepts. Any occupation involving harm is to be avoided. Gautama named five jobs that no Buddhist should accept: trade in weapons, meat, liquor, poison, and slavery. The principle of ahimsa, non-violence—as important in Buddhism as in Hinduism—informs the Buddha's proscription of these vocations. Since the vocations of butcher and meat merchant are forbidden, and believing that non-violence prohibits meat eating, many Buddhists are vegetarians. However, there is no express requirement to this effect from the Buddha. Many Buddhists out of compassion for animals do abstain from eating meat. Others, however, because of local tradition and climatic requirements do eat meat, Tibetan Buddhists, for example.

Right Effort, the sixth dimension of the Eightfold Path, calls for energetic endeavor when engaging a spiritual discipline. Personal transformation does not occur by adhering to habitual patterns or routine ways. Extraordinary effort is required to overcome the inertia of one's own conditioned ways of being and doing. One does not drift into enlightenment. As we have seen, sloth and torpor are major hindrances to spiritual realization. The Dhammapada recognizes vigilance as a fundamental difference between the immature and the wise. "The immature lose their vigilance, but the wise guard it as their greatest treasure." It continues: "Overcoming sloth through earnestness, the wise climb beyond suffering to the peaks of wisdom." The Buddha emphasized the need for effort not only in shaping behavior but, even more emphatically, in deconditioning one's mind, in meditating. "An aspirant . . . strives, generates motivation, exerts his mind, and does his best to see that unwholesome mental states that have arisen shall be expunged; that unwholesome mental states that have not arisen shall not arise; that wholesome mental states that have not arisen shall arise, and that wholesome mental states that have arisen shall be sustained, nurtured, augmented, developed, matured, and brought to fruition."[43]

Right Awareness, or mindfulness, comes next on the Eightfold Path. It requires that one be aware of the body and its sensations, of the emotions and their intensity, of the mind and its thoughts and moods. The opposite of right awareness is dull absent-mindedness. Since the quality of the mind determines the quality of the life, a lucid, vigorous, and present mind manifests in a life that is awake and spontaneous and involved. As with most features of Buddhism, this one too requires no withdrawal from ordinary life; it offers a transformational principle that can be applied at all times in all places—in so far as one is aware enough to remember to be aware. When eating, know you are eating. When walking, know you are walking. When angry, know you are angry—that in itself marks a beginning to the dissolution of anger. When sad, know you are sad—that in itself provides distance from the sadness, thereby increasing the possibility of insight into its deeper causes and compulsive forces. When happy, know you are happy—that in itself will give insight into your own personality and possibly lead to deeper understanding of the human condition.

Right Meditation concludes the Eightfold Path. Meditation, the royal road to enlightenment, is the *sine qua non* of full realization. It purifies and deepens all the other requirements of the Eightfold Path, even as they prepare for a purer and deeper meditation. The Buddha, having mastered all the dimensions of his long practice, passed through the four stages of meditation on the full moon night of his enlightenment. In the first stage, he detached from all sense objects and unwholesome states of mind. Discursive thinking slowed down; attention simply rested on passing mental images. He experienced a calming and eventual cessation of the emotions, though feelings of joy and happiness continued. A kind of zestful ease abounded. In the second stage, all conceptual and discursive activity ended and one-pointedness of mind took over; that is, attention fixed on a single mental image. Tranquility, joyful alertness, and contentedness marked his mental state. In the third stage, he was fully mindful but dispassionately so. Joy, in so far as it was an active sensation, gave way to calm happiness. A sense of equanimity and bliss prevailed. In the fourth stage, any lingering vestiges of polarity (pleasure-displeasure, joy-sorrow, elation-despondency) disappeared. Only equanimity and awareness remained. This state of consciousness marked one of the Buddha's principal realizations while sitting under the Bodhi Tree.

The earliest philosophical-psychological system of thought in Buddhism, which purports to be a systematization of the teaching and experience of the Buddha, is the Abhidharma, the 'Further' or 'Essential Teachings'. Abhidharma claims that the four dhyanas experienced by the Buddha belong to the realm of form. It identifies four additional states that belong to the formless realm. These are the state of infinite space, the state of infinite consciousness, the state of 'nothing at all', and the state of neither cognition nor its absence, i.e., the final limit of perception. Realization of the eight meditative states constitutes cessation, a state where all fetters or attachments are entirely destroyed. When it occurs in a mind marked by wisdom and compassion, cessation is identified with nirvana. Buddhism recognizes two forms of nirvana, 'with remainder' and 'without remainder'. Gautama's enlightenment under the Bodhi Tree was nirvana with remainder, i.e., with enough remaining, non-binding karma to permit him to continue living. At death, at his *parinirvana* or 'final' nirvana, no karma remained; at this time he passed from samsara to full nirvana, never more to know bondage or limitation in any form.

To try to describe the Buddha's experience of nirvana is, as Buddhists sometimes point out, comparable to a frog trying to explain dry land to tadpoles. We can only truly understand what we have experienced. The only way to know what nirvana is like is to 'wake up'. The Dhammapada agrees: "How can you describe him in human language—the Buddha, the awakened one, free from the net of desires and the pollution of passions, free from all conditioning?"[44] Even though we may not be enlightened, we are able to intuit at least some of its features. If we can see how we are entrapped by our attachments, we can 'imagine' what it would be like not to be. We often, in fact, feel most free when we see how we have not been free. Seeing our bondage is the first step in becoming free from that bondage. To the extent that awareness becomes more sensitive through meditation, we discover increasingly subtle forms of self-imprisonment, and then can undertake whatever attitudinal and behavioral changes are necessary to undermine the conditioning and habitual process that keeps us from being free, whether these are forms of ignorance, desire, or anger.

The last chapter of the Dhammapada, titled 'The Brahmin', borrows a term from Hinduism that represents the highest level of religious development. In its use of the term, the Dhammapada distinguishes between one who is Brahmin in name only and one who truly exemplifies the brahmanic state, that is, one who has reached the pinnacle of spiritual realization. Following is a compilation of phrases from the chapter that characterize the nirvanic mind of a buddha. Nirvana is "beyond the world of fragments." It is "the deathless ground of life." An enlightened person "fears neither prison nor death," "lives free from past and future," is "free from I, me, and mine." A buddha is "beyond . . . likes and dislikes," "detached," "at peace among those at war." He is "beyond good and evil," has "overcome the urge to possess even heavenly things," has "risen above the duality of the world." He exhibits "love for all." "Homeless, he is ever at home." "Wanting nothing at all, [he is] master of his body and mind, he has gone beyond time and death." The last verse of the Dhammapada epitomizes the life of the Buddha: "All that he had to do is done; he has become one with all life."[45]

The Eightfold Path is frequently divided by Buddhists into the three trainings. Right views and intention comprise training in wisdom. Right speech, conduct, and livelihood make up training in morality. Right effort, awareness, and meditation constitute training in meditation. It is worth noting that effort is linked with meditation, an activity too often assumed to be entirely passive. Some Buddhists, however, connect effort with training in morality, while others argue that it rightfully bears on all of the dimensions of the Eightfold Path. There is, of course, merit to each of these views. Finally, just as the bodhisattva perfections are to be developed simultaneously, so are the practices of the Eightfold Path since each thereby reinforces and advances the others.

The Dharma

The dharma includes the teaching of the Buddha following his enlightenment. While the Four Noble Truths and the Eightfold Path are clearly part of the dharma—the foundation, in fact—what follows are additional features that have shaped the Buddhist experience of personal transformation. The three refuges, Buddha, Dharma, and Sangha, do not represent distinct, separable categories but overlapping, interrelated dimensions of Buddhism. The Buddha told Ananda, for example, that the dharma would take his place and become the teacher of the sangha after his demise. On a previous occasion, he said to one of his followers: "Whoever sees the dharma, sees me; whoever sees me, sees the dharma." In spite of the importance of the dharma, the Buddha never saw it as an end in itself. It functioned for him as upaya, skill-in-means. He once likened it to a raft that is used to transport one from the nearer bank of a river to the farther, from conditional existence, or samsara, to liberation, or nirvana. He then asked rhetorically: "On reaching the other shore, should one pick up the raft and carry it around on one's shoulders?" "Dharma," he said, "is for crossing over, not for retaining."[46] No attachment! Not even to the teaching and practice that liberates.

In India, dharma is used broadly to designate what is meant in English by 'religion'. Religious belief and practice make up dharma. But dharma also designates universal or cosmic order and law. It refers to the fundamental laws that govern all of the processes that operate in the cosmos, from the astronomical to the subatomic. That a single word is used to designate two categories, religion and cosmos, that we ordinarily see as different, highlights the Buddhist view of their integral nature. To rightly practice Buddhism is to live in harmony with cosmic law. To become a buddha is to become one with all. Dharma, then, names how one must be, in thought, word, and deed, in order to live in perfect accord with what is.

One of the earliest Pali texts identifies the three most fundamental marks of being, and indicates their priority even to the buddhas. The passage affirms thereby that the dharma leading to buddhahood is derived from, dependent on, and one with the dharma that is the cosmic process. "Whether Buddhas arise, O priests, or whether Buddhas do not arise, it remains a fact and the fixed and necessary constitution of being, that all its constituents are transitory. This fact a Buddha discovers and masters, and when he has discovered and mastered it, he announces, teaches, publishes, proclaims, discloses, minutely explains, and makes it clear, that all the constituents of being are transitory."[47] No tenet of Buddhism receives greater emphasis then that of universal and perpetual change. Nothing, absolutely nothing, remains the same. The principle of impermanence is itself liberational; since change is inevitable, one finds freedom and contentment by accepting change. To resist change is to want life to be otherwise than it is. To resist change is to suffer.

Providing further insight into the nature of change and drawing out the transformational potential that lies in it, the Buddha taught what some claim to be his most important cognitive discovery, the doctrine of 'dependent origination', or 'co-arising'. The Buddha indicated the importance of this doctrine when he declared: "He who sees dependent arising sees the dharma."[48] Some Buddhists contend that a proper and thorough understanding of this (right) view is tantamount to enlightenment. A summary formulation of the doctrine is given several times in the early texts:

> This being, that becomes;
> From the arising of this, that arises;
> This not being, that becomes not;
> From the ceasing of this, that ceases.[49]

On the basis of this generalization of dependent arising, one might conclude that it asserts nothing more than linear causality, a perspective commonly held. The Buddhist claims much more than this, however. The more complete statement of dependent co-arising identifies the twelve pre-conditions or interrelated factors that give rise to the round of existence and human bondage in it. That there are different lists of the pre-conditioning factors, with variations in the factors named, their number, order, and starting/ending point, indicates that what is important is not the formulation so much as the insight intended by the formulation. What follows is a standard formula for presenting causal conditioning.

1. Conditioned by ignorance, karmic formations arise,
2. Conditioned by karmic formations, consciousness arises,
3. Conditioned by consciousness, psycho-physicality arises,
4. Conditioned by psycho-physicality, the six sense objects arise,
5. Conditioned by the six senses objects, contact arises,
6. Conditioned by contact, sensation arises,
7. Conditioned by sensation, desire arises,
8. Conditioned by desire, clinging arises,
9. Conditioned by clinging, becoming arises,
10. Conditioned by becoming, birth arises,
11. Conditioned by birth, decay and death arise,
12. Conditioned by decay and death, ignorance arises.

This series too, like the brief formula, attempts to convey considerably more than mere linear causation. Linear causation, as a theory of the way the world works, is a reduction of an extraordinarily complex process. Interdependent co-arising asserts that reality is a dynamic unfolding of relationships and processes, not simply a complex of isolated entities. According to dependent co-origination, at least three simultaneous operations are occurring in the process of life's unfolding. To understand the Buddhist view properly, these three must be seen to operate concurrently and interactively.

First, rather than causation being linear, it is mutual; that is, the effect of a cause is itself a cause (a contributing casual factor or force) of its cause. What something is has an effect on those forces that make it what it is. Children have a shaping effect on parents at the same time that parents are shaping their children. Shariputra, the Buddha's most scholarly disciple, illustrated this mutuality by noting how, when two sheaves of reeds lean against each other, each supports the other. If either one is pulled away, the other falls.

Buddhists have shown the mutual causation of other pairs in the twelvefold linkage, ignorance and desire, for example. According to other Buddhist analyses of the human predicament, desire is sometimes singled out as the root causal factor, and sometimes ignorance. But the two are so interrelated that they are really two ways of talking about a single factor. Beings locked in samsara are characterized as "cloaked in ignorance, tied to craving." Buddhist scholar Joanna Macy notes that "neither factor is reducible to the other because they are mutually generative: as ignorance propels our craving, so does craving mire us in ignorance." Mutuality is so central to the Buddhist understanding of causation that Buddhaghosha, an early Theravada scholar, defines dependent co-origination as the view that sees "phenomena arise together in reciprocal dependence."[50]

Buddhaghosha's use of plurality in characterizing dependent co-arising introduces the second principal aspect, the multiplicity of causal factors. Causation is not a matter of mere polarity, with each of only two factors impacting the other. Causation is multiple as well as mutual, with innumerable factors impacting each factor. Buddhism identifies twelve of the most important components that mutually interact to give rise to each of the other components in the chain. Every factor has a causal effect on every other factor. This view is particularly developed in Chinese Hua-yen Buddhism, founded by Fa-tsang (643-712 CE), who argued for the universality of the buddha nature by demonstrating the principle for his students. He set up a statue of the Buddha in the center of carefully positioned mirrors, one each at the cardinal points, the four intermediate points, the nadir, and the zenith. These points, according to the conventions of Buddhist cosmology, represent everywhere. The Buddha image was thus reflected in all the mirrors, and each of them in turn reflected in all the others, ad infinitum. The interdependency of all things is so central in Hua-yen Buddhism that it is also known as 'the teaching of totality'; every entity in the universe depends on and is conditioned by every other entity. Nothing exists in and of itself. Everything that is, is what it is, by right of everything else that is.

As we saw in the first chapter and will develop more fully now, the Vietnamese monk Thich Nhat Hanh (1926-) invented a neologism to convey this vital point.

There is a cloud floating in this sheet of paper. Without a cloud, there will be no rain; without rain, the trees cannot grow; and without trees, we cannot make paper. The cloud is essential for the paper to exist. If the cloud is not here, the sheet of paper cannot be here either. So we can say that the cloud and the paper inter-are. "Interbeing" is a word that is not in the dictionary yet.

If we look into this sheet of paper even more deeply, we can see the sunshine in it. If the sunshine is not there, the forest cannot grow .... The paper and the sunshine inter-are. And if we continue to look, we can see the logger who cut the tree .... And we see the wheat. We know the logger cannot exist without his daily bread, and therefore the wheat that became his bread is also in this sheet of paper. And the logger's father and mother are in it too.

Looking even more deeply, we can see we are in it too. This is not difficult to see, because when we look at a sheet of paper, the sheet of paper is part of our perception. Your mind is in here and mine is also. So we can say that everything is in here with this sheet of paper. You cannot point out one thing that is not here—time, space, the earth, the rain, the minerals in the soil, the sunshine, the cloud, the river, the heat. Everything co-exists with this sheet of paper. That is why I think the word interbe should be in the dictionary. "To be" is to interbe. You cannot just <u>be</u> by yourself alone. You have to interbe with every other thing. This sheet of paper is, because everything else is.[51]

The third facet of dependent origination concerns the simultaneity of causation. If causality is mutual and multiple, that is, not strictly linear, then it is not limited to serial time. Lama Govinda observes that dependent co-origination describes "a linkage which is simultaneously or together arising . . . , a timeless simultaneous becoming . . . , immediate synchronicity of complex processes." An accurate understanding of the Buddha's intended meaning requires that one see "the simultaneous cooperation" of all twelve factors, "each link representing the sum total of all the others." Govinda suggests a way of approaching timeless causality from the standpoint of conventional thought, that is, thought within the framework of time: every entity that appears "is based on an infinite past and thus on an infinity of causes, conditions and relationships, which does not exclude anything that has been or ever will come into existence."[52]

If the all-encompassing past and the entirely open, non-conditioned future are seen as the base or circumstance of all present activity, then the timelessness of causality, the eternal dimension of what is now, may be glimpsed. A kind of temporal timelessness prevails. Quantifiable time becomes a timeless quality or condition of the present. The events of the past are simultaneously present now. The coal or oil burned to turn turbines and produce the electricity now lighting a room was sunlight millions of years ago which fell on green leaves that were later buried and over the millennia transformed by pressure, heat and chemical action into fossils and then fuel. If electricity comes from a nuclear plant it is power from a star that exploded billions of years ago, even before this solar system began.

The light of antiquity is present now. William Blake seems to have known interbeing and timelessness

> To see a World in a Grain of Sand
> And a Heaven in a Wild Flower,
> Hold Infinity in the palm of your hand
> And Eternity in an hour.

Dependent origination and its three integral dimensions, reciprocal, multitudinous, and simultaneous, are not meant to deny or replace common sense views on causation but to add a more inclusive perspective, one that is non-reductive and therefore more complete. The Buddha's insight into the conditional nexus enables one to avoid simplistic assumptions about the nature of causation. It is not a view, admittedly, that can be grasped by the rational mind. The Buddha himself declared the view to be "beyond logic," and "hard to perceive . . . , deep, subtle, difficult."[53] It is an 'understanding' that is not so much thought as intuited, not so much reasoned as experienced. And, rightly understood, dependent co-arising is a view that liberates. If causality is conditional, release is possible. If we are not simply the product of parental genes and personal history, if the whole universe, past, present, and future, coalesce in who we are at any given moment, our sense of self opens and expands, our personal awareness takes on a quality of freedom and joy. We loosen our clinging to separate identity and begin to align with all that is. To truly see the universal in the particular, and the particular as process, attachment and clinging become impossible.

The second of the three fundamental characteristics of being that buddhas discover and proclaim is duhkha, sorrow, the sense that life is unsatisfactory, a perspective sufficiently discussed above as the first of the Four Noble Truths. The third mark of existence is *anatman,* 'nonself', 'nonsubstantiality', 'nonessentiality'. This position denies the existence of a permanent, unchanging, eternal self. What Hinduism affirms as the highest and ultimately the only reality, Buddhism denies outright. There is no greater divergence between the two traditions than in their respective views on the nature of the self. It is worth noting, however, that the Buddha himself did not so much deny the existence of a permanent, substantive self as he denied the possibility of finding or locating one. Later forms of Buddhism have taken a more absolute position in outright denial of the self. What is mistakenly believed to be the self is for Buddhists simply the interaction of the five factors or aggregates, the *skandhas*. The five are: (1) form, matter, or corporeality; (2) sensation or feeling, i.e., of a pleasant, unpleasant, or neutral nature; (3) perception, i.e., by means of the six senses; (4) mental formations or dispositions, i.e., karmic or conditioned tendencies; and (5) consciousness, i.e., simple awareness. Each of the skandhas is in turn composed of elements that are still further devisable, ad infinitum. There is thus nothing fixed and permanent. What is taken to be real, changeless, and substantive is actually a process of interrelationships.

The skandhas themselves exhibit the three marks of being, impermanent, unsatisfactory, and without essence, to which is often added a fourth, empty (shunya). Buddhism does not deny the sense of self, of personhood, as a useful convention for social interaction. What it denies is the existence of a fixed, changeless essence. To assume the existence of a real self is, from the Buddhist perspective, a mark of ignorance, a failure to accurately assess one's own nature. The postulation of a self is an unnecessary addition to what is actually experienced. The five constituents exhaustively account for all that is human. Buddhaghosha offers an analogy that shows how a composite, the so-called self, lacks inherent reality. We can substitute an automobile for Buddhaghosa's chariot and note that it is made up of a body, seats, wheels, an engine, "and other constituent members, placed in a certain relation to each other." A car is simply the composite of specific ingredients standing in a particular relationship to each other. Apart from the specific ingredients, which are themselves comprised of still further ingredients, and their relationship to each other, there is nothing that can be called a car. Thus, 'car' is simply a designation, a name applied to a specific arrangement of parts. Similarly, Buddhaghosha argues, 'self' is no more than "a mode of expression for the presence of the five attachment groups [skandhas], but when we come to examine the elements of being one by one, we discover that in the absolute sense there is no living entity there to form a basis for such figments as 'I am,' or 'I'."[54] Buddhaghosha avers that all we find are names, that is, the four psychic skandhas and form. What we take to be an abiding self is nothing more than name and form, empty (shunya) of permanence, of essence, of inherent reality.

Buddhism does not for a moment deny the experienced reality of thinking, feeling, willing, acting, etc. What it argues is that these common human processes do not justify the inference that there is a thinker, a feeler, a self that wills and acts, etc. There is, for example, the immediate and undeniable experience of thinking. Thinking is an eminently real subjective datum. But where is the thinker? The thinker is merely supposed, fully lacking in either subjective or objective reality. A self that thinks, feels, etc., cannot be identified. The personal sense of being a separate, independent, continuing self is a construction, albeit unconscious and conventional, of the psychophysical organism as a whole, an act of the bodymind that is also invariably a conceit, the source of all selfishness, and conse-quently of all sorrow and suffering. Shantideva (8:134) declares: "Whatever calamities there are, and whatever sorrows and fears come to the world, they are all the result of attachment to 'self'." To be without a sense of ego or separate self is to be enlightened. The Diamond Sutra affirms: "Incomparable enlightenment . . . is straightly attained by freedom from separate personal selfhood."[55]

The Buddhist dharma has been systematized philosophically and psychologically in many different forms. We will look briefly at three, Abhidharma, Madhyamika, and Dzogchen, that are especially significant and representative. Each purports to be an analysis of reality as it is, of reality in its suchness or thusness (tathata). Each is ultimately directed toward liberation, providing a comprehensive analysis of the human situation that, by means of understanding and practice, culminates in the resolution of the human predicament.

Abhidharma, the reigning system in Theravada Buddhism, is also the foundation and starting point for the development of the Mahayana and later the Vajrayana traditions. Abhidharma is a scholastic approach that focuses on the five skandhas and the twelve pre-conditions. Since we have already outlined this system of thought above, we need only name it here, and note further that it includes a comprehensive analysis of the basic building blocks of reality, known as we have seen above as dharmas. The dharmas are the 'atoms' or irreducible units of existence.

A major Mahayana school, Madhyamika, refutes what it sees as a tendency toward reification in Abhidharma, a tendency to regard compounded factors as ultimate, as being essences, and, consequently, a failure to uphold the Buddha's crucial teaching of emptiness. Madhyamika (Middle Way) applies a radical dialectical method that seeks to undermine all propositions about the nature of reality. By doing so, it promotes a middle position between such extremes as eternalism (there are eternal substances or essences) and nihilism (nothing ultimately exists). Madhyamika maintains that the identity of so-called logical opposites is not only feasible but indicative of the highest truth. Nagarjuna, the second and third-century CE founder of Madhyamika, capitalizes on the twofold truth theory that is held widely in Buddhism. In his *Fundamentals of the Middle Way*, he writes: "The teaching by the Buddhas of the *dharma* has recourse to two truths: the world-ensconced truth and the truth which is the highest sense. Those who do not know . . . the two kinds of truth do not know the profound 'point' in the teaching of the Buddha."[56] The distinction is between relative or conventional truth, on one hand, and absolute or supreme truth, on the other. Conventional truth depends on ordinary logic, ultimate truth does not. To distinguish between the two truths is not, however, to prefer one and reject the other. Each is essential.

Nagarjuna's unique contribution to Buddhist dharma rests in his identification of emptiness with interdependent origination. Entities co-arise interdependently and therefore are without self-nature or 'own-being' (*svabhava*). Since everything that is is what it is by right of relationship to other things that are also what they are by right of their relationships, ad infinitum, everything is empty of self-sufficiency, of essence. Dependent co-arising attests poignantly to emptiness. Nagarjuna not only argues that dependent co-arising affirms emptiness—this is clear on the basis of clear thinking or conventional truth—but also argues that dependent co-arising is itself empty—this is clear from the viewpoint of transcendent truth. Ultimately there is no causation, no conditioning, no relationship, and no mutuality. Such a view does not lead to nihilism, to nothingness, however, since emptiness does not deny relative existence. Though shunyata is sometimes translated 'nothingness', this is misleading. Appealing to the common sense observation that things do appear and disappear, an opponent challenged Nagarjuna by arguing that "if all existence is empty, there is no origination nor destruction." Nagarjuna responded with deeper insight and said: "If all existence is non-empty, there is no origination nor destruction."[57]

Emptiness does not deny the reality of relative things, rather that these things do not have any self-sufficient, independent, or ultimate nature. Some Chinese versions of Vimalakirti's text contain the line: "That all things do not exist ultimately is the meaning of voidness." Emptiness, then, does not negate matter; it is a statement about the nature of matter. This point is made clear in Vimalakirti's treatise where the skandhas too are seen to be empty. "Matter itself is void. Voidness does not result from the destruction of matter, but the nature of matter is itself voidness. Therefore, to speak of voidness on the one hand, and of matter, or of sensation, or of intellect, or of motivation, or of consciousness on the other—is entirely dualistic. Consciousness itself is voidness. Voidness does not result from the destruction of consciousness, but the nature of consciousness is itself voidness."[58]

The failure to understand shunyata as Buddhist understand it is due to considering emptiness from the relative standpoint where it contrasts with fullness, or plenitude. From the Buddhist perspective, emptiness is the All. D.T. Suzuki, one of the twentieth-century's foremost interpreters of Buddhism to the West, says that shunyata is "the fullness of things, containing all possibilities."[59] Emptiness is pure potentiality, the "ever-present origin" of all that ever was, is, or will be.[60] Buddhists sometimes use space as an analogy for emptiness, as we saw above. Space seems empty, but Buddhists see it as full potentiality, believing that it contains all.

Because of the tendency of the human mind to seek foundation, support, certitude, there is the danger in Buddhism that the Madhyamika position on emptiness might itself be construed as a support, a foundation on which to stand. To counteract this possibility, proponents of Madhyamika teach the 'emptiness of emptiness'. Vimalakirti points out that ideas, thoughts, mental constructions, like all things, are empty. He then observes that the concept of emptiness, being a mental construction, is itself empty. Emptiness as a concept is as non-substantive and non-ultimate as everything else.[61] The *Perfection of Wisdom in 8,000 Lines* declares: "Nowhere has the Tathagata taken his stand; for his mind has not anywhere sought for a support. He has stood neither in the conditioned, nor in the unconditioned."[62]

The Prajnaparamita (Perfection of Wisdom) texts are inarguably among the most important in Buddhism. One of the most important of these is the Heart Sutra, a text that is widely memorized and often recited. The heart of the Heart Sutra asserts: "Form is emptiness; emptiness is form. Emptiness is not other than form; form is not other than emptiness. In the same way, feeling, discrimination, compositional factors, and consciousness are empty . . . . In that way all phenomena are empty, without characteristic, unproduced, unceased, stainless, not stainless, undiminished, unfilled."[63] Masao Abe, successor to D.T. Suzuki as a principal interpreter of Buddhism to the West, especially Japanese Buddhism, affirms the integral nature of form and emptiness and the dynamic nature of emptiness when he notes: "form is ceaselessly emptied, turning into formless emptiness, and formless emptiness is ceaselessly emptied and forever freely taking form. This total *dynamic movement* of emptying, not a *static state* of emptiness, is the true meaning of shunyata."[64]

The "form is emptiness; emptiness is form" summary proclaims an identity that transcends duality without succumbing to monism. The highest truth is here expressed as unambiguously as conventional truth and language permit. Here Buddhism succinctly articulates the middle path between absolutism and nihilism, between unicity and plurality. Developing further the middle position of 'no position', the Heart Sutra alludes to the twelvefold complex of dependent co-arising: "There is no ignorance, no extinction of ignorance, [and so on] up to and including no aging and death and no extinction of aging and death. Similarly, there are no sufferings, no origins, no cessations, no paths, no wisdom, no attainment, and also no non-attainment."[65] From the perspective of Ultimacy, no assertion by means of language is adequate to reality as it is. Therefore, all assertions must be qualified by means of negation.

One of the most inclusive negations is that of nonduality. In fact, the perfection of wisdom is frequently summarized as nonduality. Hui-neng says, "Buddha-nature is nonduality."[66] Vimalakirti devotes an entire chapter to nonduality as understood by various bodhisattvas. The following excerpts are representative.

> 'Good' and 'evil' are two. Seeking neither good nor evil, the understanding of the nonduality of the significant and the meaningless is the entrance into nonduality.

Sinfulness' and 'sinlessness' are two. By means of the diamond-like wisdom that pierces to the quick, not to be bound or liberated is the entrance into nonduality.

To say, 'This is mundane' and 'That is transcendental' is dualism. This world has the nature of voidness, so there is neither transcendence nor involvement, neither progress nor standstill. Thus, neither to transcend nor to be involved, neither to go nor to stop—this is the entrance into nonduality.

Dualism is produced from obsession with self, but true understanding of self does not result in dualism.

The mendicant who is neither bound nor liberated does not experience any like or any dislike and thus he enters nonduality.

Finally, Manjushri, the Bodhisattva of Wisdom, congratulated the other bodhisattvas on their insights into nonduality but declared that their explanations were themselves dualistic. He continued: "To know no one teaching, to express nothing, to say nothing, to explain nothing, to announce nothing, to indicate nothing, and to designate nothing—that is the entrance into nonduality." Manjushri then asked Vimalakirti to give his understanding of nonduality. The text says: "Vimalakirti kept his silence, saying nothing at all."[67]

A particularly succinct summary statement on nonduality in Mahayana Buddhism is the identification of the wheel of becoming with the state of liberation: samsara is nirvana; nirvana is samsara. Vimalakirti notes: "Liberation is the equality of all things."[68] Even samsara and nirvana are equal. While the truth of this equation is undeniable from the perspective of Ultimacy, from the standpoint of relative truth distinctions remain. One can begin to glimpse how these distinctions blur, however, by noting that while liberation is immediately at hand—in that it is omnipresent, not limited to any time or place—it is not immediately realized due to the bondage that prevails in any existence marked by ignorance, greed, hatred, desire, etc. To the extent that these binding factors are released through wisdom and non-attachment, liberation and ordinary existence are experienced as non-different.

The third psychological/philosophical system we will survey is Dzogchen, a major Vajrayana school of thought and practice that was brought to Tibet in the eighth century by Padma Sambhava, an Indian Buddhist savant. Based on the Tibetan word *dzogchen*, 'great perfection', Dzogchen, as a teaching and practice lineage, is often called the Natural Great Perfection. This Natural Great Perfection is everything we experience, i.e., all that enters our awareness through our senses and arises as our thoughts. Nyoshul Kenpo Rinpoche (1932-1999), one of the foremost twentieth-century teachers of Dzogchen, notes: "The entire external phenomenal and internal noumenal universe is the great Dzogpa Chenpo," i.e., Dzogchen or Natural Great Perfection.[69] When the mind, which is the fundamental Natural Great Perfection, is cleared of obscurations, we *recognize* the Natural Great Perfection as just that.

The three phases of personal transformation in Dzogchen proceed according to ground, path, and fruition. Ground is "the fundamental innate mind of clear light" that reflects or displays all the phenomena of samsara and nirvana. Path is the purification of the mental accretions that impede realization of our innate, luminous mind. Fruition occurs when "this fundamental innate mind of clear light itself, free from obscuration," constitutes our ongoing awareness and everything is seen as Natural Great Perfection.[70] The Dzogchen path often begins with the lama, who has attained steady awareness of the liberating view, transmitting that view to his students. The path requires the students, who have now at least glimpsed the view, to practice until the view becomes their uninterrupted awareness, thereby constituting fruition. Two phases constitute the path, meditation and post-meditation. Dudjom Rinpoche (1904-1986) advises: "When meditating, as soon as thoughts arise from awareness's dynamic energy, use mindfulness to identify them: self-arising, self-liberating, like waves on water. Recognize them as such and let them go."[71] Post-meditation is carrying this same non-attachment and non-doing into everyday activities.

Dzogchen, like the Mahamudra school of thought and practice with which it is often linked, is considered the highest (*ati*) formulation of the Buddha's teaching. Even though the two lineages are distinguishable, they are frequently linked in a single teaching and practice. Nyoshul Kenpo explains: "Our tradition is more the experiential lineage, the practice lineage of the union of the Mahamudra and Dzogchen nondual streams, the inseparability of wisdom and compassion, *prajna* and *upaya*, truth and love, as a method for awakening" (89). The Ati claim is substantiated by fact that prior forms of Buddhism are incorporated into Mahamudra and Dzogchen, as seen in the prior quotation from Nyoshul Kenpo and in the following excerpts from one of his Vajra songs. In these he draws from Theravada and Madhyamika as he propounds Dzogchen:

> To abide in the natural state of emptiness
> Is the "calm abiding" of *shamatha*,
> And to perceive it vividly clear
> Is the "clear seeing" of *vipashyana*. (97)

> Everything has the nature of being empty.
> When the empty looks at the empty,
> Who is there to look at something empty?
> What is the use of many classifications,
> Such as "being empty" and "not empty,"
> As it is illusion looking at illusion,
> And delusion watching delusion? (94-95)

All discursive thought is emptiness,
And the seer of the emptiness is discursive thought.
Emptiness does not destroy discursive thought,
And discursive thought does not block emptiness. (95)

The Tibetan term for the natural mind in its crystalline lucidity is *rigpa*, also known as innate wisdom or pure presence, our primordial awareness. Surya Das and Nyoshul Kenpo note that "all the phenomena of samsara and nirvana are perfect and complete within rigpa" (78). Describing the nature of rigpa more fully, they continue:

The ultimate nature of mind is perfectly pure, profound, quiescent, luminous, uncompounded, unconditioned, uniform and undying, and free since the beginningless beginning. When we examine this mind for ourselves, it becomes apparent that its innate openness, clarity, and cognizant quality comprise what is known as innate wakefulness, primordial nondual awareness: rigpa. This is our birthright, our true nature. It is not something missing, to be sought for and obtained, but is the very heart of our original existential being. It is actually inseparable from our uncontrived everyday awareness, beyond willful alteration, free from conceptuality; unfabricated ordinary awareness, unadulterated by effort and modification—naked, fresh, vivid, and totally natural. What could be simpler than this, to rest at home and at ease in total naturalness? (78)

Dzogchen is a superb instance of the continuing and overarching argument of this book; namely, that human beings, given a proper view and practice, can gain total freedom from the limitations of the ego and the sorrows of life.

Hakuin (1686-1769)

Hakuin Ekaku lived at a time when Japan practiced isolationism and the state had virtual control of institutional religion. Corruption and moral depravity were widespread. Religion had become perfunctory. Hakuin, through his own rigorous spiritual regimen and his tireless efforts on behalf of others, succeeded in helping to revitalize a Buddhism that had become ceremonial and routine. He is widely recognized as the reviver of Rinzai Zen. Heinrich Dumoulin in his history of Zen Buddhism calls Hakuin "one of the greatest figures of Japanese Buddhism."[72]

Sugiyama Iwajiro, later to be known as Hakuin Ekaku, was born on January 19, 1686. His mother was the eldest daughter of the postmaster in the small and rather unimportant town of Hara. His father came from the samurai class and seems to have had minimal influence on his son, the youngest of five children. Hakuin's mother belonged to the Nichiren sect of Buddhism, which especially reveres the Lotus Sutra. Gifted with an exceptional memory, Hakuin reputedly was able at the age of four to recite over 300 of the songs current in his village. He once amazed others by giving a full and accurate account of a sermon he had heard on the Lotus Sutra. He was an exceptionally sensitive child. A sermon he heard on the Eight Hot Hells caused him great consternation and seems to have shaped his life for years to come. Seeing the fire heating his bath water, he became terrified and pleaded with his mother to reveal to him some way to escape the inevitable retribution he feared because of his childhood mischievousness. She assured him that Kannon, the Bodhisattva of Mercy, would save him, but he took little consolation. Convinced that he could only escape hell by forsaking the world, he wanted to become a monk. Only years later did his parents agree. Still plagued by the fear of hell, Hakuin devotedly recited a formula from the Lotus Sutra that purports to protect from water and fire. To test its efficacy the lad touched his leg with a poker from the fire.

This may have been his first lesson, a vivid and painful one, in the non-literal interpretation of scripture.

Finally convinced by their son's resolve, Hakuin's parents consented to his entrance into monastic life. He joined the Zen monks at a temple in his native town. He was fifteen years old. He had his head shaved, received ordination, and was given his monastic name, Ekaku, or Wise Crane. During these early years, he read and pondered Buddhist scriptures, especially the Lotus Sutra, and studied the Confucian classics as well. He began to doubt the superiority of Buddhism over other religions, and its efficacy to protect him from hell. His doubt became a crisis when he was nineteen and happened to read about Ganto, the ninth-century Ch'an master whose cries were reputedly heard ten miles away when he was attacked and killed by bandits. Hakuin became so distraught that he did not eat for three days and for some time his faith in Buddhism was shattered. While going through the motions of monkhood, he increasingly gave his attention to poetry, calligraphy, and painting.

Hakuin traveled to various temples and monasteries, continuing to study and develop his artistic skills. One summer day while residing at a temple headed by a poet-monk, his commitment to Buddhism was rekindled. The abbot had carried his library of Buddhist, Confucian, and Taoist texts outside to dry in the sun. Hakuin's gnawing doubt came to a head. Who should he follow: the Buddha, Confucius, or the Taoist sages? Longing for guidance, he reached for a volume and began to read about a Zen master who meditated day and night without pause. When drowsiness threatened to overcome him, he would press a sharp awl into his body to stimulate alertness through pain. Greatly encouraged by the Zen master's exceptional dedication, Hakuin decided he could best honor his mother after her recent death by redoubling his monastic determination. When he was twenty-two he moved to a different monastery where his commitment deepened even further. So intense was his resolve to do the one thing needful that he burned all his poems, calligraphy, and paintings.

Zen monastic training typically involves extensive *zazen*, 'seated meditation', *dokusan*, 'private consultation' with the *roshi*, or Zen master, formal study sessions, and daily periods of work, such as cleaning, gardening, cooking, etc. The main discipline, however, in Rinzai Zen, the branch to which Hakuin belonged, is *koan* investigation. The other major form of Zen, Soto, while sometimes using the koan, places far greater emphasis on quiet sitting. Koans are designed to puzzle and confound the rational mind. At first glance they appear to be conundrums that, with sufficient intellectual application, ought to be solvable. The intended purpose of a koan, however, is to thoroughly frustrate the reasoning mind, thereby causing it to shut down and allow a larger consciousness to appear. Such an experience is known either as *kensho*, 'seeing into one's own true nature', or *satori*, a term that is sometimes used equivalently to kensho but that may also be reserved for a more complete 'seeing' that constitutes final enlightenment.

Hakuin worked extensively with the Mu koan, usually given to monks as their first. A monk asked Joshu, "Does a dog have buddha nature or not?" Joshu said, "Mu." Mu literally means 'no' or 'nothing', but Joshu's answer is not taken to be a simple negation. It becomes the focus for a concentration that surpasses negation and affirmation, i.e., the realm of duality. In spite of his great effort, Hakuin was forced to confess: "I concentrated night and day on the Mu koan without a moment's rest, but to my great disappointment I was unable to achieve a pure and uninvolved state of undistracted meditation." His perseverance paid off, however, in his twenty-fourth year when he experienced his initial awakening.

Night and day I did not sleep; I forgot both to eat and rest. Suddenly a great doubt manifested itself before me. It was as though I were frozen solid in the midst of an ice sheet extending tens of thousands of miles. A purity filled my breast and I could neither go forward nor retreat. To all intents and purposes I was out of my mind and the Mu alone remained. Although I sat in the lecture hall and listened to the master's lecture, it was as though I were hearing a discussion from a distance outside the hall. At times it felt as though I were floating through the air.

This state lasted for several days. Then I chanced to hear the sound of the temple bell and I was suddenly transformed. It was as if a sheet of ice had been smashed or a jade tower had fallen with a crash. Suddenly I returned to my senses . . . All my former doubts vanished as though ice had melted away. In a loud voice I called: 'Wonderful, wonderful. There is no cycle of birth and death through which one must pass. There is no enlightenment one must seek. The seventeen hundred koans handed down from the past have not the slightest value whatsoever.' My pride soared up like a majestic mountain, my arrogance surged forward like the tide. Smugly I thought to myself: 'In the past two or three hundred years no one could have accomplished such a marvelous breakthrough as this.'[73]

According to custom, Hakuin wrote a short verse articulating his new-found experience and showed it to his master. Realizing full-well that Hakuin's ego had not dissolved but had become inflated, his master rebuffed him, began calling him a "poor hole-dwelling devil," and presented him with a new koan. In true Rinzai fashion, he gave Hakuin's nose a hearty twist. Somewhat later Hakuin offered another verse to his master and this time was hit twenty or thirty times and pushed off the veranda into the mud. Now with renewed determination, he applied himself to intensive study of several new koans, not even pausing to eat or sleep. Hakuin reports as follows on his next awakening experience.

Still deeply dejected, I took up my begging bowl . . . and went into the village . . . My mind was hard at work on my koans. It never left them. I stood before the gate of a house, my bowl in my hand, lost in a kind of trance. A voice from within yelled, "Go on! Go somewhere else!" But I was so preoccupied I didn't even notice it. This must have angered the resident of the house, because she suddenly appeared, flourishing a broom upside-down in her hand. She flew at me, flailing out wildly, whacking away at my head as if she was bent on dashing my brains out. My sedge hat lay in tatters. I was knocked down and ended heels up on the ground. I lost consciousness and lay like a dead man.

As I regained consciousness, my eyes opened, and as they did, I found that the unsolvable and impenetrable koans I had been working on . . . were completely penetrated. Right to the root. They had suddenly ceased to exist. I clapped my hands and laughed great shouts of laughter, frightening the people who had gathered around me.[74]

When Hakuin returned to the monastery his master immediately recognized the profound change. He authenticated Hakuin's awakening and strongly urged him to continue after-satori practice, i.e., to keep working with progressively more difficult koans. Hakuin followed this advice assiduously and toward the end of his life was able to claim that he had experienced eighteen great awakenings (satori) and innumerable lesser openings (kensho). He became one of Zen Buddhism's major advocates for after-satori practice. He once compared the resolution of koans to chopping down a huge tree ten arm's length around. "You won't do it with one swing of your axe," he argued, "but if you keep chopping away at it and do not let up, eventually, whether it wants to or not, it will suddenly come down."[75]

Hakuin, like Siddhartha, had to learn the important lesson of balance and moderation. As a result of his extreme discipline, involving minimal sleep and food, and long hours in meditation and study, Hakuin developed what he called 'Zen sickness'. He describes

191

his debilitating symptoms as follows. "My heart began to make me dizzy, my lungs became dry, both my legs felt as cold as if they were immersed in ice and snow. My ears were filled with a ringing as of the rushing waters of a swift river in a deep canyon. My liver felt weak, and in my behavior I experienced many fears. My spirit was distressed and weary, and whether sleeping or waking I always became lost in wild fancies. Both armpits were perpetually bathed in sweat, and my eyes were continually filled with tears."

Hakuin became so distraught that he actually longed for death. Today his condition would be considered a nervous breakdown. He reports having searched widely for teachers and physicians who might help him, but to no avail. Finally, he heard about an aged recluse, Hakuyu, who lived in the mountains far from human habitation. Hakuin made his way to him and was given a psychotherapeutic remedy based on the integration of the body and the mind. Drawing on Taoist principles of balance, Hakuyu informed Hakuin that health depends on keeping the upper body cool and the lower body warm and filled with 'original energy'. He prescribed for Hakuin the following visualization, to be done each night before sleeping, with the legs extended and held together. "This space below my navel, my loins and legs down to the soles of my feet are in truth my original face. There is no need of any nostrils. This space below my navel is in truth my original home. There is no need of any visits from my home. This space below my navel is in truth the Pure Land of my heart. There is no need of any other splendor. This space below my navel is in truth the Amida who am I. There is no need of preaching the Law to me."[76]

The references to original face, Pure Land, Amida, etc., were understood by Hakuin as pointed reminders of his buddha nature. He practiced this integrative visualization faithfully for three years and reported miraculous results. Nearly fifty years later he wrote:

Even though I am past seventy now my vitality is ten times as great as it was when I was thirty or forty. My mind and body are strong and I never have the feeling that I absolutely must lie down to rest. Should I want to I find no difficulty in refraining from sleep for two, three, or even seven days, without suffering any decline in my mental powers. I am surrounded by three-to five-hundred demanding students, and even though I lecture on the scriptures or on the collections of the Masters' sayings for thirty to fifty days in a row, it does not exhaust me. I am quite convinced that all this is owing to the power gained from practicing this method of introspection.[77]

Hakuin continued to travel to temples and monasteries, eager to pursue his after-satori practice and to have his realization tested by those older and more experienced than himself. In 1717, after years of near continual pilgrimage, he returned to the monastery he had entered as a youth. He found it greatly dilapidated but was able to turn it, according to one Zen scholar, into "the center of the strongest Buddhist movement of the Tokugawa period."[78]

As Hakuin's fame spread throughout Japan, hundreds of students came to subject themselves to his harsh but compassionate training. About his disciples it is said: "Their ears hear nothing but scoffs and reviling or scolding words. What touches their bodies is only angry fists and painful rods."[79] Hakuin knew from personal experience that nothing less than absolute determination is required to see into one's true nature. He once wrote that practice without the "valiant will to succeed" is about as useless "as glasses for a blind man or a comb for a [shaven] monk." He understated when he wrote that "Zen is surely not an easy thing."[80] The demand that he placed upon himself—with painful corroboration by his teachers—he in turn placed on his students. Hakuin is principally known for his revival of koan study. While he believed that one could become enlightened by other methods, those of Rinzai Zen—particularly koan study—were most effective. In one of his letters, he gives a brief explanation of how a koan works. "If you take up one koan and investigate it unceasingly your mind will die and your will will be destroyed. It is as though a vast, empty abyss lay before you, with no place to set your hands or feet. You face death and your bosom feels as though it were afire. Then suddenly you are one with the koan, and both body and mind are cast off. . . . When suddenly you return to life, there is the great joy of one who drinks the water and knows for himself whether it is hot or cold. . . . This is known as seeing into one's own nature."[81]

Hakuin personally devised a large number of koans. His koan, The Sound of One Hand, is as widely known as Mu, and frequently used as the first to be investigated. He writes:

What is the Sound of the Single Hand? When you clap together both hands a sharp sound is heard; when you raise the one hand there is neither sound nor smell. . . . If conceptions and discriminations are not mixed within it and it is quite apart from seeing, hearing, perceiving, and knowing, and if, while walking, standing, sitting, and reclining, you proceed straightforwardly without interruption in the study of this koan, then in the place where reason is exhausted and words are ended, you will suddenly pluck out the karmic root of birth and death and break down the cave of ignorance. . . . At this time the basis of mind, consciousness, and emotion is suddenly shattered; the realm of illusion . . . is overturned.[82]

Hakuin's contribution to koan study was so extensive that his method, systematized further by his students, became the dominant approach to enlightenment in Zen Buddhism. Koan study continues to be a distinctive and effective transformational tool. Hakuin died on January 18, 1769.

Lama Anagarika Govinda (1898-1985)

Ernst Lothar Hoffmann was born on May 17, 1898 in Waldheim, Germany. After his mother's death in childbirth when he was three years old, he was raised by his aunt, who had quite an international outlook. His mother's side of the family had links with South America, a great grandfather having helped in the liberation and development of Bolivia. Ernst grew up trilingual, learning from various family members German, French, and Spanish. He would later master Pali, Sanskrit, Tibetan, and English. The paternal side of the family was business oriented. Ernst's father owned a cigar factory.

In his mid-teens Ernst began reading philosophy, followed by the Christian mystics. In spite of his initial attraction to Christianity, he found himself more inclined to Buddhism after he undertook a comparative study of those two religions and Islam. His first book, which he began writing at age eighteen, was on Buddhism. He studied Buddhism in Switzerland and Italy and eventually traveled to Ceylon, now Sri Lanka, in 1929. Ernst joined a European monastic community under the leadership of a German, Nyanatiloka Thera, and took the name Brahmachari Govinda. A few months later he was ordained while on pilgrimage in Burma, now assuming the name Anagarika, 'the homeless one'. Govinda was drawn to the Theravada Buddhism of Ceylon because of the purity of the tradition. He continued his study of Pali, the early texts of Buddhism, and Theravada meditation. About this time, he attended a Buddhist convention in Darjeeling, in northeast India.

While in Darjeeling, Govinda visited a Tibetan Buddhist monastery located in the adjacent mountains. When a blizzard trapped him at the monastery for three days, the abbot permitted him to occupy one corner of the monastery temple. He later recalled finding himself "seated in the dimly lit hall of a Tibetan temple, surrounded by a pantheon of fantastic figures, some of them peaceful and benevolent, some wild and frightening, and others enigmatic and mysterious; but all full of life and colour." Many of the images and symbols were as foreign to Govinda as the Tibetan language. He asked himself, "How did I get from the placid life of Ceylon's tropical paradise into this pandemonium of a Himalayan blizzard and the strange surroundings of a Tibetan monastery?" When the storm lifted and he was free to return to Darjeeling and then back to Ceylon, he felt no desire to do so. He writes: "Some inexplicable force seemed to keep me back, and the longer I stayed on in this magic world into which I had dropped . . . , the more I felt that a hitherto unknown form of reality was revealed to me and that I was on the threshold of a new life."[83] Govinda later noted how this new reality became his own as it transformed his consciousness and led him to a deeper understanding of religion and the human situation.

> I realised that religious truth and spiritual life are more a matter of transcending our habitual consciousness than of changing our opinions or building our convictions on the strength of intellectual arguments and syllogisms, of the laws of reason, which will never lead us beyond the circle of what is already known . . . . These have always been the greatest obstacles of creative vision and of the exploration of further dimensions of consciousness and deeper realms of reality. Spiritual life is based on inner awareness and experience, which no amount of thinking [can] create, thinking and reasoning merely being a process of digestion or mental assimilation which follows.[84]

By yielding to the magnetic force of what he experienced in the temple, Govinda stayed on at the monastery and soon met Tomo Geshe Rinpoche, the saintly sage who would impact his life like no one he had ever met or ever would meet. Govinda writes that when the Rinpoche "moved through the hall a deep silence fell upon the congregation and all sat motionless as if spellbound by the magic presence of this one man, who seemed to fill the whole temple with the accumulated power gained through a long period of concentration and complete absorption." He carried himself as one who "had become one with the Buddhas." Govinda reports that when Tomo Geshe placed his hands on him as he bowed at his feet, a "stream of bliss" swept through his body and entire being. The questions he had intended to ask vanished from his mind like smoke in air. "Merely to be in this man's presence," he confesses, "seemed to be enough to dissolve all problems, to make them non-existent, like darkness in the presence of light."[85] Govinda would later receive initiation and instruction from others gurus, but none would compare with Tomo Geshe, his root guru. As a result of the empowerment and instruction received from his own root guru, Govinda would, for the rest of his life, emphasize the essential and central role of the guru-*chela* relationship.

The word guru (*blama*, Tibetan; pronounced and most often spelled 'lama') is often translated 'teacher'. A guru or lama, however, is one who imparts much more than information. "A guru," Govinda writes, "is one who has become one with his knowledge, one who is inspired and inspiring, who himself is the embodiment of what he wishes to convey and pass on."[86] Chela is commonly translated 'student' but is better rendered 'disciple', thereby suggesting something of the psychic or heart-level connection that must exist between the chela and guru. For the guru's work to prove effective the chela must open himself in unreserved trust. A guru will often test a chela's resolve and sincerity by giving him difficult tasks to perform, and postpone accepting him as a disciple. A classic instance is the eleventh-century mahasiddha, Marpa, who accepted Milarepa as a disciple only after the latter had served him for six years, repeatedly performing near superhuman tasks during this trial period. Milarepa's ordeal was especially severe because of the great suffering he had caused to others prior to his turn to Buddhism.

By means of formal initiation, the guru transmits to his disciple, not only the transformative teaching—often secret—but more important, the motive power that will enable him to apply the teaching in ways that will be fundamentally transformative. At least part of this power derives from the glimpse of the enlightened state that is conveyed to the disciple. Govinda describes this as "the power that makes one participate in an experience belonging to a higher state of consciousness and realization, which gives one a foretaste or glimpse of the aim towards which [one] strives, so that it is no more a vague ideal but an *experienced* reality."[87] The subsequent discipline of the disciple is directed toward making this fleeting glimpse a permanent reality. Govinda notes that it may take a guru several days or even weeks to prepare himself for an initiation. During this time he puts "himself in touch with the deepest sources of spiritual power through intense meditation, during which he *becomes* the embodiment of the force or quality which he wants to transmit."[88] The guru often gives the chela a personal mantra that will be used as a meditative focus. Govinda claims that the disciple, by means of the mantra, "is able at any time to summon up in himself the transmitted power, so that a permanent contact is maintained with the guru."[89] This contact continues even beyond the death of the guru.

The guru's ongoing task is to tailor instruction and guidance to the particular character and needs of his disciple. Govinda reports that Tomo Geshe, among other things, emphasized the danger lurking in criticism. "As long as we regard ourselves superior to others or look down upon the world, we cannot make any real progress. As soon, however, as we understand that we live in exactly that world which we deserve, we shall recognise the faults of others as our own—though they may appear in different form." He also revealed that "unselfish love and compassion towards all living beings [is] the first prerequisite of meditation;" it removes, if properly understood and applied, "all self-created emotional and intellectual limitations."[90] Govinda explains that the task of the guru is one of "enabling the chela to reduce his egocentricity, to free himself from all vanities, from feeling hurt and insulted, from his dependence on praise and blame.

[The guru] confronts him with the opinions, prejudices, and creeds that he has merely taken over from others."[91] The guru persistently guides the disciple toward immediate, authentic experience that is free of the distorting effects of conditioning.

The principal means used by a guru to help a disciple realize his buddha nature is meditation. Govinda characterizes meditation as "the way to re-connect the individual with the whole." It enables one to "see through the ego-complex and thus overcome the illusion of a soul or selfhood that is separate and independent of the whole."[92] In several of his books and essays, Govinda takes up the connection between individuality and universality. He argues that "individualization and universality are not mutually exclusive qualities, but rather are complementary to each other. They are like two simultaneous movements in opposite directions. Individuality pursued to its end, i.e., realized to the fullness of its possibilities, is universality. It is only when stopping halfway that individuality solidifies and shrinks to the notion of an ego that contradicts universality."[93] For individuality to become universality, the ego must relinquish its apparent individuality. The dissolution of false individuality uncovers the true individuality that is universality. As the separative functions of the ego recede, the identity of the individual and the universal emerges.

Building on the Buddha's teaching of dependent co-arising, Govinda interprets the individual-universal co-inherence in a way that parallels the great net of connections emphasized by Hua-yen Buddhism and also augments the Buddha's teaching on the great advantage of being born human.

The whole world can be compared to a mighty net of interrelations. There is nothing that is not akin to everything else in the universe and does not have a relation to it. Accordingly we can say that every individual is a crystallization point of everything the universe contains. All the powers of the universe are required to create a single human being, a single tree, or a single insect;

without the basis of all the powers of the cosmos no being can come into existence. From this point of view we have to ask ourselves whether the coming-to-be of the innumerable forms of life is not the mightiest achievement of this entire universe. And when we then consider the universe as a whole and recognize the endless emptiness that exists in both the macrocosm and the microcosm, and see how extremely rarely those crystallizations of forms occur (that we call matter), and if we then consider how much rarer still are the conditions under which living, conscious beings can develop, then perhaps we shall understand that individuality is just as essential as universality. Indeed, universality can only be experienced through individuality.

And this, Govinda argues, is the true aim of life, for the individual to discover his inherent universality. Meditation is the means by which one comes to know oneself as "a focal point in which the universe becomes aware of itself."[94]

As a Buddhist in the Vajrayana tradition, Govinda recognizes the value of ritual as a support for meditation. Since an historic and established ritual is "an external expression of internal feelings" it has the power to elicit those feelings as one participates in the ritual. Meditation can be enhanced with the use of candles, flowers, incense, water, music, or poetry. A proper meditation setting, with appropriate aids and actions, can help to simultaneously pacify and stimulate our minds and thoughts. "The collection and concentration of all our inner powers in a suitable focal point is the prerequisite for all meditative work," he counsels.[95] The objective is to find balance and harmony within and in relation to the universe. This objective can be realized by attending to the breath, which should not so much be controlled as observed. He advises reflecting on the notion, "the universe is breathing through me," and points out that "breathing teaches us we can't hold on to anything."[96] He observes that breath is not only a crucial link between the individual and the universe but also between the body and the mind. Attending to the breath marks "the first step toward the transformation of the body from the state of a more or less passively and unconsciously functioning physical organ into a vehicle or tool of a perfectly developed and enlightened mind."[97] Breath meditation also aids the process of accessing, purifying, aligning, and integrating aspects of the conscious and unconscious mind. The inner calm that ensues from following these guidelines "permits us to observe ourselves and the continuous stream of our thoughts without valuation and without fixation."[98]

A meditator must have already developed some degree of inner tranquility and skill in non-evaluation and non-attachment before undertaking the distinctive feature of Tibetan meditation, namely, visualization. Govinda says: "A spiritual discipline or meditational practice which shuns the power of imagination deprives itself of the most effective and vital means of transforming human nature."[99] Because of the power inherent in visualization, i.e., in *seeing*, Govinda stresses that this form of meditation be pursued only under personal instruction and guidance of a competent guru. Without such supervision, visualization is likely to prove ineffective, or worse, dangerous. Govinda discovered that the fierce, horrendous figures as well as the benign and beneficent ones seen in Tibetan temples are, in fact, "representations of a higher reality, born from visions and inner experience." He says that we need "to recognise all these fearful and terrifying appearances as emanations of our own mind and transformations of the force that will ultimately lead us towards enlightenment." Govinda describes his visit to a small temple that featured the deities of the dark side.

> It was dedicated to the terrible and awe-inspiring deities, the forces of dissolution and transformation, which appear destructive and frightening to those who cling to the things of this world and to their own limited existence, but which prove to be the forces of liberation to those who accept them and make use of them in the

right spirit, by realising their true nature. They are removers of obstacles, the liberators from bondage, the symbols of the ultimate mystery of self-transcendence in the ecstasy of breaking through the darkness of ignorance. They are the embodiment of the highest knowledge . . . . To [the initiated] these forces or aspects of reality are as much symbols of Enlightenment as the compassionate embodiments of Buddhas and Bodhisattvas. Indeed, they are *one* in their ultimate nature. The universal law is beneficent to those who accept it, terrible to those who try to oppose it.[100]

Whether divine or demonic, whether beneficent or malevolent, whether met in paintings, or sculpture, or in one's meditations, these beings are visual representations of deep aspects of consciousness, expressions of our essential nature, and projections of the human mind. Govinda calls attention to a warning set forth in Tibetan texts. "In all visualization we should never fall into the error of imagining that what we see is a reality outside of ourselves."[101] That these superhuman figures are mind-made must not be construed to mean that they are unreal. Their reality lies in the cosmo-psychic forces they represent and, consequently, in their ability to stimulate fundamental transformation. To the extent that the fearful is resisted, its power increases and one remains trapped in conventionality; to the extent that the fearful is recognized and accepted as a disowned dimension of one's own nature, it transfigures into a beneficent power available for transformation and transcendence. The wide appeal of Vajrayana or Tantric Buddhism lies to great extent in this profound insight.

Visualization as a means of meditation takes a variety of forms. The meditator may envision a particular bodhisattva or buddha, or the historical Buddha, sometimes in the form of the meditator's own guru. The image may be visualized in meditative posture just above the meditator's head, then descending into his body and gradually expanding until the body of the buddha-cum-guru and the meditator are one. Govinda claims: "As long as the Buddha is . . . imagined outside ourselves, we cannot realise him in our own life."[102] Figuring prominently in Tibetan meditation is the *mandala*, a Sanskrit term meaning 'circle'. A mandala usually consists of circles and squares sharing a common center which is occupied by a buddha, historical or celestial. Other buddhas or bodhisattvas are located at the cardinal points. Mandalas are often impressive works of art comprised of geometric shapes, mythic images, symbolic forms, and vibrant colors. A mandala is a macrocosmic-microcosmic map designed to facilitate personal integration, on one hand, and integration of the meditator with the cosmos, on the other hand. Thus, it aids in bringing about individual-universal identity. Govinda supplies a clue to the power of mandalas and other iconographic forms when he notes that they represent crystallizations of meditative experience; therefore, when they are artistically depicted they provide a path leading to the same realization from which they originally emerged.[103]

Mantras, power-filled words or sounds, may be envisioned or chanted as a dimension of meditation. Govinda argues that a mantra is most effective when it is accompanied by its appropriate visualization. He also contends that mere recitation of a mantra without comprehension of its deep meanings and associations severely, if not entirely, depletes its effectiveness. One of his best known books, *The Foundations of Tibetan Mysticism*, is solely devoted to the mantra *Om Mani Padme Hum*, the oldest and most important mantra of Tibetan Buddhism and one associated with Avalokiteshvara/ Chenrezi, the Bodhisattva of Compassion.[104] Mantras may or may not carry cognitive meaning. While 'om' and 'hum' have many esoteric meanings, they have no denotative meaning. 'Mani padme,' on the other hand, can be translated as 'the jewel in the lotus' and, in addition, has many symbolic connotations.

It was 1931 when Govinda first met Tomo Geshe Rinpoche and made the fundamental shift from Theravada Buddhism to Vajrayana. Until mid-1960, when he began lecturing in the West, he spent most of his time in Tibet and India, with excursions to nearby countries. Traveling often and widely, he lived up to his name, 'the homeless one'. Much of his travel in Tibet took the form of pilgrimages to remote temples and monasteries. Here, often under adverse weather conditions, he not only deepened his experiential knowledge of Buddhism, but exercised his long-standing interest in art and architecture by making detailed drawings. In this task he was assisted by his wife, Li Gotami, a Parsee woman from Bombay who had been his student years earlier when he taught at a college in Bengal. Li Gotami was also an accomplished photographer. Their artistic reproductions and photographs were widely published and displayed. Some of their work is the only surviving record of Tibetan artistic creations, due to the destruction of temples and monasteries following the Chinese invasion.

In 1938 Govinda became a naturalized citizen of British India. This status proved of no help in keeping him out of internment when the Second World War broke out. Because of his German heritage, he was arrested and forced to remain in confinement until the war ended. Soon after India's independence in August 1947, he became a citizen of India. Travel, writing, and spiritual practice occupied him during the ensuing years. By mid-1960, Govinda began to lecture in Europe and in 1968 made his first visit to America. After several lecture tours, he settled in Mill Valley, California with his wife in mid-1970. He was attracted there, he said, by the interest of the people in Buddhism. He once wrote to a friend that there are more Buddhists in American than he had met in India.[105]

Lama Anagarika Govinda is a twentieth-century Marco Polo of the spirit. Thoroughly rooted in the culture of the West, he moved to and spent most of his adult years in the East, traveling and imbibing its finest teachings. These he then brought back to the West and disseminated through more than a dozen books, a great number of articles and essays, countless lectures, and such organizations as the Arya Maitreya Mandala, which he founded in 1933 at the instigation of Tomo Geshe Rinpoche to help spread Buddhism. His scholarship is one of the main forces making Buddhism available in the West. Though Govinda diligently practiced Buddhism and possessed a profound understanding of its transformative power, he never suggested that enlightenment had become his abiding state. Shortly before his death on January 14, 1985, he wrote to a Buddhist friend in England: "Now it is up to the next generation to take Buddhism out of the . . . academic atmosphere and make it a living experience."[106] Given the strong experiential and practice dimension in his writing, his statement may have been a premonition of the continuing impact of his own contribution to Buddhism.

NOTES

1. Eknath Eswaran, trans., *The Dhammapada*. (Petaluma, Ca.: Nilgiri Press, 1985), 78.

2. Balangoda Ananda Maitreya, trans., Rose Kramer, reviser, *The Dhammapada: The Path of Truth*. (Novato, Ca.: Lotsawa, 1988), 1, 5.

3. P. Lal, trans., *The Dhammapada*. (New York: Farrar, Straus & Giroux, 1967), 45.

4. Theravada Buddhism is the only surviving sub-group of a larger branch of Buddhism known as Hinayana. The Small (hina) Vehicle, i.e., the 'lesser path of progress', is a designation applied by Mahayanists who considered themselves to represent the 'greater path of progress'.

5. For a fuller treatment of the arahant see Nathan Katz, *Buddhist Images of Human Perfection: The Arahant of the Sutta Pitaka Compared with the Bodhisattva and the Mahasiddha*. (Delhi: Motilal Banarsidass, 1982); and George D. Bond, "The Arahant: Sainthood in Theravada Buddhism," in Richard Kieckhefer and George D. Bond, eds., *Sainthood: Its Manifestations in World Religions*. (Berkeley: University of California Press, 1988), 140-171.

6. Dhammapada, Chapter 7. Cf. the translations of Easwaran, *Dhammapada*. 102-103; and Ananda Maitreya, *Dhammapada*. 25-27.

7. Translation of the title and characterization of the work are from Kate Crosby and Andrew Skilton, trans., *The Bodhicharyavatara*. (Oxford: Oxford University Press, 1996). xxx, viii.

8. Robert A. F. Thurman, trans., *The Holy Teaching of Vimalakīrti: A Mahayana Scripture*. (University Park, PA: Pennsylvania State University Press, 1976), 43, 45.

9. Quoted in Donald S. Lopez, Jr., "Sanctification on the Bodhisattva Path," in Kieckhefer and Bond, *Sainthood,* 187.

10. Unless indicated otherwise, all quotations from the Bodhicharya-vatara are from Marion L. Matics, trans., *Entering the Path of Enlightenment: The Bodhicharyavatara of the Buddhist Poet Shantideva.* (New York: Macmillan, 1970).

11. This practice is discussed further in the last chapter, "A Way of Ways."

12. A.F Price and Wong Mou-lam, trans., *The Diamond Sūtra and the Sūtra of Hui-neng.* (Boston: Shambhala, 1990), 81. All quotations from the Diamond Sūtra, the Platform Sūtra, or the Sūtra of Hui-neng are from this edition unless otherwise indicated.

13. Thurman, *Vimalakīrti,* 41.

14. Matics, *Entering the Path,* 100.

15. Quoted in Lopez, "Sanctification," 195.

16. For an excellent study of this phenomenon in the world religions see Georg Feuerstein, *Holy Madness: The Shock Tactics and Radical Teachings of Crazy-Wise Adepts, Holy Fools, and Rascal Gurus.* (New York: Paragon House, 1991).

17. Thurman, *Vimalakīrti,* 64.

18. Matics, *Entering the Path,* 50-51.

19. Richard H. Robinson and Willard L Johnson, *The Buddhist Religion: A Historical Introduction.* 3rd ed., (Belmont, Calif.: Wadsworth Publishing Co., 1982), 77.

20. Thurman, *Vimalakīrti,* 39.

21. The translation/interpretation of the two Sanskrit terms and the description of transcendental analysis are from E. Obermiller, "The Doctrine of Prajñaparamita as Exposed in the Abhisamayalamkara of Maitreya," *Acta Orientalia.* vol. 11 (1932), parts I-II, 16-17.

22. Quoted in Robinson and Johnson, *Buddhist Religion,* 226.

23. Thurman, *Vimalakīrti,* 36.

24. Ibid., 21, 83.

25. Quoted in Lopez, "Sanctification," 198.

26. Robinson and Johnson, *Buddhist Religion*, 77.

27. Quoted in Lopez, "Sanctification," 197-198.

28. Herbert V. Guenther, trans., *The Royal Song of Saraha: A Study in the History of Buddhist Thought*. (Berkeley: Shambala, 1973), 70.

29. For a perceptive study of the mahasiddha, see Reginald Ray's article under that title in Mircea Eliade, ed-in-chief, *The Encyclopedia of Religion*. vol. 9, (New York: Macmillan Publishing Co., 1987), 122-126.

30. Lama Anagarika Govinda, *A Living Buddhism for the West*. Maurice Walshe, trans., (Boston: Shambhala, 1990), 72.

31. Thurman, *Vimalakīrti*, 19, 14.

32. Price and Mou-lam, *Diamond Sūtra*, 119.

33. Quoted in Katz, *Buddhist Images*, 283.

34. Quoted in George D. Bond, "Tathagata," in Eliade, *Encyclopedia*, vol. 14, 353.

35. Easwaran, *Dhammapada*, 116-117.

36. Maitreya, *Dhammapada*, 42.

37. Quoted and slightly modified from Peter Harvey, *An Introduction to Buddhism: Teachings, History and Practices*. (Cambridge: Cambridge University Press, 1990), 24.

38. Heinrich Dumoulin, *Zen Buddhism: A History*. vol. 1, James W. Heisig and Paul Knitter, trans., (New York: Macmillan Publishing Co., 1988), 9.

39. Sengstan, the Third Zen Patriarch, "Hsin Hsin Ming" ("Verses on the Faith Mind," privately published as a pamphlet by Alan Clements, (Virginia Beach, Virginia, 1980), [2].

40. Govinda, *Living Buddhism*, 111.

41. Price and Mou-lam, *Diamond Sūtra*, 152.

42. Quoted in H. Wolfgang Schumann, *Buddhism: An Outline of its Teachings and Schools*. Georg Feuerstein, trans., (Wheaton, IL: The Theosophical Publishing House, 1974), 69.

43. Easwaran, *Dhammapada*, 81-82, 205.

44. Ibid., 132.

45. Extrapolated from Easwaran, *Dhammapada*, 195-199.

46. Quoted and slightly modified from Harvey, *Introduction to Buddhism*, 28, 31.

47. Henry Clarke Warren, trans., *Buddhism in Translation.* (New York: Atheneum, 1963), xiv; first published by Harvard University Press, 1896).

48. Quoted in David J. Kalupahana, "Pratitya-Samutpada," in Eliade, *Encyclopedia*, vol. 11, 487.

49. Quoted in Joanna Macy, *Mutual Causality in Buddhism and General Systems Theory.* (Albany, N.Y.: State University of New York Press, 1991), 39.

50. Ibid., 57.

51. Thich Nhat Hanh, *The Heart of Understanding: Commentaries on the Prajnaparamita Heart Sutra.* Peter Levitt, ed., (Berkeley, CA: Parallax Press, 1988), 3-4.

52. Govinda, *Living Buddhism*, 99; Lama Anagarika Govinda, *Creative Meditation and Multi-Dimensional Consciousness.* (Wheaton, IL: Theosophical Publishing House, 1976), 286.

53. Macy, *Mutual Causality*, 27, 45.

54. Warren, *Buddhism in Translation*, 133-134.

55. Price and Mou-lam, *Diamond Sūtra*, 44.

56. Translated in Frederick J. Streng, *Emptiness: A Study in Religious Meaning.* (Nashville, TN: Abingdon Press, 1967), 213.

57. Ibid., 215.

58. Thurman, *Vimalakīrti*, 118, 74-75.

59. D.T. Suzuki, "The Buddhist Conception of Reality," in Frederick Frank, ed., *The Buddha Eye: An Anthology of the Kyoto School.* (New York: Crossroad Publishing Co., 1991), 103. Republished from *The Eastern Buddhist.* vol. 7, no. 2 (1974), 1-21.

60. The phrase in quotation marks is from Jean Gebser, *The Ever-Present Origin.* Noel Barstad and Algis Mickunas, trans. (Athens, Ohio: Ohio University Press, 1985).

61. Thurman, *Vimalakīrti*, 43-44. See also p. 123, Thurman's notes 4-8.

62. Quoted in Edward Conze, *Buddhist Wisdom Books: Containing The Diamond Sutra and The Heart Sutra.* (New York: Harper Torchbooks, 1958), 47.

63. Translated in Donald S. Lopez, Jr., *The Heart Sutra Explained: Indian and Tibetan Commentaries.* (Albany: State University of New York Press, 1988), 57

64. Masao Abe, "Kenotic God and Dynamic Sunyata," in *The Emptying God: A Buddhist-Jewish-Christian Conversation.* John B. Cobb, Jr. and Christopher Ives, eds., (Maryknoll, N.Y.: Orbis Books, 1990), 28.

65. Lopez, *Heart Sutra.*, 95.

66. Price and Mou-lam, *Diamond Sūtra*, 77.

67. Thurman, *Vimalakīrti*, 73-77.

68. Ibid., 59.

69. Nyoshul Kenpo Rinpoche and Lama Surya Das, *Natural Great Perfection: Dzogchen Teachings and Vajra Songs.* Lama Surya Das, trans., (Ithaca, NY: Snow Lion Publications, 1995), 89. Except where indicated otherwise, all information on Dzogchen is drawn from this book, with page numbers of quotations given at the end of the quotes.

70. The Dalai Lama, *Dzogchen: The Heart Essence of the Great Perfection.* Geshe Thupten Jinpa and Richard Barron (Chokyi Nyima), trans., Patrick Gaffney, ed., (Ithaca, NY: Snow Lion Publications, 2000), 48.

71. Dudjom Jigdral Yeshe Dorje, *Wisdom Nectar: Dudjom Rinpoche's Heart Advice.* Ron Garry, trans., (Ithaca, NY: Snow Lion Publications, 2005), 114.

72. Heinrich Dumoulin, *Zen Buddhism: A History.* vol. 2, Japan. James W. Heisig and Paul Knitter, trans. (New York: Macmillan Publishing Co., 1990), 367.

73. Philip B. Yampolsky, trans., *The Zen Master Hakuin: Selected Writings.* (New York: Columbia University Press, 1971), 117-118.

74. Norman Waddell, trans., "Wild Ivy: The Spiritual Autobiography of Hakuin Ekaku," *The Eastern Buddhist.* vol. 15, no. 2 (1982), 99.

75. Norman Waddell, trans., "Talks by Hakuin Introductory to Lectures on the Records of Old Sokkō," *The Eastern Buddhist.* vol. 24, no. 1, New Series (Spring 1991), 119.

76. R.D.M. Shaw and Wilhelm Schiffer, trans., "Yasen Kanna: 'A Chat on a Boat in the Evening' by Hakuin Zenji," *Monumenta Nipponica* (Tokyo). vol. 13, nos. 1-2 (1956), 113, 109.

77. Yampolsky, *Zen Master Hakuin*, 32.

78. Dumoulin, *Zen Buddhism*, vol. 2, 375.

79. Shaw and Schiffer, "Yasen Kanna," 107.

80. Yampolsky, *Zen Master Hakuin*, 132, 177.

81. Ibid., 135-136.

82. Ibid., 164.

83. Lama Anagarika Govinda, *The Way of the White Clouds: A Buddhist Pilgrim in Tibet.* (Berkeley: Shambhala, 1966, 1970), 12-13.

84. Govinda, *White Clouds*, 16.

85. Ibid., 27-28, 33.

86. Govinda, *Living Buddhism*, 107.

87. Govinda, *White Clouds*, 26-27.

88. Ibid., 158.

89. Govinda, *Living Buddhism.* 111.

90. Govinda, *White Clouds*, 34-35.

91. Govinda, *Living Buddhism*, 121.

92. Lama Anagarika Govinda, *Buddhist Reflections.* Maurice Walshe, trans. (York Beach, Maine: Samuel Weiser, Inc., 1991), 55.

93. Govinda, *Creative Meditation*, 40.

94. Govinda, *Buddhist Reflections*, 59-60, 56.

95. Govinda, *Living Buddhism*, 132-133.
96. Helen Newman, "The Teacher Speaks on Methods: A partial account of Lama Govinda's weekend seminar at HDI," *Human Dimensions*. vol. 1, no. 4 (Buffalo: Human Dimensions Institute,1972), 38-39.
97. Govinda, *Creative Meditation*, 117.
98. Govinda, *Living Buddhism*, 133.
99. Govinda, *Creative Meditation*, 43.
100. Govinda, *White Clouds*, 54, 175, 24-25.
101. Govinda, *Buddhist Reflections*, 65.
102. Govinda, *White Clouds*, 35.
103. Lama Anagarika Govinda, *Insights of a Himalayan Pilgrim*. (Berkeley, CA: Dharma Publishing, 1991), 63.
104. Lama Anagarika Govinda, *Foundations of Tibetan Mysticism: According to the Esoteric Teachings of the Great Mantra, Om Mani Padme Hum*. (New York: Samuel Weiser, 1960, 1969).
105. Ken Winkler, *A Thousand Journeys: The Biography of Lama Anagarika Govinda*. (Longmead, England: Element Books Ltd., 1990), 166. This book and Govinda's autobiography are the principal sources for the biographical information on Lama Anagarika Govinda.
106. Ibid., 169.

IV Islam: The Mind of Submission

"He who knows himself knows his Lord."—Muhammad

"Man is endowed with this precious gift of intelligence which allows him to know the Ultimate Reality."—Seyyed Hossein Nasr

No religion has been more misunderstood and maligned than Islam. Most of what is thought to be known about this major monotheistic religion tends to be stereotypical, biased, or erroneous. Islam is commonly perceived to be an authoritarian, rigid, restrictive religion that has spread mainly by the sword. Muhammad is considered a false prophet who engaged in subterfuge and coercion to further his ends. The Koran is regarded as dull and repetitious.* Allah is thought to be wrathful and vindictive. Muslims are seen as fatalistic, uncultured, and fanatical. Each of these as characterizations is decidedly wrong.

Islam is an authentic religion that has spread during the fourteen centuries of its history over much of the world, an expansion based on

---

* A more accurate English spelling of the Muslim holy book is Qur'ān; the figure that looks like an apostrophe in this spelling denotes a short break in pronunciation between the syllables. The common English rendering of Arabic terms will be used if available. Otherwise a standard transliteration system will be used that should aid with pronunciation.

its inherent appeal to the heart and mind. Here is a proven religion that not only provides a sure pattern of religious, moral, and social action but also a worldview that answers the deepest longings of the human soul. As "the straight path" (Koran 1:6), Islam nurtures and fosters the best in humanity while warning against the dangers that delude, corrupt, and destroy. Islam's status as the second largest religion in the world is derived from its ability to meet the comprehensive needs of human nature. Regarded by some as the fastest growing religion in the world, Islam extends from Indonesia to Canada, from West Africa to China, and, of course, throughout the Middle East.

Islam is the third great monotheistic religion of the world, historically following Judaism and Christianity. It emerged out of a Judeo-Christian environment in a way comparable to Christianity's emergence out of Judaism. Because of this origin, Islam is generically a Western religion. The commonalities between these three religions are so great that one can properly speak of the Judeo-Christian-Islamic tradition. Besides worshiping the same God, the three religions acknowledge many of the same prophets, share a similar worldview, recognize sin as the essential problem of mankind, and offer comparable ways of coming into right relationship with the divine. Seeing itself as the culmination of God's revelation to Jews and Christians, Islam recognizes the divine origin of the Hebrew Bible and the New Testament, while holding the Koran to be God's final and unsurpassed revelation. Since Muslims generally know more about Judaism and Christianity than Jews and Christians know about Islam, it behooves the latter to learn more about the religion that grew from their ranks.

Muhammad (570-632 CE)

Muhammad was born on the 12th of Rabīᶜ al-Awwal in the year
of the Elephant (August 2, 570 CE).* His lineage reaches back to
Abraham through Ishmael, Abraham's first son, born of Hagar, the
Egyptian handmaiden presented to Abraham by his wife Sarah when
she was unable to bear a son. Muhammad's father was the grandson
of the founder of the aristocratic tribe that ruled Mecca, the Quraysh.
Mecca was at this time the principal religious and commercial center
of the Arabian Peninsula. Muhammad's father died before the birth
of his son. Muhammad's mother, according to the custom of the day,
sent her young son to live for extended periods in the desert with a
Bedouin tribe, a practice thought to increase health and strength.

An event known as the Opening of the Chest is usually attributed
to the time Muhammad spent in the desert as a boy. According to
traditional accounts, Muhammad was visited by two men dressed in
white, later identified by him as angels, who took him aside from his
playmates and, forcing him to the ground, cut open his chest, took out
his heart, and washed it in a basin of melted snow, thereby removing
a black clot. The angels disguised as men returned his heart to his
chest and disappeared. Muslims debate among themselves whether
the event occurred bodily or was a dream or vision. Some contend
that the extraction of the black clot signifies removal of the inclination
to sin, of ignorance, error, and unbelief. These were replaced by
wisdom, compassion, and faith. The event is understood by some
Muslims as part of his preparation for prophethood.

Muhammad's mother died when he was six years old. He became
the ward of his aged grandfather, who himself died two years later.
Muhammad then moved into the home of his uncle, Abu Talib (Abū
Tālib), father of Ali (ᶜAlī). After Muhammad's call to prophethood,

---

* The sign that looks like a small, raised 'c' is called an ᶜayn in
  Arabic and causes the adjacent vowel to be gutteralized.

Ali became one of the first converts to Islam and a major supporter of the Prophet. As a youth, Muhammad frequently joined Abu Talib on his trading missions to Syria and elsewhere. On one of these caravan journeys he met a Syrian Christian monk who, after asking him a number of questions, informed Abu Talib that Muhammad would someday become a prophet. This monk identified a mole on Muhammad's back as the physical sign of Muhammad's eventual position as the Seal of Prophethood.

As Muhammad matured and assumed increasing responsibility in the world of commerce, he came to be called al-Amin, the Trustworthy One. Because of his reputation as a person of upright character, Muhammad was called upon by the Quraysh elders to settle a dispute that arose when the Kaba (ka°ba, cube), the central sanctuary in Mecca, underwent renovation. The Black Stone, a meteorite that normally occupied one corner of the Kaba, had been removed during the repairs. The elders, vying with each other for the honor, could not agree on who would replace the Black Stone. When Muhammad appeared they agreed that he should arbitrate the matter. Muhammad suggested that the Black Stone be placed in the center of his mantle, which each of the elders would then lift so that all would share equally in replacing the sacred stone. All were satisfied when Muhammad performed the final positioning.

As a young man Muhammad came into the employ of a wealthy widow, Khadijah, who operated a caravan business. She was so impressed with Muhammad that she proposed marriage to him. He accepted the proposal; he was twenty-five and she forty at the time. During their twenty-five years of marital life, Khadijah bore two sons, both of whom died in infancy, and four daughters. Only after Khadijah's death did Muhammad take additional wives, some in order to consolidate religio-political alliances, some to offer support to widows, and some out of personal attraction. Chief among the latter was A'isha (°A'isha), daughter of Abu Bakr, an early convert and the first caliph to lead the Muslim community following Muhammad's death.

After his marriage to Khadijah, Muhammad had the leisure to devote himself more fully to matters of religion. Discontent with the idolatry that prevailed throughout most of Arabia, and with what he knew of Judaism and Christianity, Muhammad considered himself an *hanīf,* one who espoused a strict monotheism in opposition to paganism and polytheism. His spiritual practice consisted of periodic retreats, some as long as a month, to a cave close to the summit of a nearby mountain. Here Muhammad devoted himself to fasting, prayer, and meditation. On one of these retreats, when Muhammad was forty years old, he received the call to prophethood.

During the month of Ramadan in 610 CE, on what would come to be known as the Night of Power, i.e., the night on which the Koran descended from heaven to earth, Muhammad was visited by the angel Gabriel. Gabriel commanded, *'Iqra'!* Understanding the command to be 'Read', Muhammad refused since he was illiterate. Again the angel demanded and Muhammad declined. When Gabriel charged Muhammad a third time, he began to choke him. Muhammad now apparently decided that he would learn to read and, perhaps simultaneously, understood the command to be 'Recite!', an equally acceptable meaning. When Muhammad accepted Gabriel's demand, the first revelation from Allah was given to him (Koran 96:1-5): "Recite: In the Name of thy Lord who created, created Man of a blood-clot. Recite: And thy Lord is the Most Generous, who taught by the Pen, taught Man that he knew not."[1]

Muhammad was so perplexed, distraught, and weakened by his encounter with Gabriel that he had to crawl back to Mecca, all the time fearing for his sanity. He described his ordeal to Khadijah who assured him that he was not going mad. She approached her cousin who, like Muhammad, was a hanif, and told him about Muhammad's experience. He not only determined that Muhammad was called to prophethood but, knowing something of Christian scriptures, declared that Jesus had foretold Muhammad's coming, thinking apparently of John 16 where Jesus announced the coming of the *parakletos* (Greek, advocate or comforter), which in Christianity is identified as the Holy Spirit.

Revelation continued to come to Muhammad intermittently for the next twenty-three years. When receiving revelation, Muhammad would seem to be focused on an invisible presence. His face might turn red and begin to perspire. He noted a physical heaviness and would sometimes tremble and shake. Occasionally he emitted involuntary sounds; at other times his lips would move but no sounds would be heard. He sometimes felt muscular tension and pain. The force of revelation once caused a camel he was riding to fall to its knees. Muhammad believed that the strain of revelation caused his beard to turn prematurely white. After he had received a new revelation, he recited it for his companions. The individual revelations were commonly memorized, and occasionally recorded. During the caliphate of Uthman (ᶜUthmān), who assumed his office twelve years after the Prophet's death, the various revelations were assembled to form the Koran.

The seventeenth chapter of the Koran opens with a verse that Muslims believe refers to an event in Muhammad's life that is second in spiritual significance only to his call to prophethood, namely, his Night Journey to Jerusalem and Ascension to Heaven. "Glorified be He Who carried His servant by night from the Inviolable Place of Worship [i.e., Mecca] to the Far Distant Place of Worship [variously interpreted as Jerusalem or Heaven] . . . that We might show him of Our tokens!" (Koran 17:1)[2] Traditional literature has greatly expanded, with numerous variations, this terse description. The Night Journey and Ascension is generally believed to have been a single event and to have occurred a year or so before Muhammad moved from Mecca to Medina. While sleeping one night near the Kaba, the Prophet was awakened by Gabriel and told to mount a celestial steed named Buraq. Buraq is sometimes depicted with a human face, peacock tail and heavily adorned with precious jewels. En route to Jerusalem, stops were made at Mt. Sinai and Bethlehem, sites important in Judaism and Christianity, thereby confirming that Muhammad stands in the prophetic lineage of Moses and Christ.

In Jerusalem, Muhammad found the prophets and angels waiting for him to lead them in ritual prayer. After doing so, he began the ascent to heaven, leaving from a huge rock that is now housed in the Dome of the Rock, a major mosque in Jerusalem. In the first of seven heavens, Muhammad met Adam, who alternately laughed and cried as he looked to the right at his progeny in paradise and to the left at those in hell. In the second heaven, he met Jesus and John the Baptist. Other prophets welcomed him in the succeeding heavens. Finally, Muhammad left Gabriel and Buraq and continued his ascent alone on a miraculous carpet until he came into the presence of Allah Himself. After bowing to Allah in humility and submission, Muhammad was given insight into the mysteries of creation, some of which he was charged to keep secret, some of which he could reveal if he chose, and some of which he was required to convey to his community.

After leaving his audience with Allah, Muhammad descended through each of the heavens. When he met Moses, he was asked if God had issued any particular obligations for the Muslims. Muhammad replied that Allah had charged Muslims to pray fifty times each day. Moses objected that the number was too great and urged Muhammad to return to Allah and request a reduction. Muhammad traveled back and forth until the number was reduced to five. Even though Moses deemed five daily prayers still too many, Muhammad refused to request any further reduction, especially since Allah had graciously agreed to count the five as equivalent to fifty.

Muslims debate whether Muhammad's Night Journey and Ascension was a physical journey in the body or a spiritual experience in the mind. Neither interpretation is considered more correct than the other. To deny outright the fact of the Ascension, however, is unacceptable. One of Islam's most important theologians, Abu al-

Hasan al-Ashʿarī (260-324 AH/873-935 CE), attests: "We credit the tradition of the Ascent."[3] An early Muslim creed, Fiqh Akbar II, reads: "The report of the Ascension is a reality, and whosoever rejects it is an erring schismatic."[4] Muslim mystics particularly value the report of Muhammad's Ascension, often modeling their own spiritual journey on the ascent of the Prophet.

When it became apparent that Muhammad's conveying of revelation and his preaching were beginning to attract large numbers, both inside and outside Mecca, the Quraysh became alarmed. They feared that his message of monotheism would lead to the loss of their religious, economic, and political power. If the Bedouin tribes stopped coming to Mecca to worship their deities at the Kaba, a drastic fall in trade would result. The Quraysh knew that if they lost their financial power, their influence in other areas would diminish as well. Their persecution at times became severe, even making attempts against the life of the Prophet.

About the time that the opposition was at its height, a contingent of Arabs from Yathrib, a community about 210 miles north of Mecca, approached Muhammad and invited him and his followers to move to their oasis. They believed that Muhammad, given his leadership ability, would be able to resolve differences among those living in the region and successfully govern the community. Muhammad began to send Muslims gradually and secretly to Yathrib, and finally left Mecca himself along with Abu Bakr. They headed south to forestall suspicion and were followed by a herd of sheep to cover their tracks. Seeing pursuers behind them, they took refuge in a cave. When their enemies approached the cave, they saw a spider web over the entrance and concluded that no one could have recently entered. Muhammad and Abu Bakr thus escaped sure death and were able to reach Yathrib safely. The entire Muslim immigration (*hijra*) was completed in 1 AH (Anno Hijra)/622 CE, a year that officially marks the beginning of the Islamic calendar. Henceforth, Yathrib was known as Medina, after Medina an-Nabi, the City of the Prophet.

Opposition, however, did not cease after settling into Medina. Not only did the Quraysh continue their pursuit, but the Jews of Medina, and others who came to be known as the hypocrites, resisted Muhammad and his followers, and made concerted attempts against their lives. Over the next several years, Muhammad and the young Muslim community were engaged in a number of military battles, some of which they lost but most of which they won. It was when returning from a military skirmish that Muhammad made the crucial distinction between the lesser *jihād* (lit., struggle, effort) and the greater jihad, the former being the military struggle against another army and the latter being the inner struggle against one's evil tendencies.

Revelation continued to come to Muhammad while living in Medina. During this time, he promulgated laws for governing Muslim society and was successful in attracting many individuals and Bedouin tribes to Islam. Over the next eight years, Islam became so firmly planted on Arab soil that Muhammad and his followers were able to complete the annual pilgrimage to Mecca virtually unchallenged by the Quraysh. One of Muhammad's first acts on entering the city was to destroy all the idols in the Kaba and declare it henceforth to be a sanctuary dedicated solely to the worship of the one God. Two years later, on June 8, 632, Muhammad died. He was 62 years old.

The Muslim community faced its first crisis without the Prophet when Umar (ʿUmar) refused to accept the fact of Muhammad's death, alleging that he was only in hiding and would return to punish those who thought him dead. Abu Bakr intervened saying: "O men, if anyone worships Muhammad, Muhammad is dead; if anyone worships God, God is alive, immortal." He then recited a passage from the Koran (3:144/138): "Muhammad is but a messenger; messengers (the like of whom) have passed away before him. Will it be that when he dieth or is slain, ye will turn back on your heels?"[5] Abu Bakr's mature acceptance of Muhammad's death may well have prepared the way for him to be elected by the grieving Muslim community as the first of the Rightly-Guided Caliphs.

Muhammad has been depicted thus far from the standpoint of traditional Muslim biographies. Another appproach, while including the biographies with their explicit historical bent, treats the Prophet from the perspective of Muslim faith. This more comprehensive approach focuses on the meaning and significance that he holds for Muslims. Here one finds also great variation in Muslim views, further dispelling the notion that Islam is a monolithic religion that imposes rigid beliefs and practices on its adherents. Muhammad is seen to fulfill six basic roles for Muslims. Muslims are virtually of one mind in their understanding of the first three roles. Different and opposing views arise in the last three roles.

First among the roles Muhammad completes for Muslims is that of prophethood; not only is he a prophet but the Prophet, God's final prophetic spokesman and messenger. God completes His revelation to mankind in Muhammad, who stands at the end of the prophetic lineage that began with Adam and extended through 120,000 prophets before culminating in Muhammad. To deny that Muhammad is the Prophet is to be non-Muslim. Other titles given by the Koran include guide, warner, bringer of glad tidings, witness, reminder, and servant. Muslims sometimes devotionally recite a litany of 201 names of the Prophet. As a general rule, the more important someone is in the life of a people, the more names they have for him. The high regard and loving devotion that Muslims typically have for Muhammad is indicated by the fact that this writer has collected out of Muslim literature more than a thousand different names, titles, and epithets for Prophet.

Second, Muhammad is a Founder, Reformer, and Legislator. By integrating policies of government within religion, he successfully founded not only a religion but also an empire, thereby effecting basic changes in the common social and cultural practices of his day. He outlawed drunkenness, blood revenge, and infanticide.

He transformed an assemblage of fractious tribes into an orderly society founded on principles and laws of justice and equality. He moved his followers away from stark individualism and isolationism into an integrated and homogenous society. Muhammad's success in merging religion and government set the standard for Islam to become not only a religion but an entire civilization. Muslims believe that Islam is fully Islam only when it governs the state as well as leads the prayers. Sharia (*shari*c*a*, way, path), based on the Koran and the practice of the Prophet, is the comprehensive Islamic law that sets the standard for all aspects of Muslim life, from personal religion to governmental policy.

Third, Muhammad is Teacher and Exemplar. His teaching and practice, known as the *sunnah* (custom) of the Prophet, became the standard for Muslim belief and behavior. Great effort was expended by scholars to collect and authenticate Muhammad's many sayings and actions. These reports, transmitted from generation to generation, have been codified into several official collections of Hadīth (report, tradition). Hadith constitutes an authority in Islam second only to the Koran. If the Koran does not provide explicit guidance on an issue, Muslims consult Hadith to discover what Muhammad said or did about the matter.

Though he was himself illiterate, Muhammad placed high value on education. He decreed that every prisoner who taught ten Muslims to read and write should be freed. His companions remembered him saying: "Go in quest of knowledge even unto China," and "To seek knowledge is obligatory on every Muslim man and woman."[6] Muslim mystics trace some of their most profound teachings to Muhammad; for example, "He who knoweth his own self, knoweth God."[7] A teacher, however, no matter how worthy his teaching, is unworthy of emulation if he does not exemplify his teaching. Muslims believe that there was no discrepancy between Muhammad's teaching and his practice. The Koran (33:21) itself asserts: "Verily in the messenger of Allah ye have a good example." Al-Ghazzali (450-505/1058-

1111), one of Islam's most influential theologians and mystics, concludes his treatise on "The Conduct of Life as Exemplified by the Prophetic Character" by declaring: "We ask Allah to help us imitate Muhammad's character, actions, qualities, and sayings, through His grace and the ampleness of His generosity."[8] Abu Saᶜid (357-440/967-1049), a Persian mystic, claims: "I modelled my actions, outward and inward, upon the sunna of the Prophet, so that habit at last became nature."[9] Throughout history few humans have been as exhaustively and minutely emulated as Muhammad.

Four, Muhammad is Mediator and Intercessor. All Muslims readily acknowledge that Muhammad mediated the Koran. Most believe that he also mediated divine insight and guidance through his teaching and behavior. On the question of intercession, i.e., representation by another on the Day of Judgment, the record is not so clear. The Koran speaks often of intercession, but not unambiguously. Appealing to Koran and Hadith, Muslims believe that there will be no intercession, that God Himself will provide intercession, that angels, or the Koran, or Jesus, or one of the other prophets will intercede. The famous Throne Verse of the Koran (2:255/256) seems to leave the question of intercession entirely up to God: "Who is he that intercedeth with Him save by His leave?" Some Muslims, however, do believe that Muhammad will intercede and support their claim with Koranic passages, albeit interpreted, and Hadith. One of the Prophet's companions reported him saying: "I was offered a choice between intercession and having half of my community enter the Garden [Paradise]. I chose intercession because it is more general and more adequate."[10] Muslims who deny intercession outright also base their view on Hadith. A contemporary Muslim cites Muhammad's words: "O men of Quraysh, earn your own salvation; for I cannot avail you on the Day of Judgment in any way."[11] Appeal is also made to the Koran (2:48/45): "Guard yourselves against a day when no soul will in aught avail another, nor will intercession be accepted from it." The ongoing debate in Islam over intercession demonstrates the importance of textual interpretation, whether applied to scripture or other religious documents.

Five, even greater controversy exists in Islam over the role of Muhammad as a Miracle Worker. He was occasionally taunted by the people of his day to work a miracle in proof of his mission. The Koran (17:90-93/92-95) reports that he was challenged to "cause a spring to gush forth from the earth," to produce "a garden of date-palms and grapes" or a "house of gold." At such times, Allah enjoined him to retort: "My Lord be glorified: Am I naught save a mortal messenger?" The majority of Muslims contend that Muhammad, while a unique and extraordinary man, was indeed a man and thus unable to circumvent the laws of nature. At the same time, however, many Muslims believe that Muhammad did work miracles. Not only did miracles accompany his birth and death, he was often miraculously protected from danger during his lifetime. Some believe that he possessed superhuman powers, e.g., that he could see behind himself and in darkness, that he could both hear the dead speak and speak to the dead, that he could hear all languages in Arabic. Some believe that he possessed power over nature, that he could heal disease and revivify the dead.[12] Needless to say, such claims are totally denied by the majority of modern educated Muslims.

All Muslims agree, however, that there is one miracle connected with Muhammad, the miracle or inimitability of the Koran. This, of course, is not a miracle that Muhammad worked but a miracle transmitted through him. The Koran (17:88/90) claims: "Though mankind and the Jinn should assemble to produce the like of this Koran, they could not produce the like thereof though they were helpers one of another."* The miraculous nature of the Koran,

---

* Jinn (from which the word genie derives) are beings with powers somewhat less than those of angels. They may be good or evil and occupy, along with angels, the subtle world that exists between the material world and the divine world.

Muslims claim, lies both in its content and its style. An Egyptian theologian, Muhammad ᶜAbduh, asks rhetorically: "Is not the appearance of such a book, from the lips of an illiterate man, the greatest miracle and clearest evidence that it is not of human origin?"[13] Muslim scholars contend that Muhammad's personal linguistic style is markedly inferior to that of the Koran. Others argue that no matter how proficient a person may be in Arabic, to produce a passage as eloquent, felicitous, and meaningful as those of the Koran is impossible. The uniqueness of the Koran stands unchallenged among Muslims.

Six, and finally, Muhammad is recognized by some Muslims as a Transcendent Being. Muslims with a philosophic, esoteric, or mystical propensity often understand Muhammad to have primordial, metaphysical, and ontological significance. Behind the appearance of the historical man Muhammad is the Muhammadan essence. Al-Hallāj (244-309/857-922), one of the first mystics to emphasize Muhammad as a transcendent principle, affirms that "Muhammad's existence was prior even to non-existence and his name was prior to that of the 'Pen'. He was known before substances and accidents [metaphysical categories], and before the realities of 'before' and 'after'."[14] Known as the Truth, Reality, or Light of Muhammad, this essence not only undergirds all spiritual existence but the entire cosmos as well. Besides finding its fullest human expression in the Prophet of Islam, this essence sustains all that is and stands as the source and end of creation. By means of the notion of the Truth or Light of Muhammad, a conception of philosophic subtlety, Muslims articulate their understanding of the essential nature of the Prophet as identical to the deep structure of the universe in all its intricacy and complexity. The Muslim who knows and conforms to this Truth or Light of Muhammad finds that his own existence takes on cosmic significance since he lives according to the most fundamental principles of being. By means of full alignment with Muhammad as Transcendent Being, time and space are transcended as Muslims become one with Allah.

Koran

The 114 chapters of the Koran vary in length from three verses to 286 and are arranged roughly according to length, with the longer chapters appearing first and the shorter ones coming toward the end of the book (with the exception of the first chapter which is only seven verses long). Revealed, recited, and written in Arabic, Muslims commonly hold that the Koran is only fully and authentically the Koran in Arabic. Since translations are invariably interpretations, not only is there a change from the sacred language of Arabic, there is also a change in meaning, albeit perhaps subtle, whenever the Koran is rendered into another language.

To be sure, the Koran has been translated into many languages—nearly a dozen different English versions are available—but usually with some degree of reluctance. The translations are necessary in part because the majority of the world's Muslims are not Arabs. Even when Muslims do not natively speak Arabic, however, they memorize key passages from the Koran that must be known in order to fulfill their ritual obligations. Seyyed Hossein Nasr, a contemporary Muslim philosopher and mystic, notes that "the formulae of the Koran read in prayers and acts of worship must be in the sacred language of Arabic which alone enables one to penetrate into the content and be transformed by the Divine presence and grace (*barakah*) of the Divine." Commenting further on the transformative, integrative power of sacred language, Nasr observes: "The efficacy of canonical prayers, litanies, invocations, etc., is contained not only in the content but also in the very sounds and reverberations of the sacred language. Religion . . . is a method of integrating our whole being, including the psychical and the corporeal. The sacred language serves precisely as a providential means whereby man can come not only to think about the truths of religion, which is only for people of a certain type of mentality, but to participate with his whole being in a divine norm."[15]

Muslims memorize and recite in Arabic the first chapter of the Koran, often about forty times a day in the course of fulfilling the daily prayer requirement. It is also commonly recited when offering thanks for a meal and when seeking God's protection from some imminent danger. A contemporary Muslims notes: "Over a thousand times every month, the illuminating energy of this fundamental prayer from the Holy Koran is inwardly invoked by the Muslim, until it becomes a constant ringing presence in the deeper regions of awareness."[16] The universal reach of "The Opening," even in translation, is such that many outside of Islam can sense the appeal and power of this short prayer:

In the name of Allah, the Beneficent, the Merciful.

1. Praise be to Allah, Lord of the Worlds,
2. The Beneficent, the Merciful.
3. Owner of the Day of Judgment,
4. Thee (alone) we worship; Thee (alone) we ask for help.
5. Show us the straight path.
6. The path of those whom Thou hast favored;
7. Not (the path) of those who earn Thine anger nor of those who go astray.

The extent to which the Koran permeates the lives of Muslims is seen also in the frequency with which key phrases appear in their daily activities. One of the most common, "in the name of Allah, the Beneficent, the Merciful," opens every chapter of the Koran except one, and is uttered repeatedly by the devout at the commencement of all important activities. It serves to remind that Allah is compassionate, that all activities occur under his watchful gaze, that one's actions should conform to divine expectation, and that one's activities are to be dedicated to Allah. Many times a day in Muslim society one hears *insha' Allah*, "if God wills." The phrase refers to the future and acknowledges that human activity is always subject to God's will.

In traditional Islamic society, education often begins by memorizing the Koran. Small boys, more rarely girls, meet daily with the Koran master to recite portions of the Koran after him until, for those who persevere, the entire Koran—somewhat shorter in length than the New Testament—is entirely memorized. One who has memorized the Koran carries the title *hāfiz*, 'Guardian', i.e., of the Koran. Some Muslims learn to chant the Koran in a manner that is commensurate with the beauty and profundity of the text. Koranic chanting contests are sometimes held, with the most accomplished receiving the kind of acclaim that is reserved in the West for opera stars. Koranic Arabic is rhythmic and poetic, often rhyming. To hear it slowly and sonorously chanted by a devout Muslim with a trained voice, in deep concentration, is an experience capable of opening the heart and thrilling the soul, whether one is Muslim or not, whether one knows Arabic or not.

The reverence and respect Muslims have for the Koran stems from the view that it is the very Speech of Allah. Muslims reason that because Allah is eternal and uncreated, his mind and, therefore, his speech are also eternal and uncreated. This reasoning underscores the miraculous nature of the Koran, that the uncreated and eternal has entered time and space, has become part of history. In light of this view, the Koran may be seen as not so much parallel to the Bible as to Christ. In other words, the Koran is for Muslims what Christ is for Christians. The eternal, cosmically pre-existent nature of the Koran parallels the eternal, cosmically pre-existent, or logos, nature of Christ. Just as Christ, the Word of God, came into history in the form of a man, so the Koran, the Speech of God, came into history in the form of a book. As Christ is central and foundational in Christianity, the Koran is central and foundational in Islam.

A sacred text so vital in a religious tradition is obviously subject to a great deal of interpretation. Like all scriptures, the Koran contains statements that appear to differ, even contradict each other. Believers and scholars must develop tools, hermeneutical principles that will permit them to resolve apparent differences and correctly understand the text. One of these interpretive principles in the case of the Koran is abrogation. We have already seen that the Koran is progressive revelation in two senses; first, it was revealed to Muhammad many centuries after the Torah was entrusted to Jews and the Gospels were given to Christians, and, second, it was revealed to him in segments over a period of about twenty-three years. Scholars try to date the revelations since the later ones sometimes replace, or abrogate, earlier ones. The change in the direction toward which Muslims pray is one example of abrogation. Early in Koranic times, Muslims were enjoined to pray in the direction of Jerusalem; this was subsequently changed by the Koran (2:142-144/136-139) to Mecca.

Koranic exegesis falls into two broad categories, *tafsīr* (explanation, elucidation) which is primarily concerned with historical background and exoteric commentary, and *ta'wīl* (reducing to origin) which seeks the deep, inner meaning. Ta'wil moves from the exterior of the text to the interior, symbolic meaning and significance. Shiʿites (*shīʿa*, party, i.e., of Ali) who make up the smaller of the two branches of Islam, are more drawn to the deeper connotations of the Koran than are the Sunnis, who make up the larger branch. Muslim mystics, who are found among both Sunnis and Shiites, are particularly committed to deciphering the hidden meanings of the Koran. Nasr rightly establishes the transformative power of these inner meanings. "Ta'wil in the sense used by the Sufis and Shiite sages is the penetration into the symbolic . . . meaning of the text, which is not a human interpretation but reaching a divinely pre-disposed sense placed within the sacred text through which man himself becomes transformed. The symbol has an ontological reality that lies above any mental constructions. Man does not make symbols. He is transformed by them. And it is as such that the Koran, with the worlds of meaning that lie hidden in its every phrase, transforms and remakes the soul of man."[17]

Muslims frequently acknowledge that a given passage in the Koran may have more than a single meaning. The leader of a Sufi order in Turkey has said, with perhaps some exaggeration, that there are as many levels of meaning in the Koran as there are letters. The famous medieval mystic, Ibn al-ʿArabī, claimed an even greater number, and suggested how these meanings emerge: "There are infinite meanings within the verses of the Holy Koran, within every word, changing with your states and levels, knowledge and understanding."[18] The Koran (3:7/5) refers to these hidden meanings in a passage that is itself subject to widely different interpretations, one supporting and the other condemning the search for the deeper meanings. "He it is Who hath revealed unto thee (Muhammad) the Scripture wherein are clear revelations—they are the substance of the Book—and others (which are) allegorical. But those in whose hearts is doubt pursue, forsooth, that which is allegorical seeking (to cause) dissension by seeking to explain it. None knoweth its explanation save Allah. And those who are of sound instruction say: We believe therein; the whole is from our Lord; but only men of understanding really heed." Those favoring a more literal understanding of the Koran support the reading as given. Those favoring a more symbolic understanding, however, point out that since punctuation is absent in the earliest versions of the Koran, the crucial part of the text above can just as properly read: "None knoweth its explanation save Allah and those who are of sound instruction." The door is thus open to plummeting the deepest meanings of the sacred text.

It is worth noting that although the Koran, like other scriptures, gives explicit directives on interpretation, even these directives must be interpreted. Consequently, there are principles of interpretation that must be invoked even prior to those that may be stipulated by a text. In final analysis, principles of interpretation derive from outside the text to be interpreted. The meanings found in a text depend on technical expertise as well as on the nature of the person, on both what one knows and who one is. They derive from the breadth of experience of the interpreter, from one's wholeness and integrity as a human.

Nasr contends that, rightly understood, the Koran "corresponds to the very structure of reality; it corresponds in its external and inward aspects to all degrees of reality and knowledge, of being and intellection, whether it be practical or theoretical, concerned with social and active life or with metaphysical knowledge and the contemplative life."[19] Thus, in much the same way as with the Muhammadan Reality, the Koran too enables Muslims to expand beyond their restrictive egos and become identified with Reality itself. The Muslim who knows and conforms to both the explicit and implicit dimensions of Koranic truth finds that his own existence takes on cosmic significance since he lives according to the most fundamental principles of being. By means of alignment with the Koran as Transcendent Truth, both time and space are transcended as Muslims become one with Allah.

The Five Pillars

Umar reported that he was once with Muhammad when "a man with a very white garment and very black hair" approached and asked the Prophet to inform him about Islam. Muhammad replied by naming the Five Pillars: "Islam is that you should testify that there is no deity save Allah and that Muhammad is His Apostle, that you should say the prayers, pay the legal alms, fast during Ramadan, and go on pilgrimage to the House (i.e., the Kaba) if you can find a way to do so."[20]

We have seen that Islam, as a civilization centered on religion, is governed by the Sharia, a comprehensive set of principles and laws that regulate personal and social life. Sunni Islam has four orthodox systems of law. Shia Islam has its own. These schools of law agree on the most important aspects of Islam and have jurisdiction in different

Muslim countries. The legal texts, stipulating how Islamic society will operate, open with the ordinances of divine worship, the Five Pillars. For Muhammad to describe Islam as the Five Pillars and for the Sharia to begin its elaboration of the Islamic legal system with the Five Pillars indicates the exceptional status that testimony, prayer, alms-tax, fasting, and pilgrimage have in Islam.

A legally necessary feature in the performance of each pillar is intention. The Koran (33:5) declares: "There is no sin for you in the mistakes that you make unintentionally, but what your hearts purpose (that will be a sin for you)." Two of the most important Hadith collections in Islam open with a tradition from Muhammad in which he says: "Works [will be rewarded] only in accordance with the intentions, so each man will receive only according to what he intended."[21] Muhammad is also reported to have said: "The intent of the believer is of more account than his doing."[22]

Muhammad's insistence on intention reflects a genuine interiority in Islam. The quality of mind accompanying intention is also important. He admonishes: "Allah does not answer the prayer of an unmindful, inattentive heart."[23] He further underscores the importance of attentive mindfulness when he advises: "When a person is drowsy during prayers, let him go to sleep until he knows what he recites."[24] Muhammad seems to have known that transformation does not occur magically, by mindlessly fulfilling ritual obligations. Required is an alert presence, a physical/mental/emotional vigor that accompanies the sincere intention to fulfill one's spiritual discipline to the very best of one's ability.

Testimony

The foundational declaration of faith in Islam, which every Muslim must make to be Muslim, is the *Shahāda*, the testimony or confession, "There is no god but God; Muhammad is the Messenger of God." To utter these words aloud, to understand them perfectly, and to believe them in the heart with no reservation is to become a Muslim and join a community that founds itself on this profession of faith. The typical Muslim may repeat these words twenty times a day. The Shahada is declared in the Call to Prayer and in the daily prayers themselves. They are the first words whispered in the ear of the newborn child and the last words heard by the dying. Muslim life begins and ends, and is punctuated throughout, with the affirmation that God is One and Muhammad is His Apostle. The first part of the Shahada links Muslims with Jews and Christians, indeed, all monotheists; the second part historically distinguishes Muslims from other monotheists. Increasingly, however, non-Muslims are recognizing Muhammad as an authentic prophet

"There is no god but God" affirms the most important theological tenet in Islam, the doctrine of God's Unity or Oneness, *tawḥīd*. A tradition from the Prophet avows: "Say there is no divinity but the Divine and be delivered."[25] Final salvation lies in confessing God's Oneness. A Palestinian Muslim declares: "Tawhid is that which gives Islamic civilization its identity, which binds all its constituents together and thus makes of them an integral, organic body." He goes on to argue that without tawhid there is no Islam.[26] Chapter 112 of the Koran, one of the earliest revelations, consists of only four verses and is titled "at-Tawhid."

1. Say: He is Allah, the One!
2. Allah, the eternally besought of all!
3. He begeteth not nor was begotten.
4. And there is none comparable unto Him.

The third verse is a reference to Christianity, which Muslims believe distracts from the absolute Oneness of God because it considers Christ to be the Son of God and co-equal with God as a member of the Trinity. Muslims take such Koranic sayings as "Nothing is like Him" (42:11/9) with total seriousness. The unpardonable sin in Islam is *shirk* (association), giving God a partner or rival. Shirk is unpardonable because it denies the essential nature of God as the only Ultimate Reality there is. As long as a person denies God, he is not open to God and therefore cannot be forgiven.

All Muslims confess tawhid as the central doctrine of Islam. Sufis, however, are not content to simply confess God's unity doctrinally. They want to realize it experientially. The first part of the Shahada becomes for them not just a statement of belief but the fundamental truth of reality to be known personally, with absolute certainty. The declaration, "There is no god but God," is enlarged to become, "Only God is." They engage an extensive discipline that includes the Five Pillars as base but extends beyond them to incorporate, among others, what is known as *dhikr*, remembrance. The Koran (33:41) says: "Remember Allah with much remembrance." While dhikr takes different forms in various Sufi brotherhoods, one common practice is to repeat in Arabic "There is no god but God" continuously in coordination with breathing and certain head movements. The objective is to become aware of God as the only Reality.

Prayer

Salāt (ritual prayer) is sometimes translated 'worship'. It entails prescribed words in Arabic, specific body positions (standing, bowing, kneeling, and prostrating), and is to be done daily at specified times (dawn, mid-day, afternoon, dusk, and after dark). It always requires a preliminary ritual ablution. At the five set times of prayer, when the call to prayer is heard, Muslims interrupt what they are doing if they can and pray privately or, better, join others, always facing Mecca. Because of the work demands of modern times, many Muslims offer the first prayer at its prescribed time and make up the prayers missed during the day when they perform the last prayer after dark, an exception to the traditional pattern that is permissible. On Friday at noon, a special effort is made to pray at a mosque. The congregation is usually predominantly male, with the few women and children occupying a balcony or the back of the mosque.

Without chairs or pews, a mosque is typically an open room with a pulpit, a few quotations from the Koran as pictures or embossed in the walls, and always a niche in one wall identifying the direction of Mecca. In addition to the ritual prayer itself, there may be two short sermons, one treating a religious topic and the other addressing a current social or political issue. A passage from the Koran may be recited. Some may remain after the formal prayer to make up missed prayer sessions or to offer extemporary prayers. On leaving the mosque, some may place a monetary gift in a box, or hand it to needy persons waiting outside.

The importance of prayer is second only to the testimony of faith. Muslims are sometimes called by non-Muslims 'the people who pray'. An actual callus, called 'the mark of prostration' by the Koran, may form on the foreheads of those who take prayer most seriously. Salat is one of the main unifying features of Islam, giving participants a deep sense of belonging as they say the same words in the same language at the same time in the same direction to the same God.

Ritual prayer has a deeply personal and interior dimension beyond its formal and communal significance. Some see it as a process of "reintegration into the uncreated."[27] Nasr describes how prayer enables a Muslim to discover religion as *religare*, re-connecting with the divine source. The one who prays "is able to return, thanks to the words and movements which are themselves the echoes of the inner states of the Holy Prophet, back to the state of perfect servitude and nearness to the Divine which characterizes the inner journey of the Holy Prophet . . . to the Divine Presence on that nocturnal ascent which is at once the inner reality of the prayers and the prototype of spiritual realization in Islam."[28]

The four body positions of ritual prayer may be seen as symbolizing the transformative process in Islam. Standing upright in the direction of Mecca signifies recognition of Allah as One. Bowing, leaning forward with hands on knees, represents humility, the only reasonable and proper posture in the presence of God. In this position, Muslims repeats three times, "Glory to God the Mighty." Prostration, touching the prayer mat with one's forehead, indicates submission to the divine in total trust and acceptance of whatever might unfold in one's life. For the Sufi this position symbolizes complete extinction of all that separates, the dissolution of the separative ego into Ultimacy. Kneeling, a position of great stability halfway between standing and prostrating, suggests integration of divine qualities into human life. It portends a return to ordinary life more firmly based in the ways of God.

Alms-Tax

Zakāt, based on a root meaning 'to be pure', has several meanings in Arabic, 'virtue', 'giving', or 'gift'. Its most technical meaning is alms-tax or legal alms. The giving of alms is seen as a means of purification and an expression of piety. Salat and Zakat are frequently linked in the Koran; the command is given, for example, to "perform the prayer and pay the alms."[29] Prayer and alms-giving are two of the most highly valued forms of piety in Islam.

Although Zakat bears some resemblance to the Jewish and Christian tithe, it is significantly different. It is a legal requirement regulated by the Sharia, with some variation from one school of law to another. It is based on total wealth, not annual income, and is governed by rather complex formulas that vary depending on the commodities that make up one's estate, whether land, or crops, or livestock, for example. The annual payment is two-and-a-half percent for cash reserves. Zakat can be distributed through a government agency, through a local mosque, or directly to the needy. Among others, the Koran lists the following as proper recipients of Zakat: orphans, the poor, travelers, beggars, and slaves. Zakat may be considered the Muslim equivalent of the Western welfare system. A Pakistani Muslim, writes: "No state has the right to be called an Islamic state if it disregards the injunctions about Zakat, because, according to Islam, a state has no other purpose except social welfare and social welfare is impossible without Zakat."[30]

According to Hadith, a spiritualizing and extending of the principle of Zakat had begun already in the Prophet's time. Some of Muhammad's poorer companions complained that the wealthy were more able to benefit from the giving of Zakat than they were. Muhammad replied that every time one says the pious phrase that means "Glory be to Allah," one gives alms. Alms are likewise given when one says "Allah is most great," "Praise be to Allah," and "Hallelujah." On another occasion, Muhammad gave the following as examples of alms-giving: resolving troubles between two people, helping someone load baggage, and removing something harmful from a path. He added: "A good word is an alms. In every step you take while walking to prayers, there is an alms."[31]

Nasr claims that Zakat helps to realize that "the other or the neighbor *is* myself." Zakat, he argues, is a way of "creating awareness of one's inner nature shorn of artificial attachment to all that externalizes and dissipates."[32] The giving of one's possessions, coupled with the giving of oneself, is a vital ingredient in a comprehensive spiritual discipline, one that particularly contributes to detachment from materialism.

Fasting

Muhammad is reported to have said: "There is zakat for everything, and the zakat for the body is fasting."[33] Fasting (*Sawm*), like Zakat, is an exercise in sacrifice, a voluntary giving up of the lesser for the sake of the greater. Optional fast days occur throughout the Muslim year, but the most important fast by far extends throughout the entire month of Ramadan. The Koran (2:183/179) says: "Fasting is prescribed for you during a fixed number of days . . . so that you may safeguard yourselves against moral and spiritual ills."[34] From dawn to dusk, Muslims forgo food, drink, and sexual activity, and, in general, try to limit the pleasures of the senses as far as possible. Abstinence ceases after dark, though Muslims continue to practice moderation. The aged, the sick, pregnant and nursing mothers, travelers, and those whose work is especially strenuous are exempt from the fast, though they may be required to make up the lost fast days later.

Since the Muslim calendar is lunar, Ramadan revolves around the seasons. When days are short fasting is less of an ordeal; when they are long fasting is a challenging test of faithfulness. Generally, Muslims look forward to Ramadan, eager to undertake the fast in order to prove themselves obedient to divine law. Despite the solemnity of fasting, a joyous spirit extends throughout the month. Some claim they never feel better—physically, emotionally, morally, spiritually—than during Ramadan. Because all are fasting at the same time and under the same conditions, a sense of communal harmony and solidarity arises. Gratitude to Allah for his bounteous gifts also emerges; appreciation naturally grows in the absence of that which is needed and taken for granted. Muslims also see fasting as a way of doing penance for sin. A tradition from the Prophet says: "He who fasts during Ramadan with faith, seeking his reward from Allah, will have his past sins forgiven."[35]

Muslims who add an internal dimension to fasting see it as abstention from indulging in passions and desires, specifically, giving up lying, backbiting, anger, irritability, envy, jealousy, and pride. At a deeper level, it involves abstention from what might be ordinarily permitted because such states or activities distract from nearness to God. For example, even though one could justifiably extract justice when wronged, a spiritualized understanding of fasting might cause one to act mercifully with forgiveness. The deepest level of interiorized fasting requires abstention from "everything other than God." This is the level of those mystics "who see God and nothing else."[36]

When the deeper principles of fasting are interiorized, one discovers that detachment from the material world fosters a heightened sense of the spiritual world. Fasting sensitizes and expands awareness so that one comes to see and know subtle realities that otherwise tend to elude. Fasting aids in quieting the body which aids in quieting the mind, a mental quieting that is essential in order to know the spiritual world firsthand.

Pilgrimage

The last pillar, *Hajj*, is incumbent only on those who are physically and financially able to perform it. Even though the Hajj is not mandatory, most Muslims aspire to complete it at least once in their lifetime and will save for years in order to do so. Although one can make a pilgrimage to Mecca any time—in which case it is known as a visitation—the Hajj can be performed only during the first half of Dhū 'l-Hijja, the last month in the Muslim calendar. Depending on political and economic conditions in the world at the time, a million or more Muslims may converge on Mecca to retrace the steps of the Prophet, visit sites important in the emergence of Islam, and fulfill a variety of ritual acts. The most important of the pilgrimage rites include the following. Men wear two pieces of unstitched cloth wrapped around the upper and lower body; these signify equality and unity. Women may wear their traditional dress. The Kaba must be circumambulated seven times on each of at least two occasions, when beginning and ending the pilgrimage. A visit to a mountain about twelve miles from Mecca, on the ninth day of the month is required. Here one asks forgiveness for sin and offers oneself to God in service.

On the return to Mecca, pilgrims will throw stones at three pillars representing Satan and his powers of temptation. An animal will be sacrificed in commemoration of Abraham's willingness to sacrifice Ishmael (not Isaac, as in the Judeo-Christian tradition). Only if the first three rites above have been completed can the pilgrimage be considered fulfilled. Before returning to their homes, many Muslims will travel north to Medina to visit the Prophet's tomb and the site of the first mosque.

Those completing the pilgrimage, one of the world's most elaborate rituals, are henceforth known as hajjis. They return home with a deepened vision of the brotherhood, equality, and unity of Islam. For several, intense days, they joined fellow believers representing a multitude of languages, customs, lifestyles, occupations, social positions, and economic levels. They mixed with uneducated peasants and powerful government officers while wearing the same attire, visited the same holy sites, carried out the same ritual actions, prayed the same prayers, and recommitted to the One God. They return to their communities with renewed allegiance to Islam and an enlivened sense of their identity as a Muslim.

Like each of the Pillars, the activities of the hajj prove efficacious to the degree that they are carried out with pure intention. Purity of intention is best gauged by the pilgrims themselves. If they hope to make business contacts while on pilgrimage, their intention is alloyed. If they are worried about their family back home, intention is vitiated. If they assess the appearance or speculate on the wealth of other pilgrims, their intention is sullied. If they are concerned about the impression they are making on others, intention is again tainted. To move through the regimen while preoccupied with other concerns is to forgo realization of deeper meanings. Only by being totally entrenched, without distraction or wavering, can pilgrims hope they will be transported into "that inner journey to the Center which is at once nowhere and everywhere."[37]

Allah, Submission, and Salvation

The Arabic word, *islām*, is based on *salama*, which denotes 'submission' and, secondarily, 'peace'. Islam is the religion of submission to Allah that results in inner peace. 'Muslim', based on the same root, means 'one who submits, thereby finding peace'. Because Muslims believe that God causes and controls everything that happens, non-Muslims (and some Muslims) conclude that Islam is a religion of strict predestination and fatalism, that Muslims, in submitting to God, are simply resigning themselves helplessly to whatever happens. Such is far from the truth.

It is true that the Koran (14:4) teaches predetermination. "Allah sendeth whom He will astray, and guideth whom He will. He is the Mighty, the Wise." Hadith reports Muhammad saying: "When Allah creates a servant for Paradise, He bids him perform the actions of the people of Paradise and thereby causes him to enter Paradise. And when Allah creates a slave for the Fire, he bids him perform the actions of the people of the Fire and thereby causes him to enter the Fire."[38] Fiqh Akbar I, a Muslim creed formulated about 100 years after Muhammad's death, asserts: "What reaches you could not possibly have missed you; and what misses you could not possibly have reached you."[39]

But the Koran (18:30/28) also teaches free will. "Whosoever will, let him believe, and whosoever will, let him disbelieve." The same idea is set forth in a tradition conveyed by Muhammad that contains the Words of Allah: "It is your works alone for which I shall hold with you an accounting."[40] Responsibility for one's good and bad deeds makes no sense without the ability to exercise free will. One of the Prophet's companions asked him if, assuming that predestination is the whole truth, he should not simply resign himself and give up trying to be a good Muslim. Muhammad urged him to keep striving, reminded him that everyone is helped, and recited the Koran (92:5-10): "As for him who giveth and is dutiful (toward

Allah) and believeth in goodness; surely We will ease his way unto the state of ease. But as for him who hoardeth and deemeth himself independent, and disbelieveth in goodness; surely we will ease his way unto adversity." The nature of God's help is contingent on the moral and religious quality of one's life. A creed originating about the middle of the fourteenth century rejects the strict determinism of the prevailing theological system by distinguishing between the power to act and the choice of how to act. "The creating is the act of God and consists in the originating of the power in man, but the use of the originated power is the act of man."[41] The creed attempts to balance God's sovereignty and man's responsibility.

The tension between determinism and free will arises for Muslims because of the need to preserve God's absolute power, on one hand, and His justice, on the other. God's power requires that He be the *effective* Source of everything that exists and all that happens. The theology of al-Ashari, the prevailing system in Islam, emphasizes God's absolute power and consequently predestination. God's justice requires that humans be recompensed according to the quality of their lives. The Muʿtazilites, early opponents of the Asharites, call themselves the "People of Justice and Unity" and argue for free will.

Whether successful or not in resolving the logical problem between free will and determinism, Muslims exhibit in their lives both submission to God as Absolute Creator (determinism) and effort to follow "the straight path" to the best of their ability (free will). A contemporary Muslim writes: "While Islam views man's life as predestined in the sense that nothing can finally oppose the Will of God, man nonetheless has the gift of free will in that he does make choices and decisions. [He] is completely free in what is essential, that is, he can accept the Absolute and surrender himself to It, or reject God and pay the price."[42] Determinism and free will are integrated in life if not in the dualistic mind.

Thus, determinism, widespread as it is in Islam, does not cause Muslims to renounce personal responsibility or helplessly acquiesce to whatever happens. It is perhaps useful to distinguish between a determinism (predeterminism, or determinism of the future) that sets an unalterable course until the end of time, and a determinism (present determinism) that incorporates the free will of humans as already exercised in determining the reigning conditions of the present. The second form of determinism is, in fact, a necessary dimension, the larger context, within which the exercise of free will makes sense. If there was no determinism, nothing would be fixed and free will would constitute a hodgepodge of counterforces that would result in utter chaos. Submission can be seen as an active choice (free will) to conform to God's will (that which is determined, set, and unalterable). Submission to Allah, implying as it does both determinism and free will, is the Muslim form of the fundamental transformational principle that requires both acceptance and action. Only by accepting what is (submitting to what is determined) and acting (exercising free will) according to the tenets of Islam can the Muslim know the inner peace that confirms right relationship to the divine.

To construe submission to Allah as resignation to the prevailing conditions of a social order is to distort a central transformational principle of Islam. Muhammad once said: "When any one of you notices anything that is disapproved [of by Allah], let him change it with his hand, or if that is not possible then with his tongue, or if that is not possible then with his heart, though that is the weakest faith."[43] Submission is not an abdication of personal responsibility and action but a call to exercise personal responsibility in conforming to divine will and acting accordingly. Submission is based not on fatalism but trust.

Trust that the circumstances of one's life are ultimately in one's best interest is essential in all religion that would be transformative. In the absence of trust there can only be helpless resignation or stubborn resistance, neither of which is conducive to transformation. Submission is not a new relationship to the divine to be adopted, but one's original nature to be rediscovered. The Koran (30:30/29) enjoins: "Devote thyself single-mindedly to the Faith, and thus follow the nature (*fitrāh*) designed by Allah, the nature according to which He has fashioned mankind." Commenting on this natural submission, Muhammad reportedly said that every child is born a Muslim; his parents turn him into a Jew, a Christian, a Parsee (the main religion of Persia at the time). Every child is born in submission to God, in conformity to the laws that govern all existence; he is inducted into a specific religious tradition through the process of enculturation. Fitrah is understood by Muslims to designate mankind's primordial nature, to represent natural religion.

Muhammad was once asked to define religion (*ad-dīn*). He replied that it consists of three things: surrender to Allah through practice of the religion he ordained, faith or belief in the essential truth of that religion, and virtue or excellence, i.e., the supererogatory, the intensification and extension of surrender and faith beyond minimal requirement. Surrender as a distinctive feature of Islam as a religion (rather than one's inborn nature in reference to God) refers specifically to observance of the Sharia, i.e., performance of the Five Pillars and living according to the laws that govern Islam as a social, religious, and political system. Faith, as defined by the Koran (2:177/172), consists of belief in "Allah and the Last Day [i.e., Judgment Day] and the angels and the Scripture and the Prophets." According to the main current in exoteric Islam, one is Muslim in so far as one identifies with the Muslim community and believes that God is One and Muhammad is His Messenger. It is possible to violate the practice dimensions of the Sharia without ceasing to be Muslim. This does not mean, however, that a Muslim can sin with impunity. The Muslim view of sin is meant to underscore the primacy of faith over practice—in much the same way that intention is more important than action—without giving license to profligate behavior. Sin, a violation of the religious and moral standards of Islam, is by no means condoned. The primacy of faith does not minimize the seriousness of sin.

Sin in Islam is distinguished from mistakes and shortcomings, which are simply to be corrected. Sin consists of acts of willful transgression, and is contrasted in the Koran and Hadith with righteousness. The five articles of belief—Allah, Judgment, Angels, Scripture, Prophets—are named by the Koran (2:177/172) as part of righteousness. The remaining parts include proper worship, paying the alms-tax, giving to the needy, freeing slaves, keeping treaties, and finally, being "patient in tribulation and adversity and time of stress." A tradition from Muhammad says: "Righteousness is good character and sin is what wavers in your soul and about which you would not like people to discover."[44] An-Nawawī's widely circulated collection of "Forty Traditions" contains several sayings from the Prophet that give Muslims general principles by which they can gauge whether or not an act is sinful. "If it does not cause you to be ashamed, do whatever you wish." Muhammad also cautioned: "Leave that about which you are in doubt for that about which you are in no doubt."[45]

If a Muslim violates the religious and moral standards of Islam and ignores the counsel of the Prophet, he is likely to feel guilt and remorse. If he is true to his inner feelings, his remorse will prompt him to repent. If sin is turning away from God, repentance is turning back to God and the means of realigning with one's primordial, sinless nature (fitrah). The repentant Muslim, in asking for God's forgiveness, knows that two of God's Ninety-nine Beautiful Names are the Forgiver and the Forgiving. In the final tradition of an-Nawawī's collection, God promises: "O son of Adam, if you come to Me with so many sins that they nearly fill the earth, and meet Me without associating anything with Me, I will come to you with the same amount of forgiveness."[46] Muhammad once said: "One who repents from sin is like one without sin."[47]

In the Koran (20:82/84) God avers: "I am forgiving toward him who repenteth and believeth and doeth good, and afterward walketh aright." This verse suggests that for God's forgiveness to be complete the penitent Muslim must intend to live uprightly and to do good works. Another verse (27:11) makes this even clearer: "I am most forgiving, ever merciful toward him who does wrong and then substitutes good in place of evil."[48] Muhammad advised his companions to "follow up an evil deed by a good one." The Koran (11:114/116) declares that "good deeds annul bad deeds." The main deeds that authenticate the sincerity and resolve of repentance, and meet God's expectation of recompensing action, are the Pillars, especially performing the prayers, paying the alms-tax, observing the fast, and going on pilgrimage. Each of these actions enables the penitent to restore harmony in his relationship to both God and his fellow humans.

Abdullah Yusuf Ali, a Pakistani Muslim and translator of the Koran, refers to salvation as "the Supreme Achievement" and declares that "it may require the utmost effort or striving (jihad) of a lifetime." At the same time, he denies that salvation is justification by works and asserts that "at best our merits . . . amount to very little, God's mercy and grace are vast and all-embracing, His grace is beyond calculation."[49] Muhammad, while stressing the importance of individual effort, called for an underlying and comprehensive trust in God. He once said: "If a person puts his whole trust in God and confesses each morning as he leaves his house, 'I have no strength to resist evil and no power to do good except through God,' that person has his needs met, is guided, and is saved."[50] Human effort is essential if salvation is to be gained. But without God's grace and mercy, no amount of effort will lead to salvation from sin.

Salvation in Islam is not only a concern of this life; for many Muslims, perhaps most, it is even more of a concern for the Hereafter. The Koran (40:39f/42f) says: "The life of this world is but a temporary provision; and the Hereafter is the permanent abode. Whoso does evil will be requited only with the like thereof; but whoso does good, whether male or female, and is a believer, these will enter the

Garden," i.e., Paradise.[51] *Najāt* is a Koranic term meaning salvation as well as deliverance, i.e., salvation, deliverance from Hell, the Fire, a place of everlasting punishment. Another common term in Islam for salvation is *falāh*, which also means success, both in this life and the next. When Muslims hear the Call to Prayer they are invited to come to falah, to success, to salvation.

For a religion that originated in the arid desert of Arabia, a garden is a particularly fitting term for Paradise, which is often depicted in the Koran (e.g., 2:25/23) as, "Gardens underneath which rivers flow." The use of the plural suggests that Paradise is made up of various levels or states of being, different regions depending on the moral and spiritual quality of life while on earth. The Koran uses picturesque imagery in its characterization of Paradise, imagery that has been elaborated in Hadith and in the imagination of Muslims. Many interpret this imagery literally, others less so, and some understand it in an entirely metaphorical fashion. Widely divergent views on the nature of the Hereafter exist among Muslims. Orthodoxy hinges on belief in the Hereafter, not on a single understanding of the nature of either Paradise or Hell. As the Fiqh Akbar I proclaims: "Difference of opinion in the community is a token of divine mercy."[52]

Islam is a religion of community. The communal dimension is so strong that Muslims find it extremely difficult to be good Muslims outside of a Muslim community, as Muslims living in non-Muslim countries readily admit. Of the Five Pillars only the first, the Testimony of Faith, issues forth in the first person: "I witness that—'There is no god but God, and Muhammad is God's Messenger.'" Even this Testimony must be publicly confessed. The communal element in the remaining Pillars is obvious: prayer at the same time, in the same direction, with the same words; alms-tax for the benefit of the needy; fasting with others in obedience to God; and pilgrimage en masse to the holy sites of Islam's origin. Salvation too occurs in community. Admittedly, it is first and foremost individual, marking a Muslim's personal relationship to God. But identity is found by identifying with a community. For most Muslims, salvation occurs by conforming to the standards of a community whose standards are those of God.

Islamic Mysticism: The Sufis

The Shaykh of al-Azhar, head of the most important university in the Islamic world (located in Cairo, Egypt) has said that a Sufi is simply a good Muslim. As we have seen, all Muslims focus their faith in God by witnessing to his Oneness, and Sufis by striving to realize his Oneness. As a word specifying the central doctrine of Islam, tawhid implies not only the fact of Oneness but the process of becoming One. It signifies end and means. As end, it signifies God, the Transcendent One who is end as Origin and end as Goal. As means, tawhid signifies the inner unification that occurs through continual submission to Allah of all that separates from him, that is, the subjugation and sacrifice of everything in one's life that operates contrary to the singular will of the divine. Sufis engage both senses of the word. The salvation sought by Sufis is from anything and everything that might separate from God. The goal of the Sufi is not just salvation in the traditional sense but absorption into the fullness of God.

The term, *sūfī*, is derived from the Arabic word for wool. To distinguish themselves from the worldly of their day, early Sufis wore a simple dress commonly made of wool. The word may also be related to *sāfi*, pure. An early mystic of Baghdad identifies a Sufi as one "who keeps his heart pure (*sāfi*)." Since something is pure to the extent that it is devoid of elements corrupting its essential nature or impeding its natural activity, the Sufi may be said to be one who attempts to eliminate from himself everything that has accrued since birth that is foreign to his primordial nature, his fitrah.

The model of human nature that underlies the Sufi path consists of two interrelated realms, *nafs* and *rūh*. Several wideranging meanings adhere to nafs (breath, animal life, carnal desires, soul). The term may be linked broadly with psyche and more specifically with ego. Mohammad Shafii, a Muslim psychiatrist, notes that the Muslim concept of nafs covers much the same ground as the Western notion of personality, more specifically what in psychoanalysis is known as the id, ego, and superego."[53] Nafs is the ego self, the self that is driven by bodily urges, emotional demands, and mental compunctions. It is the self that sees itself as separate and needy. The other pole in the Sufi analysis of human nature is ruh or Spirit. Since this is the dimension that defines one's most essential nature and links one at the same time to the divine, it is another way of identifying one's primordial nature, fitrah. Ruh may also be designated the Self, the integral center of the whole person, the all-inclusive center to which the ego as the conscious center of the personality is related.

Sufis base their linkage of Self with God on a saying of the Prophet: "Whoso knoweth himself knoweth his Lord." A treatise attributed to the thirteenth-century Sufi, Ibn al-ᶜArabī says: "When thou 'knowest thyself' thine egoism is taken away and thou knowest that thou art not other than God." He also indicates the depth of self-knowledge required: "If thou know thyself without existence or ceasing to be, then thou knowest God: and if not, then not."[54] A Sufi, Shaykh al-ᶜAlawī, declares that "the knower of himself is stronger in Gnosis [intuitive knowledge] than the knower of his Lord." Another Sufi explains this rather surprising evaluation by drawing attention to the implicit duality in a Lord-servant relationship. Beyond this duality, he writes, is the "One-and-only Indivisible Infinitude. In other words, beyond the Personal God is the Transpersonal Self, which is what the Shaykh means by the word 'himself'."[55] For al-Alawi, then, one's Self is the transpersonal Self, God, and knowledge of this Self is supreme knowledge.

Nafs and ruh, psyche and Spirit, or ego and Self, as the basic dimensions of human nature according to Sufi psychology, account for the entire range of inner experience and outer expression, extending from base drives to sublime possibilities. The integration—i.e., the reintegration—of these poles, in submission and conformity to the will of Allah, marks the Sufi aim. An eighteenth-century Moroccan Sufi, ad-Darqāwī, claims that nafs and ruh "are but two names for one and the same thing." Rather than being essentially discordant, nafs contains the urge and power to re-align with ruh, a realignment effected through submission. He explains that the ego (nafs) separates from the Self (ruh) as a result of confusion. This confusion, which arises through forgetting one's theomorphic nature, can be overcome when "the soul [i.e., the ego] returns from the passions which [tore] it away from its virtue, its goodness, its beauty, its nobility."[56] Remembering, dhikr, is the cure for forgetting and the means of reunion. Returning to its source, the ego is reunited with the Self. Ibn al-Arabi defines nafs as "all that is beside God" and then argues that there is nothing beside God. Anything that appears other than God is illusory.[57] Illusion is dispelled by seeing clearly, by remembering one's essential nature and thereby nullifying the ignorance that keeps one separate. Al-Junayd, a famous mystic who died in the early tenth century, declares that the aim of the Sufi is to return to "the state in which he was before he was."[58]

Detachment allows the ego to discover its connection to the Self. As the ego becomes rooted in the Self, it exchanges attachment to the things of the world for simple awareness of the things of the world. Since attachment is the normal operation of the ego and awareness the natural operative mode of the Self, as the ego becomes increasingly non-attached, it appropriates the dominant function of the Self—pure awareness—and all its attendant powers and possibilities, but without identifying with or becoming attached to them. In other words, the functions and powers of the Self are freely manifested in, through, and by the ego. Martin Lings, an Englishman and a practicing Sufi, refers to this process when he characterizes the Sufi path as one that exchanges "second nature," or habitual processes, "all those habits and reactions which are strictly speaking unnatural," for "man's primordial nature, made in the image of God."[59] As the ego becomes purified and realigned to the Self, and thus detached from the world and one's own personality, the disparate drives that usually fracture and tyrannize, cease to do so. They lose their power to pull off center, away from rootedness in the Self. None of the partial 'selves' that usually imperialize is able to gain control, to monopolize the center. Harmoniously interrelated, neutralized in their otherwise scattering compulsiveness, these 'selves' begin to cooperate. The ego, freed from the contradictory pulling and pushing of insubordinate ego states, becomes empty of vested interest, of selfish objectives, and naturally subordinates itself to the Self. The Self, unobstructed by ego attachments, opens up to the Absolute, or, in traditional religious terminology, is filled with the divine. Summarizing this process, al-Junayd declares that in Sufism, "God makes thee die to thyself and become resurrected in Him."[60] A Sufi of the thirteenth and fourteenth century, Shabistarī, outlines the process poetically.

> Go sweep out the chamber of your heart.
> Make it ready to be the dwelling place of the Beloved.
> When you depart out, He will enter it.
> In you, void of yourself, will He display his beauties.[61]

According to Sufism, the ego is both the obstacle and the means for realizing the Self. As such its demands cannot be ignored or repressed. Al-Alawi advises: "Neither abandon thy soul [i.e., the ego], nor oppose it, but go along with it and search it for what it is."[62] A twentieth-century Sufi, Vilayat Inayat Khan, notes that "our very ignorance is the way He protects us from the knowledge that overwhelms, our blindness His shield from the light that burns the eyes, our ego, His prop for the delicate plants of our personalities until we know how to survive death."[63] Muslims believe that such insights extend back to the Prophet himself. Kamal al-Din, for example, observes that Muhammad's "mission was to regulate, and not to thwart, nature and its gifts."[64] The Prophet did not seek to destroy or curtail man's natural disposition but to restore its original submission and conformity to the will of God. The Sufi goal then is not to destroy the ego but to control, or better, harmonize and integrate it. Commenting on Muhammad's saying, "thy worst enemy is thy lower soul," al-Hujwīrī, the eleventh-century author of the oldest Persian text on Sufism, notes that "the purpose of mortifying the lower soul is to destroy its attributes, not to annihilate its reality." The same writer tells of a mystic who, on being inclined to amputate his sexual organs in order to rid himself of passion and lust, heard a voice in his heart whispering: "If thou do this, I swear by My glory that I will put a hundredfold lust and passion in every hair in that place."[65] The Sufi approach to personal integration and mystic union is summarized in a statement attributed to Muhammad, "my Satan has become a Muslim." The alienating and disruptive tendencies in human nature centered in the ego have submitted to and re-aligned with the unifying and harmonizing forces of human nature centered in the Self.

The ego is commonly represented by Sufis as a veil which separates man from the divine. "Thou thyself art the greatest of all veils between thee and God; when thou [i.e., the ego] has become absent from thyself [i.e., the Self], the evils implicit in thy being are annihilated in thee." This absence from ego is equivalent to presence with God. A visitor once came to the cell of Abū Yazīd al-Bistāmī, a ninth-century Persian, and called out for him. Abu Yazid replied, "Who is Abu Yazid, and where is he, and what thing is he?" When similarly called upon on another occasion, Abu Yazid rejoined, "Is anyone here except God?"[66]

Shaykh ad-Darqawi, author of the most psychologically profound treatises to be found in Sufism, declares that "nothing veils Him from us except our concern, not with existence as such, but with our own desires."[67] Abū Saʿīd, an eleventh-century Sufi, affirms that "the Sufi is he who has become purified of all desire."[68] Like the Buddhists,

Sufis have discovered the undesirability of desire. From the Sufi perspective, desire necessarily gives rise to estrangement since it represents an implicit rejection of the adequacy and completeness of the given, and consequently is a denial of the Absoluteness of the Supreme Unity, Majesty, Will, etc. It is as if the creature were saying to the Creator, "What you have created here is not good enough!" But by definition, the One, the Whole, is incapable of deficiency. And yet desire is predicated on feeling deficient. The dissatisfaction and striving that inevitably accompany the sense of deficiency, therefore, are diametrically opposed to the submission expected of Muslims.

Sufis frequently characterize themselves as those who are "in but not of the world," as those who "possess nothing and are possessed by nothing," or as those who "have possessions without being possessed." The ideal of non-attachment finds summation in the term *al-faqīr*, the poor, an almost universal designation for Sufis. While poverty in the sense of being without material possessions often accurately characterizes Sufis, it marks them more importantly in the psychospiritual sense as without attachment.

To summarize the role of desire in Sufism, we see that desire works in at least two ways to block Self-realization: first, it sets up a barrier between the person and the Real by implicitly denying the all-sufficiency of Allah and; second, it binds one to illusory realities. Desire detaches from Unity and attaches to multiplicity. It thereby causes the very opposite of the state to which Sufis aspire, namely, presence with God and absence from self.

In place of desire, Sufis cultivate contentment. While all Muslims, as we have seen, submit to Allah, Sufis extend their submission until it becomes contentment. This they do by accepting whatever befalls them, by maintaining a spirit of equanimity under all circumstances. Few have spoken more eloquently about Sufi equanimity than Abu Said. "If they are kept without clothing, they are happy; and if they are kept hungry, they are happy. Never do they reside in the house of self-will . . . . Disaster and well-being, favor and privation are the same for them . . . . If they be taken to hell, they say 'Greetings!' and if they be taken to paradise, they say 'Greetings!.' Neither does paradise cause them joy nor hell fear."[69] Pir Vilayat Khan describes the person who has attained this high degree of contentment as being "unaffected by the emotions of personal enjoyment or even repulsion, so that, for example, insulting him would not stir any emotion of resentment. Nor would any esteem rob him of his humility."[70]

Because he encouraged the use of music, song, and dance as modes of mystical practice in the Mevlevi Order he founded in the thirteenth century, Jilāl ad-Dīn ar-Rūmī became the target of harsh criticism and even legal proscriptions. One historian, noting this opposition, states: "Out of his kindly disposition, and love of peace, Jalal made no reply; and after a while all of his detractors were silenced."[71] Al-Ghazzali, one of Islam's most respected theologians, after extensive personal resistance and inner struggle, came to embrace Sufism. One of his companions described his attitudes before he became a Sufi as those of "maliciousness and roughness toward people" coupled with contempt, while afterwards he was totally unperturbed by "contradiction and attack and slander."[72] Sufis use their inner sense of contentment and discontentment to gauge the extent to which they are still preoccupied with their own personal concerns and desires. They work with the standard: "Wherever some thought of yourself is, there is hell. Wherever you are not, there is heaven."[73]

The Sharia ideal of integrating religion and society has provided Sufism with a base for merging the mystical path into ordinary life. Javad Nurbakhsh, a psychiatrist and shaykh of a Sufi order in Iran, believes that the perfection of man can only be accomplished in society, that solitude is advisable only for purposes of renewal and then only for brief periods of time.[74] Another psychiatrist and Sufi leader, A. Reza Arasteh, declares that "society and culture are a bridge for attaining the real self."[75] The monasticism that is common in other religions is virtually unknown in Islam. Ordinary life is the arena within which the Sufi gradually progresses toward personal integration and mystic union. Carefully watching his reactions to the events and situations of everyday life, he discovers how attachment binds, how desire distorts, and how self-preoccupation veils awareness. By daily submitting these debilitating ploys of the ego to the liberating and integrating power of the Self, by accepting and trusting every situation to reveal its inherent grace, the Sufi turns ordinary life into spiritual practice.

Even difficult and disturbing situations that arise in life are embraced by the aspiring Sufi. The outer circumstances and inner states that commonly elicit resistance or denial offer the serious practitioner opportunity for transformation, for gaining insight into habitual and limiting modes of being. Pir Vilayat Khan asks rhetorically: "How can one undergo transformation without being shattered?"[76] Rumi affirms: "God's mercies are often hidden in His chastisements."[77] A thirteenth-century Egyptian Sufi, Ibn ᶜAtā'illāh, writes: "Sometimes you will find more benefit in states of need than you find in fasting or ritual prayer."[78] Distress provides an opportunity for transformation. Some Sufis regard Satan as an agent of God since the trouble he supposedly creates can only be neutralized by relying on God. From another angle, the ego may be said to create distress by using—or rather, misusing—the events and circumstances that normally arise. By opening to the Self, however, i.e., by releasing self-preference, the ego is able to see its role in creating the distress. For example, the urge to defend oneself against hostility, slander, and criticism usually derives from the ego. By seeing such attacks in a larger context, without self-contraction, perhaps even with compassion, one not only defuses the hostility in the other but undermines the reactive, alienating tendencies of the ego within oneself.

Abu Yazid once cried out: "O Lord, with my egoism I cannot attain to Thee, and I cannot escape from my selfhood. What am I to do?" God answered: "O Abu Yazid, thou must win release from thy 'thouness' by following My beloved," i.e., by following Muhammad.[79] In addition to deriving a great deal of guidance and inspiration from the Koran and the practice of the Prophet, Sufis model their psychospiritual path according to Muhammad's Ascension. In a pattern similar to Muhammad's ascent through the several heavens into the presence of Allah, Sufis ascend through a number of stages or stations where they experience states appropriate to each stage. While Sufis differ on the number of stages and states, they agree that the former are permanent and acquired, i.e., the result of effort, and the latter are temporary and received, i.e., divine gifts of grace. The moral, ascetic, and spiritual disciplines, i.e., the stages, include repentance, abstinence, renunciation, poverty, patience, etc. The psychospiritual states bestowed by divine favor include love, hope, intimacy, tranquility, certitude, etc.

The disciplines and virtues extolled in the stages and states are activated and realized according to a two-fold, complementary method consisting of contraction and expansion. Contraction and expansion describe the natural rhythm of personal transformation. Contraction occurs when the qualities and characteristics that draw away from God, that keep one bound to the phenomenal world are in control, when one is under the throes of jealousy, envy, hatred, anger, fear, etc. Any sense of distress or need is a contracted state. Equally, contraction marks one's state during times of spiritual barrenness, when in spite of much longing, the divine seems absent. Expansion marks one's state when the ego conforms to the Self, when the qualities and characteristics of the Self that lead to realization of Ultimacy are in ascendance. One is in the state of expansion when relating to others in a spirit of compassion, charity, beneficence, and goodwill, when feeling joyous, peaceful, and harmonious, when aligned with God in submission and abandonment. Even though contraction and expansion are dialectical processes, they represent complementary phases in the transformational journey. To be attached to expansion and resist contraction is itself a form of contraction to be released.

Only when one is able to find God in all things, the so-called desirable and undesirable, can one transcend the alternation of contraction and expansion.

Progress through the stages and states, accompanied by contractive and expansive phases, eventuates in annihilation, i.e., annihilation of multiplicity and estrangement. Extinguished is the egoistic 'I'. Annihilation, the negative pole in the unitive experience, is complemented by a positive pole, subsistence or remaining, the sense of resting in all-prevailing Unity. Annihilation and subsistence are two ways of articulating the experience of nonduality. All debilitating elements of the ego have been eliminated; the Self remains to exercise its powers freely. The extinction of egoistic impulses equals the subsistence of the Self. Annihilation and remaining represents a conscious state in which one is aware of nothing but God, of everything as God. This was the state of Mansūr al-Hallāj (857-922 CE), the Persian Sufi martyred by his countrymen who thought he was equating himself with God when he proclaimed, "Ana al-Haqq," "I am Truth," or "I am God." Rather than claiming equality with God, al-Hallaj was testifying to the extinction of everything but God, himself included. If annihilation is a temporary state of total absorption in God alone, subsistence is the awareness that prevails when one returns to the world and finds it permeated by the divine. The customary distinction between God, world, and self disappear. There remains one unfolding, interacting reality that is entirely sacred.

All Muslims believe that the Koran teaches the Unity of God. Sufis (at least some Sufis) believe that it also teaches the Unity of Being. The Koran (57:3) declares: "He is the First and the Last, and the Outward and the Inward." Another passage (55:26-27), the Koranic basis for the annihilation/subsistence distinction, asserts: "All that is in the earth passes away; there remains only the Face of thy Lord in Majesty and Glory." Also (Koran 2:115), "Whithersoever you turn, there is the Face of God." Al-Ghazzali comments on this verse: "Each thing has two faces, a face of its own and a Face of its Lord; in respect of its own face it is nothingness, and in respect of the Face of God it is Being. Thus there is nothing in existence save only God." When the Sufi attests to Oneness of Being, he is not simply voicing a doctrine but affirming an experience. According to al-Ghazzali, the Sufi sees "directly face to face that there is nothing in existence save only God."[80] With this declaration, we see how Sufis are able to extend the Confession, "There is no god but God," to mean only God is.

By contrasting the confessions of Mansur al-Hallaj and Pharaoh, Rumi underscores the extraordinary difference that lies between seeing from the perspective of the Self and claiming from the position of the ego.

> The words, "I am truth" were light in Mansur's mouth.
> In the mouth of Pharaoh, "I am Lord Supreme" was blasphemy.
> When the illusion of seeing double is swept away,
> They who say "one" and "two" are even as they who say "One".[81]

It is not so much a particular set of words that matters, but the inner state, the attitude, the awareness from which the words derive. Intention is more important than formulation. Outwardly, Sufis may appear no different from others. Inwardly, a monumental difference abounds.

Muhyid Din ibn al-ᶜArabī (1165-1240)

Few have shaped Islamic spirituality as profoundly as Ibn al-Arabi, whose name means 'son of the Arab'. He is the author of perhaps 700 different works, principal among which are *The Meccan Revelations*, containing 560 chapters, and, his most influential work, *Bezels of Wisdom*, revealed to him in a dream. Ibn al-Arabi is commonly known as ash-Shaykh al-Akbar, 'the Greatest Master', for the depth, originality, and quantity of his writing. Something of his impact on mystical Islam is indicated by a title given to him posthumously, Muyīd Dīn, 'Revivifier of Religion'.

Ibn al-Arabi was born in Murcia, Spain. His father came from an ancient Arab lineage, was well educated, and active in government and politics. Religion occupied a central place in family life; three of his uncles were Sufis. He moved with his parents to Seville when he was eight and began a formal education, studying the traditional subjects, Koran, Koranic exegesis, Hadith, Arabic, and Islamic law. Although he was not formally initiated until he was 20 years of age, Ibn al-Arabi served a spiritual apprenticeship under two revered Sufi women, one of whom was in her mid-nineties at the time. His spiritual training entailed the study of metaphysics, cosmology, esoteric exegesis, and possibly astrology and alchemy. Since Sufism is not Sufism without practice, his discipline surely included prayer, meditation, invocation of God's name (dhikr), fasting, all-night vigils, and occasional short-term retreats. He reports spending long hours of the night in communion with the spirits of the dead in cemeteries.

The spiritual certitude and authority that Ibn al-Arabi felt, even as a young man, is reflected in his meeting with Ibn Rushd (Averroes), one of the most celebrated of Muslim philosophers, and one who was to have great influence on the development of medieval Western philosophy. Ibn al-Arabi was about 20 at the time.

> I spent a good day in Cordova at the house of Abū al-Walīd ibn Rushd. He had expressed a desire to meet with me in person, since he had heard of certain revelations I had received while in retreat, and had shown considerable astonishment concerning them. In consequence, my father, who was one of his close friends, took me with him on the pretext of business, in order to give Ibn Rushd the opportunity of making my acquaintance. I was at the time a beardless youth. As I entered the house the philosopher rose to greet me with all the signs of friendliness

and affection, and embraced me. Then he said to me, "Yes!" and showed pleasure on seeing that I had understood him. I, on the hand, being aware of the motive for his pleasure, replied, "No!" Upon this, Ibn Rushed drew back from me, his color changed and he seemed to doubt what he had thought of me. He then put to me the following question, "What solution have you found as a result of mystical illumination and divine inspiration? Does it agree with what is arrived at by speculative thought?" I replied, "Yes and No. Between the Yea and the Nay the spirits take their flight beyond matter, and the necks detach themselves from their bodies." At this Ibn Rushd became pale, and I saw him tremble as he muttered the formula, "There is no power save from God." This was because he had understood my allusion.

Sometime after 1190, Ibn al-Arabi began to travel to North Africa where he met with mystics and scholars, and frequented mosques and shrines for prayer and meditation. While in Morocco in the year 1200, he had a vision in which he was told to travel to the eastern Islamic world. He visited friends in Tunis and then went on to Alexandria and Cairo before arriving at Mecca. Here his reputation as one deeply immersed in the traditional and esoteric sciences was soon established. The learned and pious families of the city were eager to host him. While in Mecca, Ibn al-Arabi continued his study and spiritual practice. He had several experiences here that confirmed his growing sense of having a special role to play in mystical Islam.

Ibn al-Arabi returned to Cairo where he encountered so much public opposition that he was forced to leave Egypt. His esoteric ideas had been severely condemned by those who upheld the mainstream teachings of Islam. He traveled back to Mecca and then to Konya in Turkey where he mentored a disciple who later wrote commentaries on his thought. He also conveyed his teachings to other notable Sufis, including Jilāl ad-Dīn ar-Rūmī.

Until he settled permanently in Damascus in 1223, Ibn al-Arabi continued to travel back and forth to the major cities of Asia Minor and the Middle East. He was accorded great honor and respect by the political leaders of his day, which may have added to his worsening relationship with the jurists and theologians. Benefiting from the patronage of the rulers of Damascus, Ibn al-Arabi capitalized on his settled life in the city to finish his monumental *Meccan Revelations* and a major collection of poetry. During these years of maturity, he also wrote his most widely read book, *The Bezels of Wisdom*. After his death in 1240, Ibn al-Arabi's body was buried at the foot of a mountain just north of Damascus. Later a mausoleum was constructed over the site, which to this day remains a major pilgrimage center.[82]

Metaphysics

Because Ibn al-Arabi's thought is comprehensive, profound, complex, subtle, and imaginative, it is frequently called a speculative system. It is far from merely speculative, however, since it is founded on his direct, personal experience. Ibn al-Arabi's imaginal world, an intermediate region between the sphere of incorporeal spirit and the material world, was a realm of immediate experience for him. As we have seen, according to his own report the entire contents of *The Bezels of Wisdom* came to him from this realm, which includes the dream world. In chapter 367 of *The Meccan Revelations* and in his *Book of the Night Journey*, Ibn al-Arabi recounts his own personal ascension, observing that "my voyage [to Allah] was only in myself." That this was not mere fantasy unrelated to waking life is indicated in his note that "from the day I attained this station [i. e., the final station, that of pure servanthood] I have not possessed any living thing, indeed not even the clothing I wear."[83] His subjective, imaginal experience had a direct influence on how he lived his outer life. Ibn al-Arabi uses the intimately experiential term *dhawk*, tasting, to designate the authoritative knowledge that comes through personal experience, thus distinguishing this knowledge from the ordinary knowledge that is gained through the mere transmission of information. "[True] knowledge," he affirms, "comes only through tasting."[84]

Ibn al-Arabi was a metaphysician of the highest order. He understood metaphysics in a traditional sense, as "the science of Ultimate Reality" and "a wisdom which liberates."[85] It is, in fact, his investigation of being as well as beyond-being, and his understanding of the connection between being and knowledge that marks him as a traditional metaphysician. Ibn al-Arabi's fundamental metaphysical perspective is 'Oneness of Being'. William Chittick, a specialist on Ibn al-Arabi, notes that the Shaykh's "main concern is not with the mental concept of being but with the experience of God's Being, the tasting (*dhawq*) of Being, that 'finding' which is at one and the same time to perceive and to be that which truly is."[86] Similarly, R.W.J. Austin believes that Ibn al-Arabi intended to "convey the meaning of the Oneness of both Being and Perception in the perfect and complete union of the one and only Reality." He points out further that *wajada*, the key Arabic term, carries the idea "of being and therefore objectivity, and that of perception and therefore subjectivity, both of which [are] one in *the* Reality."[87] Ibn al-Arabi's central insight concerns the inseparability of being and awareness, of existence and consciousness, in Ultimacy as Source and in all who know they derive from Source. Ontology and epistemology, being and knowing, are a single reality, distinguishable but not divisible. To be is to be aware, and to be aware is to be.

Ultimacy for Ibn al-Arabi is the Essence, God in Itself, and thus irreducible to any created thing. The Essence is unknowable and unnameable. At best only negative assertions can be postulated of It since any positive propositions would be necessarily limiting and therefore incorrect. Izutsu indicates that Ibn al-Arabi distinguishes between Essence in Itself and Essence in relationship by means of *al-Ahad* and *al-Wāhid*: "The Ahad is the pure and absolute One— the reality of existence in a state of absolute undetermination, the prephenomenal in its ultimate and unconditional prephenomenality— whereas the Wahid is the same reality of existence at a stage where it begins to turn toward phenomenality." The Ahad is "the One standing beyond all determination" while the Wahid is "the One with internal articulations."[88] In some contexts, Ibn al-Arabi employs al-Haqq and Allah to distinguish between the Absolute in Itself and the Absolute in relation to created entities.

Ibn al-Arabi takes up the central ontological question, "Why is there anything rather than nothing," by quoting a tradition from Muhammad that depicts Allah speaking: "I was a Treasure but was not known. So I loved to be known, and I created the creatures and made Myself known to them."[89] Thus, love is the initiating movement that gives existence to all created things. Austin notes that mercy is "the very principle of creation by which all created things exist and by which all the latent potentialities within the 'divine mind' are released into actuality."[90] Thus we see that love and mercy, words implying movement toward another, lie at the very heart of Ibn al-Arabi's ontology and cosmogony. All-that-is emerges out of the Absolute by means of love/mercy.

Ultimate Realization

Ibn al-Arabi's concept of the Perfect Man dominates much of his thought. He treats the concept on two levels, universal and individual. In his development of the Perfect Man on the macrocosmic level, Ibn al-Arabi addresses such topics as the Truth/Reality of Muhammad, man as the image of God, and mankind as the apex of the creative hierarchy. On the microcosmic level, his thought bears on the transformation of ordinary man into perfect man. Even as saintship is prerequisite to prophethood and apostleship, so it is the basis or essential quality of the perfect man. The perfect man is a saint in the fullest sense. All that would separate him from God has been annihilated and he subsists in a state of continual awareness that God is the only reality.

No dimension of Ibn al-Arabi's concept of human perfection is more important than that of the divine names. Here we have the heart of his anthropology, his view of mankind, and his Soteriology, his view of salvation. Every human by right of being human contains all of the divine names *in potentia*. This, in fact, is what places humans at the top of the hierarchy of created beings, ahead even of angels. Only the perfect man, however, actually lives his life motivated by the divine names. He is, therefore, one "who does what is proper for what is proper as is proper," i.e., acts appropriately according to the circumstances of the moment.[91] Ibn al-Arabi notes that "the certain, enduring, perfect sage is he who treats every condition and moment in the appropriate manner, and does not confuse them."[92]

The perfect man, aware that his essential nature is constituted by all the divine names, knows himself to be in a state of balance or equilibrium vis-à-vis the divine names in their comprehensiveness. No particular name or quality rules to the exclusion of others. Proper relationships exist between names that might otherwise appear contradictory. An overall dynamic equilibrium is maintained as precedence is given, when appropriate, to beauty over wrath, generosity over justice, humility over magnificence, etc. Because of his truly comprehensive nature, the perfect man intuitively knows, given a particular circumstance or context, which divine qualities warrant manifestation. Of all beings only man, given the comprehensiveness of his nature, occupies the role of servant (*ᶜabd*) of Allah. Since the name 'Allah' itself indicates comprehensiveness for Ibn al-Arabi, only man, because of his parallel comprehensiveness, can properly serve God. Only the perfect man, wholly individuated, exhibits servanthood fully. Ibn al-Arabi writes: "Perfect man is separated from him who is not perfect by a single intangible reality, which is that his servanthood is uncontaminated by any lordship whatsoever."[93] With no sense of specialness or superiority, the perfect man cannot mis-act by injecting anything foreign into the absolute impartiality of the Absolute.

The comprehensive, harmonious qualities of the perfect man lead him to a dialectical mode of being in the world. While all humans occupy an intermediate position between the Real and the phenomenal, only the perfect man is capable of maintaining an actual and dynamic balance. Most humans 'forget' their true nature and find themselves overly drawn to the phenomenal, thus shirking their nature and responsibility as spiritual beings. The perfect man reflects the same equipoise as the Ultimate. In *The Bezels of Wisdom*, Ibn al-Arabi writes: "If you insist only on His transcendence, you restrict Him. And if you insist only on His immanence, you limit Him. If you maintain both aspects, you are right."[94] A person who operates out of the dialectical mode has a both/and perspective and is called a "Possessor of Two Eyes" by Ibn al-Arabi. The Possessor of Two Eyes upholds God's incomparability and comparability simultaneously. He understands the Absolute to both reveal and conceal Himself at one and same time. God is the Outward and the Inward. The Absolute is undivided in Itself and multiple in manifestation, simultaneously. Referring to God, the Shaykh asserts: "He is at once our identity and not our identity."[95] Ibn al-Arabi also introduces a concise formula to represent the nonduality he sees between the Real and the world, "He/not He."[96]

Perfect humans, because of their comprehensive, balanced, and nondual outlook, see God in all forms. Ibn al-Arabi points out that "the gnostic sees things in principle and in forms . . . He sees only God as being that which he sees."[97] Describing an insight gained in his own ascension, Ibn al-Arabi asserts that "God (*al-Haqq*) can only *be* in (external) reality through the form of the creature (*al-khalq*), and the creature can only be there (in reality) through the form of

God. This circularity . . . is what actually exists and is the way things are."[98] This mutuality between Creator and creature, between Source and manifestation, leads the Shaykh—given the fierce support of most Muslims to Allah's Oneness and Otherness—to a daring claim: "The perfect gnostic recognizes God in every form."[99]

Knowing full well the extent to which the theologians and the Muslim masses opposed his views, Ibn al-Arabi gives considerable attention to the way in which belief limits. The Arabic word for belief (*i'tiqād*) denotes the tying of a knot and implies a strong attachment to a particular idea. The Shaykh declares: "He who delimits God [according to his own belief] denies Him in everything other than his own delimitation, acknowledging Him only when He reveals Himself within that delimitation. But he who frees Him from all delimitation never denies Him, acknowledging Him in every form in which He appears."[100] Concisely and unambiguously, Ibn al-Arabi affirms: "In every object of worship it is God Who is worshiped."[101] The great distance between Ibn al-Arabi, the mystic, and the vast majority of Muslims, given their exoteric outlook, is best summarized in an oft-quoted poem of the Shaykh al-Akbar that links love with the full acceptance of all religious forms.

> My heart has become capable of every form:
> It is a pasture for gazelles and a convent for Christian monks,
> And a temple for idols and the pilgrim's Kaba
> And the tables of the Torah, and the book of the Koran.
> I follow the religion of Love:
> Whatever way Love's camels take,
> That is my religion and my faith.[102]

One of the most effective and widely applicable principles of transformation enunciated by Ibn al-Arabi is that of detachment. In his gentle, pastoral tract for beginners on the spiritual path, he sets forth many different attitudes to be taken and ways to live: divest yourself of worldly goods, beware of egoistic wishes, live in the present, expect no return, do not be satisfied in your spiritual state, choose less rather than more.[103] Common to all these injunctions, and others in this primer, is the disposition to disvalue, or at least, to attribute only minimal, relative value to created things. The novice is enjoined to stand free of all that might distract from the divine, to disengage from the mundane world in order to know God. In his manual on spiritual retreat, *Journey to the Lord of Power*, the Shaykh identifies several stages along the way and concludes his description of each stage with the words, "if you do not stop with this," before moving to the next stage. He notes: "If you let go . . . then He will free you from that mode." Why is detachment necessary? Because, "if you become enamored of this world, it will trip you, and you will be exiled from God."[104]

Ibn al-Arabi also introduces detachment to the exoteric, mythically oriented masses when he points out that Muhammad was able to journey steadily upward on his Ascension to Allah only by means of detachment. For example, Muhammad said to the Throne on which Allah sat, when it attempted to distract him with its *earthly* concerns: "Do not disorder for me my detachment." When Muhammad finally came to God Himself, Allah—as if reserving these insights until the very end to emphasize their importance—said to him: "I am far removed from time and place and state of being . . . , from boundaries [and] that which is limited and that which is measured." And then pointedly, "I in My perfection am far removed from anything . . . to which one may cling."[105]

One may not cling, in fact, even to the spiritual. Concluding his *Journey to the Lord of Power*, Ibn al-Arabi declares that "it is not possible for the door of the invisible world and its secrets to be opened while the heart craves for them."[106] Finally, realizing the full meaning of God's omnipresence, the spiritual adept must release all longing for God in order to become one with God here and now.

Ibn al-Arabi discovered early in life that the essential principle of transcendence and transformation is detachment. By the end of his 75 year sojourn on earth, he had confirmed through his own experience that it applies equally at the farther reaches of spiritual realization. The journey from the exterior to the interior, from the ephemeral to the Eternal, is by means of detachment. Paradoxical as it seems, only by detaching from all created things was Ibn al-Arabi able to know and declare: "Everything is He, and of Him and from Him and to Him."[107]

Irina Tweedie (1907-1999)

Irina Tweedie was born in Russia on April 20, 1907. She pursued her education in Vienna and Paris and eventually moved to England, where she was happily married to a naval officer. She became so distraught, however, by his premature death in 1954 that she considered suicide. A friend took her to the library of the Theosophical Society where she began to read about religion. She joined the Society and was an active member, traveling in 1961 to the world headquarters near Madras, India. Still unsettled and searching, Irina accepted the suggestion of a friend to seek out her spiritual master, a Sufi shaykh living on the Ganges River about halfway between Varanasi (Benaras) and Delhi. Here she met a man who would turn her life upside down and inside out over the next five years. Had the 54-year-old Irina Tweedie been able to guess how arduous and torturous her path would turn out to be, she might well have sought an easier one.

In keeping with the custom of some Sufi groups, Irina never used her spiritual master's proper name, Radha Mohan Lal, but called him, as did other followers, Bhai Sahib, Hindi for "Elder Brother." Of her first meeting she writes: "My mind . . . turned a somersault. My heart stood still for a split-second. I caught my breath. It was as if *something in me* had stood to attention and saluted. I was in the presence of a Great Man."[108] She had the distinct sense of coming home, of having known him before. When she was out of his company, however, she could not remember his face. But she could vividly recall his feet and sandals, the same feet and sandals that had belonged to the tall Indian who led her, in a dream years before, down a stony desert road, an apt figure for the journey she was about to begin. With minimal exception, Irina went daily to Bhai Sahib's home to sit for a few minutes or up to ten hours.

Bhai Sahib was a Hindu by birth but became the disciple of a Muslim Sufi at the age of fourteen. His father had belonged to the Chishti Order, a Sufi brotherhood founded in India that uses music and dance to facilitate absorption in the divine. Bhai Sahib, however, became a practitioner of the Naqshbandi Order, which eschews music and dance, preferring a silent approach to God. Bhai Sahib explained to Irina that those in his order were known as the Silent Sufis since their devotional practices were silent prayer, meditation, and dhikr. He explained also that Sufism is not a religion in the usual sense, that there are Hindu Sufis, Muslim Sufis, and Christian Sufis. Sufism, he maintained, existed before organized religions and is associated primarily with Islam because it first flourished in Arabia and Persia where Islam was the dominant religion. Similarly, in India where Hinduism is the dominant religion, Sufism has taken on some of the terminology and coloring of the Hindu religion. In essence, Bhai Sahib argued, Sufism is the religion of the Lovers of God. This view of Sufism, which sees it as a generic devotional mysticism, while widespread in India, is rejected in the Middle East, where to be a Sufi is to be a Muslim first and then a Sufi.

Bhai Sahib distinguished between two ways of coming to the divine. The path of meditation, which is easier but slower, is for the many. The path of renunciation, because it requires the sacrifice of everything, is for the few but capable of leading to God in a single lifetime. For most of his followers, some of whom had been with him for 60 years, Bhai Sahib chose the path of meditation. For Irina he chose the path of renunciation, which is also the path of love and the path of fire. He told her she was the first woman to receive the ancient training, and that many of its secrets are recorded only in untranslated Persian writings. Two other features of the Naqshbandi Order are private conversations between master and disciple on matters of psychospiritual transformation, and silent communion when each opens to and focuses on the other. Bhai Sahib often characterized his method as one of infusing love from heart to heart. He said that love is *created* by the spiritual teacher and infused in the heart of his student. Once awakened by this infusion of divine love, the heart gradually neutralizes the blocks and limitations within the disciple.

Bhai Sahib claimed that he always related to his followers out of love alone, never being displeased or angry with them, even though he might respond in apparent displeasure or anger. He distinguishes between a bad teacher and a good one:

A bad Teacher will always behave as his followers expect him to behave. If he is after personal prestige, or even money or honors, he will always be kind, benevolent, compassionate, uttering at all times wise, profound sentences; that is the conventional idea. But a good Teacher obeys a law of which the world knows nothing. As it is the nature of the fire to burn or consume, or the wind to blow, so it is with the Sat Guru [True Teacher]; he just is. He may do things which people don't understand, or may even condemn. Love does not conform to conventional ideas; Love can appear in the shape of great cruelty, great injustice, even calamity. In this respect the Sat Guru is similar to God. He cannot be judged or measured (169).

On the student side of the master-disciple relationship, absolute obedience and submission is required. The standard of submission advocated by al-Jīlī (1365-1417), a Persian mystic-poet and follower of Ibn al-Arabi, is well-known in Sufi circles. He advises the disciple who is fortunate enough to find a true shaykh to drop everything else and "be thou with him as a corpse in the ablutioner's hands. He turneth it at will, while it passive remaineth."[109] Bhai Sahib taught that real training begins only when this degree of submission has been attained. Without unwavering faith and obedience, he believed that no progress could be made. Most of Irina's training during the five years she worked with Bhai Sahib was directed toward the self-emptying that is essential to true submission. She trained to become, in the deepest sense of the term, a muslim, one who submits.

Tweedie struggled with perplexity, disappointment, and doubt during her first few weeks with Bhai Sahib. His home, his family, his surrounding, the people who came to him—all were so ordinary, so banal. How could he be a great man? Instead of answering her questions, he talked about all the money he had spent on his teacher. Was he expecting her to do the same? She contemplated leaving but decided to stay for six months. The example of a fellow disciple, a professor who had been coming to Bhai Sahib for twelve years, provided some reassurance. One night, after about three weeks, she awakened from a dream with the words resounding in her ears, "There is no other Way at all to go." She submitted to Bhai Sahib and his methods out of a compelled dedication. She knew she was exercising her own free will and also had no real choice. She submitted by necessity, the higher Self overriding the lower self.

Tweedie's approach to practice was typical of educated Westerners; she wanted to know, to comprehend, to understand. But Bhai Sahib believed that the thinking mind impedes love. In order to drive Irina beyond the mind to the heart so that the true 'teaching' from heart to heart could begin, Bhai Sahib had to frustrate her intellectual need, her mental curiosity. He refused to answer her questions, even questions she thought important. He sometimes compounded her consternation by answering the seemingly insignificant questions of others. She herself was often ignored while animated discussion with others continued on matters of moot significance.

Throughout most of the first two years under Bhai Sahib, Irina was ignored, reprimanded, insulted, ridiculed, denigrated, mocked, and falsely accused. She was called dense, stupid, and an idiot. He asked her to do silly, irrational things, like type multiple copies of inconsequential documents. She was required to give English lessons to Bhai Sahib's son. Sometimes he would see her coming, go inside his house, and close the door. She was made to sit outside the house while others were permitted in, regardless of the weather or time of day or night. She endured heat, sometimes over 110 degrees, and shivering cold; she sat through dust storms, the burning sun, and torrential rains. Only after 20 months of such treatment was she given permission to enter his home at will.

Though he did not demand it, Bhai Sahib asked Irina to give him all of her money. She gave him the proceeds from the sale of her home in England, as well as the inheritance she had received after her husband's death, a sum she had expected to use during her later years. He used some of this money to maintain himself and his family. He gave much of it to needy people who came to him for help. He was so restrictive in what he gave Irina that she sometimes had to borrow in order to pay for her room. She once lived for ten days on the equivalent of 44 cents, ate only potato soup for days, and drank only lemon water.

Irina could not ignore the difference between the way Bhai Sahib treated her and his other followers. While they were given consideration, kindness, and instruction, she was victimized by rebuff and cruelty. She was disturbed also by his penchant for saying one thing to one person and something quite different to another, and for telling her one thing and later something else. She sometimes confronted him with these contradictions. He smiled and said nothing. Irina came to learn that a competent shaykh guides and instructs according to the particular conditioning, possibilities, and capacities of each disciple. Bhai Sahib eventually explained that all his teachings are correct when seen from the right perspective. He taught according to the stage of development of each disciple, as each grows the teaching changes to accommodate the still limiting needs of the student. The creative shaykh keeps adjusting the practice until the student sees that God is the whole and only reality. What appears to be contradiction is only one more limitation, one more instance of suffering.

The effects of Irina's discipline were felt in her body, particularly her heart. Bhai Sahib explained that there are two hearts, that the quickening of the spiritual heart manifests in palpable changes in the physical heart. Irina's heart alternately raced and slowed, missed beats, and pounded erratically, sometimes so loudly she was sure others could hear it. Her whole body surged with energy. She sometimes lay awake all night watching the currents of energy coursing throughout her body. She felt an inner vibration like that of a motor, sometimes in definite parts of her body, sometimes throughout. She felt intense heat, sometimes in waves, sometimes pervasive. One night she saw a bluish-white light running along the nervous system, leaving the body and then re-entering at different points.

> This liquid light was cold but it was burning me, as if currents of hot lava were flowing through every nerve and every fiber, more and more unbearable and luminous, faster and faster. Shimmering, fluctuating, expanding and contracting, I could do nothing but lie there watching helplessly as the suffering and intense heat increased with every second . . . . It became more and more unbearable, the whole body on fire. When I concentrated on some part of my body the light and heat increased there to an intense degree. How long it lasted I do not know. When it happens [I am] in a kind of in-between state, a muddled consciousness, unaware of time, neither sleeping nor waking" (68).

Her body would sometimes shake. She experienced a weakness that hardly permitted her to stand or walk. She occasionally felt nauseous, and sometimes actually vomited. She seemed to be crying all the time, uncontrollably, occasionally in Bhai Sahib's home, more often in her own room. She often could not sleep and would spend the entire night awake. Her eyesight seemed to deteriorate. She became aware that her memory was not working properly, and was deeply disturbed because she could not think as she was accustomed to think, particularly when in the presence of Bhai Sahib. She thought she was going insane. She had severe headaches, and suffered from loneliness, despondency, and depression. She experienced intense irritation, even hatred, sometimes toward Bhai Sahib himself, and often toward innocent people. In a fit of uncontrollable rage, she once continued to beat a mouse after it was dead. As soon as she took stock of what she had done she was horrified. She became afraid of herself, and realized that she did not know who she was, did not know what lay beyond the range of her conscious understanding. One year after meeting Bhai Sahib, she confessed that it was the most trying year of her entire life.

Bhai Sahib had warned Tweedie at the outset that she would be forced to endure injustice, that she would be attacked, and that it would hurt immensely. "Unbelievable suffering of the mind and the body are necessary in order to become a saint," Bhai Sahib said (188). A shaykh can be very cruel in his effort to root out all obstacles, defects, and impurities, cruel in the same way as a surgeon opening an abscess. He reminded her that he was never really harsh with her personally but only adopted an attitude of harshness for the sake of the training. His apparent harshness was actually motivated by love. Irina asked if her suffering arose because she did not love sufficiently. Bhai Sahib replied to the contrary; she suffered because she loved deeply. He encouraged her to love even more deeply so that her suffering would increase. He believed that suffering has a redeeming and purify power. It burns off karma and expiates sin.

Bhai Sahib frequently quoted the Sufi masters, and often sang verses in Persian and translated them for Irina. One of these verses advocated the extending of honor to those who spoke critically about oneself. Irina had already discovered, contrary to all ordinary expectation, that her love for Bhai Sahib grew deeper with the suffering. The worse he treated her, the greater was the love she felt for him. She came to understand that her love for and submission to Bhai Sahib would eventually lead to love for and submission to God. She discovered through her own experience that the feeling of nearness to her teacher is the same as the feeling of nearness to God.

After Bhai Sahib's death in 1966, Irina traveled to the Himalayan foothills where she spent several months in solitary retreat. In spite of the immediate sense of loss and separation, she found that she could make contact with him, with his spirit, in meditation. Then she discovered that her sense of him, his spirit, as distinct from herself, disappeared. There was only him-herself united in God. The intense work she had done under his guidance continued to permeate her whole being. Now that the malevolent forces were neutralized and dispelled, and her limiting patterns were dissolved, her natural self, her divine self, was free to manifest. She noted that the world began to look different to her, to change in subtle but real ways. Though outwardly everything appeared the same, her inner sense of the world was profoundly softened and deepened. What had seemed so far removed was now her immediate experience. Only God is. Through being reduced to nothing, Irina came to know that there is nothing but Nothingness, and that Nothingness is God.

Irina Tweedie returned to London where she guided spiritual seekers in her home. She never considered herself a shaykh or guru but rather as one providing access to the Beyond that is here already. To the hundreds that came to her in search of guidance and direction, she shared her own journey of transformation and personal awareness of the divine. Her memories of Bhai Sahib continued to be vivid, particularly memories of his kindness. In Irina's account of Bhai Sahib's wise and loving response to a poor village woman, one sees the qualities of the perfect man as outlined by Ibn al-Arabi, particularly the quality of appropriateness. A more perfect, fitting response to a common, real-life situation is hardly imaginable.

> She was small, very thin, her face wrinkled and shrunken, as if dried up by the merciless sun and the hot winds of the plains. She was telling an endless, sorrowful litany of her troubles. Illnesses, misery, the death of her husband and most of her children. Now she was alone, useless, nobody needed her, she had nothing to hope for, nothing to live for. And she came out with the question which seemed to burn, scorching her trembling lips: "Maharaj, why did God create this world so full of troubles? Why did He create me to endure all these sufferings?" I saw him lean forward, a shimmering light in his eyes, the light of compassion I knew and loved so well. His voice was soft when he answered: "Why has He created the world? That you should be in it! Why has He created you? He is alone; He needs you!" Never will I forget the broad, blissful smile on that lined, emaciated face when she was walking away. She went happy in the knowledge that she was not alone, not really, for God needed her to keep Him company because He too was alone. Never will I forget the love that I felt then. Only a very Great Soul could have expressed so simply and convincingly one of the greatest Mysteries to a naïve, childlike village woman. The Ultimate Metaphysical Truth; that He who is Alone and Perfect, in order to realize His Perfection, created the Universe" (201-202).

Irena Tweedie died in 1999. Her influence has continued to spread through her writings and through Sufi circles that she and her students have established in Europe and the United States.

NOTES

1. *The Koran Interpreted.* Arthur J. Arberry, trans., (New York: Macmillan Co., 1955).

2. Unless otherwise indicated, quotations from the Koran are either from Marmaduke Pickthall, *The Meaning of The Glorious Koran: An Explanatory Translation.* (New York: Alfred A. Knopf, 1930), or are renderings of the author. Two different verse numbering systems are used in translations of the Koran. Pickthall uses the Cairo system, which is cited first, followed by a slash (/) and the Fluegel numbering when it differs. In most cases, the two systems agree. A second Koranic reference widely believed to refer to the Ascension is 53:13-18. The plural personal pronoun is frequently used in the Koran in reference to Allah. Muslims believe this to be the case particularly when Allah is speaking from a position of all-encompassing majesty.

3. Richard J. McCarthy, trans., *The Theology of al-Ash°arī.* (Beyrouth: Imprimerie Catholique, 1953), 250. Some dates are given first according to the Islamic calendar, dating from the Prophet's immigration to Medina in 1 Anno Hijra, then, following a slash (/), also according to the calendar of the Common Era, thus 1 A.H./622 CE. Other dates are given only according to the Western calendar.

4. A.J. Wensinck, *The Muslim Creed: Its Genesis and Historical Development.* (London: Frank Cass & Co., 1932, 1965), 197.

5. Muammad ibn Isāq, *The Life of Muhammad: A Translation of Isāq's Sūrat Rasūl Allāh.* A. Guillaume, trans., (Lahore: Pakistan Branch of Oxford University Press, 1955, 1967), 682-683.

6. Abdullah al-Mamun al-Suhrawardy, *The Sayings of Muhammad.* Wisdom of the East Series, (London: John Murray, 1941/1949), 92; °Alī ibn °Uthmān al-Jullābī al-Hujwīrī, *The Kashf al-Ma-jūb: The Oldest Persian Treatise on Sūfiism.* new. ed., Reynold A.

Nicholson, trans., E.J.W. Gibb Memorial Series, vol. 17, (London: Luzac and Co., 1936/1967), 11.

7. al-Suhrawardy, *Sayings*, 95.

8. L. Zolondek, trans., *Book XX of al-Ghazālī's Ihyā' ᶜUlūm al-Dīn.* (Leiden: E.J. Brill, 1963), 51.

9. Reynold A. Nicholson, *Studies in Islamic Mysticism.* (Cambridge: University Press, 1921/1967), 15.

10. Peter Ipema, "Muammad as Intercessor according to the Qur'ān and Hadīth," Unpublished M.A. thesis, (Hartford, Ct.: Hartford Seminary Foundation, 1969), 54, 45.

11. Ismaᶜīl Rāgī al-Fārūqī, "Islam," in *The Great Asian Religions: An Anthology.* Wing-tsit Chan, Ismaᶜīl Rāgī al-Fārūqī, Joseph M. Kitagawa, P.T. Raju, comps, (New York: Macmillan Co., 1969), 371.

12. James E. Royster, "The Meaning of Muammad for Muslims: A Phenomenological Study of Recurrent Images of the Prophet." Unpublished Ph.D. dissertation, (Hartford, Ct.: Hartford Seminary Foundation, 1970), 234-253.

13. Muhammad ᶜAbduh, *The Theology of Unity.* Isāq Musaᶜad and Kenneth Cragg, trans., (London: George Allen & Unwin, 1897/1966), 119.

14. A.E. Affifi, *The Mystical Philosophy of Muyid Dīn-ibnul ᶜArabī.* (Cambridge: University Press, 1939), 86.

15. Seyyed Hossein Nasr, *Ideals and Realities of Islam.* (Boston, Beacon Press, 1972), 44, 47.

16. Lex Hixon, *Heart of the Koran.* (Wheaton, IL: Theosophical Publishing House, 1988), 7-8.

17. Nasr, *Ideals and Realities*, 61.

18. Muhyiddin ibn ᶜArabi, "What the Student Needs," *Journal of the Muhyiddin Ibn ᶜArabi Society* (Oxford, England). vol. 5 (1986), 44.

19. Nasr, *Ideals and Realities*, 55f.

20. "The Forty Traditions of an-Nawawī," in Arthur Jeffery, ed., *A Reader on Islam.* (The Hague: Mouton and Co., 1962), 145.

21. Ibid., 144-145.
22. Reuben Levy, *The Social Structure of Islam*. (Cambridge: University Press, 1962), 219.
23. Abu Ameenah Bilal Philips, *Salvation Through Repentance (An Islamic View)*. (Riyadh: Tawheed Publications, 1990), 28.
24. Shems Friedlander, *Submission: Sayings of the Prophet Muhammad*. (New York: Harper & Row, 1977), 19.
25. Seyyed Hossein Nasr, *Knowledge and the Sacred*. (New York: Crossroad Publishing Co., 1981), 328.
26. Isma'īl Rāgī al-Fārūqī, *Tawhīd: Its Implications for Thought and Life*. Muslim Training Manual, vol. 2, (Wyncote, Pa.: International Institute of Islamic Thought, 1982), 18, 20.
27. Cyril Glassé, *The Concise Encyclopedia of Islam*. (San Francisco: Harper & Row, 1989), 349.
28. Seyyed Hossein Nasr, *Islamic Life and Thought*. (Albany: State University of New York Press, 1981), 194.
29. Koran 2:83/77; Arberry, *The Koran Interpreted*. 38.
30. Khalifa Abdul Hakim, *Islamic Ideology*. (Lahore: Institute of Islamic Culture, 1961), 273.
31. Jeffery, *Reader on Islam*. 153.
32. Nasr, *Islamic Life and Thought*. 195.
33. Friedlander, *Submission*. 71.
34. Khan, *The Quran*. 28.
35. Jamal A. Badawi, "The Obligatory Fasting of Ramadhan," *The Muslim World League Journal*. vol. 8, no. 10 (August 1981), 35,
36. Seyyed Hossein Nasr, ed., *Islamic Spirituality: Foundations*. vol. 19 in *World Spirituality: An Encyclopedic History of the Religious Quest*. (New York: Crossroad, 1987), 118-119.
37. Nasr, *Islamic Life and Thought*. 195.
38. Roland E. Miller, "The Muslim Doctrine of Salvation," *The Bulletin of Christian Institutes of Islamic Studies* (Hyderabad, India). vol. 2, nos. 1-4 (Jan.-Dec. 1980), 149.

39. A.J. Wensinck, *Muslim Creed.* (London: Frank Cass & Co., 1932/1965), 103.
40. Jeffery, *Reader on Islam.* 152.
41. W. Montgomery Watt, *Free Will and Predestination in Early Islam.* (London: Luzac and Co., 1948), 155.
42. Glassé, *Concise Encyclopedia of Islam.* 249.
43. Jeffery, *Reader on Islam,* 157.
44. Philips, *Salvation Through Repentance.* 30; also, Jeffery, *Reader on Islam,* 153-154.
45. Jeffery, *Reader on Islam.* 151, 148.
46. Ibid., 160 (rephrased).
47. Philips, *Salvation Through Repentance.* 2-3.
48. Khan, *The Quran.* 369.
49. Abdullah Yusuf Ali, trans., *The Holy Qur'ān: Text, Translation and Commentary.* (Washington, D.C.: American International Printing Co., 1946), 1469, 1465.
50. Muhammad Zafrulla Khan, trans., *Gardens of the Righteous (Riyadh as-Salihin of Imam Nawawi).* (New York: Olive Branch Press, 1989), 25 (rephrased).
51. Khan, *The Quran.* 469.
52. Wensinck, *Muslim Creed.* 104.
53. Mohammad Shafii, *Freedom from the Self: Sufism, Meditation and Psychotherapy.* (New York: Human Sciences Press, 1985), 19-44.
54. Muyī al-Dīn ibn ʿArabī, "The Treatise on Oneness," *Journal of the Royal Asiatic Society* (Malayan Branch). (October 1901), 809, 816.
55. Martin Lings, *A Sufi Saint of the Twentieth Century: Shaikh Ahmad al-ʿAlawī.* (Berkeley: University of California Press, 1971), 204-205.
56. Al-ʿArabī ad-Darqāwī, *Letters of a Sufi Master.* Titus Burckhardt, trans., (London: Perennial Books, 1973), 29-30.
57. Ibn al-ʿArabi, "Treatise on Oneness," 813.

58. A.J. Arberry, *Sufism: An Account of the Mystics of Islam.* (New York: Harper & Row, 1950), 57.

59. Martin Lings, *What is Sufism?.* (Berkeley: University of California Press, 1977), 18-19, 90.

60. Seyyed Hossein Nasr, *Sufi Essays.* (New York: Schocken Books, 1977), 69.

61. Ira Friedlander, *The Whirling Dervishes.* (New York: Macmillan Publishing Co., 1975), 23.

62. Lings, *Sufi Saint*, 213.

63. Vilayat Inayat Khan, *Toward the One.* (New York: Harper & Row, 1974), 353.

64. Kamal al-Din, "Muhammad as a Soldier," *Islamic Review and Muslim India* (Woking, England). vol. 5, no. 1 (January 1917), 29-30.

65. al-Hujwīrī, *Kashf al-Mahjūb*, 206-207, 209.

66. Ibid., 249-250, 258.

67. ad-Darqāwī, *Letters*, 3.

68. Nasr, *Sufi Essays*, 82.

69. Ibid., 79, 81.

70. Khan, *Toward the One*, 396.

71. Shemsu-'d-Dīn Ahmed el-Eflākī, *Legends of the Sufis: Selected Anecdotes from the Work Entitled "The Acts of the Adepts".* J.A. Redhouse, trans., (Wheaton: Theosophical Publishing House, 1976), 51.

72. Duncan B. Macdonald, *The Religious Attitude and Life in Islam.* (Beyrouth: Khayats, 1965), 194.

73. Price, *Persian Sufis.* 81.

74. J. Nourbakhch, "Le Soufisme, Son But et Sa Methode," *God and Man in Contemporary Islamic Thought.* Charles H. Malik, ed., (Beirut: American University, 1972), 142.

75. A. Reza Arasteh, *Rumi the Persian: Rebirth in Creativity and Love.* (Tucson: Omen Press, 1972), 17.

76. Khan, *Toward the One*, 350.

77. Whinfield, *Teachings of Rumi*, 226.

78. Ibn ᶜAtā'illāh, *Sufi Aphorisms (Kitāb al-Hikam)*. (Leiden: E.J. Brill, 1973), 49.

79. al-Hujwīrī, *Kashf al-Mahjūb*, 238.

80. A.J. Arberry, ed., *Religion in the Middle East: Three Religions in Concord and Conflict*. vol. 2 in *Islam*. (Cambridge: University Press, 1969), 255-257.

81. Whinfield, *Teachings of Rumi*, 65.

82. Biographical material is drawn mainly from R.W.J. Austin's introduction in Ibn al-ᶜArabi, *The Bezels of Wisdom*. R.W.J. Austin, trans., in *The Classics of Western Spirituality*. (New York: Paulist Press, 1980), 1-14; and Seyyed Hossein Nasr, *Three Muslim Sages*. (Cambridge: Harvard University Press, 1964), 90-97.

83. James E. Morris, "The Spiritual Ascension: Ibn ᶜArabī and the Miᶜrāj," pts. 1 and 2, *Journal of the American Oriental Society*. vol. 107 (1987), no. 4, 634; vol. 108 (1988), no. 1, 73, note 198.

84. William C. Chittick, *The Sufi Path of Knowledge: Ibn al-ᶜArabi's Metaphysics of Imagination*. (Albany: State University of New York Press, 1989), 220.

85. Seyyed Hossein Nasr, ed., *The Essential Writings of Frithjof Schuon*. (Amity, N.Y.: Amity House, 1986), 27.

86. Chittick, *Sufi Path of Knowledge*, 3.

87. Ibn al-ᶜArabi, *Bezels of Wisdom*, 26.

88. Toshihiko Izutsu, "Ibn al-ᶜArabī," in Eliade, *The Encyclopedia of Religion*. vol. 6, 556.

89. Chittick, *Sufi Path of Knowledge*, 66. Ibn ᶜArabi knew that this tradition was not included in any of the standard collections. He believed, however, that it is a sound tradition on the basis of direct perception in the imaginal world, i.e., by means of the intuition of those capable of understanding.

90. Ibn al-ᶜArabi, *Bezels of Wisdom*, 29.

91. Chittick, *Sufi Path of Knowledge*, 174.

92. Muhyiddin Ibn ᶜArabi, *Journey to the Lord of Power*. Rabia Terri Harris, trans., (London: East West Publications, 1981), 59.

93. Chittick, *Sufi Path of Knowledge*, 372.

94. Ibn al-ᶜArabi, *Bezels of Wisdom*, 75.

95. Ibid., 127.

96. Chittick, *Sufi Path of Knowledge*, 3-4, 113-115.

97. Ibn al-ᶜArabi, *Bezels of Wisdom*, 235.

98. Morris, "Spiritual Ascension," 74.

99. William C. Chittick, "Belief and Transformation: The Sufi Teachings of Ibn al-ᶜArabi," *The American Theosophist*. vol. 74 (1986) no. 5, 191.

100. Nasr, *Foundations*, 388-389.

101. Ibn al-ᶜArabi, *Bezels of Wisdom*, 78.

102. Nasr, *Three Muslim Sages*, p. 118.

103. Muhyiddin ibn ᶜArabi, "What the Student Needs," *Journal of the Muhyiddin Ibn ᶜArabi Society*. vol. 5 (1986), 33-52.

104. Ibn ᶜArabi, *Journey to the Lord*, 39-48.

105. Arthur Jeffery, "Ibn al-ᶜArabī's Shajarat al-Kawm," *Studia Islamica*. vol. 11 (1959), 154, 156, 158.

106. Ibn ᶜArabi, *Journey to the Lord*, 63.

107. Ibid., 25.

108. Irina Tweedie, *The Chasm of Fire: A Woman's Experience of Liberation through the Teaching of a Sufi Master*. (Tisbury, Wiltshire, England: Element Books, 1979), 10. Unless indicated otherwise, subsequent quotations pertaining to Irina Tweedie come from this autobiography, with the relevant page number in parentheses following the quote.

109. Lings, *Sufi Saint*, 193.

V Christianity: The Mind of Reconciliation

"You shall love the Lord your God with all your heart, and with all your soul, and with all your mind, and with all your strength."—Mark 12:30

"Do not be conformed to this world, but be transformed by the renewing of your minds."
—Romans 12:2

"Finally, beloved, whatever is true . . . , whatever is just, whatever is pure . . . , think about these things."—Phil. 4:8

A Methodological Fore-Note: Growing a Faith while Growing in Faith

Unlike previous chapters, which are written from a *strictly* phenomenological standpoint, i.e., from the perspective of an outside but sympathetic observer, this chapter is written from the viewpoint of a life-long Christian. By right of being a Christian, I have the freedom to incorporate my particular views of Christianity into the chapter and still offer it as a phenomenological presentation of the tradition, albeit an atypical one. My experience of Christianity today, as indicated in the Preface, is significantly different than it was in earlier decades. There are two reasons for this. First, having lived through perceived limitations and contradictions found in Christianity in earlier years, I could not in clear conscience present those forms in a purely descriptive way. I would have felt bound by conscience to be critical, which would be unacceptable from the phenomenological standpoint. Second, because I have changed as a Christian within Christianity, Christianity has also changed, i.e., my view of what constitutes Christianity. In other words, the growing or transformational process has been a mutual one in which each impacts the other in ways that give rise to each accommodating the other by rising to new levels of being, as a person and as a faith. Though I am the same person I have always been, I am also a different person than I used to be. Similarly, the Christianity I espouse today is both the same Christianity and a different Christianity than I knew earlier in life. An important ingredient in this mutually transforming process has been the integration of the transrational sentiments of my heart with the rational requirements of my mind. If the heart rules, religion tends to become overly emotional and a search for personal comfort and security. If the mind rules, it tends to become a cold formalism accompanied by rigid judgments.

This integration of mind and heart is an essential prerequisite for progressing through full evolutionary growth in personal religious life, ideally from exoteric through esoteric to metateric. It was, in fact, the discovery of this integration and progression in the practitioners of other religions that led to finding it also in the saints and mystics of Christianity, in Evagrios of Pontus and John Cassian in the Orthodox Church, in St. Teresa of Avila and St. John of the Cross in the Roman Catholic Church, in Jakob Boehme and George Fox in the Protestant Church. The wise and saintly Christianity of these and countless other Christians was absent from my early church experience, as it still is in many if not most churches today. Now that sectarianism is diminishing somewhat, more mutual enrichment across the historic divide between the world's religions is occurring. Indeed, from the late twentieth-century, some churches—and many

Christians unconnected to churches—have discovered a profound spirituality in the world religions and are now finding and opening to higher/deeper realizations in Christianity. Even when this new spirituality is known, however, many may be unresponsive: their level of consciousness may resist such forms (see Chapter I); rigid beliefs may rule it out, as may fear of change; there may be an unwillingness to take up the necessary discipline; and, finally, there may not be adequate guidance and support offered.

Two principal factors shape the following presentation of Christianity. First, Christianity is seen in the context of the world's religious and wisdom traditions, i.e., as a religion among religions. Therefore, common and universal principles found to operate in these traditions are seen as likely to be operating in Christianity as well. For example, in addition to Ultimacy as the focus of all authentic religious experience, another shared principle lies in the potential for life-long evolution of religious experience through multiple levels of realization, with each level bringing the practitioner into closer and closer relationship to and with Ultimacy. Second, Christianity, like all religions, contains many different and often conflicting interpretations. A standard of truth is needed in order to evaluate these views so that one can determine truth for oneself. The standard of truth employed here is: that truth is most valid that is most comprehensive and inclusive. Truth is charitably inclusive, not doctrinally or morally exclusive. In light of Jesus' affirmation (John 8:32), "the truth shall make you free," a sense of clarification, confidence, and openness should also accompany truth.

Mere familiarity and preference are not standards of truth. A universal criterion is required. In the context of this study, all religions affirm that Ultimacy, i.e., God in Christianity, is the most embracing of all realities. Therefore, one holds a position that is most God-like, or ultimate, if it accounts for all dimensions of reality without merely rejecting some on the basis of particular religious or moral grounds. To dismiss the beliefs or behaviors of others by simply branding them as erroneous or evil is inadequate. To note that a particular belief or behavior causes suffering—is afflictive and thereby limiting—is a worthy standard of evaluation. Such a standard gives rise to love and compassion, and denotes a genuinely human and humane relation to all humans, all creatures, and the world at large.

To grow in faith, to transform personally, necessitates a corresponding growth or change in how one understands one's religious tradition, one's Faith. No one can be a Christian in all the ways it is possible to be Christian. What is going to be considered most important: Jesus as teacher and exemplar, his death, the Resurrection, the on-going work of the Holy Spirit, Christ's oneness with God, the creeds of the church, or some other aspect? One's Christianity must be individualized, must correspond to one's understanding of what it means for oneself to be Christian. For integrity to ensue, one's personal faith and the Faith to which one adheres must evolve together. Since personal transformation is a central theme in this work, interspersed throughout this presentation of Christianity are interpretations and comments that facilitate this transformation. In other words, while presenting Christianity phenomenologically, the portrayal will frequently highlight dimensions of the Faith that encourage growth in faith, growth with the potential to lead from exoteric through esoteric to metateric realizations.

There is considerable precedent in Christianity for making changes in how the tradition is to be understood. Different views have marked Christianity from its beginning. Most scholars agree today that Jesus did not intend to found a new religion. He was not a founder but a revolutionary and reformer. His life and teachings released forces that led others to establish the new religion. The Jesus Movement, informed and inspired by the teachings, example, and spirit of Jesus, became Christianity because of men like Paul and Peter. Popularly, of course, Jesus is regarded as the founder of the church, but Paul and Peter played a much larger role in its initial formation. Since Paul never actually met Jesus, his views are secondhand and particularly interpretive. If Paul and his supporters had not prevailed, Christianity might have become simply a revivalist movement in Judaism or never formed at all. Nor were Christianity and the church shaped solely by the biblical writers. Greek philosophy, particularly that of Plato and his Neoplatonist followers were drawn upon in the course of developing Christian theology and mysticism.

Leaders of the church throughout history continued to fashion different forms of Christianity. The core beliefs and practices evolved over time as a result of different interpretations, and thereby became normative for the numerous churches and denominations that constitute Christianity today. The process has not and probably never will end. Like all living religions, Christianity is 'still in the making' as Christians and the church respond to new developments in the world at large. Even though there is an essential continuity, Christianity today is significantly different than it was before the Renaissance, the Enlightenment and rise of the scientific movement, or Darwin's discoveries, to name a few of the major cultural forces to which Christianity has been forced to adapt, though often grudgingly and after much debate and turmoil. Any religion that fails to be dynamic by means of such adjustments soon becomes obsolete.[1]

Further modifications occur when Christianity moves into new countries and is compelled to express itself in ways that will prove meaningful and appealing to the citizenry. While there is certainly a nucleus of commonality, the church in India looks different from the church in Korea. Christianity in Africa and Latin America presents a different face than that in Europe. An Eastern Orthodox form of Christianity introduced to China in the seventh century incorporated into itself features of Buddhism and Taoism. No religion can become or remain a world religion if it is entirely resistant to modification, unwilling to adapt to changing conditions and different cultures.

As we will see, Christianity underwent many changes over time. By right of being a living religion, it will continue to change and develop. The fact of change is inherent in the very fabric of reality.

To resist change as a matter of principle is to deny an essential feature of life itself. This being the case, every Christian has the right, while drawing on the full Christian heritage, to develop a personally meaningful and viable faith. To uphold personal integrity, a Christian must adhere to a Christianity that not only makes sense, i.e., is not irrational, but makes more than sense, i.e., transcends reason. Bishop John Shelby Spong noted that "the heart cannot worship what the mind rejects."[2] We might expand this to read: the heart cannot affirm what the mind rejects.

The Apostle Paul was well aware of the change that can occur, that should occur, in religious life. His conversion from persecutor to advocate is one indication. Another is his testimony in 1 Cor. 13:11: "When I was a child, I spoke like a child, I thought like a child, I reasoned as a child; when I became an adult, I put an end to childish ways." Paul advises (Phil. 2:12-13): "work out your own salvation with fear and trembling." Here is an indication from the New Testament itself that believers are to take an active role in the formation of their faith. Why the phrase "with fear and trembling"? Because it is a serious and momentous undertaking. Paul immediately adds, "it is God who is at work in you," that is, the Spirit of God, the Holy Spirit, is actually guiding the process. But what conditions must prevail if that is to be the case?

What is to assure that working out one's faith proceeds according to divine will? Probably nothing is more important than personal integrity, an open mind, broad experience, wide reading, and general maturity. These will be enhanced by an actual spiritual practice, the concerted application in one's daily life of the transformative principles set forth in the Bible and developed further over time. It is not enough simply to believe the doctrines or creeds, just to attend religious services and participate in rituals. One must *work out* one's faith, one must *do* the truth. Later in this and in the last chapter transformative practice is treated explicitly. Here one example may suffice. Paul declares (1 Cor. 13:5) that love "does not insist on its own way." The application of this truth penetrates to the heart of the transformational process by breaking down self-preferring patterns, overcoming the limiting and controlling power of the ego. The "renewing of your minds" (Rom. 12:2) that Paul speaks of cannot occur without steady and repeated application of this central principle. No more powerful example of self-preferential transcendence is likely to be found than in the crucifixion of Jesus.

Strictly speaking, it is impossible to be a follower or disciple of Jesus today. We cannot know the person Jesus of Nazareth today. We only know doctored reports. The Jesus Movement slowly faded away as the church of the first century began to form during the post-Easter years and has continued to develop throughout history. The only possibility today is to be (or not be) a Christian. But what kind of Christian? What is essential, what optional? Every person must decide for himself or herself. Most, of course, 'decide' by ascribing to the church with which they are familiar, the one they were born into, that their friends attend, that offers the most, perhaps socially and/or politically as well as religiously. Most likely none of these are deliberate choices. A mature and true choice will result from sincere, honest, and open inquiry. This will supply the needed information and hopefully some degree of direct experience with different expressions of Christianity. The next task is to question, to weigh, to evaluate. Here one is exercising personal discernment, an operation of the heart/mind that not only is unique to humans but which, if not exercised, diminishes the fullness of our humanness. To be fully human is to make deliberate and well-informed decisions. Otherwise, one is living someone else's life, more or less blindly following custom and tradition. Even with children and young adolescents, no one should demand how another person should be religious. No more far-reaching decision is likely to be made by an individual than how he or she is going to relate to Ultimacy, to God.

Some clergy and staunch believers may vigorously oppose the individualized method of developing a faith outlined here. They may declare: "What you're concocting is heresy. What my church espouses is true Christianity; accept it or you're not a Christian!" This ill-informed and hard line stance is little different from that of the early church authorities who prohibited gnostic texts from entering the New Testament canon. Some authorities in established institutions want compliance, not individuality; uncritical acceptance, not thoughtful questioning. Though unlikely if one follows the guidelines suggested in this chapter, there is some risk that the theological view, spiritual outlook, and personal practice worked out for oneself could be a mix of features drawn from here and there that lack cohesion and harmony. Critics of the personal approach may well declare that only a hodgepodge of disparate elements can ensue. Though the incorporation of incompatible or conflicting features is unlikely, it can be forestalled by periodically discussing one's faith with wise and spiritually mature persons of wide experience.

A summary caveat is in order. To shape a Christianity that suits one's mind and heart must, at the same time, reflect a real connection with historic Christianity. Integrity requires that it be a *Christian* faith if it is going to purport to be. To be sure, there have been many Christianities throughout history. But to conjoin disparate elements of the tradition arbitrarily, to graft on items from other religions that are ill-suited, or to introduce features that have little relevance to personal transformation within a broad Christian context, would be to depart far from authentic spirituality and the values set forth in this chapter and the book as a whole. Both the integrity of oneself and Christianity require actual continuity between personal faith and the classic features of the historic Faith.

Christianity: Two Main Principles

The founding principle of Christianity is love, God's love for mankind. As remarkable as this may seem, according to both the

Bible and the teaching of the church, love constitutes the very basis for God's revelation of Himself in and through His Son, Jesus the Christ. The scriptural basis for this originating principle is one of the most memorized verses in the New Testament, John 3:16: "God so loved the world that he gave his only Son."[3] The proper human response to this extraordinary gift is set forth in another widely memorized passage, this one known as the First Great Commandment (Mark 12:30): "You shall love the Lord your God with all you heart, and with all your soul, and with all your mind, and with all your strength." God's love for humanity, then, is to be mirrored back to God by means of a total love involving one's entire being.

Because divine love is a quality and therefore without boundary or limit, i.e., inexhaustible, it is also to mark the relationship between humans. This injunction is set forth in the Second Great Commandment (Mark 12:31): "You shall love your neighbor as yourself." The New Testament asserts that the high expectation of Christian love is made possible by right of God's initiating love. Another New Testament passage asserts (1 John 4:19) that "we love because he [God] first loved us." The ultimate implication of this divine and human love sets the standard for evaluating the quality of Christian life. This fact is clearly articulated by a Roman Catholic theologian: "Charity [love] is the principal norm for judging the perfection of the Christian life."[4] Apart from a life of love, one cannot expect to live a truly Christian life (1 John 4:8): "He who does not love does not know God." Nearly two hundred references to love are found in the New Testament. John 3:16 (quoted above) continues by noting that the purpose of God's loving gift of His Son is "so that everyone who believes in him may not perish but may have eternal life." This suggests that evangelism, the sharing of the Gospel (literally, good news) with others, follows naturally from God's Self-manifestation in and through Jesus. Some believe it is required also by the Great Commission (Matt. 28:19): "Go therefore and make disciples of all nations." Christian outreach, evangelism and missionary activity, is a second major feature that has enabled Christianity to become the largest and most widely distributed religion in the world. Virtually no country today is without some Christian presence.

Like Buddhism before it and Islam after it, Christianity began with the reforming passion of a man who has come to be recognized as its founder. While there is no convincing evidence that Jesus intended to establish a new religion, a new religion was formed around his life and mission in the decades and centuries following his death. The intensity and urgency that characterized Jesus' life and preaching became in his followers an intensity and urgency to live the life he enjoined, and an equal intensity and urgency to spread his teaching so that others might enjoy salvation and holiness in this life and eternal life in the hereafter. The "make disciples" command came to mean for many Christians, particularly those with conservative or fundamental leanings, that evangelism is as much a requirement of Christianity as is "love your neighbor." Always with conviction, and sometimes with aggression, the devout of Christianity have sought to share with others something of the transformational—or saving and sanctifying—power they have experienced in their personal relationship with Jesus the Christ. Until the rise of Islam in the seventh century, Christianity was the unrivaled missionary religion in the world.

Multiple Views and Historical Forms

Like all religious traditions, Christianity contains wide and conflicting views of faith and practice. A careful reading of the Gospels shows that even during Jesus' lifetime different views regarding him existed. For example, when he asked his disciples, "Who do people say that the Son of Man is?" they named John the Baptist as well as several Old Testament prophets. When the question was directed to the disciples themselves, Peter identified him as the Christ, a designation Jesus accepted (Matt. 16: 13-17). In the decades immediately following Jesus' death, several different groups formed around their respective memories of him and vied with each other over the correct view. Marked difference in what Jesus did and said are found in the four Gospels. As theological and moral issues came to be worked out, further differences emerged. For example, from the letters of Paul we know that some followers of Jesus, contrary to Paul's own view, believed that Gentiles must be circumcised—a unique Jewish rite—before they could be regarded as Christian.

It is a well-established principle that every event requires interpretation and interpretation depends on who one is, the extent and quality of one's total life experience. A well-educated person with extensive experience in life, including exposure to world cultures, will inevitably see and understand a specific event very differently from someone of limited education and little contact with other cultures. When the matters requiring interpretation pertain to religion, not only extensive education and wide experience is desirable but also moral integrity plus spiritual insight, openness, and sensitivity. Referring to recent biblical reinterpretations, Pope John XXIII said on his deathbed: "It is not that the gospel has changed; it is that we have begun to understand it better." He then affirmed that new readings, new interpretations, derive from wide experience: "Those who have lived as long as I have . . . [have been] enabled to compare different cultures and traditions."[5]

When an especially remarkable person or event appears in a culture, a struggle occurs in the attempt to understand and incorporate the new development into the prevailing worldview. This is done by seeing the new in terms of the old, by locating it in familiar or slightly modified intellectual and cultural forms. When there is considerable social upheaval and individual insecurity, as was the case at the time of Jesus' life and death and also during the following decades and centuries, the assimilation process takes on even more urgency. Well into the fourth century and beyond, there was constant, vigorous debate, even persecution, intrigue and murder, in an effort to establish a single understanding of the person and work of Jesus the Christ, and consequently, a single view and practice of Christianity.[6]

This objective received a huge boost when Constantine came to the Roman throne in 324 CE and declared, in an effort to unify his empire, that Christianity would henceforth be the official religion. But Constantine's declaration fell far short of actually unifying Christianity or the empire; controversy and conflict continued. In fact, the very next year he called together about 220 bishops from the Western (Latin) and Eastern (Greek) churches to form the first worldwide or ecumenical gathering of the church, the Council of Nicaea. The immediate impetus for this assembly was to deal with Arius, a priest in Alexandria, Egypt, and the heretical ideas he spawned.

The Arian heresy contends that the Son of God, while divine, is not equal to God the Father but occupies a position subordinate to God. The Nicene Creed, in declaring Jesus the Christ to be "God from God, light from light, true God from true God, begotten not made, of one substance with the Father," attempted, unsuccessfully as it turned out, to quell what had become a widespread view among some clergy and many of the laity, a view that in fact persisted for centuries and is found even in modern times. The central view of Arianism, that Jesus, the Son of God, occupies a position less lofty than God and Father, is found today in the Unitarian Church as well as among Christians who do not subscribe to all of the official beliefs of the church with which they associate.

Additional church-wide councils were convened in subsequent centuries, with Christian unity remaining a desired but elusive goal. Because of the continuing strife, persecution, and killings between the Eastern and Western branches of the church, aggravated by the Nicene and Arian issues as well as others, Christianity's semblance of unity during its first thousand years finally came to a formal end in the middle of the eleventh century. Today three major branches of Christianity exist, Orthodox, Catholic, and Protestant, with each made up of further internal divisions.

The Eastern Orthodox Church

The Eastern Orthodox Church, like the other branches of Christianity, traces its origin back to Jesus and the early apostles. The Orthodox Church is made up of a number of autonomous churches, distinguished from each other according to national identity, e.g., Russian, Coptic (Egyptian), Syrian, etc. The Greek Orthodox Church is the largest of these autonomous churches. The Eastern Orthodox Church regards itself as the One Holy Catholic Apostolic Church of the seven Ecumenical Councils (held intermittently from 325 to 787), official assemblies, as we have seen, that are called to establish correct doctrine and practice, thereby combating heresy (orthodox literally means 'right belief').

Theology in the Eastern Church falls into two forms, cataphatic, or positive theology, in which divine revelation is interpreted in terms of the categories of time and space (i.e., theology as commonly understood), and apophatic, or negative theology, where God is regarded as inconceivable, so totally other that the human mind cannot possibly understand or describe 'Him'. John of Damascus (ca. 670-750) wrote: "God is unknowable and incomprehensible and the only thing knowable of God is His unknowability and incomprehensibility."[7] These two forms of theology are essential to each other: apophatic theology keeps cataphatic theology from becoming too literalistic, and cataphatic theology keeps apophatic theology from becoming too abstract.

Arianism was never fully relinquished by the Eastern Church. This is because it wanted, without diminishing the divinity of

Jesus the Christ, to acknowledge his full humanity so that ordinary humans, by emulating him and calling on divine grace, could be transformed and elevated to a divine status like him. This doctrine, known as *theosis* or deification, enabled Athanasius, Patriarch of Alexandria in the fourth century, to declare that Jesus "was made man that we might be made God." The doctrine and practice of theosis, ranging from observance of the Sacraments plus prayer and fasting for all believers, to the added asceticism and mysticism of monks and mystics, is the means in Orthodoxy of fundamental human transformation. Here spirituality becomes lived experience and not simply formal acknowledgement.

By right of the Incarnation, the doctrine which asserts that Jesus the Christ is fully human and fully divine, Orthodox Christians undertake a spiritual pilgrimage in which each becomes increasingly holy and united with God. Theosis provides the doctrinal basis for salvation, liberation from sin and evil, and redemption, reunion with God. To avoid the delusion that one actually becomes God, Orthodoxy teaches that theosis is a union with the energies or qualities of God and not with his essence, which always remains mysterious, hidden, and unknowable.

Among other verses in the Bible, two from the Petrine letters substantiate theosis. The most explicit as promise and command is 1 Peter 1:16 which says: "You shall be holy, for I am holy." In his second letter (2 Peter 1:4) Peter urges the devout to "become participants of the divine nature."

The sacraments are central in the worship of the Eastern Church. A sacrament is a divinely instituted rite and an outer expression of an inner work, an act of grace that occurs as the officiating priest conducts the ritual according to the official prescriptions of the Church. According to the Eastern and Western Churches, grace is actually conveyed to recipients through the sacraments.

The Orthodox Church does not specify a precise number of sacraments; instead it affirms that the entire world is sacramental because of the divine presence 'hidden' in everything. Nonetheless, seven special sacraments operate in the ritual life of Orthodoxy. The most important, Holy Eucharist, is the focus of worship every Sunday and on all Holy Days. It is known as the "Sacrament of Sacraments" and is the Church's celebration of the death and resurrection of Christ. All other sacraments flow from and lead back to the Eucharist.

Baptism and Chrismation are usually performed for infants. Baptism conducts the newborn into the life of the Church. Chrismation (being made Christ-like) confirms that each child is blessed by the Spirit with certain gifts and talents that hopefully will be developed in later life. Paul lists the general fruits or gifts of the Spirit: "love, joy, peace, patience, kindness, generosity, faithfulness, gentleness, and self-control" (Gal. 5:22-23). These are the Christian virtues and justify this sacrament's name as Chrismation.

Confession is the sacrament by means of which sin is annulled and the penitent's relationship to God, as well as to others and himself, is restored. The penitent confesses his sins to God and is forgiven by God, with the priest serving as a witness and support.

In the Sacrament of Marriage, God conjoins a man and woman in a union of mutual love that also links them as a couple with both God and the Church. Marriage is a sacred vocation that calls for each partner to assist the other in growing closer to God and developing the gifts bestowed by the Holy Spirit.

According to the Sacrament of Holy Orders, clergy are ordained for special service to the Church. Three major orders are recognized: bishop, priest, and deacon. As they perform their pastoral duties, they are regarded as living icons or representatives of Christ.

Finally, the Sacrament of Holy Unction, or Anointing of the Sick, gives solace and healing to those suffering, physically, mentally, emotionally, or spiritually. The sacrament is given for any illness as well as at the time of death. It is offered to all members of the Church during Easter or Holy Week celebrations.

The Roman Catholic Church

The Roman Catholic Church and the Eastern Orthodox Church shared a common history for a millennium. However, in the middle of the eleventh century, each went its separate way, for political as well as religious reasons. Tension had been brewing between the two geographical regions of the Church for centuries, tension that came finally to center in the question of who was to receive primary allegiance, the patriarch in Constantinople (known today as Istanbul) or the pope in Rome. The year 1054 is usually cited as the date of official separation. During this year, the pope excommunicated the patriarch, who, in turn, excommunicated the pope's representatives who had served the bull, the official pronouncement of excommunication. Recriminations continued back and forth for some time before the two branches settled into their respective regions and activities.

Notwithstanding the formal separation more than a millennium ago, many common features characterize the Roman Catholic and Eastern Orthodox Churches, for example, in their understanding and celebration of the sacraments. The seven sacraments recognized as the main ones in the Eastern Church are regarded as the only ones in the Western Church. In both Churches, the sacraments are the central symbols and means of personal transformation.

In the Roman Church, the mystery of the Eucharist lies in the doctrine of transubstantiation, the belief that the wine and bread of the mass are actually changed into the real blood and body of Christ. (Two other prominent beliefs in Christianity are consubstantiation, the blood and body of Christ coexist with the wine and bread, and symbolic, the wine and bread represent the blood and body of Christ.) In the Roman Church, the mystery of transubstantiation is further underscored by the Latin phrase, *ex opere operatio,* which asserts that the efficacy of the Eucharist does not depend on either the faith or the virtue of the officiant; the mass in itself is effective in conveying the saving act of God.

The Roman Catholic Church, like the Eastern Church, practices infant baptism. Here too, baptism is for the remission of sin. In the case of infants, this is a canceling out of original sin, the inborn propensity toward sin carried forth in humans because of Adam and Eve's disobedience in the Garden of Eden. The doctrine of original sin is controversial in Christianity, with many Christians, particularly liberal Protestants, disavowing its reality. Adult baptism, while the norm in many Protestant churches, takes place in Catholicism only if there is some question regarding the legitimacy of one's original baptism.

Reconciliation, also known as Penance or Confession, is the sacrament of forgiveness for sins committed after baptism. In the case of infant baptism, the parents, godparents, or other responsible adults affirm on behalf of the child its commitment to Christ and their intent to guide the child toward a sinless and fully Christian life. If sins are committed in later life, by confessing them to a priest, the repentant Christian is relieved of guilt as the priest says, "I absolve thee from thy sins in the name of the Father and of the Son and of the Holy Spirit." He or she must promise not to sin again and be willing to make restitution, that is, to perform an act of goodness prescribed by the priest that will exemplify the person's intent to live a godly life henceforth. As a result of engaging the sacrament in a heartfelt manner, the individual is again reconciled to God, Christ, and the Church.

Confirmation is conferred immediately after Baptism or early in adolescence; in the latter case it represents a ritual passage out of childhood. The confirmed youth is expected to rely less on parental guidance for determining right and wrong and more on conscience and propriety.

Marriage is considered a vocation based on a calling from God. This view enhances the sanctity of matrimony and provides the basis for the Roman Catholic prohibition against divorce. Since procreation is one of the main purposes of marriage and because artificial contraception impedes the natural process of childbirth, the Roman Catholic Church prohibits the use of artificial contraception.

Extreme Unction is offered to the seriously ill and the dying. Like all the sacraments, this one too is derived from a practice in the early church (James 5:14): "Are any among you sick? They should call for the elders of the church and have them pray over them, anointing them with oil in the name of the Lord." The grace imparted to the sick is believed to derive from the atoning death of Christ (Matt. 8:17): "He took our infirmities and bore our diseases." When the rite is given to a dying person, it prepares the soul for eternal life.

The seventh and final sacrament, Holy Orders, ranks the clergy in a hierarchical manner. The upper level consists of the pope, the cardinals, and the archbishops. Next come bishops, priests, and deacons. In addition to a divine calling, candidates for these offices must undergo pastoral and theological training. Unlike clergy in Eastern Orthodox and Protestant Churches, Roman Catholic clergy are not permitted to marry. Celibacy has been normative since the fourth century and mandatory since the eleventh.

Throughout Roman Catholic history, there have been some who aspired to a higher spiritual life than they felt they could achieve in the clerical orders or in ordinary life. These entered religious communities where they took vows of celibacy, poverty, and obedience. From monastic orders, Christianity's greatest mystics emerged. The mystics demonstrate in their writings how they overcame the limiting bounds of the ego and united with the divine. In the next chapter, we will survey the lives and teaching of representative and exemplary mystics.

The belief and practice of the Roman Catholic Church is determined to a great extent by ecumenical councils. The most recent, Vatican II, was inaugurated by Pope John XXIII in 1962 and formally closed by Pope Paul VI three years later. This council was the first in almost a century and only the second since the Protestant Reformation in the sixteenth century. Vatican II promulgated a number of official documents designed to meet the changing conditions of the modern world without compromising the historic truth of the Church. The most significant reforms occurred in the biblical, liturgical, and ecumenical life of the Church.

The Bible came to assume a centrality in theological reflection, in seminary education, and among the laity that it never had previously. Translations by Protestant scholars were approved to be read. This increased study of the Bible by the laity led to Roman Catholic involvement in the Charismatic Movement, a Christian-wide lay movement that revived such New Testament expressions of piety as divine healing and *glossolalia* (Greek, speaking in tongues), a form of ecstatic speech believed to be an evidence of the indwelling of the Holy Spirit (cf. Acts 10:46, 19:6, 1 Cor. 12:10, 14 *passim*). The Charismatic Movement began in mainline Protestant churches, e.g., Episcopal, Lutheran, and Presbyterian, in the 1960s and then spread to Roman Catholic and Orthodox churches. It is thus an expression of Christian unity running across all three branches of Christianity.

Perhaps the most controversial change stemming from Vatican II occurred in liturgy, so controversial that significant numbers of clergy and laity left the Church. The position of the altar was reversed so that the officiating priest now faced the congregation. He recited the mass in the vernacular rather than Latin, and spoke loudly so that all could hear and hopefully understand. While this removed some mystery from the mass, it involved worshippers as never before. The priest offered bread and wine directly to the recipients, and preached from the Bible. The latter added a prophetic role, namely, speaking God's message to the people in the language of the day, rather than just the traditional priestly role of presenting the concerns of the people to God. The priestly office now took on a twofold directionality, representing God to the congregation and the congregation to God. Music also became an integral part of the liturgy. All in all, worshippers were encouraged to become active participants, not just passive observers.

Following Vatican II, the Roman Church began to take a more active role in relating to other Christian denominations. Abandoning its 'one true church' stance, it ended the millennium-long schism with the Greek Church and also sought closer relations with Protestant churches. In the spirit of ecumenicity, it became an official observer, though not a full member, in the World Council of Churches (WCC). Prior to Vatican II, the WCC was an assembly of only Orthodox and Protestant churches. Representatives from these churches have met periodically since 1910 to reflect on matters of Christianity that have divided believers throughout the centuries, thereby hoping to discover and demonstrate increased unity. With the added presence of the Roman Catholic Church, the WCC now represents all three major branches of Christianity.

Vatican II also set in motion forces that opened the Roman Church to communication with other religions. For example, Judaism is now recognized as a legitimate religion. The popular view that the Jews killed Jesus has been rejected. And anti-Semitism has been condemned. The Church now recognizes that other world religions are also paths to God. Pope John Paul II (1978-2005) called leaders of the world's major religions to Assisi, Italy, on three occasions to pray together for world peace. Breaking with papal precedence, he visited a Jewish synagogue in 1986 and later an Islamic mosque.

The doctrine of papal infallibility was first promulgated by Vatican I (1869-1870) and further defined by Vatican II. The pope, as successor of St. Peter, is regarded as infallible when he definitively addresses matters of morality and faith. Infallibility does not extend to issues of church governance or discipline, and does not mean that the pope himself is impeccable or otherwise inerrant.

Mary, the mother of Jesus, plays a more vital role in the Orthodox and Catholic Churches than in Protestantism. The Roman Church, for example, in a papal bull in 1854, set forth the doctrine of the Immaculate Conception, which declared that Mary, like Jesus, was preserved from original sin at the moment of her conception. She is also believed to have been foreordained by God at the time of creation to be Christ's most intimate associate in preparing for human redemption. In a doctrine of faith proclaimed by Pope Pius XII in 1950, known as the Assumption of the Blessed Virgin Mother, Mary is declared to have ascended to heaven in body and soul following her death. Mary is the most perfect human being created by God and second only to Christ (who is divine as well as human) as a focus of honor and reverence in the Church.

A final issue to be considered before taking up Protestantism concerns what may well be the most fundamental difference between the two largest branches of Christianity, namely, the final authority for determining matters of faith and practice. To somewhat simplify this difficult issue, for the Roman Catholic Church it is the tradition of the Church itself, for Protestantism it is the Bible. The Roman Catholic Church contends that scripture was produced by the Church and, therefore, the Church has the sole right to interpret scripture and determine truths for which there is no direct evidence in the Bible. Protestants argue that the New Testament existed first and announced the founding of the church; therefore, scripture rather than tradition is the highest authority. From this perspective it is unacceptable to introduce dogmas for which there is no biblical evidence, such as the Immaculate Conception of Mary and her Assumption to Heaven.

Of course, each branch of the church recognizes both scripture and tradition as authoritative. But which takes precedence over the other? The two views are irreconcilable since they are interpretation that cannot be resolved by appeal to any agreed upon higher authority. God, of course, would be such an authority, but God does not answer unambiguously, i.e., in a way that leaves no room for interpretation and difference. Therefore, each view, conflictive though they are, is the final authority for each branch of the church.

The Protestant Churches

During the late Middle Ages, certain moral practices, doctrinal teachings, and institutional forms had become common in the Roman Catholic Church that some monks and priests felt were contrary to biblical teaching. One of the first protesters was the Englishman, John Wycliffe (1330-1384), who believed that Holy Scripture should be available to the laity in their native language, that believers are directly responsible to God and not wholly dependent on priestly intercession, and that the papal office claimed entirely too much power for itself. He also objected to the sale of indulgences. The practice of granting indulgences had begun in the eleventh century as a way of doing penance. By drawing on the merit of the saints, the pope and the bishops claimed they had the power to remit the temporal penalty required for the remission of sin—if the penitent undertook a pilgrimage, joined a crusade, distributed alms, or gave a monetary gift to the Church, a monastery, or a charitable organization. The practice of granting indulgences soon deteriorated into a moneymaking scheme for the Church.

Joining Wycliffe in the call for reform were a number of other clergy in Europe: John Huss (1372/3-1415) in Bohemia (present day Czech Republic), who was excommunicated and then executed; Ulrich Zwingli (1484-1531) in Switzerland, killed in a war that erupted over his opposition to Rome; Martin Luther (1483-1546) in Germany, excommunicated and outlawed by imperial edict; and John Calvin (1509-1564) in France and later in Switzerland, who succeeded in turning Geneva into a virtual theocracy and enclave of protection for those opposing the Roman Catholic Church. There were other reformers as well, but foremost among them all was Martin Luther, who is usually credited with initiating the Protestant Reformation on October 31, 1517. On this date, he posted ninety-five theses on the door of the castle church in Wittenberg in opposition to the granting of indulgences.

The issue of indulgences only triggered the Protestant Reformation. The most fundamental and decisive issue between the Catholic Church and the reformers resides in their different views of the Bible. As we have just seen, the Roman Church considers the Bible, although unquestionably the revealed Word of God, to be the product of the Church—admittedly the early church, or first followers of Jesus—and, therefore, it can be interpreted properly only by the Church, or, more specifically, by those in the Church who have undergone special study of the Bible and have received ordination, namely, the priests. Briefly, in Roman Catholicism, Church takes precedence over Bible; in Protestantism, Bible takes precedence over church. The reformers affirmed with Wycliffe the right of believers to read the Bible in the vernacular and interpret it according to the dictates of their hearts and minds. From this fundamental difference emerged a number of others.

On the basis of his reading of the Bible, Luther concluded that faith should occupy a more important role in salvation than works, thus his opposition to the practice of granting indulgences. Luther added *sola* (Latin, alone) to the Bible's *fide* (Latin, faith), believing that this was consistent with the Bible's overall teaching, so that sola fide, faith alone, became a watchword of the Reformation. Justification by faith, another watchword, indicated that from the human side the only requirement for salvation was faith in the power of Christ to save. *Sola gratia*, grace alone, indicated that from the divine side there was no expectation of working for salvation, of earning it through human effort. Good deeds might follow, indeed, were expected to follow, but could play no role in effecting salvation.

In Protestantism, status differences between clergy and laity are minimized. The reformers affirmed 'the priesthood of all believers'. Every human stands in direct relationship to God and needs no formally ordained priest for access to the divine. Church polity, patterns of governance, is less hierarchic and authoritarian, more egalitarian and democratic than in Catholicism. Worship tends to be less ritualistic, more informal and spontaneous. It centers less in the Eucharist and more in the Word as read from the Bible and preached from the pulpit. Eucharist becomes the Lord's Supper or communion and more an occasion for remembering Christ than mediating him, a view based on Jesus' words (1 Cor. 11:24), "Do this in remembrance of me." The singing of hymns and gospel songs is more prominent in Protestant worship, as is participation by the laity.

These and other differences between the Protestant and Catholic Church derive, directly or indirectly, from the Protestant Spirit. While it is easiest to think of the Protestant Spirit as one of opposition, of protesting, it is also one of affirmation, of testifying for, of being *pro*-testant. During the Reformation, the reformers spoke *against* what they saw as abuses, and simultaneously *for* what they saw as biblical truth. In the deepest sense, the Protestant Spirit opposes all absolutism, all attempts to contain Ultimacy in any creed or dogma, any form or formulation. It protests all presumption of knowing, absolutely and finally, the mind of God. At the same time, the Protestant Spirit affirms the Absolute Otherness, the Absolute Unlimitedness, or Infinitude and Eternality, of Ultimacy. Because the Protestant Spirit recognizes Ultimacy as Formless and Unconditioned in Itself, it affirms the relativity of all forms and conditions used to express the nature of Ultimacy. Among some few, the Protestant Spirit rejects the notion that God revealed himself only once and will not reveal himself further. From this standpoint, the Protestant Spirit sees the divine as continually manifesting in the cosmos and in the evolutionary unfolding of human consciousness. Ironically, the Protestant Spirit in this deeper sense is less operative in the Protestant Church today than in the Roman and Eastern Churches, given the presence in these of apophatic theology and a vital mystical tradition. Neither apophaticism nor mysticism has ever played a prominent role in Protestantism, even though the Protestant Spirit, when fully understood, requires it.

Because of the Protestant emphasis on (1) the primacy of the Bible, (2) the right of every believer to read and interpret it personally, and (3) the priesthood of all believers, Protestantism has proliferated into literally hundreds of different denominations. As believers found different perspectives that were important to them in their reading of the Bible, whether based on justifiable or fanciful interpretation, they tended to form new churches. Unfortunately, many of these readings were uninformed, lacking in adequate comprehension of the cultural milieu during the early centuries of Christianity's formation, devoid of recognition of how the biblical texts were actually written, the purposes and biases of the writers, for example. Nonetheless, during the course of the historical development of Protestantism, the attitude of protest, backed by various readings of the Bible, came to be directed as much toward other Protestant churches as toward the Roman Catholic Church.

Protestant fragmentation has often been marked by a competitive, even combative, spirit. This became an embarrassment for some Christians, particularly in the context of foreign missionary activity. Sensitive missionaries asked themselves how they could invite others to become Christians when Christianity was so divided within itself, and often contentiously so. These missionaries convened the World Missionary Conference in Edinburgh in 1910, and out of this organization grew the World Council of Churches in 1948. Since then, many regional, national, and local councils have formed to carry forth the spirit of ecumenicity. A number of Protestant churches, particularly those with conservative or fundamentalist outlooks, have refused to participate in the ecumenical movement as represented by the WCC and its associates. Some of these have formed parallel organizations comprised of denominations holding similar conservative and fundamentalist perspectives. Though merger is not the specific aim of the ecumenical movement, in some instances Protestant churches with significant historical and theological similarity have actually combined institutionally to form a single church. The express purpose of the ecumenical movement, however, is to discover and manifest greater unity among Christians, in obedience to Christ's prayer (John 17:21): "that they may all be one."

The Bible

Notwithstanding differences among Christians regarding the Bible and its interpretation, accord prevails on the importance of the Bible in setting the conditions of religious life and practice. However, Christians are not entirely agreed on what books rightfully make up the biblical canon (canon derives from a Greek word meaning rule or standard). A collection of fourteen books and parts of books known as the Apocrypha (Greek, hidden, concealed) is excluded from the Protestant Bible (partly because they contain teachings contrary to those of the Reformation, for example, on purgatory and the efficacy of good works). These writings are included in the Eastern Orthodox and Roman Catholic Bibles, though even here the Bible approved for use in the Greek Orthodox Church includes four books and Psalms 151 that are absent from the Catholic Apocrypha. Generally speaking, even in Catholicism and Orthodoxy, the Apocrypha is accorded less value than the canonical books; they are considered edifying but not inspired.

Centuries of debate transpired before the Old Testament, what Jews call Torah or Tanakh, finally came to be accepted as part of the Christian Bible. Establishing the New Testament canon took equally long as Christians tried to decide which of the writings composed and circulated in the first and second century were authentic records, accurately depicting the life and work of Jesus and his earliest followers. Today, with the exception of two Eastern Orthodox Churches, one with a smaller and the other with a larger collection, all Christian churches accept the canonicity of the books now found in the New Testament.

A long and hard struggle, however, went into the final establishment of the New Testament canon. Even in the fourth century and beyond, debate and discord continued over precisely which writings should be counted as orthodox. Various Christian groups vigorously championed their particular list of authentic writings. Many works other than those finally deemed worthy of canonical status were in strong contention for inclusion. In 367, Bishop Athanasius of Alexandria circulated the first list of the books now contained in the New Testament. He forcefully denied the authenticity of contending works, even labeling some as heretical. His list was circulated widely to churches and monasteries. It is quite possible that Athanasius' condemnation of books not on his list led to the burial in Egypt of the texts that were discovered in 1947 at Nag Hammadi. The Alexandrian bishop's attempt to settle the matter once and for all was not immediately successful. Well into the sixth century some were still resisting his list and putting forth their own. For many years the status of several books (e.g., Hebrews and Revelation) remained uncertain.

The New Testament eventually came to include the twenty-seven books now found in it. These include the four gospels, the Acts of the Apostles, several letters by Paul and others, and the last book of the Bible, the Revelation (Apocalypse) of John. The first three gospels, Matthew, Mark, and Luke, are called synoptic (Greek, seeing together) gospels since there is a great deal of similarity between them in content, organization, and wording, which in some passages is identical. Most scholars believe that Mark is the earliest gospel, written around 70 CE. Matthew and Luke, written a decade or so later, used Mark in the writing of their books. Some scholars contend that they also used another source, now lost, known simply as 'Q' (from the first letter of the German word for source, *Quille*). This accounts for material that is common to Matthew and Luke but absent from Mark. The fourth gospel, John, was probably written toward the end of the first century or early in the second. While it reports many of the same events and teachings found in the synoptic gospels, it reflects less historical and more theological concern. By the end of the second century it was known as the spiritual gospel.

The Acts of the Apostles is commonly attributed to Luke and regarded as the first book of church history. It reports major events in the life of the emerging church. Twenty-one of the books making up the New Testament are epistles (Greek, *epistolos*, letter). Although fourteen of these are attributed to Paul (ca. 10-62 CE), scholars identify only seven as indisputably written by him. Most of his letters were written to encourage and instruct new Christians and help resolve problems in newly founded churches, some of which he had established or helped to establish on his three missionary journeys. No one has shaped the life and practice of the church more than Paul. Jesus unquestionably furnished the originating spirit of Christianity but Paul fashioned that spirit into a form that eventuated in the Christian religion. He was the first Christian theologian. Some of the epistles attributed to Paul (e.g., 1 and 2 Timothy) may have been written early in the second century by someone convinced that he was addressing current problems in the church as Paul would have done if he were still alive. All of the authentic Pauline writings antedate the gospels.

The last book of the Bible, the Revelation to John, written around the close of the first century, employs highly imaginative figures (dragons and multi-headed beasts) as it addresses issues of eschatology, the end of time. Among other things, the book encourages Christians to remain faithful even during times of tribulation and persecution.

The question of the New Testament canon began to take on renewed relevance around the middle of the twentieth century for three reasons: (1) the discovery of heretofore unknown documents bearing on early Christianity, (2) the vast increase in knowledge about the religious, social, and political conditions in the eastern Mediterranean world in the first century, and, partly stimulated by these discoveries, (3) the desire to establish as reliable a picture as possible of the historical Jesus, how he regarded himself, how he envisioned God, what he conceived his mission to be, what his specific teachings were. Academic scholarship and some scholars in the churches have long distinguished between the Jesus of Nazareth and the Christ of faith. Who Jesus was in himself, on one hand, and how he was envisioned by those who responded to him in faith, on the other hand, are two quite different, though related, topics.

Biblical scholarship has demonstrated quite conclusively that there are several levels in the transmission of the picture of Jesus the Christ in the New Testament record. First, what is the content of the Jesus story, what does the New Testament actually say about his person and mission? This level, crucial in its own right, is also the basis for the other levels. Second, what can we discern about the way in which Jesus was remembered and envisioned by those who knew him personally? It is important to bear in mind that three or more decades transpired between Jesus' death and the writing of the first canonical gospel. Biblical scholars apply a method of analysis known as form criticism in order to establish the way in which this oral transmission shaped the material that came to be included in the gospels. Third, what were the purposes of the gospel writers as they decided what to include and exclude from their accounts? How have they shaped their chosen material to their specific objectives? This approach to biblical scholarship is known as redaction criticism. Drawing on the insights of form criticism and redaction criticism, a contemporary scholar notes that "every story and word of Jesus has been shaped by the eyes and hands of the early church."[8]

We can see now that the distinction is not quite so clear-cut that the Protestant reformers made when they insisted on the primacy of the Bible in contrast to the Roman Catholic insistence on the primacy of the church. Even as the Bible creates the church (the Protestant position), the church creates the Bible (the Catholic position). Therefore, an unravelable but dynamic tension exists in the movement from Bible to church and from church to Bible.

As we will see soon, the dynamic movement broadens as modern biblical scholarship enters the picture; now the oscillation is between scholarship, text, and church, with each informing the others, at least to the extent that each is open to the others.

Several textual discoveries of the twentieth-century are proving crucial because they enable scholars to widen their investigation of the historical Jesus by gaining a clearer picture of first-century Palestinian life, particularly religious life. These documents also include a number of non-canonical writings that describe activities and sayings of Jesus. The Dead Sea Scrolls consist of fragments and complete scrolls discovered from 1947 to 1960 at several sites near Qumran along the northwest shore of the Dead Sea. The hundreds of texts and thousands of fragments found there shed valuable light on Palestinian Judaism at the beginning of the Christian era. This is important for New Testament scholarship since it provides further information on the religious and cultural milieu in which Jesus carried out his mission and in which the New Testament had its origin. Many expressions and concepts have surfaced that duplicate or parallel those in the New Testament, thus providing a richer context for accurate understanding and interpretation of biblical statements.

Another set of long-hidden texts is even more important for gaining a fuller understanding of the New Testament. These were discovered in 1945 at Nag Hammadi in Egypt, and consist of forty-five papyrus texts bound in thirteen codices much like modern books. These texts too have contributed a great deal of new and valuable information about early Christianity. One of the most important of these texts is the Gospel of Thomas, a collection of 114 sayings purportedly dictated by "the living Jesus." The date of this gospel is not yet established; its origin in the first century is not at all impossible. The proverbs, parables, and brief dialogues in the Gospel of Thomas are similar in content and style to those in the canonical gospels, though there is no evidence of borrowing from either direction. At least some of the passages in the Gospel of Thomas are as likely to be authentic sayings of Jesus as those in the canonical texts. The Gospel of Thomas reflects the gnostic outlook that was fairly widespread during the formative years of Christianity, both in Christian and non-Christian forms.

According to Gnosticism (Greek, *gnosis*, knowledge) salvation occurs by means of esoteric or secret knowledge. The opening verse of the Gospel of Thomas promises immortality to those who truly understand the sayings that follow. The gospel affirms that the kingdom of God is an inner kingdom and that the gnosis that overcomes death and permits entry into this kingdom is knowledge of oneself (vs. 3): "When you come to know yourselves, then you will become known, and you will realize that it is you who are the sons of the living father."[9] Gnosticism presumes a fundamental duality in life and affirms that this duality must be transcended in order to enter the kingdom (vs. 22): "When you make the two one, and when you make the inside like the outside and the outside like the inside, and the above like the below, and when you make the male and the female one and the same, so that the male not be male nor the female female . . . then you will enter [the kingdom]." The Gospel of Thomas (vss. 19, 49) affirms that the inner self pre-existed creation and will return to and enjoy eternal repose in a state beyond existence. It identifies the one who dissolves duality and knows his true inner self as a *monachos*, a solitary one. "Jesus said: 'Blessed are the solitary and elect, for you will find the kingdom. For you are from it, and to it you will return.'"

In summary, an accurate understanding of the New Testament (or any scripture) requires, in addition to familiarity with the text itself, knowledge of the composition of the specific books and the formation of the canon, broad experience in life, and evolved maturity as a human being. If this reading is to contribute to personal transformation, there must be a corresponding commitment to existential truth, regardless of its source. With these considerations in mind, we turn now to the ever-challenging question, who was this enigmatic man from Nazareth around whom a world religion has formed?

Jesus the Christ (ca. 7/6 BCE-ca. 30 CE)

No life has given rise to more Lives, more attempts to understand it by means of biography, than the life of Jesus of Nazareth. While the New Testament provides some information about Jesus, the material is insufficient to constitute a biography in the modern sense. The first of the so-called Lives appeared before the end of the eighteenth century. Since then hundreds of additional Lives have been written, a few highly speculative and fanciful, most grounded in some degree of historical research. Scholars, however, have widely different views on what constitutes valid historical information about Jesus.

Toward the end of the nineteenth century, a distinction began to be made that has continued to define scholarship since that time, namely, between the Jesus of history and the Christ of faith. The first phrase denotes the domain of rigorous, critical investigation of historical records; the second pertains to theological reflection, on one hand, and religious surrender and devotion, on the other. Marcus Borg, a contemporary New Testament scholar, upholds the distinction but prefers distinguishing between the pre-Easter Jesus and the post-Easter Jesus.[10] A few scholars, who hold an extreme position, believe that nothing can be established as irrefutably factual about Jesus. Even fewer deny that he existed, a view that requires the dismissal of what most regard as reliable historical evidence.

The most widely published and active group of scholars working on these issues is known as the Jesus Seminar. Since its founding in 1985, about two hundred scholars have met periodically, in small groups, in an effort to extrapolate the authentic sayings and deeds of Jesus from what is said about him in the canonical and non-canonical literature. The objective is to distinguish the religion *of* Jesus from the religion *about* Jesus. Using rigorous criteria of reliability, the Jesus Seminar concluded that only eighteen percent of the sayings attributed to Jesus are authentic and only sixteen percent of the deeds.[11]

These scholars and others who study the life and mission of Jesus realize full well that the canonical and non-canonical writers had their respective interests and purposes according to which they shaped their stories of Jesus. The historical task, then, is to decipher the biases of the writers and infer how these positions shaped what they say about Jesus. That this is not an easy task is seen in the disparate conclusions that Jesus scholarship reaches. One group of writers, those who hold a plenary view of biblical inspiration and therefore believe that every word has been directly revealed by God, avoid these assessments since they accept the reliability of everything in the New Testament.

The Jesus Quest, as this historico-critical enterprise is often called, results in a sizable list of summary characterizations of Jesus: Social Prophet, Charismatic Jew, Magician, Jewish Sage, Peasant Sage, Cynic Philosopher, Social Revolutionary, Religious Mystic, Eschatological Prophet, and True Messiah.[12] When these titles are joined with those commonly found in churches, such as Lord, Son of God, King of Kings, Prince of Peace, Christ Crucified, Cosmic Christ, for example, one begins to suspect that religiously speaking a rigid distinction between the Jesus of history and the Christ of faith is impossible and unwarranted.

The portrayal of Jesus the Christ that informs this chapter accepts not only the validity of the history-faith distinction but maintains that it is an essential distinction for those who want their Christianity to be based on the religion of Jesus and not simply a religion about Jesus. The aim is to develop an integral faith, one of both mind and heart, of reason and commitment. Just as these two dimensions are distinguishable yet integral to our full and balanced humanness, the Jesus of history and the Christ of faith must be distinguished *and* integrated if one is to have a full and rich Christian experience. A life based solely on the so-called facts of history would be cut off from the rich and inspiring dimensions of our total humanness. Fact should inform meaning, but meaning cannot be limited to fact. Meaning, purpose, significance, and value are the vital dimensions of our existence. These are customarily expressed through theology, doctrine, ritual, and symbol. They tend to be conveyed and understood even more powerfully, however, through stories or, more accurately, through myths.

For centuries it was believed in the West that other people have myths, we have truth. It is now well established by scholars from various disciplines, and beginning to be acknowledged by the educated public, that myth is an essential aspect of all human life. Myth is truth, truth not in the form of systematic theology or rational philosophy but in the form of story. Myth fills out historic positions and facts, expands and enriches these with meanings that acknowledge the mystery, the grandeur, the wonder of life. Myth helps us know how we fit into the universe, how we can best cooperate with each other and the natural world. Most important, myth informs self-understanding and tells us how we relate to Ultimacy. Myth tells us who we are, whence we come and where we go. Myth conveys meanings that exceed reason, that unravel the values that hide beyond paradox. Living myths enrich and expand life.

Only believers with a rigid historicist bias and naïve views of religion could feel threatened by the distinction between the Jesus of history and the Christ of faith. The distinction actually arises from the Incarnation, the doctrine according to which Jesus the Christ is believed to be fully human and fully divine, simultaneously. God always acts in and through history, i.e., the Jesus of history, while not being limited by history, i.e., the Christ of faith. God works in history as Jesus to transcend history as Christ. According to the doctrine, Christ is no less Christ because Jesus is human; and Jesus is no less Jesus because Christ is divine. In a parallel fashion, Jesus is no less Christ, and Christ is no less Jesus because of the proposal to differentiate the two. To make this distinction is not to favor one pole and disparage the other. The Incarnation is the essential, nondual insight in Christianity.

For faith, the distinction is valid and important since only faith founded on reality, on how God actually works in human lives, is worthy of being called faith. Otherwise it is not true faith but simply belief, which is often based on little more than familiarity. Belief may be no more than an opinion or idea tenaciously held and emotionally supported by the need to feel connected to a like-minded community. Faith, on the other hand, is grounded in one's total life experience and is a whole person response to life that incorporates the highest values recognized. It opens us to the divine, to revelation, to ongoing transformation. Doubt is a mortal enemy to belief but an opening to growth for faith. Faith embraces new experience and new understanding.

The distinction between Jesus and Christ is implicit rather than explicit in the following account. While a great deal of inspiration, even inspiration for personal change, can ensue from knowledge of the man Jesus of Nazareth, the fundamental transformation that has occurred in the lives of countless Christians throughout history has been effected by their relationship to Jesus the Christ. Personal transformation does not so much result from factual information about Jesus but by surrender to Christ. The historical Jesus ennobles; the Risen Christ transforms. Christians believe that Jesus, in fully embracing his humanity, transcended it as limitation and thereby manifested divinity. Jesus the Christ, the incarnation of God, provides the means by which others too can transcend the limits encountered in the human condition and thereby manifest Christlike qualities, indeed, according to some, become Christs.

Birth, Youth, Baptism

According to the biblical record, Jesus was born in the closing years of the reign of Herod the Great. His mother, Mary, had been told by the angel Gabriel that the Holy Spirit would come upon her, that she would bear a son, and that he would reign over a kingdom that would have no end. According to imperial decree, Joseph and Mary went from Nazareth to Bethlehem in order to register for a census. While in Bethlehem, Jesus was born in a stable since the inn was full. Shepherds, tending their sheep in nearby fields, were visited by angels and went immediately to worship the newborn child. Wise men from the East also learned of his birth and went to worship him, offering him expensive gifts. When Herod heard about Jesus' birth, he plotted to kill him, fearing that Jesus would someday challenge his rule. An angel warned Joseph to seek asylum in Egypt, where he remained with Mary and Jesus until Herod died.

When Jesus was twelve years old, his parents took him to Jerusalem for the feast of Passover. After the celebration, Mary and Joseph started their return to Nazareth, assuming that Jesus was with others in the travel party. Only at nightfall did they discover that he was not. Two more days passed before Jesus was located, "in the temple, sitting among the teachers, listening to them and asking them questions. And all who heard him were amazed at his understanding and his answers." When Mary told Jesus how she had worried, he replied, "Why were you searching for me? Did you not know that I must be in my Father's house?" (Luke 2:46-49).

As a young man Jesus learned about John the Baptist, who wore a garment of camel's hair, and a leather girdle around his waist, who ate locusts and honey, who traveled in the wilderness and preached "a baptism of repentance for the forgiveness of sins." Jesus went to John and asked to be baptized. Though John was reticent, he baptized Jesus in the Jordan River. When Jesus came up out of the water, he saw the heavens open and "the Spirit descending like a dove on him.

And a voice came from heaven, 'You are my Son, the Beloved; with you I am well pleased'" (Mark 1:4-11).

Mission to the Dispossessed

After his baptism, Jesus went into the desert where he fasted forty days and nights. Here he was tempted by the devil, who, taking advantage of Jesus' hunger, challenged him to prove he was the Son of God by turning stones into bread. Jesus responded by quoting from the Hebrew Bible: "One does not live by bread alone, but by every word that comes from the mouth of God." Jesus was next taken to a high pinnacle of the temple in Jerusalem and challenged to prove his sonship by jumping off to see if God would send angels to save him. Jesus again quoted Scripture: "Do not put the Lord your God to the test." Finally, the devil took him to a high mountain and showed him the kingdoms of the world, telling him that they would be his if he worshipped the devil. Jesus responded with Scripture: "Away with you, Satan! For it is written, 'Worship the Lord your God, and serve only him.'" The devil then left, defeated in his efforts. (Matt. 4:1-11)

By withstanding these temptations, Jesus proved that his relationship to God was not based on hope for personal ease or gain but on the desire to serve God alone. By refusing to use his power to satisfy his hunger, he proved his detachment from psychophysical instincts and desires. By refusing political power, he proved his freedom from common human ambitions; he was free of the need for social power or influence. By refusing an outer sign of his relationship to God, he proved that inner certitude was sufficient; he was free of the need for objective 'proof'. By withstanding the temptations, Jesus proved he was free within himself, free in respect to others, and free in relation to empirical reality. Free from attachment to self, others, and world, he was free to demonstrate the primacy of spirit in all of life.

The Gospel of Luke reports that after his spiritual exercises in the wilderness, "Jesus, filled with the power of the Spirit," returned to Galilee and began teaching in the synagogues. In his hometown of Nazareth, Jesus read from Isaiah in a synagogue service: "The spirit of the Lord is upon me, because he has anointed me to bring good news to the poor. He has sent me to proclaim release to the captives and recovery of sight to the blind, to let the oppressed go free, to proclaim the year of the Lord's favor." When Jesus applied these words to himself, some of his countrymen took offense. He answered: "No prophet is accepted in the prophet's hometown" (Luke 4:14-24).

Jesus interacted openly with tax collectors and prostitutes, the socially marginalized. He had proven, in his testing by Satan, his ability to penetrate through the screen of conventionality. He could not be swaded by the usual prejudicial standards of society, or by the common human desires for comfort, approval, and social power. He focused his unique abilities where they were needed most, and where they were most welcome.

Throughout his ministry, Jesus identified with those who suffered in body, mind, and spirit. He associated with the destitute and deformed, the sick and demon possessed, i.e., those with psychotic disabilities. He straightened crooked limbs, restored hearing, returned sight, and revived the dead. He did not perform miracles to show his power over nature but to demonstrate God's power in all dimensions of life. Even when he walked on water, calmed a storm at sea, and increased a meager supply of bread and fish to feed over 5000 people, he did so in order to meet human need, emotional and physical.

Jesus as Teacher

In his own time, Jesus was regarded as one who taught with power and conviction: "he taught them as one having authority, and not as the scribes" (Mark 1:22). Much of his teaching is found in the Sermon on the Mount (Matt. 5-7). Scholars are virtually agreed that this sermon, found as a more or less coherent presentation only in Matthew, is a compilation of Christ's teaching rather than a formal address presented on a single occasion. Following are select passages, particularly those that introduce attitudes and practices that foster personal transformation.

The Sermon on the Mount opens with the Beatitudes, several of which set forth actual practices. "Blessed are the meek, for they will inherit the earth" (Matt. 5:5). Meekness or humility is a quality to be cultivated and not simply an ideal to be affirmed. All religions extol humility as essential for personal transformation. Humility counteracts the competitive and self-aggrandizing motives of the ego. It denotes the opposite of self-cherishing; it not only affirms the equality of others but extends preference to them. To be humble is to undermine the separate self sense that prohibits us from feeling the harmony and interconnectedness that would otherwise prevail in our interpersonal relationships.

"Blessed are those who hunger and thirst for righteousness, for they will be filled" (Matt. 5:6). To "hunger and thirst for righteousness" is to give precedence to spiritual life over mundane concerns, to be so committed to personal transformation that it is never far from one's mind, to incorporate transformative principles and attitudes into one's daily activities, to set specific times aside for concentrated practice.

"Blessed are the merciful, for they will receive mercy" (Matt. 5:7). To be merciful is to love, to practice loving kindness. Three qualitatively different kinds of love are frequently cited in Christianity, each connected to a Greek word. *Eros* is sexual love and charged with emotion. *Philia,* less emotionally charged, is typically the love of spouses, of parents and children, of friend to friend. The highest and purest form of love is *agape*, divine love, self-giving love, love that expects nothing in return, love that seeks only the welfare and highest good of the other. Because of the deep empathic 'feeling with', this love does not see the 'other' as other but as oneself in the sense of Jesus' injunction (Matt. 22:39), "Love your neighbor as oneself."

"Blessed are the pure in heart, for they will see God" (Matt. 5:8). The pure in heart are those whose intentions accord fully with hungering and thirsting for righteousness, those resolutely committed to ongoing spiritual development. Kierkegaard, a nineteenth-century philosopher-theologian, captured the meaning of heart purity in the title of his book, *Purity of Heart is to Will One Thing.*[13]

The next passage shows how Jesus incorporated well-known moral and religious standards of his day into his teaching. Even more important, however, the passage demonstrates how he internalized the teachings, i.e., spiritualized them in terms of our emotional-psychological nature and extended the range of their application. The point is not so much to fulfill them literally as to develop the inner attitude they set forth.

> You have heard that it was said to those of ancient times, 'You shall not murder.' But I say to you that if you are angry with a brother or sister, you will be liable to judgment. You have heard that it was said, 'You shall not commit adultery.' But I say to you that everyone who looks at a woman with lust has already committed adultery with her in his heart. You have heard that it was said, 'An eye for an eye and a tooth for a tooth.' But I say to you, do not resist an evildoer. But if anyone strikes you on the right cheek, turn the other also. You have heard that it was said, 'You shall love your neighbor and hate your enemy.' But I say to

you, love your enemies and pray for those who persecute you. (Matt. 5:21-44)

"Be perfect, therefore, as your heavenly Father is perfect" (Matt. 5:48). The Greek word used for perfect here is *teleios*, which also means whole. To be whole is to be all inclusive—as all inclusive as God. In Aramaic, the language Jesus spoke, the meaning is: "Be complete: develop yourself to the fullest degree."[14] By combining these meanings, we see that Jesus is advocating a transformational path parallel to that outlined in this chapter: keep your life moving until it is as all-embracing as the all-inclusiveness of God.

Jesus taught that God is impartial in his relationship to humans, favoring no one person more than another. He does not parcel out his blessings based on moralistic judgments. Jesus reminded that God "makes his sun rise on the evil and on the good, and sends rain on the righteous and on the unrighteous" (Matt. 5:45). This is a particularly potent reminder of the error in the all-too-common practice of condemning those whose moral standards may be different, even less noble, than those ideally affirmed. Jesus couches his non-judgmental standard in decidedly personal terms, perhaps building on the principal that if God does not judge, what right do humans have to do so.

Do not judge, so that you may not be judged. For with the judgment you make you will be judged, and the measure you give will be the measure you get. Why do you see the speck in your neighbor's eye, but do not notice the log in your own eye? Or how can you say to your neighbor, "Let me take the speck out of your eye," while the log is in your eye? You hypocrite, first take the log out of your own eye, and then you will see clearly to take the speck out of your neighbor's eye. (Matt. 7:1-5)

Critically judging others keeps us locked into our established ego boundaries. Our likes and dislikes shield us from change, from opening our hearts and minds to reality as it is, a reality that is always bigger than our little selves. Criticism is the frontline, defensive mechanism of the ego. It is the number one strategy of the ego to protect its domain and thereby prevent the expanding awareness, acceptance, and understanding that would weaken its hold on how we engage life.

Jesus uses the principle of non-judgment to introduce the well-established psychological axiom known as projection. Projection is the dynamic expression of the shadow, a major theme in depth psychology. The shadow is the unconscious reservoir of all the aspects of ourselves that we do not like, everything about our personal nature that we want to keep hidden from ourselves and others. Projection causes us to see these undesirable qualities in others and not in ourselves. We literally project these disliked features onto others where we can more 'safely' dislike them. Psychospiritual growth proceeds by discovering in ourselves what we dislike in others (and what we admire, since projection also works with positive qualities). The stronger the emotion that accompanies the judgment of another, the more important it is for personal growth to find the corollary in oneself of that which is criticized, bring it into consciousness, acknowledge, accept, and thoroughly befriend it. This is the process of re-owning the disowned. The disowned and projected feature need not be identical to what is criticized, but it will be associated in some fashion. A kind of ruthlessly honest self-introspection is always required in order to move from the projection to the disowned feature in ourselves. Depth psychologists call projection a 100%, airtight rule. It is one of the most powerful instruments of personal transformation, and clearly noted by Jesus 2000 years ago.[15]

"In everything do to others as you would have them do to you" (Matt. 7:12). Known as the Golden Rule, this verse provides an excellent principle for ethical action. More broadly, it tells us how to interact with others in our daily life whether a moral issue is at stake or not. The Golden Rule aligns with the injunction to love others as we love ourselves. With slightly different emphases, these two teachings highlight the fact of interpersonal unity. Even in our apparent individuality we are linked to others in a single beingness. I am you; you are me; we are one. When praying and meditating with like-minded others, a melting and conjoining presence arises that unites all as one. The usual sense of being separate and unconnected dissipates. Our usual self-consciousness evaporates.

"Enter through the narrow gate; for the gate is wide and the road is easy that leads to destruction, and there are many who take it. For the gate is narrow and the road is hard that leads to life, and there are few who find it" (Matt. 7:13-14). The discipline required for transformation is arduous. The journey is likely to be lonely; our deepest sentiments and values are not likely to be those of the prevailing culture. 'Destruction' is usually understood in exoteric Christianity as Hell, a place of everlasting punishment for sinners. But it can also be seen as the suffering experienced in this life by those who live selfishly, out of their contracted egos.

"Everyone then who hears these words of mine and acts on them will be like a wise man who built his house on rock. The rain fell, the floods came, and the winds blew and beat on that house, but it did not fall, because it had been founded on rock" (Matt. 7:24-25). Jesus indicates that belief alone is not enough; acting on his teaching is required. One of the main reasons so many from the West have gravitated to Eastern religions is because these religions offer specific paths, well-defined disciplines, prescribed practices by means of which one can acknowledge and develop one's spiritual intuitions. A careful reading of the gospels demonstrates—as we are seeing—that transformational principles are abundant. They are also to be found in the writings of Paul, James, and others. Unfortunately, many forms of Christianity became so sidetracked by doctrine and ritual that actual practice, the *sine qua non* of transformation, virtually disappeared.

In his teaching, Jesus frequently used parables, short stories with a gripping appeal and a metaphorical meaning. Since parables invoke the heart and the mind, thereby actively engaging the hearer in their interpretation, they tend to drive their point deeper into consciousness. About two dozen parables are found in the synoptic gospels. A typical but particularly striking one is the parable of the Good Samaritan (Luke 10:30-37). Jesus told this parable to a lawyer who was actually testing Jesus on the scope of 'neighbor'. The lawyer wanted to know precisely who should receive the kind of love Jesus was promoting, the love of neighbor as oneself.

> A man was going down from Jerusalem to Jericho, and fell into the hands of robbers, who stripped him, beat him, and went away, leaving him half dead. Now by chance a priest was going down that road; and when he saw him, he passed by on the other side. So likewise, a Levite, when he came to the place and saw him, passed by on the other side. But a Samaritan while traveling came near him; and when he saw him, he was moved to pity. He went to him and bandaged his wounds, having poured oil and wine on them. Then he put him on his own animal, brought him to an inn, and took care of him. The next day he took out two denarii, gave them to the innkeeper, and said, 'Take care of him; and when I come back, I will repay you whatever more you spend.' Which of these three, do you think, was a neighbor to the man who fell into the hands of the robbers?

When the lawyer replied, "The one who showed him mercy," Jesus told him to "go and do likewise." The lawyer, a Pharisee, may have avoided naming the merciful traveler "the Samaritan," as Jesus had done, because of the centuries-long enmity between Jews and Samaritans. He, like most Jews of his day, probably could not conceive of a Samaritan as good. Thus, Jesus not only described an act of mercy in this parable but also, attempting to dispel a long-standing prejudice, showed how the category of neighbor includes, and therefore, eliminates enemies. According to Jesus' ethic of love, enemies too are neighbors.

Most of Jesus' parables concern the Kingdom of God, a major category in his overall teaching. His parables and sayings indicate that he thought of the Kingdom of God as a present reality and a future event, a Kingdom that is already present as well as one that will come soon, in fact, within the lifetime of some of those currently alive. Jews had long looked foreword to the coming Messiah who would establish the Kingdom of God on earth. Jesus countered the common Jewish expectation when he declared (Luke 17:20-21) that "the kingdom of God is not coming with things that can be observed," and continued, "the kingdom of God is among you." The last phrase can be translated "is within you," which is the most widely held view among Christians.

Exoterically, several views of the Kingdom exist; some believe it is a Kingdom on earth at the end of time when Christ will reign; others believe it refers to Heaven where the saved will live forever. Esoterically, the Kingdom of God names a state of consciousness realizable through higher states of awareness. Metaterically, it is a metaphor describing reality as seen with nondual awareness.

A representative parable on the Kingdom is that of the Sower (Mark 4:3-8).

A sower went out to sow. And as he sowed, some seed fell on the path, and the birds came and ate it up. Other seed fell on rocky ground, where it did not have much soil, and sprang up quickly, since it had no depth of soil. And when the sun rose, it was scorched; and since it had no root, it withered away. Other seed fell among thorns, and the thorns grew up and choked it, and it yielded no grain. Other seed fell into good soil and brought forth grain, growing up and increasing and yielding thirty and sixty and a hundredfold.

Like most of Jesus' parables, the meaning of this one is not immediately obvious. Jesus explained to his disciple why he disguised his teaching in enigmatic stories (Mark 4:11f): "To you has been given the secret of the kingdom of God, but for those outside, everything comes in parables; in order that they may indeed look, but not perceive, and may listen, but not understand." Jesus here introduces the standard esoteric principle of not offering spiritual truth to those too immature or biased to understand it properly. After explaining his reason for the use of obscure parables, Jesus indicated that the parable of the Sower describes different human responses to God's Word. Building on Jesus' deciphering for his followers, Christians see the sower as Christ, the seed as the gospel, and the ground as the response of different kinds of people.

Jesus set a high standard for those who acknowledge him as teacher and guide. "If any want to become my followers, let them deny themselves and take up their cross daily and follow me. For those who want to save their life will lose it, and those who lose their life for my sake will save it. What does it profit them if they gain the whole world, but lose or forfeit themselves" (Luke 9:23-25). Psychospiritually, 'cross' refers to subjection of the ego, the refusal to allow self-preference to override regard and loving kindness for all humans; some would say, all forms of life.

Jesus lived an exemplary life, demonstrating the quality of life expected from his followers. In his teaching and in his life he stressed humility and service. "Whoever wishes to be great among you must be your servant, and whoever wishes to be first among you must be your slave; just as the Son of man came not to be served but to serve" (Matt. 20:26-28). Discipleship, Jesus insisted, requires a deep and pervasive attitude of selfless giving. A rich young man once asked Jesus what he must do to have eternal life. Jesus replied (Matt. 19:21, 24): "If you wish to be perfect, go, sell you possessions, and give the money to the poor, . . . and then come, follow me." He went on to say: "It is easier for a camel to go through the eye of a needle than for someone who is rich to enter the kingdom of God."

Jesus knew how wealth causes attachment and thereby distracts from spiritual life. The sacrifice inherent in discipleship is indicated by Jesus when he said of himself, when answering a man who volunteered to follow him (Matt. 8:20): "Foxes have holes, and birds of the air have nests; but the Son of man has nowhere to lay his head." A literal interpretation concludes that Jesus simply had no home to which he could retire. A metaphorical interpretation reveals a broader significance: Jesus was unattached to the common sources of comfort and security. By right of his commitment to God alone, he was as free as foxes and birds.

Last Days: Trial, Crucifixion, Resurrection

Jesus' teaching and manner of living did not endear him to the traditional practitioners of established religion. He chose his disciples from the margins of society, fishermen and tax collectors, and directed most of his preaching and healing to the poor and downtrodden. He was unimpressed by honor and social status, valuing character above reputation. He accorded equal worth to Gentile and Jew, slave and free, female and male, poor and rich. His very presence was an indictment against those who preferred the status quo. He often chastised the Pharisees, Sadducees, scribes, and priests for their hypocrisy and narrow sectarian interests. When the Pharisees condemned his disciples for breaking some of their customs, such as not washing their hands before eating, he accused them of violating divine law for the sake of their traditions. Jesus openly healed on the Sabbath, in defiance of the Pharisees. The

Gospel of Matthew (21:12) reports that Jesus once "entered the temple and drove out all who were selling and buying in the temple, and he overturned the tables of the money changers and the seats of those who sold doves."

Jesus' ministry was a threat to conventional religion; he was a reformer who was seen by some, particularly those with much to lose, as a revolutionary. When he gained more and more of a following among the masses, some began to see him as a champion of the Jews against the oppression of the Romans, perhaps even as a potential king. Such views brought Jesus to the attention of the governing authorities. They had already faced popular uprisings and self-proclaimed saviors. Roman officials were alert and responsive to any perceived threat to their sovereignty and control of the populace.

Not long after his triumphal entry into Jerusalem, the day Christians celebrate as Palm Sunday, Jesus gathered his closest disciples together for a final meal in an upper room of a Jerusalem home. There he washed the feet of his disciples, demonstrating the humility and service he expected of them. Then he served them bread and wine, identifying the bread with his body and the wine with his blood. After the meal, Jesus took the disciples to Gethsemane, a secluded place where he could pray. Matthew (26:39) reports that "he threw himself on the ground and prayed, 'My Father, if it is possible, let this cup pass from me; yet not what I want but what you want.'"

Soon after Jesus' agonizing prayer, he was betrayed by Judas, one of his chosen disciples. Judas came with a crowd of people carrying weapons. Jesus was captured and taken to the Sanhedrin, a court probably comprised of both religious and political leaders. Mark (14:55, 61-62) reports that "the chief priests and the whole council were looking for testimony against Jesus to put him to death; but they found none." The high priest asked Jesus, "Are you the Messiah, the Son of the Blessed One?" Jesus replied, "I am." Jesus was then condemned as deserving death. He was blindfolded, beaten, and spit upon. Nearby, when asked if he was a follower of Jesus, Peter denied knowing him.*

Jesus was taken before Pontius Pilate, governor of Judea, and Herod Antipas, tetrarch or king of Galilee, who was visiting Jerusalem at the time. Jesus refused to defend himself, or to respond to the charges leveled against him, mainly that he stirred up the people and claimed to be King of the Jews. Neither Pilate nor Herod found any crime in Jesus worthy of death, but, pressured by the people, Pilate issued the death warrant. His soldiers took Jesus away, stripped and beat him, spit on him, put a crown of thorns on his head and ridiculed him by shouting, "Hail, King of the Jews." Jesus was taken to Golgotha, the Place of the Skull, where his hands and feet were nailed to a cross. From the cross, while being mocked and jeered, Jesus prayed (Luke 23:34): "Father, forgive them; for they do not

---

* Some biblical scholars believe that the role of "the Jews" in Jesus' death is overplayed and misleading in the gospels. They base this interpretation on the late date of the gospels, perhaps 40 years and more after the crucifixion, when Christians were trying to disassociate themselves from Jews because of the Jewish rebellion against the Romans at that time, and also because the Jews had refused to accept Jesus as a spiritual reformer rather than just a political messiah. By this time also the nascent Christian community was directing its evangelism more toward Gentiles than Jews. Further, the sympathetic portrayal of Pilate, influenced by the above motives, stands in stark contrast to his depiction as a cruel despot in other historical records. Finally, scholars who see Jesus principally as a political force believe that he was crucified because that was a method the Roman authorities preferred for those deemed a threat to security. At most it seems that only a few of the Jewish authorities were opposed to Jesus, not the masses. The anti-Semitism provoked by the view set forth in the gospels is one of the great tragedies of history.

know what they are doing." After several hours he cried out (Matt. 27:46): "My God, my God, why have you forsaken me?" Finally, he exclaimed (Luke 23:46): "Father, into your hands I commend my spirit." His body was released to a disciple, Joseph of Arimathea, who placed it in a tomb.

At dawn on the third day, a Sunday, three of Jesus' followers went to his tomb and took spices with which to anoint Jesus' body. They found the tomb empty and were told that Jesus had risen. Overwhelmed with fright, they ran to tell the other disciples, many of whom disbelieved. On several occasions during the following weeks, Jesus appeared to various followers. Some did not recognize him until he showed them the scars on his hands and feet. According to Luke 24:46-51, he appeared to some of his disciples and explained how his life and mission were a fulfillment of scripture: "Thus it is written, that the Messiah is to suffer and to rise from the dead on the third day, and that repentance and forgiveness of sins is to be proclaimed in his name to all nations." After this he led them out of the city. "While he was blessing them, he withdrew from them and was carried up into heaven." Only Luke reports the Ascension, which occurred forty days after the Resurrection.

Views of Jesus the Christ: Biblical, Theological, Psychospiritual, Metateric

Jesus himself recognized the importance of his identity being properly known. On at least one occasion, he asked his disciples (Matthew 16:13-18): "Who do people say that the Son of Man is?" Their answers included John the Baptist, Elijah, Jeremiah, and other prophets. Since all of these were dead at the time and neither Jesus nor Matthew denied reincarnation, the view must have been commonly held. Although almost universally disclaimed in churches today, reincarnation was accepted in the church for several centuries before being finally banned.

Jesus continued his query by asking: "But who do you say that I am?" Peter replied by identifying Jesus as the Christ. Jesus accepted this designation and blessed Peter by declaring that it was God who revealed the title to him. Jesus went on to say: "And I tell you, you are Peter, and on this rock I will build my church." The Greek form of Peter's name is *petros* and the Greek for rock is *petra*. Some believe Jesus was making a play on words here. Be that as it may, interpretation of Jesus' statement provides the occasion for two irreconcilable views that support the theological positions of both the Roman Catholic Church and the Protestant churches. The Roman Church believes that rock is a direct reference to Peter and that this provides the biblical basis for the papacy, Peter being the first pope. Protestants, on the other hand, believe that rock refers to the faith Peter exhibited in identifying Jesus as the Christ; therefore, personal faith in Jesus as the Christ is the foundation of the church. These conflicting views demonstrate conclusively that the issue of biblical interpretation arises outside the Bible itself and therefore must be answered outside the text by readers themselves.

Jesus often referred to himself as Son of Man and Son of God. His favorite self-designation seems to have been Son of Man, a title found eighty-two times in the four gospels and used by Jesus himself on all but two of these times. Some biblical scholars and theologians link Jesus' use of the title with its appearance in the Old Testament book of Daniel (7:13). They argue that Jesus used the designation to affirm his messianic role as one who would usher in a new kingdom of divine rule for God's people. It is equally possible, however, to understand the title as Jesus' way of identifying himself with humankind at large, of playing down distinctions between himself and others. Jesus clearly identified with the common people. There is much evidence in the gospels indicating that he regarded himself as one among many. The second self-reference Jesus used most often was Son of God.

Since everyone is a creation or child of God, this epithet also linked him with all of humanity. Even though this interpretation of these two titles is uncommon in theological and biblical circles, it accords well with a metateric understanding of the consciousness of one who has transcended duality.

The traditional and the metateric interpretations are not contradictory but closely linked. As the Messiah (Hebrew) and the Christ (Greek), i.e., the Anointed One, Jesus would have seen himself as one bringing the Kingdom of God into reality, a Kingdom founded on the equal worth of all humans, a Kingdom without social distinctions, no Jew or Gentile, no male or female, no rich or poor. Thus, both expressions, Son of Man and Son of God, reveal the absence of a self-sense that regards oneself as superior or special in reference to others. If ego is understood as the separate-self-sense, Jesus in this sense was without an ego. As we have seen, he regarded himself as intimately linked with others. His mission was dedicated to the eradication of artificial barriers, barriers created by humans, barriers not inherent in the human heart/mind.

This same mind of inclusiveness and wholeness is reflected in John 14:6: "I am the way, and the truth, and the life. No one comes to the Father except through me." Although this verse is frequently cited by exoteric Christians to support their view of Christianity as the one, true religion, other interpretations suggest something quite different. One of the reasons John wrote his gospel reaches an entirely different understanding. According to this view, the declaration reflects the particular aim of the Fourth Gospel to show that the Christians of John's day, rather than separating from and denying the Jewish faith, were affirming it through their special allegiance to Jesus as the long-awaited Messiah, much as other Jews did through Moses and the prophets.[16]

An anonymous fourteenth-century text, *Theologia Germanica*, argues that John 14:6 calls for Christians to embody the same quality of life that Christ exhibited. This is what will enable them to come to the Father. To this end, it asserts: "A man must first wholly deny himself and willingly forsake all things for God's sake, and must give up his own will, and all his natural inclinations, and purge and cleanse himself thoroughly from all sins and evil ways." The effect of this quality of life is that "God Himself becomes the man, so that nothing is left that is not God or of God;" thus, God "lives, knows, works, loves, wills, does, and refrains in the man."[17]

One can also read the text to indicate that if one is going to understand God as Father in the sense in which Jesus did, one must cultivate the same quality of mind as that of Jesus the Christ. A psychospiritual, mystical interpretation understands the text, therefore, to mean that one must have the same mind as Jesus in order to come to God as Jesus knew him. 'I' in the text refers not to the historical person, Jesus of Nazareth, but to the quality of mind that marked Jesus as the Christ, a consciousness that united him in full and perfect harmony with God. Therefore, it may be called Christ Consciousness, boundless and inclusive. It is precisely this consciousness that is the way, truth, and life. Theosis, to use the Greek Orthodox term, occurs by means of developing the mind of Christ, which is entirely possible for those willing to practice according to the teachings of the New Testament and those added by later Christians, especially the mystics. The verse that provides the title of this book supports this interpretation: "Have this mind in you that was also in Christ Jesus." (See below for further discussion.)

Christ himself prayed for his disciples to develop this consciousness that unites with God. In the prayer that John records as Jesus' last before his crucifixion, sometimes called the High Priestly Prayer, Jesus asks (John 17:11, 21): "May [they] be one, as we are one," and "As you, Father, are in me and I am in you, may they also be in us." Many years before the Fourth Gospel was written, the Apostle Paul seems to have experienced this divine indwelling. He testified (Gal. 2:20): "It is no longer I who live, but it is Christ who lives in me."

Dogma and doctrine, products of theological reflection on Christ and his mission, have proven central and determinative in Christianity. For many if not most Christians, right belief is what determines their religion. Over the centuries, a number of creeds have been crafted by theologians of the church. These testimonials of faith are designed to express and affirm the main doctrines of Christianity. Representative of these is the Nicene Creed, adopted by the Council of Nicaea in 325, which addresses, among other topics, the Incarnation and the Trinity.

I believe in one God the Father Almighty, Maker of heaven and earth, and of all things visible and invisible.

And in one Lord Jesus Christ, the only-begotten Son of God; begotten of his Father before all worlds, God of God, Light of Light, Very God of Very God; begotten, not made; being of one substance with the Father; by whom all things were made; who for us men and for our salvation came down from heaven, and was incarnate by the Holy Ghost of the Virgin Mary, and was made man; and was crucified also for us under Pontius Pilate; he suffered and was buried; and the third day he rose again according to the Scriptures; and ascended into heaven, and sitteth on the right hand of the Father; and he shall come again, with glory, to judge both the quick and the dead; whose kingdom shall have no end.

And I believe in the Holy Ghost, the Lord, and Giver of Life, who proceedeth from the Father and the Son; who with the Father and the Son together is worshipped and glorified, who spoke by the prophets; and I believe in one catholic and apostolic Church; I acknowledge one baptism for the remission of sins; and I look for the resurrection of the dead, and the life of the world to come. Amen.

While this creed is not the oldest and many others have been composed since, it is one that articulates the core beliefs of traditional Christianity. It is worth noting that creeds have both united and divided Christians; a specific creed unites those who accept its formulations while excluding those who do not. Some churches have refused to form creeds because of their divisive potential.

As seen in the Nicene Creed, theological reflection on Christ and his relation to God has given rise to the doctrines of the Incarnation and the Trinity. These are the two main and most distinctive doctrines of Christianity. While parallels are found in other religions, notably Hinduism, the Incarnation and Trinity receive distinctive interpretation in Christianity and are foundational and central. Any faith purporting to be Christian requires an interpretation of these doctrines that demonstrates some continuity with Christianity as a religion.

By right of the Incarnation, Jesus of Nazareth becomes the Christ of faith. Without the Incarnation, Christianity would not have arisen as a distinct religion. Thus, the Incarnation is the core reality and doctrine of the Christian faith. Incarnation addresses the dual nature of Jesus the Christ; asserting that he is wholly and indivisibly human and divine at one and the same time. Recognizing the essential nonduality in the seemingly two-fold nature was a brilliant discovery that releases extraordinary power for transformation.

Neither the term incarnation nor the concept appears in the New Testament. However, the building blocks for the doctrine are there. The opening chapter of the Fourth Gospel, especially the Prologue (John 1:1-5), reflects a metaphysical and spiritual view of Christ that provides scriptural support for the later formulation of the doctrine. "In the beginning was the Word, and the Word was with God, and the Word was God. He was in the beginning with God. All things came into being through him, and without him not one thing came into being. What has come into being in him was life, and the life was the light of all people. The light shines in the darkness, and the darkness did not overcome it." A few verses later (14, 18) John identifies Jesus as the pre-existent Word and adds: "No one has ever seen God. It is God the only Son, who is close to the Father's heart, who has made him known." In 14:9, John has Jesus say: "Whoever has seen me has seen the Father." Colossians (1:15, 19) refers to Christ as "the image of the invisible God," and then asserts that "in him all the fullness of God was pleased to dwell." Building on the above, Irenaeus, a second-century theologian, declared that "the Father is that which is invisible about the Son, the Son is that which is visible about the Father."[18] In summary, the orthodox view throughout the history of the church has been that Incarnation means that Jesus the Christ is a single person with two natures, neither of which diminishes the other. He is equally, wholly, and integrally divine and human.

But must incarnation be restricted to Christ? Increasing numbers of Christians are questioning if not rejecting the notion of original sin, a view that demeans our innate nature as well as the good intention of the Creator God. Why would God create humans with a depraved nature? Similarly, why would God create humans with sexuality and then declare it sinful or evil? Is a virgin birth required for humans to be born pure? Given these changing views among Christians as they attain a more rational, less mythic outlook, some are beginning to claim that every human is inherently human and divine, not just Jesus the Christ. These Christians strive for a perfect integration and expression of the two natures in themselves by drawing on several resources: (1) surrendering to Christ as the Exemplar *par excellence*, (2) drawing on the power released through Christ's life, including the Crucifixion, Resurrection and Ascension, (3) opening to the presence and guidance of the Holy Spirit, (4) adhering to the teachings and practices outlined in the New Testament and those developed by Christ's followers over the centuries.

Believing that we are born depraved and condemned is a negative and debilitating view that only a continually reinforced myth can hold in place. One can not help wondering how much of the support for the traditional view is motivated by the desire to maintain the ecclesiastical status quo. We are increasingly entering an age when many feel committed to developing a faith that is personally meaningful rather than simply believing someone else's beliefs. Questioning traditional doctrines indicates dissatisfaction with a religion centered in belief and a growing desire for an experiential relationship to and with the divine. This revisionist interpretation of the Incarnation, by extending it to all humans, adds personal responsibility and motivation to overcome and transcend those elements of our humanness that occluded the full manifestation of our divine nature, those elements, for example, that were discussed above in terms of the shadow and that will be treated below in terms of sin or estrangement. To know that divinity pervades one's humanity is to inspire great effort to more fully discover and manifest that divinity.

As seen in previous chapters, the world religions usually identify a fundamental predicament that disturbs human life and then offer a resolution. In the case of Christianity, the predicament is sin and the resolution is variously named salvation, redemption, forgiveness, justification, regeneration, atonement, sanctification. Each of these is a particular way of understanding reconciliation, the process by which sin is nullified and, therefore, the beginning of personal transformation in Christianity. Several standard activities, doctrines, and rituals—such as confession, repentance, restitution, baptism, and Eucharist—support these primary means of gaining release from the binding power of sin.

In our time, many find the notion of sin wanting, if not abhorrent, especially when it is narrowly and rigidly defined. Paul Tillich, among others, has rescued sin from obsolescence and restored it to its rightful position as a basic and undeniable feature of our individual and social human life.[19] Tillich has shown that the concept of sin is relevant in modern times. He has done this by demonstrating that every instance of so-called sin is one of estrangement, a case where a split occurs within the individual, between persons, and between the individual and God. For Tillich, existence itself implies estrangement since we are locked in time and space and, therefore, separated from the eternal and infinite. But sin compounds this separation by creating additional separations that keep us from realizing that Ultimacy is also immanent, here and now.

We have previously noted that the simple fact of being human entails having an ego, the separate-self-sense that causes one to feel disconnected and apart. Feeling distinct and separate from others is built into our humanness. Sin, however, adds enormously to this disjunction and produces guilt in the sinner, conflict and disharmony between persons, and disruption of one's relationship to God. Each of these is clearly a case of estrangement. The disruptive effect of sin, i.e., estrangement, is seen in each of the so-called Seven Deadly Sins: pride, envy, covetousness, anger, sloth, lust, and gluttony. Fear, though not thought of as sin, causes anxiety and psychic contraction that disrupts, even ruptures, one's sense of harmony and safety. The writer of 1 John 4:18 was aware of the estranging effect of fear and the healing power of love when he wrote that "perfect love casts out fear."

Within the human realm, the primary uniting force is love. In every instance of love, that which was separated becomes conjoined. Love is for humans what fusion is in the physical realm, the power of connecting and integrating. Love is the restorative power in all forms of Christianity, whether exoteric, esoteric, or metateric, the means by which reconciliation and healing occur. The root meaning of healing is making whole, that is, overcoming the disruption and division that accompanies physical illness or psychospiritual estrangement. Healing and wholeness occur through love; love restores and rejoins. Reconciliation, by whatever name, overcomes estrangement through the uniting power of love.

Early in this chapter reference was made to love as the reason for the Incarnation, for God entering history as Christ. Christians believe that the love of God is conveyed most perfectly and fully through Christ's willingness to endure crucifixion in order to provide the means by which humans might overcome the divisive nature of sin and receive the three-fold reconciliation: to God, to others, and in themselves. Various doctrines and theories have been constructed to show how crucifixion gives rise to reconciliation. These include such 'explanations' as: sacrifice, ransom, expiation, pardon, satisfaction, payment of a penalty, etc.

Though unquestioned by most conventional Christians, others find inadequacies in these views. They offend moral sensitivity because they imply a God who requires the death of an innocent person so that others, i.e., sinners, can be reconciled to him.[20] Some believe that such a view undermines the 'character' of God and weakens the dignity of humans. Not only is this undesirable and unjust, it also removes responsibility from the individual and places it on a heroic 'Savior' who lived and died in the distant past. The traditional theories of reconciliation transfer the intention to "work out one's own salvation" to simply believing that one's salvation was accomplished on the cross long ago. In this fashion, Christianity becomes a matter of belief rather than an experiential religion of ongoing personal transformation through surrender, love, humility, selfless service, and other practices.

The words of John 3:16, "God so loved the world that he gave his only Son," profoundly moves the hearts of countless Christians, even those exploring new ways of understanding the divine/human Christ whose self-giving life continues to inspire. In his letter to the church at Philippi (Phil. 2:5-8), Paul summarizes the timeless, transformational challenge to every serious Christian: "Let the same mind be in you that was in Christ Jesus, who though in the form of God, did not regard equality with God as something to be exploited, but emptied himself, taking the form of a slave, being born in human likeness. And being found in human form, he humbled himself and became obedient to the point of death—even death on a cross."

Christians who understand themselves to be equally divine and human, divine because created in the image of God, are profoundly grateful to Jesus the Christ for making this known, and for providing the perfect example of how to neutralize the human factors that tend to hide the divine. By cultivating the mind of Christ, i.e., the emptying or self-giving mind, in one's daily activities whenever there is opportunity, one becomes more Christ-like and shows forth one's divine nature. This is the altruistic mind that serves without judging the 'worthiness' of others, the mind of God who "shows no partiality" (Gal. 2:6). In a word, it is the self-giving, impartial, non-judging mind that manifests one's inherent divine nature. This is the mind that led Christ to the cross, the mind that accepts his challenge in Luke 9:23: "If any want to become my followers, let them deny themselves and take up their cross daily and follow me." This mind lives according to Paul's statement in 1 Cor. 13:4-5: "Love is patient; love is kind; love is not envious or boastful or arrogant or rude. It does not insist on its own way; it is not irritable or resentful." This mind grinds away at the self-aggrandizing ego. This is the self-denying, other-preferring mind that purifies the separate-self-sense and leads to the metateric awareness that sees all things as divine. Personal transformation does not occur by believing that an historical event two thousand years ago somehow magically enables one to be free of sin today. Rather, this impeccable state occurs by doing what Christ did and by doing it daily, by seeing the absolute equality of all humans and refusing to act on any impulse that gives oneself an advantage over others. To "know the truth" that "will make you free," one must know and live "the wisdom from above" that is "without a trace of partiality or hypocrisy" (John 8:32, James 3:17).

Resurrection and Ascension are two additional beliefs on which most Christians base their overall understanding of who Jesus the Christ was and is. Can these doctrines be redeemed from exclusive significance as traditionally understood and seen as relevant in the contemporary practice of Christianity? Yes they can, if they are understood as psychospiritual processes. Accordingly, they will be seen to occur even now within those who undergo crucifixion as indicated above. Unlike the Crucifixion, Christ's Resurrection and Ascension were not actions he undertook but events that happened to him. Similarly, resurrection and ascension will take place in the soul, the psyche, the mind of those who act self-sacrificially. These 'events' happen naturally, automatically, by grace, i.e., without direct, human intervention. They take place beyond the range of awareness even though one can be aware that they have occurred. This is clear because of the remarkable shift in one's personal felt-sense.

Crucifixion, resurrection, and ascension may occur at almost any time in our daily lives. Crucifixion occurs when one denies the ego its self-centered pursuits. This often gives rise to anxiety; one's self-sense feels threatened. In extreme instances, when one is faced with a crucial decision that causes one to feel personal 'loss', one may actually feel as if a kind of death is occurring. For example, suppose you are a staunch believer in a particular doctrine or practice of Christianity. A friend is equally devoted to different understanding and the two of you are arguing. Particularly if you are 'losing' the argument, you will feel threatened by loss, experience intense negativity, inner contraction and heatedness, and hardening of your self-sense. A decided shift will take place, however, if you have done sufficient prior transformative work and can recognize that you don't *need* to win, that the whole matter can be left to 'the will of God'—or however you prefer to name (or not name) it. If you thoroughly trust, affirming something like 'it will be as it will be', you will suddenly experience relaxation into freedom, an inner movement of openness and acceptance that can be named—and quite properly, given our psychospiritual nature—resurrection and ascension, resurrection from contraction and estrangement, and ascension to freedom and wholeness. Thus, Crucifixion, Resurrection, and Ascension become not just beliefs derived from the beliefs of others but personally experienced realities. (Relinquishing arguments with others does not mean suppressing one's convictions; it only means that one does not need others to agree in order to feel confident, safe, and whole. By accepting the fact that difference is an inevitable feature of life, and by avoiding making someone else wrong, one will reside in a higher and more inclusive state of awareness.)

As we have seen, resurrection and ascension result naturally by submitting to one's personal 'cross' when occasion presents itself, i.e., submitting to the crucifixion of one's dominating ego. In addition, through applying this practice and others over time, one eventually resurrects from lower and more restricted stages of consciousness and ascends to higher and more inclusive levels. Concerted practice leads eventually to transcendence of strictly rational levels of being to the greater inclusiveness of transrational ways of being and seeing.

Developing from the doctrine of the Incarnation is the doctrine of the Trinity, which joins the Holy Spirit with God and Christ. In several texts, the New Testament opens the door to later Trinitarian thinking by linking God the Father, Christ the Son, and the Holy Spirit. The main role of the Holy Spirit, according to Paul Tillich, is to establish spirit as the *telos* of life, the aim or goal. Tillich asserts: "*Telos* stands for an inner, essential, necessary aim, for that in which a being fulfils its own nature." He affirms that telos is "the most embracing, direct, and unrestricted symbol for the divine life."[21] The Holy Spirit pervades the cosmos as the active, divine principle of Ultimacy as Spirit. It is the channel of communication between God as Spirit, Christ as Spirit, and spirit as the essential nature of humans. The Holy Spirit instills and inspires divine qualities, the gifts of the Spirit such as love, joy, and peace.

Later theological thought grappled with the relationship between God, Christ, and Holy Spirit, eventually identifying them as three 'persons' in a single Godhead, each with distinct but overlapping roles. The Trinity reached its classical formulation in the fourth century but continues to be debated and reinterpreted to this day. The doctrine has its critics both inside and outside Christianity because it seems to depart from strict monotheism. How can Christ and the Holy Spirit each be God alongside God without this leading to three gods and weakening the singularity of the one God? Theologians admit that though Trinitarian thinking seems to contravene reason, it is not irrational or contradictory but paradoxical. Paul Tillich, for example, contends that the Trinitarian paradox "points to the fact that in God's acting finite reason is suspended but not annihilated." Paradox points "beyond the realm in which finite reason is applicable." He explains further: "Nothing divine is irrational—if irrational means contradicting reason—for reason is the finite manifestation of the divine Logos"; in other words, reason is a feature of our creation in the image of God. Tillich goes on to argue that it is "unity in a manifoldness of divine self-manifestation" that is decisive in the Trinity. Seeing God as ground (the Father), God as form (Christ), and God as act (Holy Spirit) is what "makes Trinitarian thinking meaningful."[22] God the Father is the Source of all that is, Christ is the full manifestation of God in human form, and the Holy Spirit is the active principle of the divine in humans specifically and the cosmos generally. Thus, the Trinity does not violate reason but transcends it by accounting for our lived experience, which includes but extends beyond reason. Reflection on the Trinity can disclose some of its profundity, but only from the metateric or nondual perspective can its so-called mystery be 'understood'.

Ken Wilber and the Integral Institute have introduced a way of approaching Ultimacy from the standpoint of the three-person grammatical perspective we learned in primary school.[23] Accordingly, God is related to in the first person as I, in the second person as Thou, and in the third person as He, She, or It. The model can be adapted to a new way of envisioning the Trinity, one that does not necessarily replace other Trinitarian views but enriches them by adding another perspective, a perspective of perspectives. This three-person approach is an integral understanding in which each person,

God, Christ, and Spirit, has its distinctive but overlapping role. The model provides a comprehensive understanding of Ultimacy that values each person of the Trinity and its special contribution to Christian experience.

According to the third person perspective, God as Holy Spirit is seen as the entire cosmos, embedded in the natural world and in sentient beings as that which constitutes their essence. Everything is permeated by spirit. This view sacralizes our everyday experience as we relate to others and the natural world. Environmentalism, for example, takes on a new, deeper, and more crucial significance. Our contact with other humans and living forms in particular takes on a holiness that adds meaning and value.

The second person perspective is informed by our relationship to Jesus the Christ. Here we face God as Thou, as one to whom we relate personally because of the Incarnation, because of what we have learned about God through the life of Jesus. Here we see God as personal and from this relationship spring love, devotion, and piety. We are overwhelmed by the love Jesus exemplified, seeing and feeling its melting and integrating power. Humility, gratitude, and devotion become our natural mode of life. Our spirituality becomes profoundly personal as we relate to others with increased warmth and empathy.

From the first person perspective, we face God as 'I', the one to whom Jesus referred when he said, "The Father and I are one" (John 10:30). This is God as Ultimacy. God as 'I' is the 'I' that is our deepest and most profound beingness. This is pure consciousness, distinguished from everything that otherwise is me. When we rest in pure 'I-ness', we are one with God. Awareness is boundless and timeless; time and space are transcended. This is the mystical or esoteric state where one becomes one with God and only God is. When emerging from this total oneness, we recognize that our ordinary human I is a derived I. Strictly speaking, only God is 'I'.

Summation

There is no Christianity apart from Jesus the Christ. How one thinks of him sets both the center and the parameter of one's view of Christianity. As argued earlier, there is value in distinguishing between the Jesus of history and the Christ of faith. In fact, the rational mind of the modern and postmodern period requires it. At the same time, the fullness of our experience as humans dictates that life not be limited to fact and reason. We need to find wholeness and meaningfulness in life.

Therefore, for those drawn to a transrational faith, one that honors reason without being bound by it, the reintegration of the Jesus of history and the Christ of faith becomes necessary. For those committed to the integration of heart and mind, a divided Jesus, a Jesus reduced to manhood, or a Jesus stripped of divinity, is a diluted Jesus. An integration of actual history and living myth is required for Jesus the Christ to be the Godman of faith. Jesus the Christ is the basis, the inspiration, and the power for personal transformation. He is the Exemplar who opens the door to Ultimacy. Jesus informs and Christ transforms. The Holy Spirit, unhampered by time and space, by history, by empirical limits, activates the integrated Christ as God and Jesus as man in the similarly incarnated human being, thereby releasing the transforming power of Ultimacy into the heart/mind of the surrendering, practicing Christian.

NOTES

1. See John Shelby Spong, *Why Christianity Must Change or Die:
    A Bishop Speaks to Believers in Exile.* (San Francisco: Harper,
    1998); John Shelby Spong, *A New Christianity for a New World:
    Why Traditional Faith is Dying and How a New Faith is Being
    Born.* (San Francisco: Harper, 2001).
2. John Shelby Spong, *Here I Stand: My Struggle for a Christianity
    of Integrity, Love, and Equality.* (San Francisco: Harper, 2000),
    300, 302.
3. Unless indicated otherwise, all biblical quotations are from the
    New Revised Standard Version.
4. Quoted in William Johnston, *Mystical Theology: The Science of
    Love.* (Maryknoll, NY: Orbis Books, 2004), 44.
5. http://www.vatican2.org, (accessed March 2, 2006).
6. See Richard E. Rubenstein, *When Jesus Became God: The
    Struggle to Define Christianity during the Last Days of Rome.*
    (San Diego: Harcourt, Inc., 1999).
7. Alan Richardson and John Bowden, eds., *The Westminster
    Dictionary of Christian Theology.* (Philadelphia: The Westminster
    Press, 1983), 167.
8. Marcus J. Borg, *Jesus: A New Vision.* (San Francisco: Harper,
    1987), 9.
9. Quotations are from "The Gospel of Thomas," (Thomas O.
    Lambdin, trans.) in James M. Robinson, gen. ed., *The Nag
    Hammadi Library in English.* 3rd rev. ed. (San Francisco: Harper,
    1990), 124-138.
10. Marcus Borg, *The Heart of Christianity: Rediscovering a Life
    of Faith.* (San Francisco: HarperCollins, 2003), 82-83. Other of
    Borg's books relevant to this study include: *Jesus: A New Vision.*
    (San Francisco: Harper, 1987); *Meeting Jesus Again for the First
    Time.* (San Francisco: Harper, 1994); and, with N.T. Wright, *The
    Meaning of Jesus: Two Visions.* (San Francisco: Harper, 1999).

11. Mark Allan Powell, *The Jesus Debate: Modern Historians Investigate the Life of Christ.* (Oxford, England: Lion Publishing, 1998), 80. Also published in the USA as *Jesus as a Figure in History.* (Louisville, Kentucky: Westminster John Knox Press, 1998).

12. Ibid, 60-68 et passim.

13. Soren Kierkegaard, *Purity of Heart is to Will One Thing.* (New York: Harper and Row, 1956).

14. Neil Douglas-Klotz, *The Hidden Gospel: Decoding the Spiritual Message of the Aramaic Jesus.* (Wheaton, Ill: Quest Books, 1999), 129.

15. A useful discussion of the shadow and projection can be found in Ken Wilber, *No Boundary: Eastern and Western Approaches to Personal Growth.* (Los Angeles: Center Publications, 1979).

16. John Shelby Spong, *The Sins of Scripture.* (San Francisco: Harper, 2005), 232-237.

17. James S. Cutsinger, ed., *Not of This World: A Treasury of Christian Mysticism.* (Boomington, IN: World Wisdom, 2003) 177, 180.

18. Quoted in John P. Keenan, *The Meaning of Christ: A Mahayana Theology.* (Maryknoll, NY: Orbis Books, 1989), 56.

19. Paul Tillich, *Systematic Theology: Three Volumes in One.* (New York: Harper & Row, Publishers, 1967), 2:44-59 et passim.

20. For a fuller development of this objection, see Uta Ranke-Heinemann, *Putting Away Childish Things: The Virgin Birth, the Empty Tomb, and Other Fairy Tales You Don't Need to Believe to Have a Living Faith.* Peter Heinegg (trans.), (New York: HarperCollins Publishers, 1994) 268-295.

21. Tillich, *Systematic Theology*, 1:249.

22. Ibid. 1:57; 2:284,293.

23. Ken Wilber, *Integral Spirituality: A Startling New Role for Religion in the Modern and Postmodern World.* (Boston: Integral Books, 2006) 158-161, 208; Terry Patten, et al. *My ILP Handbook: Getting Started with Integral Life Practice,* Version 1.0 (www.integralinstitute.org: Integral Institute, 2005) 70-71.

VI | Christianity: The Mind of Saints and Sages

*"I pray that you may have the power to comprehend, with all
the saints, what is the breadth and length and height and depth,
and to know the love of Christ that surpasses knowledge, so that
you may be filled with all the fullness of God."*—Eph. 3:18-19

*"Yet among the mature we do speak wisdom, though
it is not a wisdom of this age . . . . We speak God's
wisdom, secret and hidden . . . ."*—1 Cor. 2:6-7

*"The Christian of the future will be a mystic or
he will not exist at all."*—Karl Rahner

Saints and Sages Described and Distinguished

This chapter highlights and develops further the esoteric and
metateric dimensions of Christianity as seen in the lives of the
saints and sages of the tradition. The category of sage is rarely found
in Christianity and yet is a valid and necessary role to recognize.
Marcus Borg, an active member of the Jesus Seminar (mentioned in
the previous chapter), concludes that "the strongest consensus among
today's Jesus scholars" is that Jesus was "a teacher of wisdom—a

sage."[1] Because it is not a widespread view, the distinction between saints and sages is not well known in Christianity; the two holy persons are usually regarded simply as saints. This traditional way of regarding them is not invalid, but even as we have refined esotericism by singling out metateric experience and insight, making this a further category, there is merit in distinguishing between saints and sages by preferring the former title for those with unitive experience and the latter for those with nondual awareness. Both, of course, are mystics. Saints tend to think of God as personal; sages are more likely to regard Ultimacy as apersonal, neither personal nor nonpersonal, or, as we discovered in the first chapter, impersonal in Itself and personal in manifestation.

While there is great similarity in the personal values and qualities of saints and sages, and in the way they respectively live their lives, saints tend to focus on God and spirituality in the context of the church while sages orient themselves somewhat more toward life at large, including other religions. Sages are likely to be philosophically or theologically astute though probably not in a traditional way. They are less likely than saints to uphold traditional standards of belief and practice. They are more likely to push the boundaries of orthodoxy and may even be accused of heresy. Saints may have mystical visions of the divine realm while sages have insight into the most foundational and essential realities of life. To perhaps oversimplify, saints are pious and sages are wise. If a single, dominant quality is to characterize each, it is compassion or love for saints and wisdom or sagacity for sages. In some instances, the two qualities complement each other so integrally that a saint might well claim that compassion without wisdom is not truly compassion, with a sage asserting that wisdom uninformed by compassion is not really wisdom. Where love and wisdom seem balanced we may want to regard some as sagely saints and other as saintly sages.

In the Orthodox and Catholic Churches, saints have been formally recognized, are believed to reside in heaven, are worshiped or venerated, and serve as persons to whom prayers are offered. They may also be emulated. In Protestantism, saints are simply those who most thoroughly exemplify Christian values and from whom one can learn. Saints and sages in this study are ideal representatives of personal transformation. They are always mystics (though not all mystics, of course, will be saints or sages). They are offered not as objects of veneration but as examples of what is possible with sufficient commitment and discipline. Their experience, practice, and teaching are exemplary, instructive, and inspirational.

Saints and sages live highly disciplined lives; some undergo such ascetic practices as fasting and sleep reduction. They live lives of integrity and moral impeccability. They give great amounts of time to introspection, contemplation, and meditation. This contributes to their exceptional spiritual insight. Sainthood and sagehood are recognized by others, never self-proclaimed. Without a deeply ingrained and natural humility, each status is forfeited. Saints and sages know no hierarchy among humans. They associate comfortably with peasants and royalty, with poor and wealthy. They recognize the distinctions that ordinarily operate in society but attribute no ranking to them. They serve all impartially. Saints and sages have profound insight into human nature and the dynamics of life. This is reflected in the contented, peaceful, easeful, and joyful lives they live. This is what enables them to serve as guides and models for others.

In the biographical sketches of Christian saints and sages featured in this chapter, we will not distinguish between the two. As we have seen, categories and labels simultaneously foster understanding and, because they define, also limit and may be misleading. Since the development of understanding and openness are among the main objectives of this book, we will not name a specific person as a saint or sage but will suggest that certain persons exemplify the dominant qualities of one or the other. For example, among better known Christians, the lives of Francis of Assisi, Catherine of Siena, Julian of Norwich, Teresa of Avila, and John of the Cross mainly reflect the qualities of sainthood, while the lives of Origen, Evagrius, Meister Eckhart, Abhishiktananda, Thomas Merton, Bede Griffiths, and Desmond Tutu exhibit what we have identified as the predominant features of sagehood. But each of these mystics is sagacious and charitable. Each mirrors the infinite within finitude.

Saints and Sages of the New Testament

Jesus astounded those in his own hometown by the sophistication of his teaching. They were so amazed at his understanding and insights that they exclaimed (Matt. 13:54): "Where did this man get this wisdom?" Jesus taught a truth that leads to personal freedom and said to his followers (John 8:32): "If you continue in my word . . . , you will know the truth, and the truth will make you free." In one of the Beatitudes (Matt. 5:8), Jesus gave the basis for mystical awareness: "Blessed are the pure in heart, for they shall see God." "Seeing God" has taken two different turns in Christianity: (1) having visions of spiritual beings, usually in altered states of consciousness, e.g., seeing Jesus, angels, formally declared saints, etc., mainly characteristic of those we are calling saints, and (2) demonstrating exceptional insight into the realities of life and the cosmos, more the mark of sages. In both cases, "pure in heart" may be understood in modern idiom as indicating unwavering adherence to the highest moral and spiritual values and a resolute commitment to personal integrity.

Jesus' assertion (John 10:30), "The Father and I are one," is as unambiguous a mystical assertion as will be found anywhere. Similarly in John 14:11: "I am in the Father and the Father is in me." Referring to his disciples, Jesus prayed shortly before his crucifixion (John 17:11): "that they may be one, as we are one," thereby indicating that mystical realization was not something reserved for him alone. In this same High Priestly Prayer, as it is sometimes called, he also prayed (John 17:21): "As you, Father, are in me and I am in you, may they also be in us." Attesting to the timeless or eternal awareness of Jesus, John (8:58) has Jesus affirm: "Before Abraham was, I am." Minimally, this claim points to the realization among some first-century Christians that mystical awareness is not bound by historical time or geographical place.

Unlike John and the others disciples, the Apostle Paul (ca. 10-62) did not know Jesus in bodily form. He, of course, did know about Jesus from others and what he heard caused him at first to become the staunchest of persecutors. But what he came to know later of Christ through personal experience enabled him to become the staunchest of advocates. The importance of the Apostle Paul to the development of Christianity can hardly be overestimated. Sometimes called the Second Founder of the religion, he is acknowledged by conservative scholars as the author of thirteen epistles of the New Testament, one-fourth of its content, though other scholars argue that a few of these letters were probably written by followers. Paul undertook three extensive missionary journeys in his effort to found new churches. He remains unsurpassed among propagators of early Christianity.

Paul was born in Tarsus to devout Jewish parents. His earliest education probably came from his father, from whom he also learned the trade of tent making, a trade he drew upon later to support himself while spreading Christianity. Paul completed rabbinic training, and seems to have been as zealous in upholding Judaism as he would later be in spreading Christianity. He characterizes himself as one "circumcised on the eighth day, a member of the people of Israel, of the tribe of Benjamin, a Hebrew born of Hebrews; as to the law, a Pharisee; . . . as to righteousness under the law, blameless" (Phil. 3:5-6). Paul studied under one of the most famous rabbis of the time, Gamaliel, who was particularly known for his spirit of tolerance. When Peter and other apostles, because of their preaching in the name of Jesus, were brought before the Sanhedrin, a council of Jewish leaders, Gamaliel advised against harsh treatment: "If this plan or this undertaking is of human origin, it will fail; but if it is of

God, you will not be able to overthrow them—in that case you may even be found fighting against God" (Acts 5:38-39).

Paul did not absorb this spirit of tolerance from his teacher, at least not when he witnessed the dying of Stephen, a bold leader of the early church who was stoned to death for his preaching of Jesus as the Christ. Accused of speaking "blasphemous words against Moses and God," Stephen was attacked and dragged outside Jerusalem. Those stoning him "laid their coats at the feet of a young man named Saul [the Aramaic form of Paul]. While they were stoning Stephen, he prayed, 'Lord Jesus, receive my spirit.' Then he knelt down and cried out in a loud voice, 'Lord, do not hold this sin against them.' When he had said this, he died. And Saul approved of their killing him" (Acts 6:11; 7:58-60). But Paul's passive approval of the persecution of Christians soon became a zealous pursuit. It was not long until "Saul was ravaging the church by entering house after house; dragging off both men and women, he committed them to prison" (Acts 8:3). Paul openly confessed that prior to his conversion he was "as to zeal, a persecutor of the church" (Phil. 3:6).

The most complete account of Paul's dramatic conversion from chief persecutor to chief advocate is Luke's summary in Acts 9:1-19:

Meanwhile Saul, still breathing threats and murder against the disciples of the Lord, went to the high priest and asked him for letters to the synagogues at Damascus, so that if he found any who belonged to the Way, men or women, he might bring them bound to Jerusalem. Now as he was going along and approaching Damascus, suddenly a light from heaven flashed around him. He fell to the ground and heard a voice saying to him, 'Saul, Saul, why do you persecute me?' He asked, 'Who are you, Lord?' The reply came, 'I am Jesus, whom you are persecuting. But get up and enter the city, and you will be told what you are to do'. The men who were traveling with him stood speechless because they heard the voice, but saw no one. Saul got up from the ground, and though his eyes were open, he could see nothing so they led him into Damascus. For three days he was without sight and neither ate nor drank.

Now there was a disciple in Damascus named Ananias. The Lord said to him in a vision, 'Ananias'. He answered, 'Here I am, Lord'. The Lord said to him, 'Get up and go to the street called Straight, and at the house of Judas look for a man of Tarsus named Saul. At this moment he is praying, and he has seen in a vision a man named Ananias come in and lay his hands on him so that he might regain his sight'. But Ananias answered, 'Lord, I have heard from many about this man, how much evil he has done to your saints in Jerusalem; and here he has authority from the chief priests to bind all who invoke your name'. But the Lord said to him, 'Go, for he is an instrument whom I have chosen to bring my name before Gentiles and kings and before the people of Israel; I myself will show him how much he must suffer for the sake of my name'. So Ananias went and entered the house. He laid his hands on Saul and said, 'Brother Saul, the Lord Jesus, who appeared to you on your way here, has sent me so that you may regain your sight and be filled with the Holy Spirit'. And immediately something like scales fell from his eyes, and his sight was restored. Then he got up and was baptized, and after taking some food, he regained his strength.

After spending time with the Christians in Damascus, Paul began to preach the very message that had previously stirred his passionate opposition. He "became increasingly more powerful and confounded the Jews who lived in Damascus by proving that Jesus was the Messiah" (Acts 9:22). One of the effects of this preaching was that the former persecutor of Christians soon became a persecuted Christian himself. A plot against Paul's life was discovered and he was smuggled out of Damascus.

Early in his new career as a Christian and promoter of the faith, Paul spent three years in Arabia, perhaps in prayer and reflection about the radically new direction of his life, as well as in reinterpreting Jewish scripture so that it conformed to his own personal encounter with Jesus the Christ. The next quarter century he spent preaching the gospel, establishing new congregations of Christians throughout the Roman Empire, and writing letters designed to deepen the understanding and strengthen the faith of those who looked to him for guidance and support. The resolute nature of Paul's conversion may be gauged not only by his contributions to the formation of Christianity but also by the hardship and persecution he was willing to suffer in order to make these contributions. He summarizes these in a letter to the church at Corinth (2 Cor. 11:23-27).

> Five times I have received from the Jews the forty lashes minus one. Three times I was beaten with rods. Once I received a stoning. Three times I was shipwrecked; for a night and a day I was adrift at sea; on frequent journeys, in danger from rivers, danger from bandits, danger from my own people, danger from Gentiles, danger in the city, danger in the wilderness, danger at sea, danger from false brothers and sisters; in toil and hardship, through many a sleepless night, hungry and thirsty, often without food, cold and naked.

Paul's life of hardship ended in Rome where he was executed because of his faith. The details of his death are unknown. He was probably in his early fifties.

Paul's life and writings demonstrate that one need not have personal contact with a person to be profoundly influenced by him. Paul is unsurpassed among New Testament writers in the depth of his spiritual experience with Jesus the Christ. That this was a mystical connection is strongly suggested by his frequent use (about 150 times) of such phrases as "in Christ," "in the Lord," and "through Christ." The vision that led to his conversion may be regarded as mystical in the broad sense of the term. Another vision was of an even more elusive nature in that it did not lend itself to capture in words. Perhaps in an effort to avoid any suggestion of boasting, Paul introduces this vision without specific reference to himself (2 Cor. 12:2-4). "I know a person in Christ who fourteen years ago was caught up to the third heaven—whether in the body or out of the body I do not know; God knows. And I know that such a person—whether in the body or out of the body I do not know; God knows—was caught up into Paradise and heard things that are not to be told, that no mortal is permitted to repeat."

One of Paul's boldest statements concerning the extent to which Christ infused and ruled his life is found in Gal. 2:20: "it is no longer I who live, but it is Christ who lives in me." Paul's claim derived from his commitment and effort to imitate Christ in his own life, a charge he extended to others. In 1 Cor. 11:1 he wrote: "Be imitators of me, as I am of Christ." As Paul realized and taught, submitting to Christ as teacher and exemplar enables followers of Jesus to build on their inherent birthright as Children of God—that is, being created in the image of God—so that image eventually becomes likeness. This is the process of theosis or divination which, as we saw in the previous chapter, came to play an increasingly important role in subsequent Christianity, especially in its Eastern forms. Imitation is a psychospiritual practice which, when pursued with humility and reliance on grace, becomes not just conformity to Christ but life "in Christ". Faithfully and fully modeling one's inner and outer life on Jesus the Christ leads to the development of Christ consciousness.[2]

Paul's submission to Christ, coupled with his profound understanding of human nature and the psychospiritual process, enabled him to develop this abiding sense of oneness with Christ. The text from which this book takes its title is one such insight into both who Christ was and how transformation occurs (Phil. 2:5-8): "Have this mind in you that was also in Christ Jesus, who, though he was in the form of God, did not regard equality with God something to be grasped, but emptied himself, taking the form of a servant, being born in human likeness. And being found in human form, he humbled himself and became obedient to the point of death—even death on a cross."[3]

As discussed in the prior chapter, the transformational process entails developing one's inherent, divine nature by subjugating and neutralizing the self-preferential dimensions of one's conditioned nature. The Christian method of doing this—which parallels practices in the other world religions—is by following the example of Christ who humbly served others, even sacrificing his life in a resolute refusal to claim any privilege for himself that was not available to others. For the contemporary Christian, as we saw, this means sacrificing one's ego, one's separate and preferred self-sense. It is a daily, constant, on-going practice. As our ego diminishes, our divine nature manifests. In terms of growing a life that exhibits the highest values of personal transformation, no practice is more important than this one. We will return to it in the last chapter.

In Phil. 4:8, Paul underscores the importance of keeping positive thoughts in one's mind: "Whatever is true, whatever is honorable, whatever is just, whatever is pure, whatever is pleasing, whatever is commendable, if there is any excellence and if there is anything worthy of praise, think about these things." In the preceding verse, he notes that "the peace of God, which surpasses all understanding, will guard your hearts and your minds in Christ Jesus."

Paul knew the importance of harmony between the heart and the mind and emphasized throughout his ministry the values commonly associated with each.

Given the role that love plays in Christianity—i.e., the *raison d'être* for Christianity, as we saw at the beginning of the last chapter—it is fitting to include here the fullest, single expression in the New Testament of the importance and nature of the love expected of a Christian, namely the description given by the Apostle Paul in 1 Cor. 13:1-13, a paean to love unsurpassed in world literature.

> If I speak in the tongues of mortals and of angels, but do not have love, I am a noisy gong or a clanging cymbal. And if I have prophetic powers, and understand all mysteries and all knowledge, and if I have all faith, so as to remove mountains, but do not have love, I am nothing. If I give away all my possessions, and if I hand over my body to be burned, but do not have love, I gain nothing.

> Love is patient; love is kind; love is not envious or boastful or arrogant or rude. It does not insist on its own way; it is not irritable or resentful; it does not rejoice in wrongdoing, but rejoices in the truth. It bears all things, believes all things, hopes all things, endures all things.

> Love never ends. But as for prophecies, they will come to an end; as for tongues, they will cease; as for knowledge, it will come to an end. For we know only in part, and we prophesy only in part; but when the complete comes, the partial will come to an end. When I was a child, I spoke like a child, I thought like a child, I reasoned like a child; when I became an adult, I put an end to childish ways. For now we see in a mirror, dimly, but then we will see face to face. Now I know only in part; then I will know fully, even as I have been fully known. And now faith, hope, and love abide, these three; and the greatest of these is love.

Paul might well have been the best educated Christian of the first century. He knew the value of learning but also the dangers if not tempered by love. He may have been drawing from his own preconversion self-sense when he declared in 1 Cor. 8:1: "Knowledge puffs up, but love builds up." Perhaps from a practical standpoint, knowing that love is available to everyone while knowledge is not, Paul clearly gave priority to the former. It is doubtful that he would have denied the preferablity of an integration of the two, an integration that might be seen as wisdom and love tempering each other.

The letter of James is sometimes categorized as Christian wisdom literature because it speaks openly of "the wisdom from above" and links this wisdom with universal qualities of high morality. "The wisdom from above is first pure, then peaceable, gentle, willing to yield, full of mercy and good fruits, without a trace of partiality or hypocrisy." (Jas. 3:17). James' phrase "willing to yield" is equivalent to Paul's note that love does not insist on its own way. Here we meet one of the most effective practices to humble the self-assertive ego. The wisdom to which Paul and James refer is not simply a matter of knowing but of embodying truth in one's entire life. We are reminded here of the view of Yeats and Blake mentioned in the Preface that while the highest truth may not lend itself to clear formulation, it can be lived. Wisdom, as James understands it, involves doing the truth. His letter is a call to action, emphasizing works as well as faith and admonishing readers to "be doers of the word, and not merely hearers." (Jas. 1:22).

Saints and Sages in the Ancient Church

Clement of Alexandria (ca. 150-ca. 215)

The term 'mystical' was introduced into the Christian vocabulary by Clement of Alexandria, head of the Catechetical School, a kind of Christian university that taught the cultured and well educated in Egypt. He was also the first to develop such ideas as true gnosis, the vision of God, divine unknowability, union, and deification, all notions that he inherited from Greek philosophy, especially Plato and Plotinus, and integrated into his view of Christian mysticism. These became central notions that were expanded in more systematic ways by later mystics. Because of Clement's influence on the development of later Christian mysticism, some have named him "the founder of Christian mysticism."

As a philosopher, theologian, and mystic, Clement was committed to the realization of wisdom. He wrote: "We define wisdom as certain knowledge, a sure and unbreakable gnosis of divine and human realities, comprehending the present, past and future."[4] This wisdom is the vision of God seen or realized by gnostics who "keep on always moving to higher and yet higher regions, until they no longer greet the Divine vision in or by means of mirrors, but feast forever on the uncloying, never-ending sight, radiant in its transparent clearness."[5] Clement also notes that this is the "vision of the pure in heart."[6] The mirror reference is derived from Paul's notion that seeing by means of a mirror is seeing dimly, as in 1 Cor. 13:12 above. This true gnosis, or vision of God by the pure in heart, can be realized fully only in heaven but, even then, only if considerable progress is made here on earth in the development of moral perfection and the faithful practice of the virtues. According to Clement, we realize theosis and become divinized as we become "assimilated to God by a participation in moral excellence."[7] Crucial to this is the cultivation of *apatheia*, passionlessness or detachment, a notion and practice that we have seen emphasized in other religions as well. Mystical apatheia bears no relationship to the current meaning of apathy. Instead, it refers to an inner state of serenity as one acts authentically out of such dispositions as kindness, charity, benevolence, generosity, i.e., acts in the spirit of agape, divine or unconditional love. Finally, we may note that Clement of Alexandria was also the first to stress the necessity of both contemplation and action, another of his themes developed further by later mystics.

Origen (ca. 185-ca. 254)

Origen was a student of Clement and succeeded him as head of the Catechetical School in Alexandria. He is the first Christian scholar and teacher to be born of Christian parents and is widely recognized as the first systematic theologian. Some of Origen's views were controversial, but among later mystics his spiritual insight and teaching outweighed any apparent weakness in doctrinal orthodoxy. In addition to mystical, his writing spanned exegetical, doctrinal, devotional, and polemical works. Some estimate that he produced as many as 6,000 volumes or papyrus rolls, most of which were destroyed in the sixth century after his condemnation for heresy. Like Clement and many others yet to come, he developed his biblical interpretations and theology in the context of Greek philosophy, particularly that of Plato and his Neoplatonic interpreters. Because of the importance of this philosophy in forming the metaphysical structure of Christianity in coming centuries, it is essential to have at least a brief introduction to its most salient features in the following two paragraphs before returning to Origen.

Plato (ca. 428-ca. 348 BCE) formulated the basic thesis of most Western philosophy by postulating that there are Forms or Ideas in the eternal, transcendent realm that govern the transient, contingent phenomena that make up the time and space realm. Plotinus (ca. 205-270), founder of Neoplatonism, created an elaborated Platonic view that enabled Christian philosophers, theologians, and mystics to develop a metaphysical framework for Christianity. Plotinus postulated a descending order of three hypostases or realities that link the two realms. Following Plato, he called the highest in the hierarchy "the One" or "the Good," an ineffable first principle from which derive in descending order Mind and third Soul. Soul in turn generates a quasi-hypostasis, Nature, which is, of course, the material world that makes up the context of our ordinary life. Each downward realm is more fragmented, limited, and contingent than its superior.

Each realm correlates with a level of consciousness which enables humans, as microcosms of the macrocosm, to access the higher realms in an ascending return to the One, itself the supreme goal of human life. The ascent begins with the Soul, the seat of discursive thought where humans think dualistically and linearly and, therefore, are able to interact with the natural world. Next is *Nous* or Mind as intuitive consciousness; it is "thought-thinking-itself," a kind of "unity-in-diversity" where each thought is present in every other, thereby reflecting the One from which it derives. Ultimately, mystical consciousness affords unity with the One. The ascent to the One is possible through contemplation, which, according to Plotinus, enables each level of consciousness to receive the essential quality of its superior. Ascension names the entire hierarchy of simultaneous procession and return, of emanation and reversion. The downward-flow/upward reversion is simultaneous because it is logical rather than chronological.[8] In our continued synopses of the Church Fathers, we will see the manner and extent to which they appropriated and modified Plato and the Neoplatonists.

Origen searched the Bible for the "secret and hidden things of God." This caused him to be much in demand as a preacher but also to become a controversial figure, both in his lifetime and beyond.[9] He developed an allegorical or anagogic method of interpreting scripture. This opened the door to greatly extending the spiritual understanding of biblical texts. According to Origen—and in this he is followed by the Church Fathers as well as a form of biblical reading practiced even today—a merely rational or academic reading of the Bible will not reveal its mystic or deep spiritual significance. This requires a heartfelt approach involving humility, love, and prayerfulness, all the while reading and reflecting on God's Word as if it is being spoken to one personally in terms of one's immediate life situation.

Origen identified three levels of biblical meaning related to the three dimensions of human beings, body, soul, and spirit. "The simple man may be edified by what we may call the flesh of scripture [i.e., the obvious or literal level] . . . ; while the man who has made some progress may be edified by its soul, as it were; and the man who is perfect . . . may be edified by the spiritual law."[10] Origen's commentary on the Song of Songs (or Song of Solomon) illustrates his threefold interpretation. The first level is obviously about the wedding of a bride and groom who are passionately in love. The second level reveals Christ's love for the church. The third or mystical level unfolds the deep thirsting of the human spirit to become one with the Spirit of God.

Origen's three levels of biblical meaning are parallel to his three stages of development in Christian life, moral, natural, and contemplative. He found each of these focused in a particular book of the Old Testament. The moral level refers to behavior and is developed in Proverbs. The natural level relates to intellectual activity and is expressed in Ecclesiastes. The contemplative level pertains to spiritual union with God and is found in the allegorical interpretation of the Song of Songs. Through the influence of Neoplatonism and Dionysius (see below), Origen's three stages were eventually reformulated as purgative, illuminative, and unitive. This formulation has been normative in Christian views of personal transformation for many centuries, including contemporary times.[11]

Origen held a view in which humankind, prior to the creation of the material world, resided in an original state of full unity with, in, and as God. Calling this the "first heaven," Origen indicates that this is a spiritual state and notes further that it "is our mind, which is also itself spirit."[12] This first creation was made up of "intellects," each one created according to the principles and image of the Logos. This is the Logos or Word introduced in the Prologue to the Gospel of John where it is also identified with Christ. Each of these intellects had a spiritual, non-material body and resided in blissful contemplation of God. Each intellect was given freedom so that the goodness created in them by the good God could be maintained and even enhanced. A process of withdrawal from this goodness occurred as the intellects became slothful and negligent in preserving their God-given goodness. This development led to the creation of the material universe and the fall of the intellects into the world as we know it.

This descent provides the background for the ascent that marks the spiritual journey back to full communion with, in, and as God. Origen believed that "the end is always like the beginning." The creation of the material world and the fall into it did not constitute a punishment but an opportunity to discover one's deepest nature and take an active part in contemplating the goodness of God. Central to this goodness is God's unsurpassable love. In his commentary on the Song of Solomon, Origen wrote: "the power of love is none other than that which leads the soul from earth to the lofty heights of heaven; . . . the highest beatitude can only be attained under the stimulus of love's desire." The word used for love here is eros, eros understood in a non-sexual way as the deep yearning that is satisfied only through union with its object which, for Origen and others in the Greek philosophical tradition, is God. McGinn, author of a multi-volume history of Christian mysticism, comments: "God himself must be Eros if the eros implanted in us is what returns us to him."[13]

Origen centralizes eros by basing it on the view set forth in both the Bible (cf. 2 Cor. 3:18) and among the Platonists, "like can only be known by like." By understanding eros in this fashion, Origen is able to derive a great deal of mystical truth from the Song of Solomon. The spiritual journey is one of detaching and purifying the eros that desires the things of the world so that it becomes like the Eros of God whose yearning for communion with humanity caused him to send Christ to earth to show the way back to God. In this way, the image of God that was created in mankind is transformed into likeness; as a result, theosis, or divinization, occurs. In one of his polemical works, Origen wrote: "Christians see that with Jesus human and divine nature begin to be woven together, so that by fellowship with divinity human nature might become divine, not only in Jesus, but also in all those who believe and go on to undertake the life which Jesus taught."[14]

Origen thought of the mystical journey in terms of the gnosis constituted by mystical vision. The realization of gnosis was a higher awareness than that of the ordinary Christian. As we have seen, it was not solely intellectual but also contained an affective quality represented by eros. Both intellectual and affective qualities are to be found in the mind. Origen believed that God is "Mind" and that humans are essentially minds. It is by means of the mind that the hidden mysteries of God and Christ are deciphered in the Bible and realized by the mystic. One authority on Origen put the matter succinctly: "It is the mind that makes us like God and by the action of the mind that we become once again fully godlike."[15]

The Cappadocian Fathers

Origen was a major influence on the three Cappadocian fathers of the ancient church: Basil the Great (330-379), his younger brother Gregory of Nyssa (ca. 335-ca. 395), and their friend, Gregory of Nazianzus (329-389).* All three became bishops and were major figures in the fight against emerging heresies, particularly Arianism which, from the standpoint of orthodoxy, tended to minimize Christ's divine nature. Each also contributed to the continuing development of mystical thought and practice.

Basil the Great was a firm believer in self-discipline; in addition to rigorous study, he engaged a life of poverty, manual work, and prayer. He withdrew for a time from a settled life to travel throughout Egypt and Syria visiting monasteries. Drawing from this experience and his own practice of asceticism, he founded several monasteries and wrote two sets of guidelines for monastic life, the *Longer Rule* and

---

* The region known as Cappadocia in the fourth century is now part of Turkey.

the *Shorter Rule*. These are written in a question and answer format and became the basis for the entire development of monasticism in the Eastern Church. Later, through their influence on Benedict of Nursia (ca. 480-550) and his *Rule* for monastics, they helped form monasticism in the Western Church. Basil the Great's *Rules* departed from the extreme austerity and hermetic or solitary life that he found in much of the monasticism of Egypt and Syria. He taught cenobitic or communal forms of monasticism, with monks and nuns involved in regular work activities in order to support life in community. Throughout history, the monasteries and convents of both branches of the church have been the principal centers for the development of deep spirituality and mysticism.

Like the other Cappadocians, the mind and spirit of Gregory of Nazianzus was permeated by the teachings of the Bible, by the spiritual and philosophical ideas of Neoplatonism, by an ascetic way of life, and by mystical aspiration. Gregory retired to the wilderness and spent four or five years in silence and contemplation. He became an accomplished orator and poet. In the final decade of his life, he published about 400 poems that reflect the paramount issues in his life, including poems on theological as well as psychospiritual topics. In an autobiographical poem, he described the inner life of his soul in an original manner that came to be paralleled in Augustine's more famous *Confessions*. Even though he was drawn into the clerical and episcopal life of the church against his natural preference for solitude and contemplation, Gregory assumed an exceptionally important and active position, taking on a role reminiscent of the Old Testament prophets in his denunciation of laxity and waywardness among the clergy of his day.

Gregory of Nazianzus made major contributions in the ongoing doctrinal debates of his age. He participated in the ecumenical councils of the time that formulated the official creeds of the Church and wrote theological treatises, among them several orations that, among other matters, clarified the finer nuances of the doctrine of the Trinity. Because of the Arian challenge, no theological issue of the day quite matched the importance of carefully delineating the relation between God, Christ, and the Holy Spirit. Each of the Cappadocians participated in the debates, but we will highlight the contributions of Gregory of Nazianzus. To set the context and delicacy of the doctrine, he quoted Plato who taught that "it is difficult to conceive God, but to define Him in words is an impossibility," and then added "in my opinion it is impossible to express Him and yet more impossible to conceive Him." He continued: "what God is in nature and essence no man ever yet has discovered or can discover."[16] The challenge of the Trinity is to show how God can be simultaneously one and three and to thereby defend Christianity as a monotheistic faith against charges of polytheism. The Cappadocians did this by distinguishing between essence (Greek, *ousia*) and being (*hypostasis*). The Father, the Son, and the Holy Spirit are three separate beings. Each is particular, with individual characteristics. Thus, they are three distinct *hypostases.* But they are simultaneously and unambiguously one and the same in essence; they are *homoousios.* As a theologically sophisticated poet, Gregory of Nazianzus personalizes this by affirming: "No sooner do I conceive of the One than I am illumined by the splendor of the Three; no sooner do I distinguish Them than I am carried back to the One." He continues: "For us there is but One God, the Father of whom are all things; and One Lord Jesus Christ by whom are all things; and One Holy Spirit in whom are all things." Gregory draws a useful analogy by noting that three different persons will be clearly distinct from each other in their personalities and characteristics while at the same time identical in their essence as humans.[17] It is worth noting, particularly in the context of this book, that the trinitarian doctrine represents an effort to express in theological language what mystics know experientially, i.e., the diminishment and dissolution of boundaries culminating in a sense of the presence of God.

Among the Cappadocian fathers, Gregory of Nyssa was the most systematic in his mystical and theological writings. According to him, each human being possesses "a divine image-likeness in the mind, the free will, and virtues." But this image-likeness becomes disrupted by sin and this breaks the harmony between God and humans. However, Christ heals this disruption and disharmony by means of his divine/human nature. The mystic path, drawing on the work of Christ and the entire biblical tradition, enables an individual to be restored to the original divine image-likeness. Gregory writes: "If a man's heart has been purified from every creature and [all] unruly affections, he will see the Image of the Divine Nature in his own beauty. . . . For He Who made you did at the same time endow your nature with . . . the likeness of the glories of His own Nature." Gregory clarifies: "the Godhead is purity, freedom from passion, and separation from all evil. If therefore these things be in you, God is indeed in you." The consequence of this is that "you are able to perceive what is invisible to those who are not purified, because you have been cleansed; . . . and so you see the blessed vision radiant in the pure heaven of your heart."[18]

Among the numerous writings of Gregory of Nyssa, his *Life of Moses* stands out as a sterling example of the transformational value that can be elicited with an analogical interpretation of the Bible. No narrative in the Old Testament matches the exodus from Egypt in providing striking parallels to the human predicament and its resolution. These extend from the dangers and trials faced in Egypt and the wilderness, through the burning bush revelation, to the two ascents up the mountain, first into the darkness of the cloud and then into the even darker darkness where God is met. The entire journey of Moses and the Hebrews from Egypt to Mount Sinai exemplifies the path of human beings away from the temptations of the world, through the purifying of inner afflictions, especially the passions of attachment, to the revelation of God in the mysterious divine darkness. This ascent into impenetrable darkness represents the ultimate divine unknowability which was affirmed by the Christian saints and sages we have already met, and will be avowed again and again by mystics we will yet meet

Gregory of Nyssa produced the first systematic apophatic theology in Christian history. The most distinctive mark of his negative theology is the doctrine of *epektasis* (Greek, reaching forward), summarized by one scholar as "an endless longing for God, continually satisfied yet always yearning for more."[19] Since God is by definition infinite there can be no endpoint in one's seeking him, either in this life or in heaven. Gregory believed that "the continual development of life to what is better is the soul's way to perfection."[20] He added: "this is truly perfection: never to stop growing toward what is better and never placing any limit on perfection."[21] Gregory also wrote commentaries on the love depicted in the Song of Solomon. He underscored the paradoxical nature of the love that leads into the divine darkness, a love that is both a presence and an absence: "She [the soul] realizes that her sought-after love is known only in her impossibility to comprehend his essence."[22] There is therefore an elusive unknowing 'knowing' in the love that is ever-present in the ever-yearning that draws the mystic into the divine darkness.

Evagrius Ponticus, also Evagrios of Pontus (ca. 345-399)

Evagrius was born in Pontus, a region along the Black Sea in what is now Turkey. He was educated by and closely associated with each of the Cappadocian fathers. In 380, he went to Constantinople where he worked closely with Gregory of Nazianzus in preparing material on the divinity of the three persons of the Trinity for the Council of Constantinople that took place the following year. It was this Council that formulated the official doctrine of the Trinity that has become standard in the creeds of both the eastern and western churches. Not long after the Council, Evagrius was forced to flee from the city because of threats from the husband of an aristocratic woman with whom he was having an amorous alliance. He made his way to Jerusalem where he came under the influence of a pious and wealthy woman, Melania, who convinced him that his lapse and humiliation were part of God's plan for his life. Because of her influence, Evagrius went to the Egyptian desert and came under the guidance of the senior monks there. After two years, he moved even further into the desert where he lived for the rest of his life among the hermit colonies. It was not long until he became recognized as one of the most prominent leaders of the ascetic monks, a role he assumed because of his wisdom, humility, and insight into spirituality and human psychology. In addition to mentoring novice monks, he rendered his insights into written form. In this respect, some of his most poignant writing was in the form of "centuries," collections of one hundred short aphorisms, each called a "chapter" and grouped under three headings: practical matters, prayer, and mystical insight (gnosis). The practice of the novice monks and nuns was to memorize one of these chapters each morning and reflect on it throughout the day.

The three categories of Evagrius' writing reflect three stages in the spiritual journey: (1) overcoming the emotions, called passions by Evagrius, that impede the unfolding of one's spirituality, (2) understanding and growing in spirituality through contemplation of the natural order, and (3) prayer and contemplation oriented toward ascension to the imageless, mystical union with God. Each stage prepares for the next but anticipates it as well, i.e., includes and manifests features of the next. One is alert to all three even while focusing on one.

Writing as a monk for monks and nuns, Evagrius championed a life of rigorous asceticism in the *Praktikos,* his manual of practical advice for the novice monastics. Unassuming dress, a simple diet, frequent fasting and prayer vigils, and ongoing assiduous self-examination make up the minimum expectation, all of this designed to break attachment to materiality and worldliness. Evagrius is famous for his catalog of the "eight passionate thoughts" which, if not controlled, keep the mind in constant disturbance so that prayer is impossible. (These eight were revised to seven by one of Evagrius' principle students, John Cassian, and have come to be known by Christians as the seven deadly sins.) Evagrius' eight passions are: gluttony, lust, greed, dejection, anger, indolence, opinionatedness, and pride. Over time, these negative emotions can be neutralized by means of reading sacred literature, all-night vigils, fasting, physical labor, solitude, and persistent prayer. Gentle acts of love are particularly effective in overcoming the debilitating passions. Anger, an especially disruptive emotion, can be controlled by chanting the psalms, by acts of penance, and by giving alms. Evagrius' sound understanding of human nature and his practicality are seen in his counsel: "You need to put all these things into practice in good order and at the right time, otherwise it will be an erratic and short-lived response, and this will cause more harm than good."[23]

Subjugation of the negative emotions is essential for the development of apatheia, dispassion. Like a good counselor and guide, Evagrius provides markers that enable the aspiring monk and nun to recognize that their practice is bearing fruit. He observes: "The man who is progressing in the ascetic life diminishes the force of passions. The man progressing in contemplation diminishes his ignorance. As regards the passions, the time will come when they will be entirely destroyed. In the matter of ignorance, however, one type will have an end, but another type will not." What is the ignorance that will not end? The limits of the human mind as well as humility require that one must always acknowledge mystery and unknowing in reference to Ultimacy. In matters of Ultimacy, claims of knowing are sure signs of arrogance. Paralleling the view of others, Evagrius holds that the highest experience of God is contentless, is without thought or image, therefore, a form of ignorance. With this contention of ongoing ignorance, Evagrius is affirming Gregory of Nyssa's view concerning the endlessness of yearning; even when finding some satisfaction in one's movement toward the divine, one yearns for more and more as one reaches toward the infinite.

Evagrius offers another mark of progress when he notes that "the proof of *apatheia* is had when the spirit begins to see its own light, when it remains in a state of tranquility in the presence of the images during sleep and when it maintains its calm as it beholds the affairs of life." Perhaps the most crucial of the progress indicators is Evagrius' observation that "a man who has established the virtues in himself and is entirely permeated with them no longer remembers the law or commandments or punishment. Rather, he says and does what excellent habit suggests." The virtues have become entirely internalized. In the previous chapter, we noted that agape, divine or unconditional love, is the highest and purest form of love recognized in Christianity. Evagrius contends that "*agape* is the progeny of *apatheia*," in other words, unconditional love is born out of dispassion, out of nonattachment.[24] When acts of charity are consistently performed from the background of stable apatheia, one is prepared to more fully engage contemplative prayer, which itself leads to imageless mystical union with God.

Evagrius' teaching on natural contemplation is the second phase in his map of the spiritual journey. The objective here is "to see God in all things—to discern, in and through each created reality, the divine presence that is within it and at the same time beyond."[25] To support this view, Evagrius drew from St. Anthony, one of the great monks of the desert whose successful battle with temptation has become legendary. When asked how he got along without books, St. Anthony replied that his book was the created order and was always available for reading. All of nature is sacramental. This second stage in the journey also entails contemplation of the angels and the role they play in the purification process. Another important aspect of this kind of contemplation is meditation on the inner meanings of the Bible. Since this initial form of contemplation involves the discursive mind and operates within the domain of multiplicity, it is distinct from the level of pure, imageless contemplation and the pervasive peacefulness of the highest stage.

Evagrius' *Chapters on Prayer* ranks among the most comprehensive and penetrating descriptions of what is involved in the ascent to the divine. This work marks the entrance to the third stage in Evagrius' transformational process. Perhaps to indicate the indispensable importance of prayer and contemplation, Evagrius apparently did not want to limit himself to the standard century of aphorisms; in this case he exceeded them by 53. By way of introducing his thoughts on prayer, we can do no better than offer a selection of aphorisms from his *Chapters on Prayer.*[26]

9. Stand resolute, fully intent on your prayer. Pay no heed to the concerns and thoughts that might arise the while. They do nothing better than disturb and upset you so as to dissolve the fixity of your purpose.

22. The man who stores up injuries and resentments and yet fancies that he prays might as well draw water from a well and pour it into a cask that is full of holes.

34. What greater thing is there than to converse intimately with God and to be preoccupied with his company?

38. In your prayer seek only after justice and the kingdom of God, that is to say, after virtue and true spiritual knowledge.

39. It is a part of justice that you should pray not only for your own purification but also for that of every man.

52. The state of prayer can be aptly described as a habitual state of imperturbable calm (*apatheia*). It snatches to the heights of

intelligible reality the spirit which loves wisdom and which is truly spiritualized by the most intense love.

59. The man who worships in Spirit and Truth no longer honors the Creator: because of his works, but praises him because of himself.

92. Train yourself like a skilled athlete. You must learn not to become anxious even if you should see some sudden apparition, or some sword pointed at you, or a beam of light leaping toward your face. Even though you should see some hideous and bloody figure, still stand firm, and in no wise give way to the fear that clutches at your heart.

97. Crashing sounds and roars and voices and beatings—all of these, coming from the devils, are heard by the man who pursues the practice of pure prayer.

98. At the time of these temptations make use of short and intense prayer.

105. Despise the needs of the body while you are engaged in prayer lest you do some damage to that unsurpassed gift that you gain by prayer due to the sting of some flea or even a louse, fly or mosquito.

114. Do not by any means strive to fashion some image or visualize some form at the time of prayer.

116. Vainglory is the source of the illusions of your mind. When it exerts its influence on the mind it attempts to enclose the Divinity in form and figure.

Evagrius believed that prayer and theology were essential to each other. He wrote: "If you are a theologian, you truly pray. If you truly pray, you are a theologian."[27] Theology was not the product of study but of prayer. He declared that "in prayer one receives from God true knowledge about God; that is *theognosis*," literally, knowledge of God.[28] That Evagrius inclined toward apophatic theology—that he was, in fact, opposed to kataphatic descriptions of God—is made unambiguously clear by his concise admonition: "Never define the divine."[29] Aphorisms 114 and 116 quoted above make this apparent, as do many other of Evagrius' assertions. Not only in contemplation but also in theology the tendency to reduce God to mental formulations must be eschewed.

The eminent practicality of Evagrius' writing is apparent. He was equally adept in his speculative theological expositions, although for some they tended to press the parameters of acceptable doctrine. The descriptions of his own profound mystical experiences also sometimes gave rise to questions regarding his orthodoxy. One scholar notes that "Evagrius is a pure mystic" and thereby claims that "the mystical teaching of Evagrius in its fully developed consistency stands essentially closer to Buddhism than to Christianity."[30] A brief look at his cosmology and soteriology, for example, will indicate something of his creative and innovative thought.[31]

According to Evagrius, there were two creations. The first, "a single undivided, integral whole whose nature was pure intelligence," was created by "a simple unity." Because of the failure to abide in the pure contemplation of God, many individualized bodies arose that were "more or less material, more or less dark, more or less thick" depending on the degree of negligence and therefore guilt. This was the second creation, including the cosmos and the material world as we know it. Angels and demons were created at the same time. The bodies of angels are made of fire and are relatively light and free of the density of matter. Human bodies are heavier, are thickened by passion, sensuality, and anger. Beneath humans in the descending scale are demons whose bodies are thick with destructive passions and devoid of light. Their bodies are made of air and are icy cold. They are the forces with which humans must contend as they neutralize the passions. The body at each level is also a soul which is constituted by varying degrees of intelligence and ignorance depending on its status as angel, human, or demon. The fall into the second creation is called a movement by Evagrius, and is not so much punishment as opportunity to become purified through contemplation of God. This enables a return to the original state as pure intelligence resting in uninterrupted union with God. The teaching of Evagrius explored above is the means by which this return is made possible.

What is the role of Christ in this worldview? He was the one intelligence that did not neglect contemplation and thereby forfeit the pure knowledge or gnosis that united him to God. All of the second creation was the work of Christ. "The multifaceted wisdom with which the second creation is achieved fills all things and provides the rational creatures with their proper object for . . . the contemplation of nature which leads to an increase of the knowledge of God." The Incarnation is another indication of the beneficent and salvational work of Christ. Christ's work is not limited to humans. His domain extends throughout the entire second creation so that, in the end, even demons will become purified. According to Evagrius, salvation is so comprehensive and inclusive that all creatures will eventually return to their original state of union with God, which will then become unity.

From this brief survey of Evagrius' practical and theoretical writing, it is easy to see how some of his views would have disturbed the ultra-orthodox. He had studied the innovative thought of Origen with the Cappadocian fathers and pursued it further among the Origenist *intelligentsia* of the desert. Because of his advocacy of Origenist theology, Evagrius was condemned by the Second Ecumenical Council of Constantinople in 553. His speculative writing caused some of his works to be banned and even destroyed. Fortunately, many escaped the censors by being translated into Syrian and Armenian, or by being published under the name of a different author. Evagrius combined the intellectual tradition of Origen with his own intellectual creativity, and embraced the daily needs of ascetic monks and nuns needing guidance in their psychospiritual journeys. Among Christians oriented toward a disciplined and mystical life, Evagrius' departure from a strict orthodoxy has proven far less significant than his insight into and teaching on the inner processes of spiritual development.

Augustine (354-430)

Augustine is one of Christianity's most prolific and oft-quoted sages. Theologians and philosophers continue to mark their own positions by declaring them to be either in harmony with Augustine or different from him. We know a great deal about the inner life of Augustine because of his frank revelations in *Confessions*, the first full-length Christian autobiography ever written and one that is now acknowledged as a classic. He was born in North Africa (in what today is Algeria) to a pagan father and a Christian mother, Monica, who has become exemplary in Christianity because of her persistent prayers for her spirited and independent son, prayers for his salvation that abated only after his conversion. Following his education in the fundamentals of Christianity, Augustine turned away from the religion of his pious mother and toward philosophy. He preferred its emphasis on reason rather than faith, which he had come to regard as mere superstition.

This initial commitment to the life of the mind occurred through Augustine's reading of Cicero's *Hortensius*, from which he learned, as he states in his Confessions (3.4): "to love and seek and pursue and hold fast and strongly embrace wisdom itself, wherever found."[32] Partly because it also claimed to be founded on reason rather than faith, Augustine became a Manichaean at an early age. (Manichaeism, a major rival of Christianity, was established in the third century by Mani, a Persian who based his system on an absolute dualism between spirit and matter, good and evil.) Augustine eventually became disenchanted with Manichaeism after coming to regard much of its mythology, in spite of claims to the contrary, as rationally baseless. He finally, after nine years, turned away from the Manichaeans on reading the Neoplatonists, especially Plotinus, and their mystical interpretation of Platonic philosophy.

Augustine was deeply influenced by Plotinus, whom he felt offered reasonable and appealing answers to the fundamental questions of life without an elaborate and fantastic mythology. The metaphysics of Plotinus shaped Augustine's personal experience, biblical interpretation, and theology throughout his life. From the Neoplatonists he learned the threefold process of contemplation that enabled him to explore his inner nature and gain a direct awareness of God: (1) withdrawal from the sense world, (2) descent into the depths of the soul, and (3) ascent to divine realities.[33] In this manner, he discovered a higher reality within himself that he could address in the words, "eternal truth and true love and beloved eternity; you are my God."[34]

Augustine eventually moved beyond his total commitment to Neoplatonism, even while incorporating some of its features into his embrace of Christianity. This move occurred after he realized that philosophy, while it led to an intellectual discovery of truth, failed to provide a means of coming to a life-changing realization of truth. Augustine continued to affirm a noetic, or knowledge, quality to spirituality. The ascent to God always has an intellectual as well as affective dimension; knowing and love are conjoined.

Augustine's newly gained respect for Christianity came largely through the mentoring and preaching of Ambrose, then Bishop of Milan. Augustine was impressed with the symbolic, metaphorical interpretation of scripture given by Ambrose, who justified his hermeneutical approach by quoting Paul, "The letter kills, the spirit gives life" (2 Cor. 3:6). Augustine commented: "Those texts which, taken literally, seemed to contain perverse teaching he would expound spiritually." This approach enabled Augustine to acknowledge that Ambrose "did not say anything that I felt to be a difficulty." Though Ambrose proved to be the catalyst leading to his intellectual appreciation of Christianity, Augustine continued to resist conversion. As he says: "I kept my heart from giving any assent" (6.4).

During the time that Augustine's mind was committed to the search for truth, that is, even from his teen years, his heart sought pleasure, not the least of which was sensual. He admits to "fornications," to "carnal concupiscence," to "sensual folly," to "an insatiable sexual desire" (2.2, 6.12). For fifteen years from the age of seventeen, he kept a concubine, who eventually bore him a son. Being of low social status, she was sent away in preparation for Augustine's arranged marriage with one who would advance his social and professional ambitions. Because his betrothed was too young to marry according to Roman law, Augustine sought another sexual alliance. He admits: "As I was not a lover of marriage but a slave of lust, I procured another woman, not of course as a wife" (6.15).

About this period of his life, not long before his conversion, Augustine addressed God: "As I became unhappier, you came closer. Your right hand was by me, already prepared to snatch me out of the filth, and to clean me up. But I did not know it" (6.16). Through the influence of Ambrose, Augustine took up a serious reading of the Bible. "With avid intensity I seized the sacred writings of your Spirit and especially the apostle Paul. Where at one time I used to think he contradicted himself . . . , [now] the problems simply vanished . . . . I began reading and found that all the truth I had read in the Platonists was stated here, together with the commendation of your grace" (7.21). Before discovering the higher realties, however, he experienced a great deal of turmoil, multiple wills at war with each other. The inner split was reducible to spirit against flesh, good against evil, and the law of God against the lawlessness of man.

Augustine's inner crisis moved beyond the point of containment during a period when he and his long-time friend, Alypius, were staying in Milan, Italy. When trying to put into words for Alypius the inner dilemma he was suffering, Augustine realized that his inner struggle was erupting in physical symptoms: "My uttered words said less about the state of my mind than my forehead, cheeks, eyes, color, and tone of voice . . . I tore my hair . . . I struck my forehead . . . I intertwined my fingers and clasped my knee." His gestures were erratic and feeble. He was profoundly agitated, inwardly and outwardly. He began to cry uncontrollably. Even though he was besieged with remorse over the licentious life he had lived, he felt powerless to free himself from the grip of his past. Shortly after throwing himself down under a fig tree in the garden behind the house he shared with Alypius, he heard a child's voice repeating over and over again, "Pick up and read. Pick up and read." Concerning this event, Augustine wrote:

> At once my countenance changed . . . I checked the flood of tears and stood up. I interpreted [the words] as a divine command to me to open the book and read the first chapter I might find. I hurried back to the place where Alypius was sitting. There I had put down the book of the apostle when I got up. I seized it, opened it and in silence read the first passage on which my eyes lit: "Not in riots and drunken parties, not in eroticism and indecencies, not in strife and rivalry, but put on the Lord Jesus Christ and make no provision for the flesh in its lusts" (Romans 13:13f) . . . At once, with the last words of this sentence, it was as if a light of relief from all anxiety flooded into my heart. All the shadows of doubt were dispelled. (8.8-12)

With this experience, Augustine turned to Christianity. The long dilemma that had marked his life, the split between the world and Christianity now came to an end. Reflecting on the differences between his life before and after his conversion, Augustine discovered a principle that came to constitute a major theme of his lifelong work as a theologian and bishop, a theme so important that he introduces it in the first paragraph of his *Confessions*: "You have made us for yourself, and our heart is restless until it rests in you" (1.1).

Augustine was so prolific that it is highly unlikely that any scholar today has read all of his theological treatises, commentaries on the Bible, homilies, letters, etc. His writings reflect influence from Plotinus, Origen, the Cappadocian Fathers and other predecessors. Building on their work, Augustine interpreted and creatively extended their insights. The theology he produced, like that of many of his forerunners and successors, was mystical because it enabled believers to experience the presence of God, not because it necessarily led to union or nonduality. In the early centuries of Christianity, the mystical was that which unlocked the mysteries of scripture in ways that elicited spiritual awareness, thereby providing insight into the mysteries of God and a sense of his immediacy.

Augustine's most systematic theological work is *The Trinity,* which consists of 15 books written over a period of about that many years. In one of his homilies, he boldly declared: "The God within is the God above."[35] *The Trinity* is a creative and detailed exposition of how this is the case. This God-within/God-above equation can be personally validated, he claimed, by means of one's own trinitarian image as it enables one to attain, through grace, the divine vision. Like the mystical theologians before him, Augustine believed that humans carry an image and likeness of their creator in their very nature. For him, this image and likeness is analogous to the Trinity as represented in the Godhead by Father, Son, and Holy Spirit. The highest and most noble feature of the soul is the mind, analogous to the Father. Knowledge and word issue or proceed from the mind and are analogous to Christ who is Wisdom and Word (*logos*). The third is love, the special but not exclusive providence of the Holy Spirit. This triune structure may also be labeled memory, intelligence, and will. Though the three are particular and distinct, they are of a single substance or essence. They are three in one.

According to Augustine, all humans carry this trinitarian imprint, but a crucial difference exists between those who recognize this and ascend to the divine vision and those who do not. "Hence this trinity of the mind is not on that account the image of God because the mind remembers itself, understands itself, and loves itself, but because it can also remember, understand and love him by whom it was made. And when it does so, it becomes wise; but if it does not, even though it remembers itself, knows itself, and loves itself, it is foolish."[36] Augustine makes an important distinction between knowledge (Latin, *scientia*) and wisdom (*sapientia*). Knowledge, important in its own domain, is concerned with the empirical world, the world we know by means of our five senses. Wisdom, on the other hand, ensues from contemplation of eternal realities. The transformational process is one of relinquishing our usual attachment to the corporeal world, i.e., to knowledge, and developing wisdom by contemplating that which is not confined to time and space. As we progressively detach from material things, grace draws us to the eternal. For Augustine, grace is a power that attracts us to God to the extent that we take "delight in righteousness."[37] In the end, a dialectical movement exists between knowledge and wisdom because we continue to be involved in the world by means of love, a love that becomes purified as we exercise apatheia, passionlessness or nonattachment, and thereby grow in wisdom. Thus, unconditional love derives from wisdom and informs our action.

For Augustine, true wisdom is always informed by love. True love is a wise love. Love and charity are closely linked with knowledge and wisdom. Because God is love one comes to know God by means of love and acts of charity. Augustine wrote: "The more ardently we love God, the more certainly and calmly do we see him."[38] He believed that we could so intimately know God that the usual gulf between God as transcendent and God as immanent would fade away. In another of his more substantive works, *The City of God*, he asserted: "God will be so known by us and so present to our eyes that . . . he will be seen by each of us in each of us, seen by each in his neighbour and each in himself."[39]

Augustine trenchantly exclaimed: "Love and do what you will." At first glance, the injunction seems to grant license to behave any way one might want. However, consideration of Augustine's other words on love quickly corrects this mistaken notion. For example, he immediately qualified the above sanction by writing: "If you keep silent, keep silent by love, if you speak, speak by love; if you correct, correct by love; if you pardon, pardon by love: Let love's root be within you, and from that root nothing but good can spring."[40] The root of love, of course, is God. To love God is to love neighbor. And to love neighbor is to love God. Augustine noted: "This is because one who loves his neighbor must necessarily first have love for Love itself. But 'God is Love, and he who abides in Love, abides in God' (1 John 4:16)."[41] Rather than allowing profligate behavior, Augustine's statement provides the only truly just basis for ethical action. If one acts out of love as set forth by Jesus, Paul, James and others in the Bible, one can act only in the best interests of the other. Divine love, Augustine believed, actually gives precedence to the other. Such a love abides "in the one who does not in this life seek his own interests." Here Augustine refers to Phil. 2:4: "Let each of you look not to your own interests, but to the interests of others."[42] Love was so integral to Christianity for Augustine that he declared: "There would have been no reason for Jesus to come except for charity."[43]

We have seen how important the Trinity was for Augustine, the role it played in his view of the transcendent God and simultaneously the way in which it parallels human nature in terms of mind/memory, knowledge/understanding, and will/love. Augustine formulates our image and likeness to God in terms of these parallels. He also taught that love is central to each person of the Trinity. A contemporary authority on the Bishop of Hippo summarized the matter concisely:

"As love, the Father is the principle of creation and providence; as love, the Word is the principle of conversion and illumination; and the Spirit as the principle of love is the principle of return to the Father."[44]

Augustine's spiritual therapy, his program of personal transformation, has been implicit in much of what we have discovered in his exposition of Christianity. After an initial conversion, continued growth occurs by gradual progress in purify the image and likeness of God within. In *The Trinity*, Augustine offered a prayer to this end: "Give me strength to seek, you who have made me find you and given me the hope of finding you more and more. My strength and my infirmity are in your sight: preserve the one, and heal the other. My knowledge and my ignorance are in your sight; where you have opened to me, receive me as I enter; where you have closed, open to me as I knock."[45] And finally, "May I remember You, understand You, and love You. Increase these gifts in me until You have re-formed me completely."[46]

Saints and Sages in the Middle Ages

Dionysius (sometimes Denys) the Areopagite, also Pseudo-Dionysius (ca. 500)

The unknown author of the mystical writings we will consider here took the name of Paul's convert in Athens when the apostle preached a sermon there based on an inscription he saw on an altar in the city, "To an unknown god" (see Acts 17:22-23, 34). Scholars have concluded that the author was probably a Syrian monk writing at the end of the fifth century or early in the sixth. No mystical author from the East has had a greater impact on the development of Western mysticism than Dionysius. Like the Church Fathers we have already reviewed, Dionysius developed his mystical system in terms of Neoplatonic views.

Dionysius refers to other documents he wrote, but only four treatises and ten letters, all relatively brief, are available today. The shortest and most important treatise is *The Mystical Theology*, five short chapters that summarize what can and cannot be known about God. The Areopagite is credited with being the first to formulate the precise expression, mystical theology. Here we meet his elaborate apophaticism or negative theology. Probably no other single work exceeds this one in profundity and impact on the development of subsequent Christian mysticism. *The Divine Names* is devoted mainly to Dionysius' kataphatic or positive theology where he develops in a philosophical way some of the names of God found in the Bible, e.g., Good, Being, Life, and Wisdom. Here too, though in a less comprehensive way, apophatic or negative theology is employed so that in this work, as in his entire corpus, God is presented both revealed and hidden. *The Celestial Hierarchy* introduces a Neoplatonic term and concept, namely hierarchy, that has proven to be a major systematizing principle in Western thought broadly as well as specifically in Christian thought. This work outlines a descending pattern of celestial beings that, like all hierarchies, provides a means of contemplation that enables "beings to be as like as possible to God and be at one with him."[47] Finally, *The Ecclesiastical Hierarchy* interprets the liturgy and offices of the church as sacred symbols that allow one who contemplates them properly to ascend from the merely perceptible to the intellectual or conceptual level.

Dionysius was influenced by Proclus (410-485), onetime head of the Academy in Athens, the main center for teaching Neoplatonism. Perhaps because Proclus preferred triads to dyads, Dionysius identifies three levels in his hierarchy, God, the angelic or celestial, and the ecclesiastical. Each of these is divided into further triads. As we might expect, the upper level takes the form of Father, Son, and Holy Spirit. The next level consists of seraphim, cherubim, and thrones with archangels, angels, and others following so that, in the end, three subcategories make up the second level. Finally, the ecclesial level breaks down into liturgy, officiants, and participants with each of these divided into further triads.

Plato's belief that a median or linking power must be present between opposites led the Neoplatonists to identify three dynamic phases in their hierarchy: between the process of proceeding (from God) and returning (to God) is that of remaining. This basic principle operating throughout the triadic hierarchies leads Dionysius to declare, in the summary of McGinn, that "the unknown God always remains super-eminently identical with himself, while overflowing into differentiation in his effects in order eventually to regain identity by reversion."[48] This dynamic process allows the contemplative to understand how symbolic, metaphorical, and anagogic interpretations enable consciousness to ascend from the material realm through intervening levels to ultimate oneness in the One.

Paul Rorem, an authority on Dionysius, clarifies the basic pattern of the Areopagite's view of the upward transformational process as it leads from biblical and liturgical symbols to union or divinization (theosis).[49]

> The Dionysian interpretation of scriptural and liturgical symbolism incorporates negation within the anagogical or uplifting journey, for such interpretation must negate and thus transcend the superficial appearance of the symbols in order to rise up to their higher, conceptual meanings. Then even the loftiest interpretations and purest conceptions must also be negated and abandoned in the final, silent approach to the ineffable and transcendent God beyond all speech and thought.

It is perhaps worth noting that since everything in the cosmos is ultimately an emanation of Ultimacy (as argued in the first chapter) everything making up the empirical world of time and space is capable, when utilizing the Dionysian scheme, of uplifting one to Ultimacy Itself. As we have seen and will see, some mystics make this very claim. The unique property of symbols is both to conceal and to reveal.

As we might expect, Dionysius held an attitude and perspective that represents an extremely high level of personal transformation and insight. At the same time, his system made room for those at different levels of realization and spiritual aspiration. In the opening lines of *The Divine Names*, he writes: "The things of God are revealed to each mind in proportion to its capacities; and the divine goodness is such that, out of concern for our salvation, it deals out the immeasurable and infinite in limited measures." Identifying the ultimate Source of these modified revelations and the variation in their manifestations, Dionysius writes: "Source of perfection for those being made perfect, source of divinity for those being deified, principle of simplicity for those turning toward simplicity, point of unity for those made one; transcendentally, beyond what is, it is the Source of every source."[50]

Its brevity notwithstanding, *The Mystical Theology* represents the epitome of Dionysius' thought. This highly influential work is the key to his method and suggests the structure of his entire corpus. Because of the precision and clarity of its expression, and its occasional poetic beauty, we can do no better than share some of its insights in quoted form. In the opening poem, addressed to the Trinity, the author prays:

> Lead us up beyond unknowing and light,
> up to the farthest, highest peak of mystic scripture,
> where the mysteries of God's Word
> lie simple, absolute and unchangeable
> in the brilliant darkness of a hidden silence.

> Amid the deepest shadow
> they pour overwhelming light
> on what is most manifest.

Amid the wholly unsensed and unseen
they completely fill our sightless minds
with treasures beyond all beauty.[51]

The Areopagite continues by advising the seeker "to leave behind you everything perceived and understood, everything perceptible and understandable, all that is not and all that is, and with your understanding laid aside, to strive upward as much as you can toward union with him who is beyond all being and knowledge. By an undivided and absolute abandonment of yourself and everything, shedding all and freed from all, you will be uplifted to the ray of the divine shadow which is above everything that is."[52] To approach the divine darkness, one must relinquish thoughts of all that impacts the physical senses as well as all thinking that normally occupies the mind. The perceptual and the conceptual must be released and transcended. Dionysius attempts to describe the indescribable as the seeker enters "the truly mysterious darkness of unknowing. Here, renouncing all that the mind may conceive, wrapped entirely in the intangible and the invisible, he belongs completely to him who is beyond everything. Here, being neither oneself nor someone else, one is supremely united by a completely unknowing inactivity of all knowledge, and knows beyond the mind by knowing nothing."[53] Here is pure, unadulterated apophaticism, not to be so emphatically set forth again in a single Christian text until the fourteenth century, again by an unknown author whose work, *The Cloud of Unknowing,* reflects much from the Dionysian corpus.

Bernard of Clairvaux (1090-1153)

Bernard grew up in a devout Roman Catholic family in the Burgundy region of France. With his brothers and several others, he joined the Cistercian monastic order in Cîteaux in 1113. Here he furthered his theological studies and deepened his spiritual life. After two years, he was sent to Clairvaux to establish a monastery there and in another two years became its abbot. By the end of the twelfth century, 530 Cistercian abbeys had been founded, about 60 of them by Bernard himself and most of the others with his active support. The Cistercian monks lived by the *Rule of St. Benedict,* the main spiritual values of which are humility and obedience to God. One of the Cistercian modifications of monastic life was to emphasize the value of physical labor, thereby adding farming activities to the daily routine of the monks. Bernard himself was canonized in 1174, little more than 20 years after his death. Attesting to the extraordinary influence he had, not only on the growth of Christian mysticism during medieval times, but on its entire subsequent development, he was declared a "Doctor of the Church" in 1820.

Bernard produced a mystical theology of knowledge and love, of head and heart. He connected these domains to the Trinity by noting that Christ enlightens the mind while the Holy Spirit purifies the heart, the affections and emotions. If knowledge is separated from love, only a kind of worldly wisdom is possible. One or the other, knowledge or love, may take precedence at any given time, resulting in a different mode of contemplative awareness depending on whether the mind or love is in ascendance. Bernard explains: "There are two forms of ecstasy of divine contemplation, the one in intellect, the other in affect, the one in light, the other in heat [*fervor* is the Latin; intensity of affection might be a better rendering], the one in knowledge, the other in devotion." Ideally, balanced cooperation between love and the intellect—"spiritual affection . . . joined with spiritual understanding"—is essential if one is to attain an unmistakable and authentic sense of the divine presence.[54]

Bernard of Clairvaux's descriptions of the soul's relationship to God are among the finest in Western mystical literature. Like most of his predecessors, he believed that Christian life begins with self-knowledge, the knowledge that although we are created in the divine image, our realization of the image is damaged by sin. Thus we are simultaneously like and unlike our Creator. Drawing from and building on the work of Gregory the Great, Augustine, and others, Bernard elaborated the psychospiritual means by which the soul, given its distinctive, created nature, can come to know and experience the love of God and recover its original image and likeness. Even though full recovery can occur only in the hereafter, a transforming and liberating experience of God's love is possible here and now, but only through the cooperation of human will and divine grace.

Bernard was a prolific writer. We will draw mainly from his two most important mystical works, *On the Love of God* and *Sermons on the Song of Songs*. The abbot of Clairvaux begins the first work by treating the how and why of loving God. He argues that "God himself is the reason for loving God; and the way to love him is without a way."[55] Throughout this book, the author stresses that love for God must be pure, must be unalloyed by any expectation or sentiment other than God himself. If God is loved with any expectation of gain, the purity of that love is diminished.

Bernard analyzes love in terms of four degrees or stages. The first stage concerns one's love of oneself for oneself. Untempered by Christ's example and teaching, such a love is clearly egoistic. Concerning this first stage, Bernard says that it is acceptable to love oneself as long as one loves others equally. Bernard points out further that one cannot love one's neighbor *perfectly* if one does not first love God. The second stage occurs when one loves God but for one's own benefit. This stage is deficient compared to the pure love yet to be realized. The third stage, the love of God for God's sake, might seem to be the final stage, but not according to Bernard. The abbot notes: "He who trusts in the Lord not because He is good to him, but simply because He is good truly loves God for God's sake and not for his own." The fourth stage arises when one loves oneself for God's sake. At this stage, self-interest has disappeared, self-centeredness has vanished, one sees as God sees. One has realized what Paul said about himself when he declared: "It is no longer I who live, but it is Christ who lives in me" (Gal. 2:20). Bernard exclaims: "To lose yourself as though you did not exist and to have no sense of yourself, to be emptied out of yourself and almost annihilated, belongs to heavenly not to a human love." He asserts: "To love in this way is to become like God." This is theosis, divination. Bernard notes that "it is necessary for human affection to dissolve in some ineffable way, and be poured into the will of God." He then asks rhetorically, "How will God be all in all if anything of man remain[s] in man?"[56]

Bernard's *Sermons on the Song of Songs*, a classic in Christian mysticism, is unsurpassed in the depth and comprehensiveness of its spiritual insights. Following Origen, Gregory of Nyssa and others, Bernard finds that the Old Testament Song of Songs, when interpreted allegorically as an account of the love between Christ and the devoted Christian, offers invaluable insight into the soul's path as it journeys into the presence of God. The abbot's eighty-six sermons on the Song of Songs reach only into the opening verses of the third chapter (there are eight chapters in the biblical book), undoubtedly due in part to his exegetical method of finding the meaning of the whole in each part. This approach allowed him to elaborate the basic ideas of the Song in many different ways. Even as he produced his teaching on the book in sermonic form, Bernard developed his theology for the mystical journey. For example, he bridged the spiritual and material worlds by teaching that Christ gave up his physical form on the Cross for a spiritual end, thereby indicating how those who identify with the body/mind can also manifest the spirit, i.e., by disidentifying with the body and the ego (the intense drive to preserve one's identity).

In order to further link the human and divine realms, Bernard offered a theological anthropology, a view of how human nature is structured that accounts for both estrangement from and reconciliation to God. As for many of his predecessors, the ordering pattern in human nature that provides the rationale for the mystical journey is found by Bernard in Genesis 1:26: "Let us make humankind in our image, according to our likeness." Bernard contends that the image of God in humankind lies in our freedom of choice. This freedom enables us to decide on a personal course of action by means of sound judgment based on reason. Unhappily, our likeness to God has been lost because of the pride that causes us to draw away him rather than acknowledge our complete dependence on him. Through the grace offered by Christ, however, reconciliation is possible. If free will is used rightly, God's grace will restore the prior status that was vitiated by sin/estrangement.

Some scholars believe that Bernard gave different interpretations of the image and likeness theme in his various writings. Anticipating this critique, the abbot of Clairvaux offers a liberal position: "any single divine text will not be off the mark if it gives rise to different understandings that can be adapted to the diverse needs and purposes of souls." Bernard's views on image and likeness are entirely rational and consistent in terms of a threefold process of psychospiritual transformation: first of all, *formation,* i.e., creation according to the image and likeness of God; second, *deformation*, i.e., violation of this solidarity with God through sin; and finally, *reformation*, i.e., restoration to our original unity with God through the grace of Christ.[57]

Bernard's twenty-third sermon in *Sermons on the Song of Songs* illustrates the allegorical method of biblical interpretation and the spiritual meanings he derives from this love poem. The key verse is Song of Songs 1:4: "The King has brought me into his chambers" (28).[58] Bernard develops his theme according to three chambers or rooms that are mentioned: (1) garden, regarded as a chamber; (2) storeroom, also called cellars; and (3) bedroom. The garden represents the historical sense of scripture; the storeroom signifies the moral sense. Bernard points out that "nature has made men equal" but this natural, moral nature has been "corrupted by pride" (30). He continues: "Our primary task is to tame this willfulness of character by submission [so that] . . . the stubborn will, worn down by the hard and prolonged schooling of experienced mentors, is humbled and healed" (30). The development of humility is the necessary starting point that allows one to reach moral maturity.

Bernard takes up the third room by noting that "the bedroom of the King is to be sought in the mystery of divine contemplation" (31). We see the generosity of spirit that marks Bernard of Clairvaux in his declaration that the king, because he has a queen as well as concubines and maidens, actually has several bedrooms: "All do not experience the delight of the Bridegroom's private visit in the same room; the Father has different arrangement for each" (31). He explains that each finds "the place and destination suited to her merits until the grace of contemplation allows her to advance further and share in the happiness of her Lord, to explore her Bridegroom's secret charms" (32). We would not expect Bernard—a citizen of the twelfth century—to do so, but today one could properly interpret the bridegroom's many rooms in a liberal way by noting that the rooms represents the different temperaments and levels of realization of those seeking nearness to God. A further interpretation in an ecumenical context might see the many rooms as the many churches of Christianity and/or the many religions practiced by humankind; thus, none are barred from the mystical journey and the hope of unity with Ultimacy. Christ's assertion in John 14:2, "in my Father's house there are many dwelling places," opens to this same interpretation.

Bernard confesses that he personally entered the bedroom of the bridegroom: "Alas! How rare the time, and how short the stay!" (33). Here one experiences something previously unknown: "This is a vision that charms rather than terrifies; that does not arouse an inquisitive restlessness, but restrains it; that calms rather than wearies. Here one may indeed be at rest" (33). This last line is reminiscent of the opening line in Augustine's *Confessions* where he declares that the human heart is restless until it rests in God. Writing from his own experience in the inner chamber of the bridegroom, Bernard confesses that it is "the only place where peace reigns" (34).

Augustine himself was exceptional in the early centuries of Christianity because of the full and frank descriptions of his personal, spiritual experience. Most Church Fathers were more reticent. Bernard of Clairvaux's forthright accounts of his own experiences in the presence of God may well have contributed to the increase in such descriptions in following centuries.

We have seen how Bernard valued the intellect and understanding. He claimed in several of his writings that actual experience is required if one is to truly understand. For example, in one of his sermons he attests: "In matters of this kind, understanding can follow only where experience leads" (185).[59] A number of Church Fathers had named the natural order, the world itself, as a second divine revelation that, when read rightly, shows God's intention for his creation. Bernard maintained the two-scripture view as well but added a third book, the book of experience. With his three-book view, he claims that humans can come to know God's will by accurately reading and understanding nature, scripture, and experience.

A few of Bernard of Clairvaux's insights into the nature of love, how the contemplative is to love God and to love others, will aptly conclude our introduction to him.

A person is present to God to the extent that the person loves him. (190)

It was only from the movement of my heart that I understood his presence. (193)

The Lord is present in the power that transforms you and the love that inflames you. (192)

God is the reason for loving God, the measure of loving him is to love without measure. (195)

Pure love has no self-interest. (198)

It is its own merit, its own reward. Love has no cause or fruit beyond itself: its fruit is its use. I love because I love. I love that I may love. (199)

Meister Eckhart (1260-1328)

Among the medieval mystics, none stands out more than Meister Eckhart. Highly popular in Germany and France during his lifetime and the years immediately following, his reputation all but disappeared for several centuries. This may have been due to official Roman Catholic opposition to him during the latter years of his life when some of his writings were deemed heretical. In modern times, however, interest in his work has increased to such an extent that many now regard him as one of the most revered mystics of all time. In fact, a move is presently underway in the Catholic Church to canonize him. Because of the universality and inclusiveness of his outlook, as well as his great influence today, we will accord him somewhat more coverage than others in this chapter.

Meister Eckhart was a teacher, preacher, and administrator in the Dominican Order, an order founded in the early thirteenth century by a group of preaching friars who also championed sound theological scholarship. The Meister's considerable influence is derived from two groups of writings, Latin and German. His Latin works include exegetical commentaries on the Bible and carefully executed philosophical-theological treatises. His German works consist mainly of two kinds: (1) sermons, many of which were preached to the Beguines, ascetic and pious laywomen who lived in loosely organized houses patterned after convents, and (2) treatises composed for purposes of consolation or instruction. As might be expected, Meister Eckhart's vernacular works are more creative and daring in expression than his formally written Latin works. Though foundational to all his writing, the Bible was particularly significant in his sermons. Here he exhibits an extraordinary creativity in his interpretation of specific passages, using metaphorical and allegorical interpretations that reflect his deep thought and personal experience. Each set of writings, the formal and the sermonic, affords insight into his mind and heart.

Although he stressed the importance of personal experience, Meister Eckhart was reluctant to speak about his own private experiences. Although rare in his writing, one does occasionally find the personal pronoun. "Here God's ground is my ground and my ground is God's ground. Here I live from my own as God lives from His own." Again, "God and I are one. Through knowledge I take God into myself, through love I enter into God."[60] Some interpreters believe that the enigmatic phrase, "pregnant with Nothing," in Meister Eckhart's sermon on Paul's Damascus Road blindness is itself the record of a personal experience, written in the third person as Paul himself occasionally did (e.g., 2 Cor. 12:2-4.). Eckhart writes: "It appeared to a man as in a dream—it was a waking dream—that he became pregnant with Nothing like a woman with child, and in that Nothing God was born."[61] Finally, by means of an analogy, Meister Eckhart affirms that direct and immediate experience is the source of certain knowledge: "If a person lives in a beautifully painted house, other people who have never been inside may indeed have opinions about it; but the one whose house it is *knows*. In the same way I am certain that I live and that God lives."[62]

Metaphysics

Drawing on the Greek philosophical tradition, mainly Plato and the Neoplatonists, Meister Eckhart was a metaphysician of the highest order. The Greek metaphysicians were not philosophers in the sense of thinkers only, as is so often the case today. For them, metaphysics (literally, that which is beyond the physical realm) leads to both understanding and realization. Meister Eckhart believed that an accurate view of reality is an essential feature in the transformational process. His attraction to metaphysics in the two-fold sense of a *knowledge of Ultimate Reality* and a *wisdom that saves* is what makes him a traditional metaphysician. His investigation into being as well as beyond-being, i.e., into existence and that which is beyond existence, and his understanding of the connection between being and knowledge are also vital to his metaphysics.

In one of his Latin works, Eckhart asserts: "Existence is God."[63] His declaration that existence—i.e., all that makes up reality—is God does not mean that he held a pantheistic view; for him the existence that marks all created things is borrowed. Insofar as anything exists, its existence is derived and therefore the existent entity is not self-sufficient. Created things are in themselves nothing: "Everything created is nothing of itself."[64] Eckhart also declares God to be Nothing when he attributes existence to creatures. If existence or being is attributed to creatures then it must be denied of God; therefore, in relationship to the beingness of created entities, God is Nothing.[65] In maintaining that God is Nothing, Eckhart is also asserting that God is purity of being, or the very beingness of being. His Nothingness of God is analogous to Buddhism's emptiness, thereby, among other things, indicating that Ultimacy is beyond all conceptual indication. He refuses to reduce God to the same status of existence as humans while maintaining a mysterious and essential oneness between God and humans.

Eckhart identifies God as *intelligere* (depending on context, intellect, intelligence, understanding, knowing) and equates this with God's very beingness or existence. He finds an essential identity between being and knowing in God. While the discursive mind distinguishes between them, in the unity of the divine they are one. To be is to know and to know is to be. And, according to the widespread macrocosm/microcosm homology of esoteric thought, "as above, so below," in man too consciousness is reality and reality is consciousness. Therefore, in God and man, when man is in union with God as Ultimacy, the being and consciousness of each is a single being and consciousness. "Where isness is not understanding, there is never unity," Eckhart claims.[66]

Eckhart distinguishes between the God that is commonly recognized in religion, on the one hand, and God as a reality prior to this known God, on the other hand, i.e., between God and Godhead. "Before there were creatures, God was not 'God': He was That which He was. But when creatures came into existence and received their *created* being, then God was not 'God' in Himself—He was 'God' in creatures." Even more boldly, the Meister exclaims: "Let us pray to God that we may be free of God that we may gain the truth and enjoy it eternally, there where the highest angel, the fly and the soul are equal," that is, where Absolute Oneness prevails.[67] A noted Eckhart scholar summarizes that Godhead "signifies God as He is in Himself, apart from any name we give to Him and apart from His relation to creatures."[68] In terms of the view of Ultimacy set forth in the first chapter, the Godhead of Eckhart is Ultimacy in itself, unmanifested. The Godhead cannot be named since all naming necessarily limits. While Eckhart prefers apophatism to kataphatism, he also recognizes that negation too limits that to which it is applied. Therefore, he believes it necessary to negate negation when referring to the Godhead. "The negation of negation," he writes "is the purest affirmation and the fullness of the term affirmed."[69]

Godhead in itself is totally without internal demarcations or external boundaries. Attempting to take this into account, Eckhart describes creation in terms of boiling and boiling over. Boiling marks the arising of the persons of the Trinity and boiling over accounts, in Eckhart's scheme, for the production of all created things.[70] Thus, all distinctive entities have their ultimate origin in the Godhead and take on created status by right of emanating from and flowing out of the Godhead. This flowing from does not, however, constitute absolute separation. "When the Father begat all creatures," Eckhart exclaims, "He begat me also, and I flowed out with all creatures and yet remained in the Father." He illustrates his point by noting how the very words he is speaking remain in him even while flowing out to his audience.[71] One scholar regards this "remaining in" as Eckhart's "expression of the authentic and altogether orthodox doctrine of panentheism . . . that all is in God and God is in all."[72]

In his German sermons, Eckhart uses *ursprunc* (literally, springing forth) to designate creation, the movement of entities out of the Godhead. Creation results from an inner pressure and is seen as a kind of eruption. One Eckhart scholar introduces the term 'dehiscence' to describe Eckhart's sense of creation. Dehiscence refers to the bursting forth of seeds from their mature pods or fruits. He writes: "God, man, and the world unveil themselves in their first 'dehiscence' . . . from their origin, without a why."[73] Eckhart does not postulate a motive for the creative process. *Sunder warumbe*, without a why, is Eckhart's final 'motive', i.e., motiveless motive, for creation. It is also man's only proper motive for worshipping the divine. The only entirely acceptable reason for loving God, Eckhart asserts, is because he is God.[74]

With this consideration we move from view of reality to transformation, from *exitus* (exit)—how God moves out of Himself to manifest Himself in creation—to *reditus* (return)—humanity's gradual ascent back to God by means of grace. To use more contemporary terms for this circular process, God's unfolding of Himself in creation is the process of involution (God involves Himself in creation) and mankind's return to God is the process of evolution (humans evolve to God).[75]

Ultimate Realization

Meister Eckhart's entire soteriology is inspired by the promise set forth in 2 Corinthians 3:18: "We shall be completely transformed and changed into God."[76] Commenting on this assurance, he declares: "I am so changed into him that he produces his being in me as one, not just similar."[77] As he begins to delineate the process more fully, he notes: "When a man accommodates himself barely to God, with love, he is un-formed, then informed and transformed in the divine uniformity wherein he is one with God."[78] He clarifies that the higher powers of the soul, i.e., will, reason, memory, "are not God, but were created in the soul and with the soul, [and therefore] must be stripped of themselves and transformed into God alone, and born in God and from God, so that God alone may be their father, for in this way they are also sons of God and the only-begotten son of God."[79] This passage introduces two principal dimensions of the return to God. These are the birth (*geburt*) of the Son (or Word) in the soul, and the breakthrough (*durchbruch*) to the Godhead. Eckhart also names here what is required of humans if this process is to occur, namely, stripping, or detachment, as he more frequently calls it.

Before taking up these key concepts in Eckhart's understanding of the transformational process, it may be well to discuss his notion of the Nobleman, designated also the Good Man, the Just Man, etc.* It is the Nobleman who has experienced the birth of the Son in the soul and broken through to the Godhead. He, and only he, can say, "God and I, we are one. I accept God into me in knowing; I go into God in loving."[80] (Note the same paralleling of knowledge and love that we saw in Bernard of Clairvaux and other Church Fathers.) In his sermon on the Nobleman, Eckhart underscores the oneness that

---

* Gender neutral language was unknown in the thirteenth century. Today we know that terms like just, good, noble apply equally to women.

marks the relationship between this kind of man and God. As he lives in the world and moves among his fellow humans, "the nobleman takes and draws all his being, life and blessedness from God, by God and in God." In a sermon on justice, Eckhart writes that the "just person is one who is conformed and transformed into justice. The just person lives in God and God in him," and seeks nothing for himself.[81]

Indicating that the Just Man is one who acts appropriately within prevailing conditions, Meister Eckhart introduces a quote from the *Institutes* of Justinian: "That man is just who gives everyone what belongs to him." He then elaborates by noting that the just are "those who give God what is his, and the saints and the angels what is theirs, and their fellow man what is his." This quality of appropriateness in daily living is the Just Man's way of honoring God, possible only in the total absence of ego, which always carries a multitude of biases and preferences. Those honor God, Eckhart avers, "who have wholly gone out of themselves, and who do not seek for what is theirs in anything . . . , who are not looking beneath themselves or above themselves or beside themselves or at themselves, who are not desiring possessions or honors or ease or pleasure or profit or inwardness or holiness or reward or the kingdom of heaven."[82]

While the ontological presence of God permeates every human, i.e., is inherent in human nature, the birth of the Son/Word in the soul is conditional. The prerequisite condition is that of honoring God, of total selflessness, absolute humility. "If God is to enter, the creature must exit."[83] Eckhart is referring not only to the outer dimensions of life, one's personality, relationships, activities, but also to "the soul's foundation . . . , its most hidden part," there where no creature, or action, or knowledge, or image can enter, the place of silence and unknowing.[84] With this condition of emptiness and silence prevailing, the Birth of the Son in the soul may take place. In a brief but daring disquisition on this mystical birth, Eckhart writes:

The Father gives birth to His Son in the soul in the very same way as He gives birth to him in eternity . . . . The Father begets His Son unceasingly, and furthermore, I say, He begets me as His Son and the same Son. I say even more: not only does He beget me as His Son, but He begets me as Himself and Himself as me, and me as His being and His nature . . . . All that God works is one: therefore He begets me as His Son without any difference.[85]

In *The Book of Divine Consolation*, Eckhart explains what he means by this birth of the Son in the soul: "I am the son of everything which forms me and gives birth to me in its image and likeness."[86] The birth of the Son in the soul means that one has become so completely purified of creatureliness that God's nature and will are free to manifest in and through oneself without any obstruction. One lives in perfect conformity with the dynamic movement of the divine in time and space. This birth in the soul has real implications for both the inner and outer person. The Meister notes: "A man so fashioned, God's son, [is] good as the son of goodness, just as the son of justice."[87]

The second major category according to which Meister Eckhart discusses the return of the soul to its Origin is the breakthrough (durchbruch) to the Godhead. In a sermon treating this theme, Eckhart identifies the Intellect as the higher power of the mind/soul (*sele*) that rests at nothing short of returning to its Ground. "It aspires," he claims, "to God not as he is the Holy Spirit nor as he is the Son: it flees from the Son. Nor does it want God inasmuch as he is God. Why? Because, as such, he still carries a name . . . . It wants him as he is the marrow . . . , the nucleus . . . , the root . . . from which goodness exudes."[88] In another sermon, the Meister declares that "the spark in the soul, which has never touched either time or place . . . , rejects all created things, and wants nothing but its naked God, as he is in himself." This spark or light, he further asserts, "is not content with the Father or the Son or the Holy Spirit . . . , is not content with the divine nature's generative or fruitful qualities . . . , is not content with the simple divine essence in its repose." Instead, this light wants "to know the source of this essence, it wants to go into the simple ground, into the quiet desert, into which distinction never gazed." He concludes his description of this final and total retreat into the Godhead by noting that "in the innermost part, where no one dwells, there is contentment for that light, and there it is more inward than it can be to itself, for this ground is a simple silence, in itself immovable, and by this immovability all things are moved."[89]

Reference has been made several times to detachment, which turns out to be one of the most crucial and emphasized themes in Eckhart's preaching and teaching. In fact, in his list of four subjects he is "wont to speak about," Eckhart lists detachment (*abegesheidenheit*, Middle High German; *abgeshiedenheit*, Modern German) as the first.[90] In his treatise *On Detachment,* he declares that he finds "no other virtue better than a pure detachment from all things." He sees it as the source of all virtue. The Meister says that true detachment calls "for the spirit to stand as immovable against whatever may chance to it of joy and sorrow, honor, shame and disgrace, as a mountain of lead stands before a little breath of wind."

Detachment for Eckhart does not mean unconcerned distance from the cares of others. His view does not lead him to advocate withdrawal from society or renunciation of acts of kindness. "The outer man may be active," he argues, while "the inner man remains wholly free and immovable."[91] Eckhart was not one to countenance quietism or rapturous ecstasy as ends in themselves. In his sermon on Mary and Martha, he openly favors Martha as the one who has integrated a contemplative awareness with an active life.[92] Elsewhere, Meister Eckhart argues that if a person is in a state of rapture and comes to know of a sick man in need of a bowl of soup, it is "far better . . . out of love to desist from this [rapture] and to serve the poor man."[93]

Detachment for Eckhart is not just from the tangibles of the outer world. It is also, and even more important, an inner orientation of the psyche that opens up timelessly to what is, what has been, and what will be. "It is not enough for a man's disposition to be detached just for the present moment when he wants to be bound to God, but he must have a well-exercised detachment from what is past and from what is yet to come."[94] True detachment excludes nostalgia and regret, anticipation and longing. As a condition of inwardness during contemplation, detachment requires retreat from feeling, intention, thought, imagery, memory, indeed, from the myriad of subjective 'objects' that typically constitute inner awareness. "A person should be removed from all senses and turn all his powers inward, and attain forgetfulness of all things and of himself."[95] Eckhart points out that "just as no multiplicity can disturb God, nothing can disturb or fragment [the detached] man, for he is one in that One where all multiplicity is one and is one unmultiplicity."[96]

The Meister outlines the unconditional demands of detachment in unambiguous terms in his homily on the poor in spirit (Matthew 5:3). "A poor man," he says, "wants nothing, and knows nothing, and has nothing." To want nothing means that a person must be "as free of his own created will as he was when he did not exist." Eckhart argues that as long as "you have a will to fulfill God's will, and a longing for God and for eternity, then you are not poor; for a poor man is one who has a will and longing for nothing." Second, "a man should be set as free of his own knowing as he was when he was not." This means that he is "to live as if he does not even know that he is not in any way living for himself or for the truth or for God. Rather, he should be so free of all knowing that he does not know or experience or grasp that God lives in him." Finally, "having nothing," for Eckhart, does not refer to external possessions but to a place within where God reigns and works. "Poverty of spirit is for a man to keep so free of God and of all his works that if God wishes to work in the soul, he himself is the place in which he [works] . . . . God is his own worker in himself."[97]

A second major notion that Eckhart uses to convey this total abandonment to and reliance on God is 'letting-go' or 'letting-be' (*gelazenheit*, Mid. High Ger.; *gelassenheit*, Mod. Ger.). Analyzing Eckhart's unique use of the term, one scholar prefers to render it in English as 'releasement' and concludes that it conveys several key notions: voluntary emptying of both outer and inner life (things and images), death to individuality and birth to beingness in general, and release of one's own distinctiveness.[98] All of this is implied when Eckhart declares: "Where the creature ends, there God begins to be. God asks only that you get out of his way, in so far as you are creature, and let him be God in you."[99]

Living according to the principles of detachment and letting-be results in living "without a why" (sunder warumbe), thereby paralleling God's motiveless creating. Eckhart argues that as long as "you perform your works for the sake of the kingdom of heaven, or for God's sake, or for the sake of your eternal blessedness" you have not come to the deepest and most correct understanding. He refers to one's innermost being where "God's ground is my ground, and my ground is God's ground" and says that "it is out of this inner ground that you should perform all your works without asking, 'Why?'"[100] Elsewhere he indicates that one should love God because of God, truth because of truth, justice because of justice, and goodness because of goodness.[101] The 17th century mystical poet Angelus Silesius aptly conveys this essential perspective of Meister Eckhart:

> The rose is without why; it blooms because it blooms;
> It cares not for itself; asks not if it's seen.[102]

A renowned Eckhart scholar observes that a person who "lives without a why is able to find God in all things."[103] Commenting on 1 John 4:9, "We live in Him," Meister Eckhart expounds: "We must understand Him equally in all things, in one not more than another, for He is equally in all things."[104] Eckhart here acknowledges experientially what he elsewhere treats ontologically as one pole of God's dialectical relationship to beings, namely, God's indistinctness from all distinct entities, given the unity of being; existence is God.[105] Showing the connection between detachment and awareness of God, Eckhart notes that "whoever really and truly has God, he has him everywhere, in the street and in company with everyone, just as much as in church or in solitary places." Such a person has God present in his dispositions, intentions, and love; indeed, "has God essentially [and thus] grasps God divinely." This means that "God shines in all things [and] forms himself for the man out of all things." Such a person "grasps everything as divine and as greater than things in themselves are" (since things are, apart from God, nothing). For the Nobleman, the Just Man, whose entire life, inner and outer, is marked by detachment, letting-be, and without why, "all things become . . . nothing but God."[106]

Meister Eckhart was fully aware of the duality that marks the immediate experience of all humans. Unlike most, however, he refused to accept this duality—particularly pernicious as the precondition of all conflict and suffering—as necessary to the human condition. Instead, he constructed a metaphysical and transformational system founded on his own personal experience that moves from the obviousness of duality through the tension and ambiguity of a dialectic to the harmony of union and, finally, to identity in Ultimacy/Godhead. With transformative principles and powers encoded in the cosmos—and made clear and effective through the grace of the Word—he saw human nature as entirely capable of undertaking this transformative journey from finitude to infinity, provided, of course, that such fundamental and essential principles as detachment and releasement are not simply affirmed but actually practiced.

Finally, while the Meister's metaphysical system is a challenge to understand, the transformative practices he set forth are an even greater challenge to embody and put into daily practice. That the two, theory and practice, are linked is indicated by Meister Eckhart in his declaration: "He who wants to understand my teaching of releasement must himself be perfectly released."[107]

Saints and Sages in Modern Times

Teresa of Avila (1515-1582)

Teresa de Cepeda y Ahumada was born in central Spain to a moderately wealthy merchant and his second wife. At the early age of seven, she fantasized becoming a martyr with her older brother as a quick way of gaining heaven. Realizing the suffering this would bring to their parents, they decided instead to take up the practice of hermits while remaining at home. During adolescence, Teresa's interests turned more to worldly matters, reading romance novels, wearing perfume, and fine clothes. She entered a convent in her mid-teens but returned home after a year and a half due to poor health. Her deepest longings, however, remained in the convent. At the age of twenty one, she became a Carmelite nun in Avila, her native town. Teresa took naturally to the cultivation of a life of prayer. Just a few years after embarking on her religious vocation, she reported exceptional spiritual experiences, occasionally even union with the divine. Her practice of prayer contributed to a sensitizing of her consciousness and her conscience.

> I was living an extremely burdensome life, because in prayer I understood more clearly my faults. On the one hand God was calling me; on the other hand I was following the world. All the things of God made me happy; those of the world held me bound.

It seems I desired to harmonize these two contraries—so inimical to one another—such as are the spiritual life and sensory joys, pleasures, and pastimes. In prayer I was having great trouble, for my spirit was not proceeding as lord but as slave. And so I was not able to shut myself within myself (which was my whole manner of procedure in prayer); instead, I shut within myself a thousand vanities. (90-91)[108]

While there were periods when Teresa did not experience this pull in opposite directions, she nonetheless reports that "for more than eighteen of the twenty-eight years since I began prayer, I suffered this battle and conflict between friendship with God and friendship with the world" (95). On two occasions in 1554, Teresa underwent conversion experiences that led to the healing of her inner split. Concerning the first of these, she wrote:

One day entering the oratory I saw a statue they had borrowed for a certain feast to be celebrated in the house. It represented the much wounded Christ and was very devotional so that beholding it I was utterly distressed in seeing Him that way, for it well represented what He suffered for us. I felt so keenly aware of how poorly I thanked Him for those wounds that, it seems to me, my heart broke. Beseeching Him to strengthen me once and for all that I might not offend Him, I threw myself down before Him with the greatest outpouring of tears. (100-101)

The second conversion occurred while reading Augustine's *Confessions*. She so completely identified with Augustine's contrition and release in his experience of conversion in the Milan garden that she wrote: "It only seemed to me, according to what I felt in my heart, that it was I the Lord called" (103). After these two conversion events, Teresa found herself wanting to spend more time in contemplation, coupled with a natural turning away from "occasions of sin."

These two turning points notwithstanding, Teresa's spiritual life was one of gradual development, marked by a rhythm of progress and regression, of bliss and sorrow. She confessed as much when she refers longingly to others who remained steady after being called, "whereas in my case I had turned back so often that I was worn out from it." Reflecting on these years from the vantage point of her spiritual maturity, Teresa discovered the cause of her fluctuation. Her failure to remain steadfastly committed to God came about, "as it appears to me now, because I did not put all my trust in His Majesty and lose completely the trust I had in myself. I searched for a remedy, I made attempts, but I didn't understand that all is of little benefit if we do not take away completely the trust we have in ourselves and place it in God" (100).

Teresa's prayer life continued to develop and her spiritual insight to deepen. She drew heavily from devotional and mystical literature for her own process and was deeply grieved when the Spanish Inquisition led to a ban on much of this literature. Teresa reported that at this time Christ appeared to her and said that he would give her "a living book." She then began to receive visions and experiences of union that prompted her to eventually write an account of her life. In this work, she outlined the four stages of prayer and compared them to four ways by which a garden may be watered. To pull water up from the bottom of a well by a rope and bucket is the most difficult way to water a garden, and indicates the difficulty in the beginning practice of prayer when one struggles to overcome distractions and keep the mind focused. Here one must also isolate oneself from others in hope of minimizing distractions. A somewhat easier way to secure water from a well is by means of a wheel and a bucket. Teresa wrote: "Here the soul begins to recollect itself and comes to touch on the supernatural, to which it could never attain by it own efforts" (113).[109] The operation of grace becomes more obvious in this second stage, called the prayer of quiet, and one experiences a state of solace even if one continues to pray for a long time.

The third stage, wrote Teresa, is like watering a garden by directing to it the water from a brook or river. The water flows over the garden with minimal labor. Prayer now occurs as if one's reason, memory, and will are asleep. There is "an almost complete death to all the things of this world and an enjoyment of God," and the "pleasures, sweetness, and delight are incomparably greater than in the former state of prayer." Teresa described the results of this quality of prayer as "a glorious folly, a heavenly madness, in which true wisdom is acquired" (115). Teresa compared the final stage of prayer, the prayer of union, to a garden that is watered by rain. The gardener now does no work. In this fourth stage, all distraction has vanished and there is a sense of "enjoyment without any understanding of the thing in which the soul is rejoicing" (116). All the faculties are suspended except for the will which is occupied only in loving. While wondering and pondering about the state of the soul at this time, the Lord appeared to Teresa and said: "It dies wholly to itself, my daughter, in order that it may give itself more and more to me. It is not itself that lives, but I. As it cannot comprehend what it understands, it understands by not understanding" (116-117). Teresa's fourfold analysis of prayer, especially from the standpoint of effort and grace, is one of the most perceptive in the entire body of Christian mystical literature.

The Interior Castle, which is based on Teresa's lifelong journey toward and in Ultimacy, is the product of her mature reflection. Here she outlines the path that leads away from attachment to the world by means of passing through the seven rooms that make up the castle. The castle represents the soul and each room is a level of spiritual development. In each of these rooms or dwelling places, there are many other rooms, above, below, to the side, thus suggesting the complexity of human nature, of varied capacities and different ways of being. In the center of the castle, God dwells. The journey into and through the soul to its very center is a process of self-discovery, of self-knowing, as well as transcendence to ever higher levels. The entrance to the soul is through prayer. Prayer is the means by which the mystery of the soul and God is penetrated. Outside the castle are those who feel no attraction to the divine, those who are caught up entirely in the life of the world and sensuality.

The first dwelling place inside the castle is comprised of those who have good intentions and who pray occasionally, but who are nevertheless absorbed with matters of wealth, prestige, security, etc. The second dwelling place contains rooms for those who have made some real though reserved steps into a life of prayer. God's grace reaches them mainly through objective means, such as literature, sermons, and inspiring friendships. Occupying the third dwelling place are those who persevere in prayer, who attempt to live according to God's will, who avoid sin, who practice self-discipline, who extend charity to those in need. Here abide those widely regarded as good Christians. Most do not venture further, however, because of their contentment with the fulfillment of the formal requirements of religion. Their attachment to wealth, honor, security, health, and comfort—in other words, their unquestioned assumption of the prevailing values of their culture—serves to block their way to further journeying.

The inner pilgrimage thus far has been in the domain of exoteric religion. The last four dwelling places of the interior castle comprise the esoteric or mystical dimension of religion. In the fourth dwelling place, infused prayer begins; here grace operates more fully. Teresa softens the usual contrast between works and grace by distinguishing between consolations which begin in human action and end in divine response and spiritual delights which originate in God and overflow into human nature. At this stage of the journey, one endeavors to let go of intellectual activity while guarding against self-recrimination for being unable to do so without faltering. Teresa encourages the traveler by noting that the wandering mind is characteristic of the human condition, as natural as eating and sleeping. One finds rest in the prayer of quiet, or peace in the divine presence, even while the mind continues its habitual activity.

The fifth dwelling place is marked by the prayer of union. Here the human faculties become silent. In the absence of their activity comes a certitude that God and the soul fuse into each other. Teresa contends that if anyone lacks certainty of this conjoining of the soul with God, "what he has experienced is not union of the whole soul with God but only union of one of the faculties or some one of the many other kinds of favor which God grants the soul."[110] The highly spiritual nature of life in this room, however, does not justify a lessening of involvement in ordinary existence. Humility, love of neighbor, exercise of virtue, and the conscientious carrying out of ordinary tasks continue to be expected.

In the sixth room, a number of exceptional mystical experiences occur. The spiritual betrothal takes place here. Great courage and fortitude are required if the soul is to become wed to the divine. Inner and outer trials must be faced and overcome. One must be untouched by both criticism and praise. One must willingly accept suffering and illness. One must work through any fears that arise, such as the fear of self-deception or of divine rejection. The betrothal itself is marked by such rapture that the ordinary senses are suspended. But with the loss of consciousness of the outer world comes increased insight into the divine mysteries.

That which was hidden from the soul in the prior rooms becomes known in the seventh, though by means of a new kind of knowing. Here one is graced with an intellectual vision of the Trinity. Teresa writes: "The three persons of the most Blessed Trinity reveal themselves, preceded by an illumination that shines on the spirit like a most dazzling cloud of light" (454).[111] This description is plainly different from that of Moses on Mt. Sinai, particularly as interpreted by Gregory of Nyssa, Dionysius and others. In this respect, Teresa comments: "He [God] may manifest himself in a different way to other people" (455). Though Teresa refers explicitly to the Trinity here, her overall spiritual journey is decidedly Christocentric. In this respect, she notes that even here in the seventh room, the spiritual marriage takes place as a perfect union, not with the Eternal Logos of John's Gospel, as one might expect given the ethereal quality of this level of mystical experience, but more 'concretely' with the Word Incarnate. In other words, this profound meeting of the divine in the depths of the soul is marked by the mutual indwelling of the human and divine, a thoroughgoing integration of what conventional Christianity regards as mutually exclusive. Rightly understood, the human and the divine become integral to each other. Teresa warns that an absorption in the divinity of Christ that results in failure to honor his humanity causes one to forfeit full realization of the last two dwelling places. She concludes that the purpose of the entire journey is to empower one to live like Christ and produce works comparable to his.

Teresa is intent on depicting her experience in the seventh room as qualitatively different from that in earlier rooms. "Here God appears in the soul's center, not by an imaginary but by an intellectual vision far more delicate than those seen before." The soul now "feels a supreme delight" and witnesses the Lord's "heavenly glory in a far more subtle way than by any vision or spiritual delight." Teresa distinguishes between spiritual betrothal and spiritual marriage by noting that the former can be dissolved but not the latter, "where the soul always remains in its center with its God" (456). She illustrates the former by means of two wax candles coming together to form a single light but that are still capable of being separated as candles. Spiritual marriage, on the other hand, is analogous to "rain falling from heaven into a river or stream, becoming one and same liquid, so that the river and rain water cannot be divided" (457).

Teresa was the first female saint to be made a Doctor of the Church. It is evident that her account of the journey into the soul is far from merely theoretical. It is undeniably autobiographical, with the transition to each dwelling place seen as a deepening of her spiritual experience, a transformation to a more transcendent level of being. Throughout her mature years, Teresa felt a deep aspiration to guide her nuns in ways that would allow them to reach the same heights of spiritual awareness as herself. In her final comments on the journey into and through the interior castle, she cites a principal that has become virtually universal among those traversing the mystical path. "Without doubt," she writes, "if we empty ourselves of all that belongs to the creature [by means of dispassion or nonattachment], depriving ourselves of it for the love of God, that same Lord will fill us with himself" (458).

John Wesley (1703-1791)

The previous chapter indicated that Christian mysticism has been pursued in the Eastern and Catholic churches but hardly at all among Protestants. Spiritual development in Protestantism proceeds more in terms of devotion, piety, and holiness, often according to the doctrine and experience of sanctification (literally, to make holy). Far greater emphasis is given to initial conversion among Protestants than on steady and continual progress in spirituality with the objective of coming to a mystical experience of unity with God. All of the saints and sages previously discussed have been from the Orthodox and Catholic traditions. It is fitting to consider at least one Protestant. John Wesley, founder of the Methodist Church, one of the main Protestant denominations, may be regarded as representative.

John was one of nineteen children, nearly half of whom failed to live beyond infancy. His father was a priest, though a non-conforming one, in the Church of England. His mother was a woman of exceptional strength of character who instilled discipline and order in her children. John was a hard-working and competent student who mastered several languages, ancient and modern. He read widely and was especially drawn to the devotional literature of such classical Christian writers as Thomas à Kempis, Jeremy Taylor, and William Law. John was ordained a priest in the Church of England in 1728, and with his brother, Charles, took on leadership of a group that called itself the Holy Club. This group met regularly to assist and encourage each other in the study and practice of their faith. Because of the structured patterns and disciplined practices of the group, they came to be called Methodists by outsiders.

Wesley declared that for the first ten years of his life, he unquestioningly adhered to the strict teaching of his parents that a person "could only be saved by universal obedience, by keeping all the commandments of God."[112] In spite of this emphasis, in the ensuing six or seven years, he was negligent. He admits to being "almost continually guilty of outward sins," though not scandalous ones. During this time, he based his sense of personal salvation on the fact that he did not live as bad a life as others and, in addition, went to church, read the Bible, and said his prayers. Much the same pattern continued during his university years. Still, he had not "so much as a notion of inward holiness." During his early twenties, he read Thomas à Kempis and came "to see that true religion was seated in the heart and that God's law extended to all our thoughts as well as words and actions." As a result, he increased his effort and set out on "a new life." He spent an hour or two daily in "religious retirement," took communion weekly, guarded against sin in word and deed, strove and prayed for inward holiness. He observed: "Doing so much and living so good a life, I doubted not but I was a good Christian." Throughout his twenties and thirties he redoubled his efforts, limiting his friendship to those who were similarly religious, watching more carefully against sin, studying more diligently, preaching to the masses, visiting prisons, helping the poor, tending to the sick, practicing self-denial, observing frequent fasts, sometimes persecuted for his zeal, and often barred from preaching in the established churches. In spite of Wesley's extraordinary effort to keep God's law he lacked assurance of salvation.

In 1735 John and Charles set sail for Georgia under the auspices of the Society for the Propagation of the Gospel in Foreign Parts.

Though their intent was to convert the American Indians to Christianity, they actually worked mainly with white colonists. In Georgia, John continued to be influenced by the Moravians, pious European Christians whom he had first met on the ship to the Colonies. Their faith profoundly impressed and humbled him when, with calm fearlessness, they faced the threat of death during a violent storm. In Georgia one of their leaders pointedly asked John, "Do you know Jesus Christ?" John answered, "I know that he is the savior of the world." The Moravian responded, "True, but do you know that he has saved you?" John had to admit that he lacked this assurance. His several encounters with the Moravians prepared for the conversion experience he was to undergo after returning to London in 1738.

About a month before his conversion, Wesley met Peter Bohler, a German Moravian, and readily agreed with him that faith is "a sure trust and confidence which a man hath in God, that through the merits of Christ his sins are forgiven and he [is] reconciled to . . . God." He also acknowledged that happiness and holiness follow from this faith and forgiveness. But Wesley had difficulty understanding how conversion could be "an instantaneous work . . . , how a man could at once be thus turned from darkness to light, from sin and misery to righteousness and joy." He restudied the scriptures on this very point and was surprised to discover "scarce any instances there of other than *instantaneous* conversions." After meeting several persons who claimed to have been converted instantaneously, and whose lives exemplified the qualities of redemption, particularly assurance and joy, Wesley became convinced, at least intellectually, that sudden conversion was not only biblically correct but experientially possible.

Gradually, through his discussion with Moravian friends and his rereading of the Bible, Wesley came to realize that he had been attempting all along to win salvation by means of his good works, his own righteousness. He resolved to end the long "struggle between nature and grace" by praying continually for "justifying, saving faith, a full reliance on the blood of Christ shed for *me*, a trust in him, as

my Christ, as *my* sole justification, sanctification, and redemption."
On May 24, 1738, Wesley went, unwillingly he says, to a gathering on
Aldersgate Street of devout believers, many of them Moravians. Here
he listened to a reading of the preface to Martin Luther's commentary
on Romans. Wesley wrote: "About a quarter before nine, while he
[Luther] was describing the change which God works in the heart
through faith in Christ, I felt my heart strangely warmed. I felt I did
trust in Christ, Christ alone for salvation; and an assurance was given
me that he had taken away my sins, even mine, and saved me from
the law of sin and death."

Even though Wesley regarded this experience as the decisive
turning point in his life-long commitment to Christ, he continued to
be confronted with doubts and temptations. When he questioned why
his conversion was not accompanied by joy, he learned that peace and
victory over sin are what is essential, that "God sometimes giveth,
sometimes withholdest [transports of joy] according to the counsels
of his own will." Wesley admits to being faced with temptations and
to resisting them again and again, with the graceful help of God.
Before his conversion, he sometimes fell victim to temptation. Now,
"fighting with all my might under the law, as well as under grace," he
claimed to always withstand them. When Wesley felt that the devil
was causing him to doubt because there were not more discernible
changes resulting from his conversion, he responded: "I know not.
But this I know, I have *now peace with God.* And *I sin not today*,
and Jesus my Master has forbid me to take thought for the morrow,"
a reference to Christ's injunction, "Do not worry about tomorrow"
(Matthew 6:34).

Wesley's Aldersgate experience was not so much a crowning
achievement as a turning point that empowered him to "go on
from faith to faith and from strength to strength." He read the
Church Fathers and was familiar with the mystical tradition in
both the Orthodox and Catholic churches. He was less interested in
uncommon states of consciousness and more interested in the total

quality of life. Consequently, he interpreted the mystical life in terms "entire sanctification," a further intervention on the part of God that results in Christian perfection, "whereby God dwells completely in the believer and enables full love of God and neighbour."[113] He understood the injunction in Matthew 5:48 to be, with God's help, a realizable ideal: "Be perfect . . . as your heavenly Father is perfect." Sanctification, for Wesley, was a second work of grace following justification that enabled one to live free of sin and to perfectly love God and others. It sometimes occurred instantly and was recognized as a 'second blessing' following redemption. In other cases, sanctification developed over time through discipleship, "a renewal of our minds in the image of God; a recovery of the divine likeness; a still-increasing conformity of heart and life to the pattern of our most holy Redeemer."[114]

We have seen the significance of grace for Wesley in his own conversion. Undoubtedly drawing from this experience, he relentlessly disclaimed any hint of "works-righteousness" throughout his entire life. "All the blessings which God hath bestowed upon man are of his mere grace, bounty, or favour: his free, undeserved favour, favour altogether undeserved, man having no claim to the least of his mercies." He believed, however, that humans play a cooperative role in the operation of grace, that grace is mediated through faith. More specifically, he taught that grace comes through "the instituted means of grace," activities on the part of believers that open them to the reception of God's grace. These include prayer, private and communal; reading and meditating on scripture as well as hearing it read; participating in the Lord's Supper or Eucharist; fasting; joining with other Christians for worship, study, reflection, encouragement and correction, and, of course, upright behavior.[115]

As a brother and lifelong associate with John, Charles Wesley imbibed the same spirit as his brother and, in addition, possessed exceptional poetic talent. Among the many hymns he composed is "Love Divine, All Loves Excelling," a fitting conclusion to our brief

introduction to John Wesley and the form of Christian spirituality
he championed.[116]

> Love Divine, all loves excelling, Joy of Heav'n, to earth come down:
> Fix in us thy humble dwelling, All thy faithful mercies crown.
> Jesus, thou art all compassion, Pure, unbounded love thou art;
> Visit us with thy salvation, Enter every trembling heart.
>
> Breathe, O breathe thy loving Spirit Into every troubled breast;
> Let us all in thee inherit, Let us find the promised rest.
> Take away our bent to sinning; Alpha and Omega be;
> End of faith, as its beginning, Set our hearts at liberty.
>
> Finish, then, thy new creation; Pure and spotless let us be:
> Let us see thy great salvation Perfectly restored in thee:
> Changed from glory into glory Till in heav'n we take our place,
> Till we cast our crowns before thee, Lost in wonder, love and praise.

Thomas Merton (1915-1968)

Merton was born in southern France to an American mother and
a New Zealander father. Both parents were artists. His mother died
when he was six and his father about ten years later. His life in several
countries (France, Bermuda, USA, and England) during his early years
may have contributed to his later worldwide interests and concerns.
Merton's adolescent and early adult years were marked by a zestful,
bohemian lifestyle. During at least part of this time he considered
himself an atheist. He began his university education at Cambridge
but transferred to Columbia University in New York, a move probably
related to his involvement with a young woman who became pregnant.
He was able to discern years later how his time at Columbia prepared
him for conversion. He wrote: "God brought me and a half a dozen

others together at Columbia, and made us friends, in such a way that our friendship would work powerfully to rescue us from the confusion and the misery in which we had come to find ourselves."[117]

Benefiting from hindsight and a more mature understanding of human nature and the way God works, Merton identified several of the factors that contributed to his conversion. One was his discovery of the notion of aseity, a quality applicable to God alone, which refers to "the power of a being to exist absolutely in virtue of itself." This awareness that "God is Being Itself," that God enjoys "complete independence not only as regards everything outside but also as regards everything within Himself," Merton wrote, "was to revolutionize my whole life."

Another vital influence was Mark Van Doren, both his friendship and his courses on literature, especially one on Shakespeare which Merton says was "the best course I ever had at college." The course carried special meaning for Merton because it was not taught as a sterile academic subject but concerned itself with "life, death, time, love, sorrow, fear, wisdom, suffering, eternity."

Merton met a Hindu guru who, while reticent to talk much about Hinduism, on one occasion said: "There are many beautiful mystical books written by the Christians. You should read St. Augustine's *Confessions*, and *The Imitation of Christ* by Thomas à Kempis." Merton had already been reading some in Eastern mysticism, but this advice opened the door to mysticism in Christianity, particularly in Roman Catholicism. Merton's graduate thesis, "Nature and Art in William Blake," also influenced his conversion. He describes his thesis as "a study of Blake's reaction against every kind of literalism and naturalism and narrow, classical realism in art," a reaction which sprang from Blake's "own ideal which was essentially mystical and supernatural." The effect of this study, Merton says, was to "cure me of all the naturalism and materialism in my own philosophy, besides resolving all the inconsistencies and self-contradictions that had persisted in my mind for years."

Writing from the vantage point of his early monastic career, Merton opens his autobiography, *The Seven Storey Mountain,* with the following summary description of the deep-rooted split he discovered in his own nature just prior to his conversion: "Free by nature, in the image of God, I was nevertheless the prisoner of my own violence and my own selfishness, in the image of the world into which I was born. That world was the picture of Hell, full of men like myself, loving God and yet hating Him; born to love Him, living instead in fear and hopeless self-contradictory hungers."

The decisive act of conversion for Merton was precipitated by his reading about the conversion of Gerald Manley Hopkins. Merton wrote:

> All of a sudden, something began to stir within me, something began to push me, to prompt me. It was a movement that spoke like a voice. "What are you waiting for?" it said. "Why are you sitting here? Why do you still hesitate? You know what you ought to do? Why don't you do it?" I stirred in the chair, I lit a cigarette, looked out the window at the rain, tried to shut the voice up. "Don't act on impulse," I thought. "This is crazy. This is not rational. Read your book . . . ." Suddenly, I could bear it no longer. I put down the book, and got into my raincoat, and started down the stairs. I went out into the street . . . . And then everything inside me began to sing—to sing with peace, to sing with strength and to sing with conviction.

Merton walked to a nearby Roman Catholic Church and told the priest he wanted to become a Catholic. He was given several books to read and invited to return twice a week for instruction in the fundamentals of Christianity and Catholicism. While undergoing his two months of preparation, Merton looked forward to his formal induction into the church, a ritual that would include baptism, confession, and communion. During the ceremony itself, which took place when he was twenty-three years old, Merton felt that a momentous transformation was taking place. He exclaimed: "What mountains were falling from my shoulders! What scales of dark night were peeling off my intellect to let in the inward vision of God and His truth!" From this time on, the orientation of Merton's life changed dramatically and diametrically: "Now I had entered into the everlasting movement of that gravitation which is the very life and spirit of God: God's own gravitation towards the depths of His own infinite nature."

Merton had numerous transformative experiences that deepened and broadened his initial turn toward the divine and away from a worldly life. One of these took place twenty years after his conversion and shattered his separate self sense. It also left him with a sense of the falsity of the common distinction between the sacred and the profane. Merton remembered the exact location in a southern city in the middle of a busy shopping center. He wrote: "I was suddenly overwhelmed with the realization that I loved all those people, that they were mine and I theirs, that we could not be alien to one another even though we were total strangers. It was like waking from a dream of separateness, of spurious self-isolation in a special world, the world of renunciation and supposed holiness. The whole illusion of a separate, holy existence is a dream." Merton clarified further: "It was as if I suddenly saw the secret beauty of their hearts, the depths of their hearts where neither sin nor desire nor self-knowledge can reach, the core of their reality, the person that each one is in God's eyes."[118] A man-made boundary in Merton's mind fell away. This new insight enabled Merton to resolve the oft-perceived polarity between so-called other-worldly mysticism and active involvement in the realities of ordinary existence. It allowed him to integrate his hermitical and contemplative life, on one hand, with passionate concern for and action in matters of social justice, on the other hand, an integration that became his hallmark as a twentieth-century monk.

Merton's conversion continued to deepen and expand right up to the last week of his life. On December 10, 1968, he died from accidental electrocution in Bangkok shortly after giving an address at a conference on interreligious monastic life. His visit just a few days earlier to the Buddhist sculptures at Polonnaruwa, Sri Lanka, had precipitated a profound recognition that was both transcultural and deeply transpersonal. He wrote:

> I am able to approach the Buddhas barefoot and undisturbed, my feet in wet grass, wet sand. Then the silence of the extraordinary faces. The great smiles. Huge and yet subtle. Filled with every possibility, questioning nothing, knowing everything, rejecting nothing, the peace not of emotional resignation but of Madhyamika, of sunyata [emptiness], that has seen through every question without trying to discredit anyone or anything—*without refutation*—without establishing some other argument . . . . Looking at these figures I was suddenly, almost forcibly, jerked clean out of the habitual, half-tied vision of things, and an inner clarity, as if exploding from the rocks themselves, became evident and obvious . . . . All problems are resolved and everything is clear, simply because what matters is clear. The rock, all matter, all life, is charged with dharmakaya [the realm of truth] . . . . Everything is emptiness and everything is compassion. I don't know when in my life I have ever had such a sense of beauty and spiritual validity running together in one aesthetic illumination . . . . I have now seen and pierced through the surface and have got beyond the shadow and the disguise . . . . It is clear, pure, complete. It says everything; it needs nothing. And because it needs nothing it can afford to be silent, unnoticed, undiscovered.[119]

No twentieth-century Christian monk and mystic has had a greater impact on the American populace than Thomas Merton. Untold numbers of persons, Roman Catholic, Protestant, and secular, have responded positively to his numerous books. His broad appeal in no way reflects a watering down of the Christian life. We will conclude this brief overview of Merton as a mystic by simply listing some of his insights into contemplation, the essential means in Christianity (as we have repeatedly seen) of coming to ultimate realization.[120]

> Contemplation is the highest expression of man's intellectual and spiritual life. It is that life itself, fully awake, fully active, fully aware that it is alive. It is spiritual wonder. It is spontaneous awe at the sacredness of life, of being. (1)

> It is a vivid realization of the fact that life and being in us proceed from an invisible, transcendent and infinitely abundant Source. (1)

> It *knows* the Source, obscurely, inexplicably, but with a certitude that goes both beyond reason and beyond simple faith . . . . [It is] a knowledge too deep to be grasped in images, in words or even in clear concepts. (1)

> [Contemplation is] an awakening to the Real within all that is real. A vivid awareness of infinite Being at the roots of our own limited being. An awareness of our contingent reality as received, as a present from God, as a free gift of love. (3)

> We do not see God in contemplation—we *know* Him by love: for He is pure Love and when we taste the experience of loving God for His own sake alone, we know by experience Who and What He is. (268)

> Where contemplation becomes what it is really meant to be, it is no longer something infused by God into a created subject, so much as God living in God and identifying a created life with His own Life so that there is nothing left of any significance but God living in God. (284)

Henri Le Saux/Abhishiktananda (1910-1973)

"Now I am ready, if the Lord wills, to remain forever a Hindu-Christian monk. Solitude, silence, poverty."[121] So wrote the French monk, Dom Henri Le Saux, just a few years after coming to India where he took the name Abhishiktananda, Bliss of the Anointed (Christ). His new name attests to his endeavor "to integrate into Christianity the monastic tradition of India."[122] J.D.M. Stuart, a friend and colleague in India, calls him a "Christian advaitin," i.e., a Christian nondualist.[123] Shortly after Abhishiktananda's death, his French disciple, Marc Chaduc (who took the name, Ajatananda, Bliss of the Unborn), said of him: "His spiritual path essentially consisted in the complete appropriation of the advaitic experience of the Upanishadic rishis [sages], without however losing hold of his own rootedness in the Christian tradition."[124] Abhishiktananda not only remained faithful to his interfaith commitment but spent a quarter of a century in India exploring the depths where faith meets faith and becomes realization. Raimundo Panikkar, another close friend of Swami Abhishiktananda, says he is "one of the most authentic witnesses of our times of the encounter in depth between Christian and Eastern spiritualities."[125]

Monasticism, a religious vocation in both Hinduism and Christianity, provided the external context for Abhishiktananda's inner exploration. His interiority led to depth experiences that he attempted to express in meaningful intellectual form, fully recognizing the impossibility of doing so. Finally, in the last months of his life, Abhishiktananda came to a realization of the Supreme beyond all form and formulation. Each of these dimensions of his spiritual journey will be taken up, after a brief biographical introduction.

Henri Le Saux was born in 1910 in the Brittany region of France. At the age of nineteen he entered a Benedictine monastery and, after studying theology, was ordained a priest. During this time he developed an intense affection for India and its spirituality, even studying English, Tamil, and the Upanishads in hope of someday going to India. Finally, in 1948, after fifteen years of preparation and waiting, he arrived in the country that was to remain his home for the rest of his life. Here, in 1950, he and Father Jules Monchanin, a senior French monk of similar outlook, founded the Satchitananda Ashram in South India for the express purpose of integrating Christianity and the Indian monastic tradition.

Within months of his arrival in India, Swami Abhishiktananda traveled with Father Monchanin to Arunachala, the holy mountain in South India, to meet Ramana Maharshi, the most renowned saint in twentieth-century India (as we have seen). This meeting proved a turning point in Abhishiktananda's life since it marked the beginning of his lifelong involvement in advaita (nonduality). Of this initial meeting, Abhishiktananda wrote: "Even before my mind was able to recognize the fact, and still less to express it, the invisible halo of this Sage had been perceived by something in me deeper than any words. Unknown harmonies awoke in my heart . . . . It was as if the very soul of India penetrated to the very depths of my own soul and held mysterious communion with it. It was a call which pierced through everything, rent it in pieces and opened a mighty abyss."[126]

Abhishiktananda saw Ramana Maharshi one more time, and was planning a third visit in April 1950 when he learned of Ramana's death. But the spirit of the saint and of Arunachala had already worked their effect. Abhishiktananda returned a number of times over the next several years to fast and meditate in the caves of the holy mountain, sometimes up to a month at a time secluded in ascetic withdrawal. During these years, prior to his last visit to Arunachala in March 1956, Abhishiktananda met and spent time with Gnanananda, "a perfect echo of Sri Ramana's teaching," who resided at a small ashram a short bus ride from Arunachala.

Abhishiktananda could not have anticipated the effect that his meeting with Gnanananda would have on him. In his two visits to

Ramana Maharshi, no words had been exchanged and, according to his own admission, he "had not yet penetrated sufficiently within to be capable of tuning in directly to the mysterious language of silence." By now, however, he had gained enough competence in Tamil to be able to talk with Gnanananda and, even more important, had learned the value of communication beyond words. Writing in the third person, Abhishiktananda summarized his first meeting as follows:

> He had come here out of curiosity and yet the few words the old man had spoken to him had gone right to his heart. These words had uncovered depths which he had never suspected . . . . He had learned nothing new on the level of words or concepts. Yet it had all been repeated in such a way that an ineffable communication had been established between the master and himself in the depths of the one as of the other. It seemed . . . that everything the guru was saying to him was welling up directly from the most intimate recesses of his own heart . . . . He realized that the allegiance which he had never freely yielded to anyone in his life was now given automatically to Gnanananda.

The importance of this relationship to Gnanananda is indicated by Abhishiktananda's assertion that "advaita remains forever incomprehensible to him who has not first lived it existentially in his meeting with the guru."[127]

For about a decade beginning in the latter 1950s, Swami Abhishiktananda divided his time between Shantivanam (Forest of Peace, another name for the ashram he cofounded) in South India and the Himalayas in the North. His travels frequently took him to spiritual retreats, study conferences, and inter-faith meetings. Finally, in 1968, he moved into a small hermitage he himself established not far from the main source of the Ganges in the Himalayas. Here he spent most of his time in contemplation, but also in writing and giving spiritual counsel, especially to a few close disciples.

After nearly twenty years of monastic life in Europe, Abhishiktananda continued to live as a monk in India but now under the rubric of a sannyasi, one who renounces or detaches from the intellectual, social, and material worlds, from everything considered legitimate and necessary in ordinary life. Abhishiktananda summarizes: "Believe me, it is above all in the mystery of *sannyasa* that India and the Church will meet, will discover themselves in the most secret and hidden part of their hearts, in the place where they are each most truly themselves, in the mystery of their origin in which every outward manifestation is rooted."[128]

As we have seen, sannyasa also refers to the final stage of life in the Hindu four-fold classification, following those of studenthood, home-making/family-rearing, and withdrawal from society. But Swami Abhishiktananda argues that sannyasa is beyond all stages of life: "It belongs to no category whatever, and cannot be undertaken along with anything else. It is truly transcendent, as God himself transcends all, being apart from all, beyond all, and yet immanent in all without any duality."[129] There is nothing external to identify the sannyasi (although he may wear saffron-colored clothes). He conforms to no pattern, no rule, no expectation. He is in fact unrecognizable except by one who is himself completely renounced, and thus completely free. For others he may appear puzzling, paradoxical. There is something about him that is mysteriously attractive, a centered composure, an aloof presence. And yet, at the same time, he may shatter preconceived notions about the appearance, the demeanor, the ideas of a 'holy man'. For he knows no conventions. Aligned as he is with Ultimacy, nothing relative marks him or contains him.

Abhishiktananda asserts: "The call to complete renunciation cuts across all dharmas [religions, social duties] and disregards all frontiers . . . . The call . . . corresponds to a powerful instinct, so deep-rooted in the human heart . . . that it is anterior to every religious formulation."[130] Because the call comes from Ultimacy, beyond all boundaries, response to the call itself transcends all boundaries, even the most sacrosanct. "The monk is the one who is . . . bound by nothing."[131] The only function of religion in reference to the sannyasi is that of allowing him to be himself; it can in no way legislate or control. It cannot, in fact, even bestow the status of renunciant. It can only recognize what is divinely bestowed, what is self-claimed.[132] He is the 'drop-out'. At the same time, from his own perspective, his so-called renunciation is no 'big deal'; it is perfectly natural and ordinary. He is simply being himself, simply being.

Using a term that characterized the attitude of the early Christian monks toward the world, Abhishiktananda regards the sannyasa ideal as acosmic, "in but not of the world." Acosm marks the sannyasi's complete non-attachment to the material things, activities, and common concerns of the world. If a monk "feels that he has some duty or obligation towards anyone else, whether it be self-chosen or imposed on him by others, he has fallen away from the true ideal of sannyasa, and no longer performs the essential function for which he was set apart from society—to witness to the one true Absolute."[133] Swami Abhishiktananda does not deny that priestly, scholarly, social, medical, etc., concerns and duties rightfully fall within the scope of monasticism. He rather argues that there must always be some monks who are not forced into vocations of 'usefulness'. The role of the 'excused' monk is "non-role and his function non-function."[134] Some must always be allowed simply to witness to the Absolute, simply to be.

Depth Experience

Swami Abhishiktananda began his explorations in silence with little forethought or expectation but soon discovered the practice to be "the bearer of grace beyond price."[135] As he explains, silence begins with the avoidance of all verbalization but soon moves to the banishment of all "useless thoughts and desires," and finally becomes the absence of "any thought, even the highest."[136] Not speaking is but the deliberately created condition that begins the process of turning away from preoccupation with the outer world. This leads to a heightened sensitivity, "a clarity and transparency which otherwise is scarcely conceivable," culminating in "the unconditional solitude of the Alone, deep within."[137] This comprehensive silence of the mind is "the supreme act of man" and "the only expression adequate to the mystery" therein met. The silence that begins with the non-pronunciation of words becomes "a silence that contains the plenitude of all words." The practitioner of this silence experiences "an essential incapacity to express . . . this Presence that transcends the mind and immerses it into its primordial abysses." In fact, there is also, at the deepest level, "no longer a person to speak."[138]

Silence prepares for, leads to, and is interiority. And interiority is essential to the deepest realization. When Abhishiktananda inquired about Ramana Maharshi's experience and teaching he was told that "no one will ever understand the Maharshi until he has reached the point of realization at which the Maharshi was. If you want to know exactly what the Maharshi thought, you must yourself become what he was."[139] Abhishiktananda claims that "the grace of India is essentially a grace of call—calling to introversion." This immersion into interiority, however, is not by means of imagination, speculation, emotion, or intellect.[140] Apart from the practice of interiority, Abhishiktananda observes that "the whole day long I am busy with myself, seeing, hearing, acting, doing, thinking . . . . My I is always inevitably connected with something else, this something else carries me constantly away from myself into the whirlpool of thoughts, feelings, actions."[141] Interiority comes about by reversing this process. Abhishiktananda writes:

> When a man accepts to go beyond phenomena—that is, conditioning, time and becoming—he is as it were carried away

irresistibly to a Source unknown and inexpressible: Source of himself, source of all. He is engulfed in a mystery which is more interior to himself than anything he is ever able to feel, think, conceive or imagine. It is a mystery which juts out on all sides and compasses all, which inside calls to an abyss ever deeper, to the innermost centre of himself and of the universe, to both the origin and the ultimate reach of all human experience."[142]

Finally, this interiority goes beyond itself: "At the profoundest depth of the inwardness, there no longer exists a within or without but only the uncircumscribable ocean of the unique Mystery, present everywhere."[143]

Contemplation or meditation plays a crucial role in interiority. Abhishiktananda's own inner journey was shaped principally by the meditative approach of Ramana Maharshi and Gnanananda. The former taught self-inquiry, the search for the 'I' by means of response to the question, "Who am I?" This is the essential, eternal I, the I beyond the phenomenal, conditional I. This I is the changeless I, identical at age 60 and 6, untouched by time. Abhishiktananda explained Ramana Maharshi's method: "It consists in trying to find out at every instant, in every act, who in truth it is that lives, thinks and acts . . . . It is a matter of constantly, relentlessly pursuing this consciousness of oneself which hides behind the phenomena and the events of the psychic life, of discovering it, seizing it in its original purity before anything else has covered it over or adulterated it." He continues: "This means in fact trying to reach one's self, one's identity, beyond and beneath the level of manifestation."[144] Gnanananda regarded meditation as the royal road to realization, the one essential method. When asked to explain he often recited Tamil verses:

Return within to the place where there is nothing
and take care that nothing comes in.

Penetrate to the depths of yourself,

to the place where thought no longer exists

and take care that no thought raises its head!

There where nothing exists is Fullness!

There where nothing is seen is the Vision of Being!

There where nothing appears any longer

is the sudden appearing of the Self![145]

Beatrice Bruteau, a scholar familiar with Abhishiktananda and advaita, clarifies further this approach to the Self that was shared by Ramana and Gnanananda, and practiced by Abhishiktananda. "In this . . . meditation the important thing is to preserve the sense of active, subjective existence: not passive, not objective, and not essence—not *what* one is but only *that* one is. The meditation is not *reflection on* oneself, for that would be doubling the consciousness, so that one part of it became an object of knowledge for another part which is the subject doing the knowing. . . . Just coincide with the subjective awareness in the very act of being aware."[146]

Referring to the Self (atman), the substantive reality that is central, foundational, and all-inclusive in Hinduism, Swami Abhishiktananda observed that "knowledge of the Self can only be learnt through interior recollection within the depth of the Self." He unequivocally connects the interior exploration of oneself with the discovery of God: "Whoever has not found himself within himself has not yet found God; and whoever has not found God within himself has not yet found himself."[147] Interiorization leads to an experience of Self, of I, of God, of Presence, of Being, all terms which Abhishiktananda uses interchangeably to designate the Undesignatable. He wrote: "When this experience has hit a man one can say that he is 'done for', at least with regard to all the ways in which he has so far sought to express himself and be aware of himself. The I of his phenomenal consciousness has to all intents and purposes disappeared . . . . His ego, which has been circumscribed and shut in on itself, has been consumed by this implacable devouring flame. There is now no place left in him for the least self-seeking or self-centredness."[148]

Swami Abhishiktananda believed that ultimately only God is, that the sense of separate selfhood is an illusion. He attested: "God alone is in the first person. If it is to be true, our inner experience of God should be of him as a first person, the one and only I . . . . He is only to be found in the experience of my own I, which is a participation (and not an outward projection) of the I of God."[149] Bruteau said of this depth experience: "If I come to the bottom of my selfhood and find the ultimate 'I', I must find That which is continuously infusing existence into me, That which is the Source of all existence and all 'I-ness', the Original I AM, which is making my 'I' to be an 'I' by loving it into existence as an 'I', from the inside."[150] This deep I, claimed Abhishiktananda, is "discovered to be free from all the limitations of the everyday world." To be sure it "expresses itself in exterior and interior perceptions but it transcends them all and in its inmost essence . . . is totally independent of them." The trans-spatiality of this Self is affirmed by Abhishiktananda when he pointed out that "by becoming more and more aware of the divine Presence in the secret place of our heart . . . we become more and more aware of that same divine Presence surrounding us on all sides."[151]

Abhishiktananda knew well the omnipresence of the divine. He drew from the Isa Upanishad to note that "nothing exists that is not atman," the Self. And then averred that "it is precisely this truth that Jesus revealed to us by incarnating himself, 'true God of true God'."[152] In his *Guhantara* ("he who dwells in the cave")—a work characterized by Father Monchanin as "a spiritual essay born of the silence"—Abhishiktananda, speaking of Christ, wrote: "In the whole world there is no form which is not yours, which does not conceal you from the ignorant and reveal you to the one who knows." With clarity and specificity, he asserted that "God . . . is fully present in the tiniest speck of matter or moment of time, . . . in the most trivial event in the world . . . [as well as in] the life of an individual."[153]

At the same time, paradoxically, Swami Abhishiktananda declared that "God is beyond all things." It is the essential role of the sannyasi to remind "men by his solitude and by his very freedom that no word can possibly express who God is." The sannyasi himself "passes beyond and bursts open all manifestations, *murtis* [images], expressions of the divine which are essentially relative." Abhishiktananda 'resolves' the paradox by arguing that since God has no form, He can manifest Himself in any form. "Nothing 'comprehends' him, but he shines through everything and makes himself known in everything. No form may be considered unworthy to be his sign, for there is really no form at all which could worthily signify him." The paradox, of course, stands. Abhishiktananda attested to the ultimate inexplicability when he referred to "the incomprehensible duality and non-duality, at one and the same time, of being, of God." In summary: "He is in everything, yet he is beyond everything."[154]

One of the essential functions of advaita, according to Abhishiktananda, lies in its perpetual denial that any formulation is adequate to the divine.

> Advaita is . . . a relentless reminder that God—and therefore also the acts of God—can never be wholly contained in our concepts. It is a healthy and permanently necessary reminder of the importance of the 'way of negation'. It condemns, and at the same time frees us from the idolatry of the intellect, in which our laziness and pride perpetually threaten to engulf us. It rejects the self-satisfied, characteristically bourgeois, reliance on institutions and rites which, however indispensable and sacramentally effective they may be, nevertheless are only signs.[155]

Abhishiktananda firmly believed that "God is none of the things that man thinks about him, nothing that man experiences of him. Only in this 'nothing', in pure naked faith, is he truly found." Drawing from St. John of the Cross, Swami Abhishiktananda noted that "the ultimate act of union and perfect love is an act so spiritual that nothing in our created nature is able to feel it or lay hold of it, to understand or express it." He affirmed the same truth by quoting Gregory the Great's characterization of St. Benedict: "He was possessed of an ignorance which knew all, and a wisdom which knew nothing."[156]

Intellectual Ventures

Swami Abhishiktananda's apophaticism did not prohibit him from grappling with intellectual issues. He was theologically and philosophically astute, so astute in fact that he clearly recognized the limits of theology and philosophy. These limits lie in their tendency to objectify, to project, to make other that which is only existentially real by means of deep introspection and direct experience. In the last year of his life, Abhishiktananda wrote in his journal: "As long as I consider the Trinity apart from me . . . it is speculation and abstraction." He believed that "the knowledge of the Self can only be learnt through interior recollection within the depth of the Self."[157] The Swami set a high standard when he declared that "all speech about the Self which does not spring spontaneously out of the depths is delusion and a lie." In reference to his various writings, he once confided to a close friend that "it is all biography."[158] Hindus who have read Abhishiktananda's work conclude that he surely must have known that about which he wrote.

It was Swami Abhishiktananda's lived experience that required, given his personal courage and honesty, his commitment to Christ and to advaita to be, in each case, complete and unreserved. In his diary in 1971, he wrote: "Whether I will or not, I am fundamentally tied to Christ Jesus and so to the ecclesial *Koinonia* (communion). It is in Him that the 'Mystery' revealed itself to me . . . . It is through his image, his symbols, that I know God." About the same time he also wrote: "If I say that I believe in Christ, that means that Christ is God for me. God-for-me, because there is no abstract God." Even while affirming his allegiance to Christ, Abhishiktananda also attested to the reality and truth of his advaitic experience. He stated that "it is impossible to deny the advaitic experience" and underscored the extent to which this "radical purification" challenges traditional religious expressions and forms.

Abhishiktananda felt deeply the tension between Christianity and advaita. He was forced by the overwhelming truth of his own experience to witness to the "coexistence of the Upanishads and the Gospel together within the same Heart." Again he declared: "I recognize the same Mystery which I have adored from the beginning under the symbol of Christ also under the myth of Narayana, of Krishna, of the Purusha."[159] He is not using the term myth here in the popular sense of false but rather in the technical sense of true though not in terms of history or science but true as unfathomable and yet undeniable experience. Swami Abhishiktananda was convinced that "the problem of Advaita-Christianity appears on the notional level." He contended: "There is no real contradiction between Advaita and Christianity, but only between . . . the premature and inadequate syntheses put forward on both sides by those who imagine that experience can be confined within their definitions. Only the man who is ready to go to the end in the experience both in the Christian faith and of Advaita will find the solution to the apparent antinomy."[160]

Fully aware of the inevitability of conditioning—intellectual, psychological, cultural—Swami Abhishiktananda espoused a tentative and open position when interpreting and comparing different religious experiences and views. He even asked rhetorically: "If Jesus had been born in an advaitin milieu, would not the expression of his experience have been wholly different?" He frequently called attention to the way in which Judaic, Hellenistic and Greco-Roman worldviews shaped Christian forms. In December 1971, just two years before his death, he wrote: "The Gospel message is not bound to the Jewish world in which it was disclosed. Its universal and ontic value burns and melts the wax cells of the Judeo-Greek world in which this honey is stored."[161] Thus, a clear distinction must be made between the ineffable experience of truth and the time/space conditioning of the expressions of this truth. This level of understanding, coupled with his honesty and courage, enabled Abhishiktananda to affirm the simultaneous truth of his Christ and advaitic experience, to see them as an instance of differentiated nonduality.

Even while acknowledging the impossibility of adequate formulations, Abhishiktananda explored options for intellectually understanding the experiential identity he found between his Christian and advaitic experiences. Because he understood the Trinity as the "most immediate reality that exists"—and not as "an abstract concept"—it could serve as a model and a symbol to express his deepest experience. He articulated his experience of the Trinitarian mystery in the advaita context in terms of the Hindu philosophico-spiritual perspective of Satchitananda or *Sat* (Being), *Chit* (Awareness), and *Ananda* (Bliss), these fundamental realities also representing for him, Father, Son, and Holy Spirit.

Abhishiktananda explains that his Christian Satchitananda in terms of the Trinity "involves a double 'procession'." By this he means that there is a double movement in God, one involving Christ or the Word which represents God revealing himself and the other the Holy Spirit or God as unknowable. He writes: "The first procession is the existential foundation of everything that appears manifold in this world. The second reveals in everything the mystery of *ekatvam*, unity, non-duality . . . . And it is this double mystery, the very mystery of Being, which from the deepest recesses of his own consciousness, recalls man to himself—to Being, to Awareness of being, to the infinite Bliss of being.[162]

Abhishiktananda believed that the nondual experience is known in life at large in the experience of love, most evidently in altruistic, selfless love. In true love there is a surpassing of thought, and consequently of the contradictions that so often inform thought. Odette Baumer-Despeigne, who had a long and profound correspondence with Abhishiktananda, summarized his sense of the dissolving power of love: "The act of pure love is what awakes. Advaita, non-duality, is not an intellectual discovery, but an attitude of the soul. It is much more the impossibility of saying 'Two' than the affirmation of 'One'. What is the use of saying 'One' in one's thought, if one says 'Two' in one's life? To say 'One' in one's life: that is Love."[163]

Abhishiktananda knew this melting effect of love first hand in his relationship with Marc Chaduc/Ajatananda, his French disciple. It is also seen—and even more strikingly since the communion transcends cultural and religious barriers—in the relationship that existed between him and Swami Chidananda, head of the Divine Life Society and director of a major Hindu ashram in Rishikesh. When the two men met, though coming from different 'worlds', they simply laughed, "through the sheer joy of being united in the Spirit."[164] In their laughter lies a powerful symbol for nonduality, for the ultimate absence of all barriers and distinctions. That laughter exemplifies transcendence in immanence, not-two at the personal level.

Supreme Awakening

While in a Rishikesh bazaar on July 14, 1973, Swami Abhishiktananda suffered a heart attack, an experience which he called "an extraordinary spiritual adventure." In his diary a few months later he wrote: "Seeing myself so helpless, incapable of any thought or movement, I was released from being identified with this 'I' which until then had thought, willed, rushed about, was anxious about each and everything. Disconnection! That whole consciousness in which I habitually lived was no longer mine, but I, I still was." Raimundo Panikkar received a letter from Abhishiktananda in which he explained: "A door opened in heaven when I was lying on the pavement, but a heaven which was not the opposite of earth, but something which was neither life nor death, but simply 'being,' 'awakening' beyond all myths and symbols. This Awakening was a total explosion." A few days after his heart attack he experienced "something like the marvelous solution of an equation"—he discovered the Grail. He wrote: "At bottom the quest for the Grail is nothing else but the quest for Self. A unique quest signified in all the myths and symbols. It is one's own self that one is seeking through all. And in this quest one runs in every direction, whereas the Grail is here, nearby, one has only to open one's eyes."[165]

From Rishikesh, Swami Abhishiktananda was taken to a nursing home in Indore where he died on December 7, 1973. Baumer-Despeigne visited him during his final months and described "the transparence of his whole being to the inner Mystery, the divine Presence . . . the extraordinary radiance of his smile, of his countenance glowing with Light." In a published letter—addressed to Swami Abhishiktananda on the second anniversary of his death—Panikkar conveyed his perception of Abhishiktananda's final realization: "In the last period of your life you found an equilibrium between incarnation and transcendence . . . , a balance between extreme . . . historicity and extreme acosmism . . . . What you achieved is, to me, genuine Advaita: the dynamic overcoming of all dvandvas (dualisms) without falling into monism, the existential overcoming of separation (sin) without theistic reductionism; in other words: authentic redemption."[166] And, we might add—in the spirit of Abhishiktananda—authentic liberation, enlightenment, full releasement, full realization. Each of these, of course, is a metaphor for the ultimate, indescribable awareness.

NOTES

1. Marcus Borg, *Meeting Jesus Again for the First Time: The Historical Jesus and the Heart of Contemporary Faith.* (San Francisco: HarperSanFrancisco: 1994) 69.

2. Gordon S. Wakefield, ed., *The Westminster Dictionary of Christian Spirituality.* (Philadelphia: The Westminster Press, 1983) 208f. See also the classic work by Thomas à Kempis, *The Imitation of Christ.* Numerous editions are available.

3. This translation combines the rendering in the Revised Standard Version and the New Revised Standard Version.

4. Quoted in Bernard McGinn, *The Foundations of Mysticism. The Presence of God: A History of Western Christian Mysticism.* vol. 1, (New York: Crossroad Publishing Co., 1991) 104.

5. James S. Cutsinger, ed., *Not of This World: A Treasury of Christian Mysticism.* (Bloomington, IN: World Wisdom, 2003) 69.

6. Ibid.

7. John R. Tyson, ed., *Invitation to Christian Spirituality: An Ecumenical Anthology.* (New York: Oxford University Press, 1999) 71.

8. The treatment of Platonism and Neoplatonism is drawn mainly from Anthony Flew, ed., *A Dictionary of Philosophy.* rev. 2nd ed. (New York: St. Martin's Press, 1984) 268-278.

9. Ursula King, *Christian Mystics: Their Lives and Legacies throughout the Ages.* (Mahwah, NJ: Paulist Press/HiddenSpring, 2001) 34f.

10. From Origen's *On First Principles*, quoted in McGinn, *Foundations*, 111.

11. Bradley P. Holt, *Thirsty for God: A Brief History of Christian Spirituality* 2nd ed. (Minneapolis Fortress Press, 2005) 59.

12. Quoted in McGinn, *Foundations*, 113. The treatment of Origen's view of creation and the return to God is drawn from McGinn's study, 112-128.

13. McGinn, *Foundations*, 119.

14. Quoted in Ibid., 128.

15. Anthony Meredith, "Origen" in Cheslyn Jones, Geoffrey Wainwright, Edward Yarnold, eds., *The Study of Spirituality.* (New York: Oxford University Press, 1986) 118f.

16. Quoted in Bernard McGinn, John Meyendorff, and Jean Leclercq, eds. *Christian Spirituality: Origins to the Twelfth Century.* vol. 16, *World Spirituality: An Encyclopedic History of the Religious Quest,* (New York: Crossroad Publishing Co., 1988) 262.

17. Ibid., 265, 268.

18. Ibid., 71-74.

19. Andrew Louth, "The Cappadocians," in *Study of Spirituality.* 167.

20. King, *Christian Mystics.* 48f.

21. Cutsinger, *Not of This World.* 176.

22. McGinn, *Foundations*, 141.

23. Quoted in John Anthony McGuckin, *Standing in God's Holy Fire: The Byzantine Tradition.* (Maryknoll, NY: Orbis Books, 2001) 45.

24. Aphorisms nos. 87, 64, 70, 81 in Evagrius Ponticus, *The Praktikos [and] Chapters on Prayer.* John Eudes Bamberger, trans., intro., notes, Cistercian Studies Series, no. 4, 33-37.

25. McGinn, Meyendorff, Leclercq, *Christian Spirituality*, I, 398.

26. Ponticus, *Praktikos,* 57-74.

27. Cutsinger, *Not of This World*, 61.

28. William Johnston, *Mystical Theology: The Science of Love.* (New York: Orbis Books, 1995) 17.

29. Quoted in Belden C.Lane, *The Solace of Fierce Landscapes: Exploring Desert and Mountain Spirituality.* (Oxford: Oxford University Press, 1998), 77.

30. H. Urs von Balthasar, "The Metaphysics and Mystical Theology of Evagrius," *Monastic Studies.* vol. 3, 1965, pp. 195-193.

31. Discussion of Evagrius' cosmology and soteriology is from Ponticus, *Praktikos,* lxxv-lxxxi.

32. Unless indicated otherwise, quotations from Augustine's *Confessions* are from Saint Augustine, *Confessions.* Henry Chadwick, trans. (Oxford: Oxford University Press, 1991).

33. McGinn, *Foundations.* 233, 237.

34. John Peter Kenney, *The Mysticism of Saint Augustine: Rereading the Confessions.* (New York: Routledge, 2005) 3.

35. Quoted in Ibid., 242.

36. Quoted in Ibid., 247.

37. Andrew Louth, "Augustine," *Study of Spirituality*, 143-144.

38. Quoted in McGinn, *Foundations,* 259.

39. Louth, "Augustine," 145.

40. Mary T. Clark trans., intro., *Augustine of Hippo: Selected Writings. The Classics of Western Spirituality: A Library of the Great Spiritual Masters.* (New York: Paulist Press, 1984) 305.

41. Quoted in McGinn, *Foundations,* 246.

42. Clark, *Augustine of Hippo,* 245.

43. Ibid., 301.

44. McGinn, Meyendorff, Leclercq, *Christian Spirituality*, 283.

45. Quoted in Bernard McGinn, ed. and intro., *The Essential Writings of Christian Mysticism.* (New York: The Modern Library, 2006) 196.

46. Quoted in McGinn, Meyendorff, Leclercq, *Christian Spirituality,* 284.

47. Quoted in McGinn, *Foundations*, 165.

48. Ibid., 162-63.

49. McGinn, Meyendorff, Leclercq, *Christian Spirituality*, 133.

50. Colm Luibheid, trans., Paul Rorem, forward, notes, collaboration, Paul Roques, preface, et al., *Pseudo-Dionysius: The Complete*

Works. The Classics of Western Spirituality: A Library of Great Spiritual Masters. (New York: Paulist Press, 1987) 49, 51.

51. Ibid., 135.

52. Ibid.

53. Ibid., 137.

54. Unless indicated otherwise, the following treatment of Bernard of Clairvaux is based on Bernard McGinn's masterful and multi-volumn study, *The Presence of God: A History of Western Christian Mysticism,* specifically vol. 2, *The Growth of Mysticism.* (New York: Crossroad Publishing Company, 1994, 158-224) 202. Page numbers in this range that follow quotations are from this source.

55. McGinn, *Essential Writings,* 434.

56. References to Bernard's four stages of love as found in *On the Love of God* are drawn from Tyson, *Invitation,* 149-152.

57. McGinn, *Growth,* 172.

58. Page references are to McGinn, *Essential Writings,* 27-34.

59. Page references are to McGinn, *Growth,* 185-199.

60. Maurice O'Connell Walshe, trans. and ed., *Meister Eckhart: Sermons and Treatises.* 3 vols. (Dorset, England: Element Books, 1978), 1:117, 2:136.

61. Ibid., 1:157-158.

62. Matthew Fox, intro. and comm., *Breakthrough: Meister Eckhart's Creation Spirituality in New Translation.* (Garden City, N.Y.: Image Books, 1980), 140.

63. Meister Eckhart, *Parisian Questions and Prologues.* trans. and intro., Armand A. Maurer, (Toronto: Pontifical Institute of Mediaeval Studies, 1974), 93; Edmund Colledge, "Meister Eckhart: His Time and His Writings," *The Thomist.* 42 (April 1978): 244.

64. Bernard McGinn, ed., *Meister Eckhart: Teacher and Preacher, Classics of Western Spirituality.* (New York: Paulist Press, 1986), 153.

65. Ibid., 396.

66. C.F. Kelley, *Meister Eckhart on Divine Knowledge.* (New Haven, Conn.: Yale University Press, 1977), 147.

67. Walshe, *Sermons and Treatises*, 2:271.

68. John D. Caputo, "Fundamental Themes in Meister Eckhart's Mysticism," *The Thomist.* 42 (April 1978): 211.

69. Bernard McGinn, "The God beyond God: Theology and Mysticism in the Thought of Meister Eckhart," *Journal of Religion.* 61 (January 1981): 8; See also Eckhart, *Parisian Questions*, 33.

70. McGinn, *Teacher and Preacher*, 391.

71. James M. Clark, *Meister Eckhart: An Introduction to the Study of His Works with Anthology of His Sermons.* (London: Thomas Nelson and Sons, 1957), 212.

72. Fox, *Breakthrough*, 72.

73. Reiner Schurmann, *Meister Eckhart: Mystic and Philosopher.* (Bloomington: Indiana University Press, 1978), 112; see 111-21.

74. Walshe, *Sermons and Treatises*, 1:98.

75. See Ken Wilber, *Integral Spirituality: A Startling New Role for Religion in the Modern and Postmodern World.* (Boston and London: Integral Books, 2006), 215f; See also Frank Visser, *Ken Wilber: Thought as Passion.* (Albany, NY: State University of New York Press, 2003), 292, n. 6.

76. Translation of biblical texts are those of Eckhart himself, as rendered into English by the scholar whose work is consulted.

77. Edmund Colledge and Bernard McGinn, trans. and intro., *The Essential Sermons, Commentaries, Treatises, and Defense, Classics of Western Spirituality.* (New York: Paulist Press, 1981) 188. For a discussion of Meister Eckhart's use of 2 Cor. 3:18, see Karl G. Kertz, "Meister Eckhart's Teaching on the Birth of the Divine World of the Soul," *Traditio.* 15 (1959):359-360.

78. Walshe, *Sermons and Treatises*, 2:119.

79. James M. Clark and John V. Skinner, *Meister Eckhart: Selected Treatises and Sermons Translated from Latin and German with*

an Introduction and Notes. (London: Faber and Faber, 1958), 111. For a discussion of why this passage ought not to have been construed as heretical by his adversaries, see Colledge, "Meister Eckhart: His Time and Writings," 249-250.

80. Colledge and McGinn, *Essential Sermons*, 188.

81. Ibid., 246; Fox, *Breakthrough*, 464.

82. Colledge and McGinn, *Essential Sermons*, 185.

83. Richard Kieckhefer, "Meister Eckhart's Conception of Union with God," *Harvard Theological Review.* 71 (July-October 1978): 210f.

84. Fox, *Breakthrough*, 294.

85. Walshe, *Sermons and Treatises*, 2:135. This is one of the many teachings of Meister Eckhart that was formally condemned in the papal bull of 1329, In agro dominico. See Colledge and McGinn, *Essential Sermons*, 79.

86. Clark and Skinner, *Selected Treatises*, 111.

87. Ibid. See Robert K. C. Forman, *Meister Eckhart: The Mystic as Theologian.* Warwick, NY: Amity House, 1991, chap. 6; Caputo, "Fundamental Themes," 217-22.

88. Schurmann, *Mystic and Philosopher*, 57.

89. Colledge and McGinn, *Essential Sermons*, 198.

90. Walshe, *Sermons and Treatises*, 1:177; also McGinn, "God Beyond God," 4.

91. Colledge and McGinn, *Essential Sermons*, 258-94 passim.

92. McGinn, *Teacher and Preacher*, 338-44.

93. Kieckhefer, "Meister Eckhart's Conception of Union," 222.

94. Colledge and McGinn, *Essential Sermons*, 276.

95. Kieckhefer, "Meister Eckhart's Conception of Union," 221.

96. Colledge and McGinn, *Essential Sermons*, 252.

97. Ibid., 199-203 passim.

98. Schurmann, *Mystic and Philosopher*, 210.

99. Raymond B. Blackney, *Meister Eckhart: A Modern Translation.* (New York: Harper and Row, 1941), 127. For a discussion of

"letting be," as well as a comprehensive look at Meister Eckhart's influence on a twentieth-century philosopher, see John D. Caputo, *The Mystical Element in Heidegger's Thought*. (Athens: Ohio University, 1978), 118-27.

100. Colledge and McGinn, *Essential Sermons*, 183.

101. Reiner Schurmann, "The Loss of the Origin in Soto Zen and in Meister Eckhart," *The Thomist*. 42 (April 1978): 307.

102. Caputo, *Mystical Element*, 61. For further indication of Meister Eckhart's influence on Angelus Silesius, the pen name of Johann Scheffler (1624-77), see ibid., index; Frederick Franck, trans., *The Book of Angelus Silesius*. (Santa Fe, N.M.: Bear and Company, 1985); Maria Shrady, trans. and foreword, and Josef Schmidt, intro. and notes, *Angelus Silesius: The Cherubinic Wanderer, Classics of Western Spirituality*. (New York: Paulist Press, 1986). Johann Scheffler, a convert to the Roman Catholic Church from Lutheranism, did not acknowledge his indebtedness to Meister Eckhart, which is understandable in light of the Meister's heretical status in the Church. More surprising is the fact that neither of these two modern books on Angelus Silesius reveals this dependence either.

103. Bernard McGinn, "Meister Eckhart: An Introduction," in Paul E. Szarmach ed., *An Introduction to the Medieval Mystics of Europe*. (Albany: State University of New York, 1984), 253.

104. Clark, *Meister Eckhart: Introduction*, 235.

105. McGinn, *Teacher and Preacher*, 187; see also McGinn, "God Beyond God," 7.

106. Colledge and McGinn, *Essential Sermons*, 251-54 passim.

107. Schurmann, *Mystic and Philosopher*, xv.

108. Unless indicated otherwise, quotations are from Kieran Kavanaugh and Otilio Rodriguez, trans., *The Collected Works of St Teresa of Avila*. vol. 1, (Washington, D,C.: Institute of Carmelite Studies, 1987) 90f, 95, 100f, 103, 100.

109. McGinn, *Christian Mysticism*, 110-117.

110. Cutsinger, *Not of This World*, 187.

111. Quotations depicting Teresa's experience in the seventh room are from *The Interior Castle* as found in McGinn, *Christian Mysticism*, 452-459.

112. Unless indicated otherwise, quotations are from John Wesley's *Journal* as found in Albert C. Outler ed., *John Wesley.* (New York: Oxford University Press, 1964) 53-69.

113. Wakefield, *Westminster Dictionary*, 395.

114. Quoted in Louis Dupré and Don E. Saliers, eds. *Christian Spirituality: Post-Reformation and Modern.* vol. 18, *World Spirituality: An Encyclopedic History of the Religious Quest.* (New York: Crossroad Publishing Co., 1989), 358.

115. Ibid., 363, 367.

116. *Hymnal of the Church of God.* (Anderson, IN: Gospel Trumpet Company, 1953), 98.

117. All quotations, unless indicated otherwise, are from Thomas Merton, *The Seven Story Mountain.* (New York: Harcourt, Brace & World, 1948) 178, 172-173, 180, 198, 202, 3, 215-216, 223, 225.

118. Thomas Merton, *Conjectures of a Guilty Bystander.* (Cardin City: Doubleday, 1966) 140, 142.

119. Naomi Burton, Patrick Hart, James Laughlin, eds., *The Asian Journal of Thomas Merton.* (New York: New Directions Books, 1973) 233-236. Some students of Merton's life debate among themselves about the precise nature of Merton's experience at Polonnaruwa, whether it was mainly aesthetic or spiritual. Since the experience was one of reality beyond categories, the debate seems pointless. Merton's own characterization, "one aesthetic illumination," suggests that the beauty of the sculpture served to elicit illumination, to a seeing beyond the visual. Underscoring the ineffability of such experiences, he admitted that his description was "not at all adequate" (230).

120. Thomas Merton, *New Seeds of Contemplation.* (New York: New Directions Publishing Corporation, 1961) 1-297.

121. Abhishiktananda, *The Secret of Arunachala*. (Delhi: I.S.P.C.K., 1979), 26 n. 4.

122. Abhishiktananda, *Secret*, viii.

123. J.D.M. Stuart, "Abhishiktananda on Inner Awakening," *Vidyajyoti*. (Delhi), 46(November 1982), 497.

124. Ajatananda, "Foreword," in Abhishiktananda, *The Further Shore*. (Delhi: I.S.P.C.K.,1984), ix.

125. Raimundo Panikkar, "Letter to Abhishiktananda—On Eastern-Western Monasticism," *Studies in Formative Spirituality*. 3, no.3 (1982), 427.

126. Abhishiktananda, *Secret*, 8-9.

127. Abhishiktananda, *Guru and Disciple*. Heather Sandeman, trans., (London: S.P.C.K., 1974), 36, 28, 26-27, 29.

128. Ibid., 162.

129. Abhishiktananda, *Further Shore*, 4.

130. Ibid., 27; Henri Le Saux/Abhishiktananda, *The Eyes of Light*. André Gozier and Joseph Lamarié, eds., (Danville, NJ: Dimension Books, 1983), 74.

131. Abhishiktananda, *Guru and Disciple*, 165.

132. Abhishiktananda, *Further Shore*, 31.

133. Ibid., 13.

134. Abhishiktananda, *Eyes of Light*, 138.

135. Abhishiktananda, *Secret of Arunachala*, 28.

136. Abhishiktananda, *Prayer*. (Delhi: I.S.P.C.K., 1979) 52.

137. Abhishiktananda, *Secret of Arunachala*, 30.

138. Abhishiktananda, *Eyes of Light*, 41, 111, 39, 23.

139. Abhishiktananda, *Secret of Arunachala*, 41.

140. Abhishiktananda, *Eyes of Light*, 68-70.

141. Abhishiktananda, *Further Shore*, 111.

142. Abhishiktananda, "Experience of God in Eastern Religions," *Cistercian Studies*. 4 (1974) 150.

143. Abhishiktananda, *Eyes of Light*, 43.

144. Abhishiktananda, *Saccidananda: A Christian Approach to Advaitic Experience.* J.D.M. Stuart, ed., (Delhi: I.S.P.C.K., 1984) 34; cf. "Experience of God," 154.

145. Abhishiktananda, *Guru and Disciple*, 87-88, 109.

146. Beatrice Bruteau, "In the Cave of the Heart: Silence and Realization," *New Blackfriars.* Summer 1984, 307-308.

147. Abhishiktananda, *Secret of Arunachala*, xi; and "Experience of God" 154-156.

148. Abhishiktananda, *Guru and Disciple*, 11.

149. Abhishiktananda, *Prayer*, 84.

150. Bruteau, "Cave of the Heart," 312.

151. Abhishiktananda, *Further Shore*, 94; *Guru and Disciple*, 101; *Prayer*, 25; *Eyes of Light*, 44.

152. Abhishiktananda, *Hindu-Christian Meeting Point: Within the Cave of the Heart.* Sarah Grant, trans., (Delhi: I.S.P.C.K., 1976) 90.

153. Abhishiktananda, *Secret*, ix-x; *Saccidananda,* 129.

154. Abhishiktananda, *Guru and Disciple*, 167; *Prayer*, 16; *Eyes of Light*, 147; *Hindu-Christian*, 54.

155. Abhishiktananda, *Hindu-Christian*, 96.

156. Ibid.; *Further Shore*, 39; *Hindu-Christian*, 70.

157. Abhishiktananda, *Eyes of Light*, 179; *Further Shore*, 47.

158. Abhishiktananda, *Further Shore*, 47; Odette Baumer-Despeigne, "The Spiritual Journey of Henri Le Saux—Abhishiktananda," *Cistercian Studies.* 4 (1983) 310.

159. Baumer-Despeigne, "Spiritual Journey," 324-325; Abhishiktananda, *Secret,* 92; *Saccidananda*, 66-67; *Eyes of Light*, 175; Baumer-Despeigne, "Spiritual Journey," 317, 325.

160. Pannikar, "Letter to Abhishiktananda," 430; Abhishiktananda, *Hindu-Christian*, 97.

161. Abhishiktananda, *Eyes of Light,* 177; Baumer-Despeigne, "Spiritual Journey," 325.

162. Baumer-Despeigne, "Spiritual Journey," 117; Abhishiktananda, *Hindu-Christian*, 88-89; For a fuller discussion see Abhishiktananda, *Saccidananda*, 163-192. Saccidananda is the Tamil spelling in English of Satchitananda which is the Sanskrit and Hindi form common in North India.

163. Baumer-Despeigne, "Spiritual Journey," 320.

164. Vandana, *Gurus, Ashrams and Christians*. (Madras: Christian Literature Society, 1980) 18; cf. also Emmanuel Vattakuzhy, *Indian Christian Sannyasa and Swami Abhishiktananda*. (Bangalore: Theological Publications in India, 1981) 93, 238.

165. Baumer-Despeigne, "Spiritual Journey," 328; Panikkar, "Letter to Abhishiktananda," 437; Abhishiktananda, Eyes of Light, 180.

166. Baumer-Despeigne, "Spiritual Journey," 329; Panikkar, "Letter to Abhishiktananda," 447-448.

VII   A Way of Ways

The Way of Actionless Action, the Way of Loving Devotion, the Way of Insightful Knowing: These—and other Ways—Lead to Liberation.—Hinduism

The Four Noble Truths and the Eightfold Path Lead to Enlightenment.—Buddhism

"I am the Way, and the Truth, and the Life."
—Jesus (John 14:6)

"Lead us on the Straight Path, the Path of Those Whom Thou Hast Favored."—(Koran 1:5-6)

Is there a Way to Higher Realization?

According to some, there is no *way* leading to ultimate realization, no methods, techniques, practices that will enable us to eventually arrive at that ultimate awareness that has provided the focus of this book. In the first chapter, for example, we saw that Ramana Maharshi maintained that "there is . . . neither path nor achievement."[1] Terence Gray/Wei Wu Wei, an Irish aristocrat cum Buddhist-Taoist philosopher, goes even further: "any kind of action, practice or intentional procedure is an unsurmountable barrier to . . .

awakening."[2] This view is actually and necessarily the case because the so-called *realized* state is our natural state, always and already. We cannot come to that which we essentially and abidingly are. However, even though this pristine state of openness and clarity is our deepest heritage, it doesn't constitute our ordinary awareness, it doesn't *seem* to be our natural state.

Ramana Maharshi urged his devotees to practice self-inquiry, to search for the origin of the I-thought by tracing it to its source. This search is aided, he claimed, by giving up the "habit of identifying yourself with the non-self. All effort is only for that."[3] And Wei Wu Wei declared that "habit and practice are a necessary prelude to conscious experience of our reality." He also agreed with the Maharshi when he said that "the abandonment of identification with an inexistent individual self" is what is required.[4] From these two highly realized individuals, we learn that practice is a process of unlearning, of undoing the conditioning that keeps us from knowing our real self.

No one knows how transformation actually occurs. We can't feel it happening. It takes place beyond the range of awareness. We usually discover that it has occurred—only after a period of time. When we notice, for example, that something that used to bother us no longer does, we can be pretty sure that some transformation has taken place. The issue relates to the tension between works and grace that we've seen in some of the religions investigated. Affirmation of both works and grace, without knowing how they complement each other, is one way of 'resolving' the tension. Nothing we can do makes transformation occur—that's the grace part—but if we don't do anything, we're not likely to see much change in our understanding, feelings, or behavior. While our work doesn't cause transformation, it clears the way so that grace can operate.

On a parallel and lighter note, an exchange between news reporters and Ben Hogan, the famous golf champion of the last century, is suggestive. When asked how he was able to win so many tournaments, Hogan answered, "I guess I'm just lucky." The reporters retorted: "But we see you practicing a great deal of time." Hogan replied: "Well, the more I practice, the luckier I get!" The Zen teacher, Baker Roshi, put it similarly when he noted that enlightenment is actually an accident and meditation makes one accident prone.

What we are born with, our soul's code and genetic composition, plus the conditioning that inevitably occurs during the normal course of life, occlude, hide, and supervene our truest nature.[5] Each of the religions and wisdom traditions has an explanation for the emergence of this universal predicament: karma, asravas, ignorance, disobedience, sin, etc. A more contemporary model for understanding how and why this suppression of our true birthright occurs can be seen in the fact and operation of the ego. This is not ego as the central operating system of our conscious life—the standard definition in psychology—but the ego as the separate self sense, the ever present but unnoticed assumption that we are apart from (rather than a part of, or better, one with) everything that is.

While this sense of being separate seems like a predetermined state of being, an essential and inevitable fact of human life, it is actually a process; it is something we are continually doing. The ego comes into existence and functions by means of fear, more specifically by contraction, by pulling back and building walls. As we saw in the first chapter, there are no boundaries in reality, in the natural world or in consciousness itself. We create them and impose them on that which is essentially interrelated, integral, and single, i.e., on the interactive, unfolding, and unitive process that is life. Whenever we feel threatened or insecure, however, we pull away from the totality of whatever we are experiencing.

The way we transform is by deconstructing the barriers we ourselves have unknowingly concocted and projected onto reality. Since we have done it, we have to undo it. Therefore, the principles and practices of personal transformation consist of views and methods that aid in seeing and removing the blockages that we—with the ready help of our entire culture—have set up to hide our original and pristine state, our God-given nature, to use traditional religious terminology. Concisely, we practice in order to discover what we already are and have always been.

The main principles and practices that facilitate personal transformation have been set forth above in the survey of the world's four great religions and their respective wisdom traditions. In this final chapter, we will return to some of these from a more generic or universal standpoint. That is, we will see them as essentially human ways of transformation that need not be seen as the exclusive property of a particular religion. And, we will see how opening to other religions can profoundly enrich our lives. Some of these practices require that we set aside specific periods of time in order to focus and practice; others can be incorporated into the normal course of our daily activities.

Two positions held by the author that are more assumed than argued in this book are that: (1) each of the major religions provides all the means necessary to come to full realization and (2) each religion can benefit greatly from acquaintance and dialogue with other religions. The importance of practice is recognized in each religion, but none quite equals Buddhism in terms of its emphasis on doing the work that leads to higher realization. Given this stress, Buddhism may be regarded as the religion of practice. Arnold Toynbee, one of the most famous and insightful historians of the twentieth-century, said that when historians of the future look back at our time, they will highlight "the momentous human discovery of the encounter between Christianity and Buddhism."[6]

Considerable benefit has already come to Christian and Buddhist monks and nuns through their conversations in recent years. This final chapter will draw mainly from these two traditions as we focus on ways of transformation and ultimate realization. Two Buddhist texts are particularly relevant. Shantideva's *The Way of the*

Bodhisattva, as we've seen, directs itself to developing the awakened mind with chapters of specific instruction on awareness, patience, effort, meditation, and wisdom. Chekawa's *The Seven-Point Mind Training (lojong)*, based on Atisha's original teaching in eleventh-century Tibet, focuses on the cultivation of the enlightened heart/mind. Topics addressed include: maintaining practice throughout life, transforming adversity into the path, measuring progress, and guidelines for mind training (the literal meaning of lojong). Several contemporary editions and commentaries on each of these works are listed in the endnotes.[7]

A View that Conforms to Reality

The forces of secularity and scientism so thoroughly dominate awareness today that vast numbers of people are indisposed to giving careful, critical thought to the basic issues of human life: What is my inborn nature?, What is the meaning and purpose of life?, How to deal with temptation and the fact of evil?, Is death the end?, Is there a better way than what I happen to believe? So overwhelming are many cultural forces today that innumerable people remain unaware of the extent to which a spiritual understanding would enrich their lives. It is difficult to imagine how those so oriented could possibly experience true happiness, occasional times of pleasure and fun, of course, but not a deep and enduring sense of contentment and joy.

Picture a huge, powerful man walking along hand in hand with a cooperative person on one side and an uncooperative, continually resisting person on the other. Both will move along at the same rate as the all-powerful man; one will keep pace and be content and happy, the other will struggle, try to pull away, and be discontent and unhappy. Figuratively, both persons 'prove' the ultimacy, the irresistibility, of the principles and laws governing life, one positively, the other negatively. Similarly, one can move through life with an erroneous view of reality and encounter a great deal of frustration and discomfort, or one can work out a view of the Kosmos and a set of practices that foster inner contentment and happiness.

The Buddha discouraged idle speculation about the nature of reality. He was uninterested, for example, in knowing how creation took place. He illustrated by referring to someone struck by a poisonous arrow who, rather than immediately seeking medical intervention, wanted to find out who shot the arrow and what kind of poison was used. The imperative issue is to get rid of whatever is life-threatening and embark on that which insures health, whether physical or spiritual. For the Buddha and his followers, this urgency led to the Four Noble Truths and the Eightfold Path. These were covered in the chapter on Buddhism; here we need only note that the first step in the Eightfold Path is right view. The Buddha and informed Buddhists know that no matter what one's practice may be, if it is not in harmony with the totality of the way things are, it cannot lead to the anticipated results.

David Steindle-Rast, a contemporary Benedictine monk active in intermonastic dialogue, summarizes: "Experience cannot be separated from the conceptual framework one brings to it . . . . Our frame of mind frames what we experience."[8] In even more concise form, perspective determines perception. Our mindset, what we hold to be reality, determines what we perceive. If we don't have an accurate understanding of how life works and harmonize our actions with that understanding, we will experience ongoing frustration and disappointment in life and wonder why unquenchable happiness eludes us.

Alfred North Whitehead, founder of a modern approach to philosophy known as Process Thought, stated the matter succinctly: "As we think, we live." A spokesperson for this view, Charles Birch, clarified helpfully: "Deep within us is an image or picture of reality, whether consciously articulated or not, which more than anything else shapes how we live."[9] We all carry within our mind/heart an implicit or explicit view of reality, how the world works, how we can best get what we *most deeply* want from this world, in a word, what life's all about. The more accurate our understanding and the more appropriate our behavior, the more likely we are to experience supreme happiness.

There is no single right view of reality. Four have been briefly presented in the chapters on the four great religions. And in each religion, there are alternative views. It is important to note that the principles and laws that govern reality are not so narrow and rigid that variations in understanding are ruled out. This is stated religiously in Islam according to a Hadith Qudsi, a saying from Muhammad that is believed to contain the words of God, who is said to have declared: "I am as My servant thinks I am." The Bhagavad Gita records Krishna as saying: "In whatever way men approach Me, I am gracious to them" (4:11). These statements are not to be interpreted, of course, with license. What is crucial is for each person to become as informed as possible and reflect on and personally test whatever appears *to be real*.

Spirit and grace permeate the universe and are available to everyone at any time. Since Spirit pervades the entire Kosmos, including each of us personally, no one is beyond the reach of spirituality. Clues on how to open to Spirit have been given throughout this book. Required is sensitivity to what one is actually experiencing and a willingness to allow new feelings and glimpses of truth to emerge. This is where doubt directed to inherited and established views may be the threshold to a truth that frees; "You will know the truth, and the truth will make you free" (John 8:32). Two further reminders are in order: first, Meister Eckhart's conclusion that God's will is that toward which a person's heart is most sincerely and repeatedly inclined, and second, life is a journey, an opportunity for ongoing learning and growth.

Awareness—Meditation, Contemplation, Prayer

The transformational journey may be aptly described as a process of continually expanding and sensitizing awareness. Awareness constitutes our life, what we see, hear, feel, taste, touch, and think. We cannot include in our view of reality anything that does not impinge upon our awareness. Only what we know shapes our life, negatively or positively. Admittedly, there is much that influences our lives beyond our immediate awareness. But it is only when we recognize such factors that we can take action in respect to them, welcoming, enhancing, altering, or rejecting them.

Even though the term meditation predominates in the East and contemplation in the West, the two designations represent comparable processes. We have seen that meditation or contemplation may be considered generically and simply as a means of self-exploration. It is a way of becoming directly aware of what is occurring in one's mind and developing increased skill in nullifying the habitual processes that impede the fullness, truthfulness, and happiness of our lives. Innumerable ways of meditating have been devised. In addition to the use of imagination and guided meditations are two widespread approaches that involve concentration and mindfulness.

Concentration on a single object (physical or mental) requires one to gently bring the mind back to the object when it wanders from it. The objective here is to focus the mind so that we are not undermined by the conditioned, habitual, and impulsive movements of an undisciplined mind. In the process of meditating in this way, we learn just how much the mind 'has a mind of its own' and how little we deliberately determine the content and direction of our mind. We gradually learn to exercise some control over our thinking and feeling by means of this concentrative method.

The second method, mindfulness, is the practice of paying attention to whatever appears in the mind without attaching to it.

One does not cling to any thought or image by thinking about it, or following it along as it develops more or less on its own. Thoughts and images are allowed to simply arise, remain awhile, and disappear, all according to their own dynamic and rhythm. In this process, one develops the pure witnessing power of consciousness.

Through each method, the mind eventually becomes quiet and one is able to sense and rest into the 'silent' space that surrounds thoughts and images. Thus, by beginning with a natural though limited skill we all possess, we discover as that skill develops and rises to heightened levels of awareness that the delimited now/here of time and space becomes subsumed into the Now/Here of the eternal and infinite. The nonduality of the sacred and profane, of the spiritual and the secular, in fact, of all so-called opposites, becomes apparent, obvious, and undeniable. From this large and inclusive view, reality is harmonious and perfect, without accident or defect. The erstwhile sense of separation is replaced by the unitive awakened awareness within which all arises.

The above overview of meditation should not be construed to suggest that the process is either simple or quick. For nearly all of us, a very real discipline is required that will entail a commitment of time as well as supportive practices to be applied in daily life, at school, in the workplace, on the sports field, in the shopping mall. And, the time spent in quiet, solitary meditation is essential.

Empirical studies have shown that meditation accelerates the transformative process. In fact, it is unlikely that one will move from exoteric through esoteric to metateric religion without considerable experience in meditation. Research has demonstrated that four years of meditation has the potential for enabling one to move up two stages in the developmental scale based on the work of Ken Wilber that was introduced in chapter one.[10] There are many additional ways of meditating and no lack of helpful books on the subject, both scholarly works analyzing the processes and benefits of meditation, as well as books detailing methods of meditation and ways of resolving any difficulties that may arise. A representative list of instructional books may be found in the endnotes.[11]

Prayer is typically a central activity in exoteric religion and takes several forms, thanksgiving, praise and adoration, petition (asking something specific for oneself; health, for example), intercession (prayer on behalf of others), and confession/expiation (acknowledging one's sins and asking for forgiveness). In esoteric religion, prayer takes the form of contemplation or meditation. In metateric spirituality, prayer becomes one's way of life. One's whole life is informed by the spirit of "your will be done" (Matt. 6:10). Referring to this kind of prayer, Meister Eckhart says: "prayer consists of nothing but being uniform with God."[12]

Prayer in this deepest and most comprehensive sense brings one into whole-person communion with God/Ultimacy, and simultaneously into harmonious and supportive alignment with life as it actually unfolds. Love and wisdom are brought to bear on situations and events as they arise. There is no thought of 'miraculous intervention', only that the love, wisdom, and justice inherent in the natural order be operative along with one's own alliance with these qualities. Here one has begun to "pray without ceasing" (1 Thess. 5:17). The biblical injunction is impossible if prayer is understood only in the exoteric and esoteric ways of being religious. Brother Lawrence, a Carmelite layman in seventeenth-century France, described his efforts to fulfill this injunction in a small book that has become a Christian classic, *The Practice of the Presence of God*. Modern versions are available that add to Brother Lawrence's description of his attempts to do what may seem impossible. Several helpful books on prayer are listed under this endnote.[13]

Essential Qualities and Virtues

That we are integral beings by birthright and potential is seen in the profound and mysterious interconnection among the qualities and virtues that mark our lives. Experience demonstrates that the development of one quality or virtue affects the development of others. Even though we distinguish between them and have seemingly precise definitions for each, we discover over time that as we work to strengthen or purify one of them, a corresponding strengthening and purifying occurs in others. We will see evidence of this mutuality as we investigate specific virtues and qualities.

Without honesty and courage, one is unlikely to transform. One must be ruthlessly willing to accept and face all facets of one's character and personality. Any hedging in order to maintain one's public face, one's reputation, one's idealized sense of self will severely limit, possibly even undermine, whatever else one may do in hope of becoming more religious, more spiritual, a better person. Required is a sensitive, careful, and thorough understanding and acceptance of oneself as one actually is.

The ego may be the cleverest element in one's constitution; it knows how to reign, how to keep its position, and will employ any means necessary to stay in control. Rigorous honesty coupled with self-knowledge enables one to discern the blatant and subtle operations of the ego. When one sees egoic separation occurring, if there is sufficient commitment to personal transformation and sufficient knowledge about the means of transformation, one can then enact the remedy. The remedy always requires, in one form or another, the virtue of humility. In fact, humility and honesty are interconnected; if one is truly humble, there is nothing to defend or to hide and, therefore, one can readily acknowledge what is actually the case.

It may be argued justifiably that the cultivation of humility is the primary means by which the ego as the separate-self sense is dissolved and nullified. In this way, humility becomes simultaneously practice and goal. It is, in fact, our natural condition since all humans are born equal so far as our humanity is concerned. Any elevation of oneself above others is a violation of the natural birthright of all humanity. Anything other than humility is pretense, and arbitrarily separative. The New Revised Standard Version of the New Testament passage from which the title of this book is derived uses the two expressions "emptied himself" and "humbled himself" to describe Christ's action, first, in the Incarnation and, second, in the Crucifixion. The passage seems to be saying that self-emptying or humility is the definitive feature of Christ's life from beginning to end.

In the last chapter, we learned that Meister Eckhart praised detachment as the most essential practice in personal transformation, and linked detachment with humility. He noted that perfect detachment cannot exist without perfect humility and that the latter ends in the dissolution of self. He also claimed—with 'tongue in cheek' we may imagine—that "in God there is detachment *and* humility, in so far as we can speak of God having virtues."[14] He then added that two virtues are better than one. The merit for us in Eckhart's discussion is that we gain a sense of the extraordinary importance of humility in the transformational process, and the power it has to transform how we see ourselves as a human among humans. On an even larger scale, true humility enables us to see our rightful place in the universe as one being among a multitude of beings.

Perhaps more pointedly, we see that humility is an action on our part, an action that undermines the lifelong action of erecting and holding a sense of separateness—with its obvious or hidden tone of superiority—i.e., the action of the ego. Therefore, humility is properly considered not as an abstract quality but an action. Heeding the example of Christ, we must *act*ually empty ourselves, *act*ually humble ourselves.

The lojong exercises of Tibetan Buddhism give specific steps one can take to develop humility. First of all, we need to note that lojong literally refers to training the heart and mind. One of the books on lojong listed in the endnotes makes this clear in its title: *The Practice of Lojong: Cultivating Compassion through Training the Mind.* The underlying objective of lojong concerns the activation of the mind and the heart, i.e., learning to live lovingly and compassionately by means of the mind. Lojong instruction begins with the injunction to train in the preliminaries. The author of the above text, Traleg Kyabgon, notes that "one of the most important preliminaries, the one that takes precedence over all the others, is the quality of interested humility." He points out that "interested humility" keeps us alert and involved in the action of transformation as well as open to fresh learning. We thus avoid becoming lax and sporadic in our practice, as well as arrogant and jaded. A story is told in Zen about a learned Westerner who visited a temple in Japan in hope of learning something about the Zen way of life. The abbot gave the newcomer a cup into which he began to pour tea. He continued to pour even when the cup was full and tea was spilling over. The visitor cried out, "Stop, it's too full," whereupon the abbot replied, "And so are you." Kyabgon affirms: "Without curiosity and humility nothing can be retained or absorbed because our minds are already too full of judgments and prejudices."[15]

In his letter to the church at Philippi, Paul enjoins: "In humility regard others as better than yourselves" (Phil 2:3). In the next verse, he admonishes: "Look not to your own interests, but to the interests of others." Rarely do readers realize that these verses set forth specific practices. Buddhism offers a meditative technique named *tonglen* (literally, sending and receiving) by which these admonitions can not only be heeded but employed as a powerful tool for grinding away at the ego, for overcoming our implicit self-cherishing. Tonglen describes a process by which one purposively takes in negativity and suffering from others and dispatches that which is positive and healthful to them. The undesirable is embraced and replaced with the beneficial.

The American Buddhist nun, Pema Chödrön, describes the tonglen method: "Sending and taking should be practiced alternately.

These two should ride the breath." Riding the breath means that one sends on exhalation and receives on inhalation. Chödrön recommends that one begin tonglen with oneself: "Begin the sequence of sending and taking with yourself."[16] In other words, be compassionate toward your own shortcomings and 'undesirable' qualities. When they come up, be gentle and loving, as you would with a child who has been overtaken with similar emotional states—without, of course, any reactive criticism that may arise.

This practice gives a specific method for preparing and acting in reference to the Second Great Commandment: "You shall love your neighbor as yourself" (Matt. 22:39). Expounding further on tonglen, Shantideva referred to the equality of self and others and declared: "Because we are all equal in wanting to experience happiness and avoid suffering, I should cherish all beings as I do myself."[17] These Buddhist teachings and the Christian commandment derive their authenticity from the interconnectedness of human life; as we benefit ourselves we benefit others; as we benefit others we benefit ourselves.

Sending and receiving is best begun by visualizing a small group of persons who hold nothing but your best interests in mind, who love you unconditionally, and wish for you only the best. They may be deceased or living. This small group of four to six can be made up of family members, spiritual leaders, a special friend or teacher, anyone who doesn't judge you but only values and loves you. Picture yourself in their presence and in receipt of their undivided attention, appreciation, and love. Bask in the richness of their affection for a few minutes and allow your heart to fill with positive feelings. Continue to receive this while visualizing and turning your attention toward someone to whom you want to extend unconditional love, initially someone you know well and for whom you have strong feelings of love.

Buddhist texts often recommend beginning with one's mother since deep feelings of love for her are probably well established. While holding in mind your mother's selfless love and appreciation for you, begin drawing from her and breathing into yourself any unworthy emotion, action, or pain that may have occasionally manifested, perhaps picturing these as a dark and cold flow of energy. Follow this by breathing out from your heart, light, warmth and corresponding positive emotions, actions, and concern for her total wellbeing. Stay with this exchange as long as it feels appropriate.

You may next focus on other family members, close friends, acquaintances, those for whom you feel no particular regard, and move next to persons with whom you have problems, and finally, those you dislike and perhaps even regard as enemies. It is best not to send and receive with those for whom you feel negativity until you have made progress in developing some degree of nondiscriminating love, even if this is a matter of years. This kind of love will grow as you are able to empathize with another on the basis of their life situation and not your own.

Sending and receiving can be adapted to a brief exchange between oneself and another, like a prayer during the day when one thinks of another or, as outlined above, can be an elaborate and lengthy exchange with many people that may extend for hours. There are many other variations suggested in the Buddhist texts listed in the endnotes. A useful modification of tonglen is to send to others whatever particular joy one may happen to experience, since everyone likes a lighthearted and upbeat moment. Also, when undergoing discomfort or pain one may be reminded of the many who are enduring severe suffering and even life-threatening illness. One can also, of course, after gaining a little experience, create additional ways of taking on the suffering and negativity of others and replacing them with positive qualities. As an actual practice supportive of specific acts of love, sending and receiving contributes to the formation of a sense of loving kindness and regard for the well-being of others. While this inner purification, intention, and heartfelt concern may give rise to transformational results for others through the medium of consciousness itself, it will simultaneously enhance the loving quality and effectiveness of whatever direct acts of love one may personally extend to another.

The quality of love to be developed is often described as unconditional, i.e., without any reservations regarding the worthiness of the other and without any requirement that the other do this or that to warrant loving kindness. Lao Tzu, the great sage of ancient China, stated the matter clearly and emphatically: "The first practice is the practice of undiscriminating virtue: take care of those who are deserving; also, and equally, take care of those who are not."[18] A Zen Buddhist put the matter well when he referred to an "unconditional love beyond discriminatory justice." He found this quality of love exhibited in the self-emptying of Christ.[19] Applying this kind of love causes one to empathize with and be concerned for the immoral person as well as the moral, for the criminal as well as the victim. According to a statement about Christ attributed to St. Francis of Assisi, the love he lived was without moralistic limitation: "The priest and the prostitute—they weigh the same before the Son's immaculate being."[20]

Demeaning those of so-called lesser moral standards is a somewhat disguised way of upholding one's own superiority. In fact, all criticism stems from the separative ego and its drive to be preeminent. Unrestricted love can occur only between equals. If one feels ever so slightly superior to another in any sense, interaction with that person will be diminished no matter how hard one may try to conceal it. To feel above others, obviously or subtly, is to make them feel below. Such a feeling undermines the heart-to-heart disposition that is truly healing and reduces the exchange to little more than a business transaction. Relating with love to criminals and immoral people does not mean condoning their actions or excusing them from the legal consequences of their actions. It rather means relating to them with the dignity they deserve as human beings and working compassionately toward their reconciliation with and reincorporation into society.

Jesus taught that his followers should love their enemies. This 'difficult' requirement becomes somewhat easier to apply if one approaches it in terms of a Buddhist practice. A fourteenth-century Tibetan monk wrote in his book, *The Thirty-seven Practices of Bodhisattvas*: "Even if someone broadcast all kinds of unpleasant remarks about you . . . , in return, with a loving mind, speak of his good qualities."[21] The way of the bodhisattva entails seeing one's enemies as one's teachers, comparable in this respect to the Buddha himself. Christ and the Buddha gave the instruction; so-called enemies provide opportunities to apply the teaching.

Shantideva observed that "my enemy is the cause of my accumulating the merit of patience because without him there is no patience to practice." He also extolled patience as the remedy for anger: "There is no virtuous practice greater than patience; therefore, I will never get angry with those who cause me suffering."[22] The Dalai Lama recognized the centrality of patience when he affirmed that "if we truly wish to progress, there is no practice more important than patience."[23] From the Christian tradition, Pope Gregory the Great declared that "patience is the root and guardian of all the virtues."

Shantideva's manual of practice for the development of wisdom and compassion devotes a whole chapter to overcoming anger by means of patience. It is obvious that wisdom and compassion are impossible in the face of anger. But how does patience subdue and eliminate anger? The source and essence of anger resides in the unwillingness (perhaps the inability when in the throes of strong emotion) to allow what is to be as it is but instead to force one's own will on the situation. We get angry when we don't get what we want. Anger arises from the ego, the sense of being separate, of being needy and wanting life to go the way one wants it to go.

Another effective way of undermining the ego is to see it for what it is, to be aware of its operation. As an arbitrarily walled off area of 'I', of Self, of all-inclusive Consciousness, of Ultimacy, the ego is necessarily partial, less than whole, and consequently deficient, inadequate, and needy. At the same time that it is constricting awareness, it is building a mass of preferences based on familiarity and the need to ensure its continuance, i.e., to feel secure. In a futile effort to fill the void that this process inevitably entails, the ego attempts to draw to itself (by means of likes, desires, cravings, greed) everything that it believes will enhance its position, and to push away (by means of dislikes, opposition, hatred, fighting, destruction) everything that is threatening. These two, attraction and repulsion, are the dynamic processes that keep the ego in place. The ego tries to find meaningfulness and fulfillment by attempting to become the All by filling itself with everything it likes while simultaneously rejecting everything it dislikes. This accounts for the insatiable appetite and continual discontent, the gnawing sense of meaninglessness and emptiness. To remedy this condition, the transformational process dissolves the contracted state of the ego by disidentifying and detaching from all that the ego has built into itself in its failing attempt to find security and permanence.

Another valuable insight into the nature of the ego that helps undermine it is the realization that it always takes things personally. Ego and personal are virtually synonymous. If one can see the ego simply as conditioned reactivity and the result of habitual formations, its operations are weakened. This is difficult because we are accustomed to interpreting nearly everything that happens as benefiting or hampering our 'personal' well-being. Our self-cherishing stance ensures this.

It is helpful also to note that egos mutually reinforce each other. By not reacting to ego activity in others, one relaxes the ego in oneself. Jesus set a high standard and gave specific ways of overcoming the ego when he said "do good to those who hate you" (Luke 6:27). Responding with kindness in the face of meanness or criticism is effective in countering the ego in oneself, and holds the possibility of changing enemies into friends, but neither result will occur if the response entails any hint of superiority. Arguing to establish one's own view or action as right or better is a sure sign of the ego at work. An effective antidote to egoistic reactivity lies in a willingness to be wrong, especially to be perceived as wrong even if one is not. 'Losing face' is a fate like death to the ego but a powerful means of countering its activities and gaining increased freedom. Relinquishing the need to be right is to drop an arbitrary, self-imposed burden and to experience a new openness and a new freshness in life.

When one becomes aware of the ego and its tricks, it ceases to function as the ego and becomes simply an old, conditioned reaction of the mind. The delimiting effects of the ego begin immediately to diminish when it is seen for what it is. The mental and behavioral pattern may persist for a time because of the momentum of habit, but every time the ego is seen for what it is, its power lessens.

Reference has been made frequently in these pages to actionless action, non-craving, asceticism, detachment, dispassion, and corollary perspectives and actions designed to undermine the ego and foster alignment with Ultimacy, however it may be conceived. One final reference will suffice, this one from Saint John of the Cross, the sixteenth-century associate of Saint Teresa of Avila and author of several classic mystical texts. The stanzas in question are often referred to by the Spanish word *nada*, nothing, the operative term in the passage—and the essential requirement, i.e., hold onto nothing/ release everything in the effort to diminish and dissolve the ego.

> To reach satisfaction in all, desire it . . . in nothing.
> To come to the knowledge of all, desire the knowledge of nothing.
> To come to possess all, desire the possession of nothing.
> To arrive at being all, desire to be nothing.[24]

There are many additional dispositions, attitudes, and actions with the two-fold capacity to undermine the ego's self-agrandizement and simultaneously enhancing harmony and oneness with Ultimacy. A select few of these are: gratitude, forgiveness, generosity, tolerance (not simply tolerating but charitably allowing and valuing others and their beliefs and practices as long as they aren't perpetuating violence—and even then, responding with charity and understanding), gentleness, peacefulness, and equanimity. Each of these is a spiritual quality that may or may not issue in specific acts.

There remain five actions which, if carried out with the right inward stance (i.e., marked by the qualities mentioned in this chapter and throughout the book), carry great power to reduce self-cherishing. These five are friendliness, courtesy, kindness, helpfulness, and service. Individually and combined as a way of life, they carry a twofold power to transform: (1) they affirm the equality of self and other, thereby undermining self-cherishing and (2) they are actual practice, thereby conjoining intention with action and building integrity.

Integral Transformational Practice

An integral approach overcomes the fractures in our lives. It enables us to resolve debilitating dilemmas and contradictory values. It heals disjunction and restores an easeful flow to life. It facilitates the development of a balanced, harmonious, and broadly inclusive life. Because we are composed of multiple, interacting systems and are constantly interacting with other people, a comprehensive integral approach to personal transformation is necessary if we hope to develop to our fullest potential and live constructively and harmoniously with others.

Integral practice is a unique approach to personal transformation. While elements of it have existed in the East for centuries, its development as a distinct and comprehensive program emerged in the Western world at the end of the twentieth and beginning of the twenty-first centuries. Integral practice expands psychospiritual transformation to include the mind and the body. George Leonard and

Michael Murphy published their manual for "Integral Transformative Practice" (ITP) in 1995. They gave the book the title, *The Life We Are Given*, and indicated its comprehensiveness with the subtitle, *A Long-Term Program for Realizing the Potential of Body, Mind, Heart, and Soul.*[25] Specific practices are given in the book for developing each of these four areas, and practice groups have been established across the country. There are, of course, countless resources available for further work in each of the areas—books, magazines, workshops, retreats, and ongoing practice groups.

Even more comprehensive is "Integral Life Practice" (ILP), inaugurated by the Integral Institute in 2005. It is built around Core Modules that focus on body, mind, spirit, and shadow. In addition, there are auxiliary modules on ethics, sex, work, emotions, and relationships. An ILP Starter Kit is available that gives specific practices that can be adjusted to one's personal interests and available time.[26] Included in the kit are substantive booklets, CDs, DVDs, and a wall chart. Ongoing guidance and development of ILP is available through the Integral Institute, which has also published a complete book on integral practices.[27]

Because relatively little has been said about shadow work in this book, and because it is so important in an integral transformational program, we will briefly address ways in which one can work with one's own shadow elements in order to gain greater clarity in self-understanding, engage with others more harmoniously, and recover repressed energy so that life is lived more exuberantly.

The healing and integrating approach to the shadow in Integral Life Practice revolves around the "3-2-1 Process" which refers to third person (he, she, it), second person (you), and first person (I, me). In terms of actual practice, this means that after identifying a denied and hidden feature in one's persona (by means of, for example, dreams, strong emotion, unusual errors in speech), one then moves through three phases by first "facing it" (in the third person as "she, he, or it"), then "talking to it" (in the second person as "you"), and finally, "being it" (by identifying with and embracing it as "me"). One can talk through the process (with or without a trusted person present) or write it out in a journal.

Just a little work with the shadow will demonstrate how insightful and freeing it can be. To be effective, however, shadow work requires absolute honesty, which means that there must be no editing or coloring of what is sensed inwardly. The presence of a trusted friend with some degree of insight and experience can be helpful in spotting where one may be slipping away from the truth. Shadow work is humbling because its purpose is to replace our ideal face, which is often a product of the inflated and devious ego, with the authentic self.

The work of Byron Katie is another way of deconstructing the shadow that can be used either as an alternative to the 3-2-1 process or along with it.[28] Katie's approach moves progressively through a number of questions that are to be answered without any censorship: Who angers, irritates, saddens, or frustrates me, and why?, How do I want them to change? What do they need to do for me to be happy? After answering these and a few other questions, one investigates the verity and validity of the underlying assumptions and beliefs reflected in the answers. One then looks at how one reacts to these in life. Next, one considers how one would feel without these negative thoughts. Finally, and this is the most powerful and transformative aspect of the work, one turns the statements and beliefs about the other person around by seeing them as referring to oneself.

By doing shadow work, we discover that what we thought was a defect in someone else is actually a denied aspect of our own self. The projection is brought back home, thereby giving us an opportunity to accept and embrace formerly 'unknown' aspects of our total self. In this fashion, our fractured self is healed and integrity is enhanced.

A Viewless View

Early in this chapter we took up the importance of having a view of the Kosmos that is accurate and meaningful. In this final section—for the reader's thoughtful and 'heartful' contemplation—we consider what some, including this writer, contend is the ultimate 'view' of the world we live in and Ultimacy, i.e., a concise, summary affirmation of the summit of human transformation culminating in perfect accord/unity with what is.

"Form is emptiness, emptiness is form; emptiness is not other than form, form too is not other than emptiness."[29]

Speaking nondualistically, Jesus acknowledged, "The Father and I are one" (John 10:30).

Similarly speaking, Ramana Maharshi confirmed, "The world is illusory. Only Brahman is real. Brahman is the world."

Meister Eckhart declared: "The eye in which I see God is the same eye in which God sees me. My eye and God's eye are one eye and one seeing, one knowing and one loving."[30]

Jesus affirmed: "Your eye is the lamp of your I. If your eye is healthy, your whole I is full of light" (Luke 11:34).[31]

St. Francis of Assisi said: "What we are looking for is what is looking."[32]

A contemporary teacher, Steven Gray/Adyashanti pointed out: "It's almost as simple as turning awareness back on itself to realize what it is that's looking through this mask right now."[33]

Muslim mystic al-Hallaj announced, "When I saw my Lord with the eye of the heart and asked who He was, I heard the reply, 'You.'"[34]

Paraphrasing slightly what we learned from William Blake in Chapter I: "If the doors of perception were cleansed, we would see everything as it is—infinite."

The 12th century Zen monk, Wu-men stated: "One instant is eternity, eternity is the now. When you see through this one instant, you see through the one who sees."[35]

'I' is Ultimacy. All else is consequent; all else is contingent. Only Ultimacy is.

To use traditional religious language—but a nontraditional concept—all of life occurs, exactly as it occurs, within, as, and of the divine.

Each of these statements is commentary on the others. Each affirms nonduality. As such, each is a radical realization of the root meaning of the word religion, namely, to bind back, to reconnect, to see through and beyond the seeming split in reality. And each emerges from a heart/mind that manifests selfless love and compassion integrated with all-embracing wisdom. Regardless of prevailing circumstances, the inevitable consequence of this quality of life is nothing less than supreme happiness and profound contentment, even while seeking the welfare of all.

NOTES

1. Arthur Osborne, ed., *The Collected Works of Ramana Maharshi.* (London: Rider, 1969), 93.

2. Wei Wu Wei, *Open Secret.* (Boulder, CO: Sentient Publications, 2004), 97.

3. Bharati Mirchandani, ed., *Heart is Thy Name, Oh Lord: Moments of Silence with Sri Ramana Maharshi.* (Tiruvannamalai, Tamalnadu, India: Sri Ramanashramam, 2006), 101.

4. Wei Wu Wei, *Ask the Awakened: The Negative Way.* (Boulder, CO: Sentient Publications, 2002), 18.

5. For a lucid survey of the power of one's soul code, see James Hillman, *The Soul's Code: In Search of Character and Calling.* (New York: Random House, 1996).

6. Quoted in Akizuki Ryōmin, "Christian-Buddhist Dialogue," *Inter-Religio.* no. 14 (Fall 1988), 39.

7. Representative books on *The Way of the Bodhisattva*:

> *A Guide to the Bodhisattva's Way of Life.* Stephen Batchelor, trans., (Dharamsala: India: Library of Tibetan Works and Archives, 1979).
>
> Shantideva, *Guide to the Bodhisattva's Way of Life: How to Enjoy a Life of Great Meaning and Altruism.* Geshe Kelsang Gyatso and Neil Elliott, trans., (Glen Spey, NY: Tharpa Publications, 2002).
>
> Santideva, *The Bodhicharyavatara.* Kate Crosby and Andrew Skilton, trans., (New York: Oxford University Press, 1996).
>
> Shantideva, *The Way of the Bodhisattva.* The Padmakara Translation Group, trans., (Boston: Shambhala, 1997).
>
> Surya Das, Lama, *Buddha Is as Buddha Does: The Ten Original Practices for Enlightened Living.* (New York: HarperSanFrancisco, 2007).

Tenzin Gyatso, The Fourteenth Dalai Lama, *A Flash of Lightening in the Dark of Night: A Guide to the Bodhisattva's Way of Life.* The Padmakara Translation Group, trans., (Boston: Shambhala, 1994).

Representative books on *The Seven-Point Mind Training*:

Pema Chödrön, *Start Where Your Are: A Guide to Compassionate Living.* (Boston: Shambhala, 2001).

Dilgo Khyentse, *Enlightened Courage: An Explanation of Atisha's Seven Point Mind Training.* The Padmakara Translation Group, trans., (Ithaca, NY: Snow Lion Publications, 1993).

Traleg Kyabgon, *The Practice of Lojong: Cultivating Compassion through Training the Mind.* (Boston: Shambhala, 2007).

Osho, *The Book of Wisdom: Discourses on Atisha's Seven Points of Mind Training.* 2nd ed., (Pune, India: Tao Publishing, 1993).

B. Alan Wallace, *The Seven-Point Mind Training.* Zara Houshmand, ed. (Ithaca, NY: Snow Lion Publications, 1992).

8. David Steindle-Rast, *Bulletin of the North American Board for East-West Dialogue.* no. 30 (October 1987), ll.

9. Charles Birch, *Science and Soul.* (Sydney, Australia: University of New South Wales Press, 2008), 114.

10. Ken Wilber, *The Eye of Spirit: An Integral Vision for a World Gone Slightly Mad* in *The Collected Works of Ken Wilber.* vol. 7, (Boston: Shambhala, 2000), 625-652; Ken Wilber, *Integral Spirituality: A Startling New Role for Religion in the Modern and Postmodern World.* (Boston: Integral Books, 2006), 137-138, 196-197.

11. Representative books on meditation:

> Joseph Goldstein, *The Experience of Insight*. (Boston: Shambhala, 1983).
>
> Daniel Goleman, *The Meditative Mind: The Varieties of Meditative Experience*. (New York: Putnam/Tarcher, 1988).
>
> William Johnston, *Silent Music: The Science of Meditation*. (New York: Harper Row, 1974).
>
> Dennis Genpo Merzel, *Big Mind, Big Heart: Finding Your Way*. (Salt Lake City, UT: Big Mind Publishing, 2007).
>
> Henepola Gunaratana, *Mindfulness in Plain English*. updated and expanded ed., (Somerville, MA: Wisdom Publications, 2002).
>
> Jonathan C. Smith, *Meditation: A Sensible Guide to a Timeless Discipline*. (Champaign, IL: Research Press, 1986).
>
> Jon Kabat-Zinn, *Wherever You Go, There You Are: Mindfulness Meditation in Everyday Life*. (New York: Hyperion, 2005).

12. Maurice O'Connell Walshe, trans. and ed., *Meister Eckhart: Sermons and Treatises*. vol. III, (Dorset, England: Element Books, 1978), 126.

13. Representative books on prayer:

> Abhishiktananda, *Prayer*. (New Delhi: Abhishiktananda Society, 1989).
>
> Brother Lawrence, *The Practice of the Presence of God*. (New Kensington, PA: Whitaker House, 1982).
>
> Frank Laubach, *Practicing His Presence*. vol. 1, *The Library of Christian Classics*. (Seedsower, 1988).
>
> Thomas Keating, *Intimacy with God: An Introduction to Centering Prayer*. (New York: Crossroad Publishing, 2006).

Basil Pennington, *Centering Prayer: Renewing an Ancient Christian Prayer Form*. (New York: Doubleday, 1980).

14. Walshe, *Meister Eckhart: Sermons and Treatises*, vol. 3, 118-119.
15. Traleg Kyabgon, *The Practice of Lojong: Cultivating Compassion through Training the Mind. (Boston: Shambhala, 2007), 16*.
16. Chödrön, *Start Where Your Are*, 33.
17. Shantideva, *Guide to the Bodhisattva's Way*, 128.
18. Brian Walker, *Hua Hu Ching: The Unknown Teachings of Lao Tzu.* rev. ed., (New York: HarperCollins, 1994), 4.
19. Quoted in William Johnston, *Mystical Theology: The Science of Love. (*Maryknoll, NY: Orbis Books, 2004), 119.
20. Daniel Ladinsky, trans., *Love Poems from God.* (New York: Penquin Compass, 2002), 35.
21. Gyelsay Togmay Sangpo, *The Thirty-seven Practices of Bodhisattvas*. Geshe Sonam Rinchen, commentary, Ruth Sonam, trans., ed., (Ithaca, NY: Snow Lion Publications, 1997), 47.
22. Shantideva, *Guide to the Bodhisattva's Way*, 86.
23. Tenzin Gyatso, *A Flash of Lightning*, 70.
24. Quoted in Johnston, *Mystical Theology*, 122.
25. George Leonard and Michael Murphy, *The Life We Are Given: A Long-Term Program for Realizing the Potential of Body, Mind, Heart, and Soul*. (New York: Jeremy P. Tarcher/Putnam, 1995).
26. For further information, go to www.integralinstitute.org.
27. Ken Wilber *et al., Integral Life Practice: A 21*[st] *Century Blueprint for Physical Health, Emotional Balance, Mental Clarity, and Spiritual Awakening.* (Boston: Integral Books, 2008).
28. Byron Katie and Stephen Mitchell, *Loving What Is: Four Questions That Can Change Your Life.* (New York: Three Rivers Press, 2002). Also, www.thework.com.
29. Tenzin Gyatso, *Essence of the Heart Sutra: The Dalai Lama's Heart of Wisdom Teaching.* (Boston: Wisdom Publications, 2002), 60.

30. Bernard McGinn, ed., *Meister Eckhart: Teacher and Preacher,* in *Classics of Western Spirituality: A Library of the Great Spiritual Masters.* (New York: Paulist Press, 1986), 270.

31. Metateric translation by the author. Cf. Matt. 5:29, the import of which can be rendered idiomatically as: "If one's eye does not see truly, one's whole life will be forfeited." For further justification of these interpretations, see Gerhard Kittel and Gerhard Friedrich, *Theological Dictionary of the New Testament.* Abridged in one volume by Geoffrey W. Bromiley, trans., (Grand Rapids, MI: William B. Eerdmans Publishing Company, 1985), 1145.

32. http://thinkexist.com/quotes/st._francis_of_assisi/

33. Steven Donoso, A Quiet Revolution: An Interview with Adyashanti,"*Shift: At the Frontier of Consciousness.* (Spring 2009, No. 22), 35.

34. For a slightly different formulation, see Huston Smith, *Tales of Wonder: Adventures Chasing the Divine, an Autobiography.* (New York: HarperCollins Publishers, 2009), 147-148.

35. http://dzogchen.org. Weekly Words of Wisdom chosen by Lama Surya Das, April 6, 2009.

Glossary*

A

Abd, A. I.—lit. 'servant'; often part of a name, e.g., Abdallah, meaning 'servant of God'.

Abegesheidenheit, Middle High Grm., Abgeshiedenheit, Modern Grm. C.—lit. 'detachment'; first and foremost virtue for Meister Eckhart, the source of all other values.

Abhidhamma, P., Abhidharma, Sk. B. lit. 'essential teachings'; the earliest system of Buddhist psycho-philosophical thought; see dhamma.

---

* Key to Glossary Abbreviations

Religions—			lit.—	literally
	B	Buddhism		
	C	Christianity		
	H	Hinduism		
	I	Islam		

Languages—		
	A	Arabic
	Grm	German
	Grk	Greek
	J	Japanese
	L	Latin
	P	Pali
	Sk	Sanskrit
	S	Spanish
	Tb	Tibetan

Advaita Vedanta, Sk. H.—lit. 'nondual' (advaita) and 'end or goal of the Vedas' (Vedanta); one of Hinduism's most profound and comprehensive religious philosophies; formulated in the ninth century by Shankara (see index).

Agape, Grk. C.—divine love; selfless love; unconditional love that seeks only the welfare of the other.

Agni, Sk. H.—Vedic god of fire.

Ahad, A. I.—lit. 'one'; for Ibn al-Arabi, Ultimacy in Itself; see wahid.

Aham Brahman Asmi, Sk. H.—lit. "I am Brahman"; one's objective in reciting the mantra.

Ahimsa, Sk. H. B.—lit. 'non-hurt', i.e., noninjury or non-violence; avoidance of inflicting any form of pain on a sentient creature.

Allah, A. I.—lit. 'the God'; the principle reference to God in Islam.

Anatman, Sk., Anatta, P. B.—absence of a self, nonsubstantiality, nothing exists independent of other factors; basic difference of Buddhism with Hinduism and its atman (see) view.

Apatheia, Grk. C.—lit. 'dispassion, detachment'; term used in the early church for the ideal of nonattachment.

Apophatic Theology, Grk. C—negative theology; the view that God cannot be known by the rational mind or conventional ways of thinking; positive assertions about the nature of God are necessarily limiting and therefore inappropriate.

Arahant, P., Arhat, Sk. B.—lit. 'the worthy one'; the most highly realized in Theravada Buddhism; the saint who will enter Nirbbanna (see) and return no more to the samsaric (see) realm.

Arjuna, Sk. H.—main protagonist in the Bhagavad Gita who, as a member of the warrior caste, is faced with the dilemma of acting against his own conscience and going to war.

Artha, Sk. H.—material wealth; the second life value in Hinduism, particularly applicable during the second or householder stage of life. Financial well-being in Hinduism is commendable as long as its pursuit does not violate moral standards.

Asanas, Sk. H.—body postures that make up Hatha Yoga; one of the practices in Raja Yoga.

Ashram, Ashrama, Sk. H.—a center for religious practice, a monastery or hermitage.

Ashtanga Yoga, Sk. H.—lit. 'eight-limbed yoga'; another name for Raja Yoga.

Asrava, Sk., Asava, P. B.—lit. 'outflows'; mental-emotional defilements that cause distortions in one's views and practice; must be extinguished for enlightenment to ensue.

Ati, Sk. B.—lit. 'highest'; applied by some to the Dzogchen (see) school as the highest teachings of the Buddha.

Atma, Atman, Sk. H.—the changeless, immortal self or soul believed by Hindus to be equivalent to Brahman.

Aum, Sk. H. B.—alternate spelling for om; popular and common mantra denoting creation and wholeness; the vibratory sound giving rise to the universe.

Avadhuta Gita, Sk. H.—a nondual text that extols the life-style and practice of the avadhuta (see).

Avadhuta, Sk. H.—lit. 'cast off', thus, the naked one; one who is bound by nothing, who lives a totally free life.

Avatar, Avatara, Sk. H.—lit. 'descent'; incarnation; mainly said of Krishna as the incarnation of Vishnu.

B

Barakah, A. I.—lit. 'blessing'; blessing and power of divine presence; grace.

Bhagavad Gita, Sk. H.—lit. 'Song of the Lord', the most widely read and influential sacred text for Hindus.

Bhajans, H.—devotional singing and music.

Bhakta, Sk. H.—one who practices bhakti, or devotional, yoga.

Bhakti Yoga, Sk., H.—practice based on liberation by means of loving devotion directed to one's chosen deity (see ishta devata).

Blama, Tb. B.—lit. 'none above'; more often spelled and pronounced 'lama'; a Tibetan Buddhist teacher or guru.

Bodhi, Sk. P. B.—lit. 'awakened'; enlightened; in Mahayana Buddhism, bodhi derives from the nondual perspective that sees the unity of samsara and nirvana and all apparent dualities.

Bodhicharyavatara, Sk. B.—The Way of the Bodhisattva; training manual for bodhisattvas.

Bodhichitta, Sk. B.—lit. 'the awakened mind'; the mind of enlightenment that has integrated wisdom and compassion.

Bodhisattva, Sk. B.—lit. 'a being of enlightenment'; bodhisattvas have attained nirvana but postpone it out of compassion for others.

Brahma, Sk. H.—the Creator God.

Brahman Nirguna, Sk. H.—lit. 'without attributes, qualities, limitation'; nothing can be postulated of Brahman Nirguna.

Brahman Saguna, Sk. H.—lit. 'with attributes'; manifestation of Brahman Nirguna.

Brahman, Sk. H.—favored name for God in Hinduism; the transcendental source of all that is.

Brahmanda, Sk. H.—lit. 'the egg of Brahma'; the manifest world; one of an infinite number of cosmoses.

Brahmin, Sk. H.—a member of the priestly caste, the highest in the traditional fourfold caste system.

Buddha, Sk. P. B.—lit. 'the awakened one'; one who sees reality as it is; title given to Gautama Siddhartha following his enlightenment.

Buddhi Yoga, Sk. H.—lit. 'awakened' yoga; a practice that combines laya, mantra, and kundalini yoga into a single discipline.

C

Cataphatic Theology, Grk. C.—positive theology; traditional ways of talking about God by attributing to him qualities and features that are known to humans.

Chakras, Sk. H.—the psychospiritual energy centers along the spine through which the kundalini (see) rises.

Chela, Sk. H. B.—lit. 'servant'; used for a student or disciple who is in a learning relationship with a guru or teacher.

Classical Yoga—See Raja Yoga.

D

Dana, Sk. B.—lit. 'giving'; i.e., generosity; the first quality to be mastered by a bodhisattva.

Darshan, Darshana, Sk. H.—lit. 'viewing'; sitting in the presence of a holy person in order to venerate him or her and receive instruction and/or blessing.

Dhammapada, P. Dharmapada, Sk. B.—widely read text containing the earliest teachings of the Buddha.

Dhamma, P. Dharma, Sk. H.B.—the third value/objective in Hinduism's fourfold classification of life values; also covers a range of overlapping activities and objectives, i.e., religion, righteousness, ritual performance, moral obligation, social duty; in Buddhism, dharma also refers to absolute truth and reality, as in dharmakaya (see).

Dharmakaya, Sk. B.—the body of truth; the transcendental realm, Ultimacy; the true and essential nature of buddhas; the supreme realm of the trikaya.

Dhawk, A. I.—lit. 'tasting'; term used by Ibn al-Arabi to designate the authoritative knowing that comes through direct experience in contrast to mere information.

Dhikr, A. I.—lit 'remembering'; reciting one or more of God's names repeatedly; 'Remember Allah with much remembrance' (Koran 33:41).

Dhyana, Sk. H. B.—concentration, contemplation, meditation; essential method for investigating the mind and developing wisdom.

Din, A. I.—generic religion.

Dokusan, J. B.—private meeting for instruction between a disciple and teacher in Zen Buddhism.

Duhkha, Sk., Dukkha, P. B.—suffering, discontent; all that is conditioned since everything changes; the first of the Four Noble Truths and one of the three fundamental marks of existence.

Durchbruch, Grm. C.—lit. 'breakthrough'; breakthrough to the Godhead; second phase in the return to God/Godhead; according to Meister Eckhart (see Index).

Dzogchen, Tb. B.—lit. 'great perfection'; central teaching in one of the major Tibetan schools of Buddhism; everything that arises is perfect as it is; sometimes rendered 'natural great perfection'.

E

Ekatvam, Sk. H.—unity, nonduality; the ability to see the divine in all things and all things in oneself.

Epektasis, Grk. C.—lit. 'reaching forward'; continual longing for God's presence; ongoing development toward the soul's perfection.

Epistolos, Grk. C.—lit. 'letter'; used in reference to the letters that make up a substantial part of the New Testament; most of these were written by Paul to churches he founded and aided.

Eros, Grk. C.—erotic love; sensual love (in the threefold Christian analysis); in some systems of thought, it is an ascending force which inclines toward higher and more inclusive perspectives; some forms of Christian mysticism recognize eros as the love that leads to union with God.

Ex Opere Operatio, L. C.—lit. 'through the performance of the work'; used in the Roman Church to note that the efficacy of a sacrament derives from God's grace and not from the human instrument.

Exitus, L. C.—lit. 'exit'; according to Meister Eckhart, the movement of God out of Himself into the created realm; see reditus.

F

Falah, A. I.—a common term for salvation in Islam; also carries the meaning of success, in this life and the next.

Faqir, A. I.—lit. 'one who is poor'; synonym for a sufi; carries the sense of nonattachment for Sufis.

Fitrah, A. I.—inborn nature; conveys the sense that to submit to God is a natural act; Muhammad claimed that every child is born a Muslim and is made otherwise by his parents.

G

Geburt, Grm. C.—lit. 'birth'; birth of the Son (or Word) in the soul; first phase of the return to God according to Meister Eckhart (see Index).

Gelassenheit, Modern Grm., Gelazenheit, Middle High Grm. C.—lit. 'letting-go, letting-be'; along with detachment, the means of totally abandoning oneself to God, of relying on God alone; according to Meister Eckhart's (see Index) system of thought and practice.

Glossolalia, Grk. C.—speaking in tongues; ecstatic speech in a language not of human invention; believed by some Christians to be evidence of the indwelling of the Holy Spirit; also found in religions other than Christianity.

Gnosis, Grk. C.—lit. 'knowledge'; refers not to learned knowledge but to intuitive insight; esoteric and metateric understanding.

Gnosticism, Grk. C.—system of thought and practice centering in gnosis (see); the noncanonical Gospel of Thomas sets forth a gnostic view.

Godhead, C.—Meister Eckhart's term for Ultimacy.

Gunas, Sk. H.—lit. 'basic quality', constituents of Prakriti (see Samkhya) which in various combinations make up the entire natural order; the three basic gunas are sometimes rendered consciousness, activity, dullness, sometimes positive, neutral, and negative, etc.

H

Hadith, A. I.—lit. 'report, tradition'; secondary source of law in Islam following the Koran; based on the sayings and actions of Muhammad.

Hafiz, A. I.—lit. 'guardian', i.e., of the Koran; title given to one who has memorized the entire Koran.

Hajj, A. I.—pilgrimage to Mecca; required only of those physically and financially able; must be made during the official month for the Hajj, otherwise it is simply a visit to Mecca; numerous prescribed activities occur, including several circumambulations of the Kaba (see).

Hanif, A. I.—someone who believed in a single God rather than the polytheism prevailing during Muhammad's day; a monotheist.

Haqq, A. I.—truth, reality in the absolute sense; one of the names of Allah.

Harijans, Sk. H.—lit. 'children of God'; name given by Gandhi to those historically known as untouchables because they were outside the formal caste system and considered ritually impure. Harijans perform tasks considered unclean, such as tanning leather, removing human waste, etc.

Hatha Yoga, Sk. H.—liberation by means of control over the body and breath, thereby gaining heightened consciousness.

Heterodox, Grk. C.—'wrong belief'; holding beliefs that are not acceptable, that depart from tradition; opposite of orthodox.

Hijra, A. I.—lit. 'immigration', sometimes misleadingly 'flight'; mass movement of Muslims from Mecca to Medina in 1 AH (Anno Hijra)/622 CE; marks the beginning of the Islamic calendar.

Holon, Grk.—lit. 'whole'; a word introduced by Arthur Koestler conveying the notion that everything is simultaneously a whole containing parts and itself a part of an even greater, more inclusive whole. Reality consists of holons ad infinitum.

Homo-ousios, Grk. C.—lit. 'same essence'; view that the three persons of the Christian trinity are identical in essence; see ousia.

Hypostasis, Grk. C.—lit. 'being'; the three persons of the Christian trinity are separate in their beingness; see ousia.

I

Incarnation, L. C.—'in (the form of) flesh'; doctrine stipulating that Jesus the Christ is God in human form, fully human and fully divine; Hindui view which maintains that there have been many incarnations (see avatara).

Indra, Sk. H.—the most important sky god in the Vedic pantheon, young and robust, slayer of the evil dragon that withholds the life-giving monsoon rains.

Insha' Allah, A. I.—lit. 'if God wills'; common saying among Muslims indicating dependence on God.

Intellegere, L. C.—lit. (depending on context) 'intellect, intelligence, understanding, knowing'; Meister Eckhart equates this with God's beingness/existence.

Inter-being,—nothing exists in isolation; everything is derived from, related to, and dissolved by and into factors and forces other than itself; strictly speaking, it is misleading to simply say that things are; properly speaking, all things inter-are.

Iqra, A. I.—lit. 'recite, read'; the angel Gabriel's command to Muhammad that became the earliest revelation in the Koran.

Ishta devata, Sk. H.—lit. 'chosen deity'; god or goddess that a Hindu chooses as his or her personal deity.

Ishvara, Sk. H.—lit. 'Personal Lord'; supreme ruler of a cosmos who, for this cosmos, projects himself as Brahma (Creator God), Vishnu (Preserver God), Shiva (Destroyer God).

Islam, A. I.—based on the root 'salama' which carries the twofold meaning of 'submission' and 'peace'; thus, Islam is the religion of peace by means of submission to Allah.

I'tiqad, A. I.—lit. 'belief'; denotes the tying of a knot and strong attachment; common stance in conventional Islam but challenged

496

and disclaimed by Ibn al-Arabi who saw beliefs about Allah as necessarily limiting and misleading.

J

Jihad, A. I.—lit. 'struggle, effort', commonly rendered 'holy war'; spiritualized to refer to the battle within against evil or negative qualities.

Jivan Mukta, Sk. H.—one who is liberated while still alive.

Jnana Yoga, Sk. H.—practice leading to liberation by means of knowledge (jnana); not knowledge in the sense of information, or even intellectual understanding, but profound intuitive insight; see gnosis.

K

Kaba, A. I.—lit. 'cube'; name given the ancient, polytheistic temple in Mecca; re-consecrated as the geographical direction of prayer for Muslims; see Hajj.

Kama Sutra, Sk. H.—a collection of comments on love-making that treats sexual pleasure in an objective and reverential fashion.

Kama, Sk. H.—sexual love or more broadly pleasure; the first of the four values or goals that Hinduism upholds as worthy and desirable.

Kamma, P. Karma, Sk. H. B.—lit. 'deed', 'action'; both physical and mental; that which is based on and results from one's deeds; the law of cause and effect that sustains the ongoing, cyclical process.

Karma Yoga, Sk. H.—practice based on liberation by means of action; two forms: (1) proper fulfillment of caste duty leads to rebirth in a higher caste; failure to fulfill caste requirements causes descent to a lower caste; (2) all action must be performed without attachment to the fruits or results of the action.

Kataphatic, Grk. C.—See Cataphatic

Karuna, Sk. P. H. B.—lit. 'compassion'; active empathy that works to relieve the suffering of all sentient beings; essential quality of bodhisattvas.

Kensho, J. B.—lit. 'seeing nature'; seeing one's true nature, i.e., awakening; Zen term for the enlightenment experience; sometimes used to designate an initial and temporary awakening that yet needs to be permanently established.

Khalq, A. I.—lit. 'creature'; technical term for Ibn al-Arabi who asserts that God (Haqq) appears in time and space as creature (khalq) even as creatures are represented transcendentally by God (Haqq).

Khanda, P. B.—lit. 'group, aggregate'; refers to the five factors that are believed in Buddhism to constitute the entirety of human personhood; the five are form or matter, sensation or feeling, perception by means of the senses, mental formations, and consciousness or awareness; there is nothing substantial or permanent. Cf. skandha

Koan, J. B.—lit. 'public notice'; question or paradox given to a student by a Zen teacher that is designed to confound the rational mind and cause it to transcend to nondualistic awareness; example, 'who were you before your mother and father were?'

Koinonia, Grk. C.—lit. 'communion, fellowship'; used by Abhishiktananda to indicate his loyalty to the Christian community.

Koran, A. I.—lit. 'reading, recitation'; common anglicized spelling of Qur'ān; sacred scripture of Muslims; believed to have been directly revealed to Muhammad from God through the agency of the angel Gabriel.

Kosmos, Grk. C.—lit. 'cosmos'; used technically to include not only the cosmos but all that is real, the transcendent realm as well as the material-energetic.

Krishna, Sk. H.—incarnation of Vishnu; principle god of the Bhagavad Gita.

Kriya Yoga, Sk. H.—lit. 'yoga of deed, effort'; another name for Raja Yoga (see).

Kshanti, Sk. B.—commonly translated as 'patience' but sometimes as 'tolerance'; the third paramita (see) of the bodhisattva path; patience and tolerance are antidotes to anger and essential to the exercise of compassion.

Kshatriya, Sk. H.—the second caste in the fourfold classification; consists of those with governing and military responsibilities.

Kundalini Yoga, Sk. H.—a yoga that likens the energy locked at the base of the spine to a coiled snake which, when raised through the psychospiritual energy centers (see chakra) along the spine, thereby clearing and energizing them, leads to liberation.

L

Lama, Tb. B.—teacher, guru; see blama.

Laya Yoga, Sk. H.—liberational approach involving breath control and veneration of a deity.

Lila, Sk. H. B.—lit. 'play', or 'sport'; regarded by many Hindus as God's reason for creating the cosmos.

Logos, Grk. C.—lit. 'word'; logos appears frequently in Western philosophical-theological discourse and carries a variety of nuanced meanings; the Gospel of John opens with the phrase, 'in the beginning was the logos'; frequently associated with intuitive, esoteric, and gnostic views.

Lojong, Tb. B.—lit. 'mind training'; disciplinary practice in Tibetan Buddhism.

M

Mahasiddha, Sk. B.—lit. 'one with great powers'; the enlightenment ideal in Tibetan Buddhism; parallel to the bodhisattva in Mahayana Buddhism but tending more to demonstrate magical powers.

Mahayana, Sk. B.—lit. 'the great vehicle'; the largest school of Buddhism; open to new interpretations and adaptations of the Buddha's teachings.

Maheshvara, Sk. H.—lit. 'Supreme or Eternal Lord'; form of Brahman Saguna that produces out of itself by means of maya (see) innumerable brahmandas (see) and an equal number of Ishvaras (see), each of which rules over a single cosmos.

Mandala, Sk. H. B.—lit. 'circle'; diagram, often composed of concentric circles, squares, and triangles that depict key symbols and can serve as focus for meditation.

Mantra Yoga, Sk. H.—devotional recitation of a mantra (see); traditionally given to a disciple in a special ritual.

Mantra, Sk. H. B.—sacred sound symbol that sets up an energetic vibration that contributes to a change in consciousness; may or may not have intellectual significance; examples, 'om'; 'om mani padme hum' (see).

Margas, Sk. H.—lit. 'paths'; disciplines and practices that lead to liberation.

Maya, Sk. H. B.—lit. 'illusion, appearance'; the ability of Brahman to reveal and conceal itself at one and the same time; denotes the unreality or mere appearance of all that makes up the ordinary world.

Metateric, Grk.—derived from the root, meta, meaning 'after', 'along with', 'beyond'. Metateric is the most inclusive way of being religious or spiritual; nondualistic and inclusive of the authentic features of both exoteric and esoteric religion; coined by the author to distinguish the nondualistic perspective from other worldviews and ways of being religious/spiritual.

Moksha, Sk. H.—release or liberation from the wheel of becoming and bondage; overcoming the bonds of karma; the special focus during the fourth stage of life, that of the sannyasi (see).

Monacos, Grk. C.—lit. 'solitary one'; identified in the gnostic Gospel of Thomas as one who is a nondualist by right of knowing his or her true self.

Murti, Sk. H. B.—lit. 'image, idol'; an object of worship for exotericists; a symbol or manifestation of God for esotericists and metatericists.

Muslim, A. I.—conveys the sense of 'one who submits (to Allah) thereby finding peace' (see Islam); a member of the Islamic religion.

Mysterium tremendum et fascinans, L.—all-powerful and awe-inspiring mystery experienced when encountering God.

N

Nada, Sp. C.—lit. 'nothing'; key term used by Saint John of the Cross that aligns with detachment, dispassion, non-craving, etc. as essential for ultimate realization.

Nafs, A. I.—central concept among Sufis; numerous meanings and connotations, e.g., breath, instinct, carnal desire, soul, psyche, ego; that which must be subjected and purified in order to enter into union with God; contrasted with ruh (see).

Najat, A. I.—salvation, deliverance, i.e., from everlasting punishment.

Nataraj, Sk. H.—lit. 'King of the Dance'; manifestation of Shiva who, iconographically dancing in a cosmic ring of fire, has taken on the three cosmic functions of creation, preservation, and destruction.

Neti, neti, Sk. H.—lit. 'not this, not that'; said of any attempt to describe Ultimacy in Hinduism, i.e., Brahman Nirguna.

Nibbanna, P. B.—lit. 'extinction', i.e., extinction of the asravas (see) and the sense of separateness; the state of liberation or enlightenment; see Nirvana.

Nirmanakaya, Sk. B.—earthly form taken by buddhas as they appear in time and space; see trikaya.

Nirodha, Sk. B.—lit. 'destruction, cessation'; the annihilation of craving and desire and thus the end of suffering; the third of the Four Noble Truths; sometimes equated with nirvana.

Nirvana, Sk. H. B.—lit. 'extinction', i.e., extinction of the asravas (see) and the sense of separateness; the state of liberation or enlightenment.

Nirvikalpa Samadhi, Sk. H.—complete identification with Ultimacy, total absorption; a nondual state in which there is no content in consciousness, no relationship, no other, no thought.

Nirvrita Sk. B.—bodhisattva state of supreme happiness and contentment due to his or her continual exercise of generosity until there is nothing further that can or need be given.

Nous, Grk. C.—lit. 'mind'; used in the sense of non-discursive thought; intuitive insight that recognizes unity in diversity; key notion in Plotinus and subsequent Christian mystical theology.

O

Om Mani Padme Hum, Sk. B.—common mantra in Buddhism; numerous significances, e.g., "Om, the Jewel is in the Lotus, Hum."

Om, Sk. H. B.—popular and common mantra denoting creation and wholeness; the vibratory sound giving rise to the universe.

Orthodox, Grk. C.—lit. 'right belief'; holding traditional beliefs; not heterodox (see) or heretical.

Ousia, Grk. C.—lit. 'essence'; term used in the context of clarifying the Christian doctrine of the trinity; contrasted with hypostasis (see) to argue that the three persons, God, Christ, and Holy Spirit, are separate beings but with a common essence; they are homo-ousios (see).

P

Pandharpur, H.—a town near Poona/Puni in Maharashtra State in which is located the image of the deity worshipped by Tukaram.

Panduranga, H.—one of several names for the deity worshipped by Tukaram.

Parakletos, Grk. C.—lit. 'advocate, comforter'; Jesus announced the coming of such a one; some Muslims regarded Muhammad as fulfilling the role.

Paramitas, Sk. B.—usually translated 'perfections'; the essential qualities or virtues, often six or ten in number, that are mastered by bodhisattvas.

Parinibanna, P., Parinirvana, Sk. B.—synonym for nirvana; sometimes used for total extinction at death to distinguish it from nirvana while living.

Petra, Grk. C.—lit. 'rock'; see Petros; a play on words in which Jesus says to Peter that he will build the church on 'this rock'; scholars continue to debate whether rock refers to Peter himself (Roman Catholic view) or to the faith Peter exhibited in claiming Jesus as the Christ (Protestant view).

Petros, Grk. C.—lit. 'Peter'; see petra.

Philia, Grk. C.—familial love; bonding force of friendship (in the threefold Christian analysis of love).

Prajna, Sk. B.—lit. 'wisdom'; insight into the emptiness of all things, i.e., to the absence of independent existence; an essential quality of bodhisattvas; the sixth and culminating quality in the six-fold classification of paramitas.

Prakriti, Sk. H.—see Samkhya.

Purusha, Sk. H.—see Samkhya.

Q

Q,—abbreviation for Quille; see next entry.

Quille, Grm. C.—lit. 'source'; refers to a lost source used by Matthew and Luke in the composition of their Gospels; a view held by some biblical scholars.

R

Raja Yoga, Sk. H.—lit. 'the royal unitive discipline'; liberational system formulated by Patanjali involving eight disciplinary practices.

Reditus, L. C.—lit. 'return'; humanity's gradual ascent back to God according to the system of Meister Eckhart; see exitus.

Relegere, L. C.—lit. 'to attend to, to observe carefully'; see religio.

Religare, L. C.—'to re-connect, to bind to'; see religio.

Religio, L. C.—root from which the English word religion is derived; the English word religion, like religio, is derived from either religare (to re-connect, to bind to) or relegere (to attend to, to observe carefully).

Rigpa, Tb. B.—pure awareness; key notion in Dzogchen (see) Buddhism characterizing the natural mind as crystalline lucidity.

Roshi, J. B.—lit. 'old (i.e. venerable) master'; Zen master or teacher.

Ruh, A. I.—central concept among Sufis; Spirit; sometimes linked with fitrah (see); perhaps best rendered 'Self' in the sense of Muhammad's saying, 'Whoso knoweth himself knoweth his Lord'; contrasted with nafs (see).

S

Sahaja Samadhi, Sk. H.—preferred name by some Hindu schools for the highest state of realization; thorough integration of one's own liberation with active involvement in the outer world; metateric realization.

Sahaja, Sk. B.—lit. 'natural'; also sometimes rendered coemergence, even spontaneity; indicative of supreme realization and the metateric view.

Salat, A. I.—lit. 'ritual prayer'; sometimes rendered 'worship'; offered five times a day by the devout; uses memorized words.

Samadhi, Sk. H.B.—lit. 'making firm', higher state of consciousness carrying the sense of standing deeply and undistractedly within one's true nature; denotes absorption in God or Ultimacy.

Sambogakaya, Sk. B.—the intermediate trikaya (see); the 'buddha paradise'; the celestial sphere where buddhas reside in great power and glory.

Samkhya, Sk. H.—a religio-philosophical systems of Hinduism that postulates two fundamental, metaphysical realities, Spirit (Purusha) and Nature or Matter (Prakriti); the liberational goal is to detach from matter and merge into pure Spirit.

Samsara, Sk. H. B.—the endless wheel of change, becoming, suffering, birth, and death; realm of bondage that entraps Hindus and Buddhist and thereby constitutes their basic predicament in life.

Sangha, Sk. H. B.—lit. 'crowd, host'; in Hinduism, a group gathered around a guru for teaching; in Buddhism, narrowly, the monastic community of monks and nuns, and broadly, the entire community of Buddhists.

Sannyasa, Sk. H.—fourth stage of life during which a Hindu renounces possessions, family, all usual relations and lives for ultimate realization alone; often entails continual travel and/or residence in an ashram (see).

Sannyasi, Sannyasin, Sk. H.—one who renounces ordinary life and takes up the fourth stage of life; renunciant.

Sapientia, L. C.—wisdom; Augustine distinguishes wisdom from knowledge; wisdom results from the contemplation of eternal and infinite realities; contrasted with scientia (see).

Sat, Chit, Ananda, also Satchitananda, Sk. H.—lit. 'existence, consciousness, bliss'; fundamental attributes of Brahman Saguna; as one word may be used as name of a sage or saintly person.

Satori, J. B.—Zen term for enlightenment; can be synonymous with kensho (see) or represent a more permanent and final enlightenment.

Savikalpa Samadhi, Sk. H.—a state of consciousness in which one relates to God in a subject-object manner.

Sawm, A. I.—fasting; observed during daylight hours of Ramadan, the month designated for communal fasting; eating is permitted before the sun rises and after it sets; children, the ill, and the aged are exempt.

Scientia, L. C.—knowledge; Augustine distinguishes knowledge from wisdom; knowledge concerns only the empirical world, the world of the five senses; see sapientia.

Sele, Grm. C.—lit. 'soul, mind'; the higher power of the soul/mind, the Intellect, seeks nothing less than returning to God/Godhead according to the system of Meister Eckhart.

Shahada, A. I.—the Muslim testimony or confession of faith, 'There is no god but God; Muhammad is the Messenger of God', by means of which, when made publically, one becomes a Muslim.

Shakti, Sk. H.—lit. 'power, force, energy'; consort of Shiva; personification of primal energy.

Shamatha, Sk. B.—tranquility; the inner quietness that is prerequisite to gaining clear vision.

Sharia, A. I.—lit. 'way, path'; Islamic law; based primarily on the Koran.

Shi'a, Shi'ite, A. I.—lit. 'party', i.e. of 'Ali; smaller of the two main branches of Islam; because of their view that the leadership of Muslims following Muhammad's death should be someone from his family lineage, the Shi'a separated from the Sunnis (see).

Shila, Sk. B.—morality; the ethical precepts that guide Buddhists; the second paramita (see) for bodhisattvas (see) that, while informed by conventional standards, is ultimately guided only by wisdom and compassion.

Shirk, A. I.—giving God an associate, a rival; unpardonable sin in Islam; see tawhid.

Shiva, Sk. H.—the Destroyer God.

Shudra, Sk. H.—the fourth and lowest group in the caste structure; unskilled workers, artisans, laborers, and servants.

Shunya, Shunyata, Sk. B.—lit. 'emptiness, void'; everything is empty of self-identity; nothing has an independent existence; a central notion in Buddhism; see anatman, skandha, svabhava.

Siddhis, Sk. B.—magical powers that instruct and facilitate the liberation of those still bound in the earthly realm.

Skandha, Sk. B.—lit. 'group, aggregate'; refers to the five factors that are believed in Buddhism to constitute the entirety of human personhood; the five are form or matter, sensation or feeling, perception by means of the senses, mental formations, and consciousness or awareness; there is nothing substantial or permanent; see khanda.

Sola Fide, L. C.—lit. 'faith alone'; view promoted by Martin Luther; salvation occurs only by faith and not be works.

Sola Gratia, L. C.—lit. 'grace alone'; salvation is a gift of God and not the result of good works.

Soma, Sk. H.—Vedic earth god; name of a plant and an ecstasy-inducing drink made from the juice of the plant, used in Vedic rituals.

Soteriology, Grk. C.—the study of salvation; what it is, how it occurs, what its fruits are.

Sufi, A. I.—a Muslim mystic; may be derived from the Arabic word for wool, which was the common dress of early Muslim mystics; may be derived from the Arabic word for pure, safi.

Sunder Warumbe, Grm. C.—lit. 'without a why'; Meister Eckhart's expression for God's motiveless creation.

Sunnah, A. I.—lit. 'custom'; customary practices, habits, and sayings of Muhammad; gave rise to extensive texts (see Hadith) from which many Muslims derive their personal behavioral patterns.

Sunni, A. I.—the larger branch of Islam; maintained that leadership of the Muslim community should fall on the person most qualified, without reference to Muhammad's family lineage, as maintained by the Shi'a (see).

Svabhava, Sk. B.—lit. 'own-being, self-nature'; according to Buddhism nothing has svabhava; nothing is self-existenct; see anatman, skandha.

Synoptic, Grk. C.—lit. 'seeing together'; refers to Mathew, Mark, and Luke; when they are seen side-by-side, many passages of identical and similar content are discovered.

T

Tafsir, A. I.—lit. 'explanation, elucidation'; Koranic exposition concerned primarily with historical background and literal or exoteric meaning.

Tanha, P. B.—see Trishna; briefly, desire.

Tat tvam asi. Sk. H.—lit. 'that art thou', indicates identity with Ultimacy.

Tathagata, Sk. P. B.—title of the Buddha indicating that he knows the tahata (see), the suchness/thusness of reality.

Tathata, Sk. B.—lit. 'thusness', 'suchness'; reality is as it is; characterizes reality in itself and as itself, without human distortion.

Tawhid, A. I.—unity, oneness; the central and most basic belief in Islam; to associate anything with God is anathema in Islam (see shirk).

Ta'wil, A. I.—Interpretation of the Koran that seeks the interior, deeper meanings; uncovering the esoteric and metateric significances.

Telos, Grk. C.—lit. 'end, goal, result'; the notion that there is an inherent, subtle energetic aim in the life process that guides it toward a goal; the Christian theologian, Paul Tillich, identifies this force as divine.

Theognosis, Grk. C.—lit. 'knowledge of God'; view of Evagrius that in prayer God gives true knowledge of himself.

Theosis, Grk. C.—'deification'; to become Godlike; manifesting the qualities of God but not his essence, i.e., not actually becoming God; particularly prominent in the Eastern Orthodox Church.

Theravada, P. B.—lit. 'the way of the elders'; the earliest form of Buddhism; the school of Buddhism that most emphasizes the traditions of the Buddha and his earliest followers.

Tonglen, Tb. B.—lit. 'sending and receiving'; meditative practice of taking in the negativity and suffering of others and sending positivity and wellbeing to them.

Trikaya, Sk. B.—the three bodies doctrine; a metaphysical analysis that identifies three forms or realms of Buddhist manifestation, nirmanakaya, sambhogakaya, and dharmakaya (see each); there are different interpretations of the trikaya.

Trishna, Sk. B.—lit. 'craving, desire'; wanting reality to be otherwise than it is; cause of suffering and discontent; the second of the Four Noble; see tanha.

U

Ultimacy,—the source, sustenance, empowerment, and eventual dissolution of all that is; an absolutely all-inclusive term. For religious practitioners, the central referent in religion is Ultimacy, though innumerable other names, titles, and attributes may be applied.

Upanishad, Sk. H.—lit. 'to sit down near'; refers to the practice of seekers finding a sage and sitting down near him to learn methods that lead to realization; a vast compendium of spiritual insight that contains much of Hinduism's deepest reflection on religion; more than a hundred texts make up this group; only about twelve are regarded as principal Upanishads.

Upaya, Sk. B.—skill in means; methods by which bodhisattvas (see) aid those victimized by samsara (see); sometimes listed among the paramitas (see).

Urspung, Grm. C.—lit. 'springing forth'; Meister Eckhart's term for creation as it 'springs forth' from the Godhead.

V

Vaishya, Sk. H.—the third caste, the members of which represent commercial, industrial, and agricultural operations.

Vajrayana, Sk. B.—lit. 'the diamond vehicle'; the third major school of Buddhism; also known as Tibetan Buddhism and Mantrayana Buddhism due to its considerable use of mantras (see) in meditation practices and rituals.

Varuna, Sk. H.—Vedic celestial god; grants forgiveness of sin.

Vedas, Sk. H.—lit. 'knowledge', the earliest and for most Hindus the most authoritative scriptures; the Rig Veda is the oldest and most authoritative of the four Vedas.

Vipashyana, Sk., Vipassana, P. B.—insight, clear seeing, i.e., into the true nature of things, thus, emptiness; name for one of the central and basic forms of meditation in Buddhism.

Virya, Sk. B.—vigor, energy, exertion; the fourth perfection developed by bodhisattvas (see); denotes the energetic activity exhibited by bodhisattvas on behalf of those suffering under the conditions of samsara (see).

Vishnu, Sk. H.—the Preserver God.

Vitthoba, H.—a form of Vishnu; one of several names for the god worshipped by Tukaram (see Index).

Viveka, Sk. H.—lit. 'discrimination, discernment', essential requirement in Advaita Vedanta (see).

W

Wahid, A. I.—lit. 'one'; for Ibn al-Arabi, God in manifestation; see ahad.

Wajada, A. I.—notion of Ibn al-Arabi linking subjectivity and objectivity, perception and being, consciousness and existence, thus asserting the nonduality of reality.

Y

Yoga Sutra, text authored/compiled by Patanjali, perhaps in the 2nd century CE; basis of Raja Yoga (see).

Yoga, Sk. H. B.—lit. 'yoke', i.e., the yoke that links oxen, thus indicating union; the yogas are sets of practices that lead to oneness with the divine.

Yogi, Yogini (fem), Sk. H.—a practitioner of yoga.

Z

Zakat, A. I.—lit. 'gift, giving, virtue'; required generosity in the form of legal alms or alms-tax; Muslims also make voluntary donations.

Zazen, J. B.—lit. 'sitting concentration'; meditation; central practice in Zen Buddhism.

Zen, J. B.—major Japanese form of Buddhism; the term 'zen' is derived from the Chinese 'ch'an' which in turn comes from the Sanskrit 'dhyana'; all three terms mean meditation.

Bibliography

A

Abbot, Justin E., *Stotramala*. Poona, India: Scottish Mission Industries, 1929.

ᶜAbduh, Muhammad, *The Theology of Unity*. Isāq Musaᶜad and Kenneth Cragg, trans., London: George Allen & Unwin, 1897, 1966.

Abe, Masao, "Kenotic God and Dynamic Sunyata," in *The Emptying God: A Buddhist-Jewish-Christian Conversation*. John B. Cobb, Jr. and Christopher Ives, eds., Maryknoll, N.Y.: Orbis Books, 1990.

Abhishiktananda, "Experience of God in Eastern Religions," *Cistercian Studies*. 4 (1974).

_____, *Guru and Disciple*. Heather Sandeman, trans., London: S.P.C.K., 1974.

_____, *Hindu-Christian Meeting Point: Within the Cave of the Heart*. Sarah Grant, trans., Delhi: I.S.P.C.K., 1976.

_____, *Prayer*. New Delhi: Abhishiktananda Society, 1989.

_____, *Saccidananda: A Christian Approach to Advaitic Experience*. J.D.M. Stuart, ed., Delhi: I.S.P.C.K., 1984.

_____, *The Further Shore*, Delhi: I.S.P.C.K.,1984.

_____, *The Secret of Arunachala*. Delhi: I.S.P.C.K., 1979.

ad-Darqāwī, al-ᶜArabī, *Letters of a Sufi Master*. Titus Burckhardt, trans., London: Perennial Books,   1973.

Affifi, A.E., *The Mystical Philosophy of Muyid Dīn-ibnul ᶜArabī*. Cambridge: University Press, 1939.

al-ᶜArabi, Ibn, *The Bezels of Wisdom*. R.W.J. Austin, trans., in *The Classics of Western Spirituality: A Library of the Great Spiritual Masters*. New York: Paulist Press, 1980.

ᶜArabi, Muhyiddin Ibn *Journey to the Lord of Power*. Rabia Terri Harris, trans., London: East West Publications, 1981.

ᶜArabi, Muhyiddin ibn, "What the Student Needs," *Journal of the Muhyiddin Ibn ᶜArabi Society* (Oxford, England). vol. 5 (1986).

ᶜArabī, Muyī al-Dīn ibn, "The Treatise on Oneness," *Journal of the Royal Asiatic Society* (Malayan Branch). October 1901.

al-Din, Kamal, "Muhammad as a Soldier," *Islamic Review and Muslim India*. (Woking, England). vol. 5, no. 1 (January 1917).

al-Fārūqī, Ismaᶜīl Rāgī, "Islam," in *The Great Asian Religions: An Anthology*. Wing-tsit Chan, Ismaᶜīl Rāgī al-Fārūqī, Joseph M. Kitagawa, P.T. Raju, comps, New York: Macmillan Co., 1969.

_____, *Tawḥīd: Its Implications for Thought and Life*. Muslim Training Manual, vol. 2, Wyncote, Pa.: International Institute of Islamic Thought, 1982.

Ali, Abdullah Yusuf, trans., *The Holy Qur'ān: Text, Translation and Commentary*. Washington, D.C.: American International Printing Co., 1946.

ᶜAlī ibn ᶜUthmān al-Jullābī al-Hujwīrī, *The Kashf al-Mahjūb: The Oldest Persian Treatise on Ṣūfiism*. new. ed., Reynold A. Nicholson, trans., E.J.W. Gibb Memorial Series, vol. 17, London: Luzac and Co., 1936/1967.

al-Suhrawardy, Abdullah al-Mamun, *The Sayings of Muhammad*. Wisdom of the East Series, London: John Murray, 1941/1949.

Ananda Maitreya, Balangoda, trans., Rose Kramer, reviser, The Dhammapada: *The Path of Truth*. Novato, Ca.: Lotsawa, 1988.

Arasteh, A. Reza, *Rumi the Persian: Rebirth in Creativity and Love*. Tucson: Omen Press, 1972.

Arberry, A.J., ed., *Religion in the Middle East: Three Religions in Concord and Conflict*. Cambridge: University Press, 1969.

_____, *Sufism: An Account of the Mystics of Islam*. New York: Harper & Row, 1950.

Arberry, Arthur J., trans., *The Koran Interpreted*. New York: Macmillan Co., 1955.

Ashokananda, Swami, trans., *Avadhuta Gita*. Madras, India: Sri Ramakrishna Math, 1981.

ᶜAtā'illāh, Ibn, *Sufi Aphorisms (Kitāb al-Hikam)*. Leiden: E.J. Brill, 1973.

Augustine, *Confessions*, Henry Chadwick, trans. Oxford: Oxford University Press, 1991.

B

Bache, Christopher M., *Dark Night, Early Dawn: Steps to a Deep Ecology of Mind*. Albany, NY: State University of New York Press, 2000, 26.

Badawi, Jamal A., "The Obligatory Fasting of Ramadhan," *The Muslim World League Journal*. vol. 8, no. 10 (August 1981).

Batchelor, Stephan, trans., *A Guide to the Bodhisattva's Way of Life*. Dharamsala: India: Library of Tibetan Works and Archives, 1979.

Baumer-Despeigne, Odette, "The Spiritual Journey of Henri Le Saux—Abhishiktananda," *Cistercian Studies*. 4 (1983).

Beck, Don and Christopher C. Cowan, *Spiral Dynamics: Mastering Values, Leadership, and Change, Exploring the New Science of Memetics*. Malden, MA: Blackwell, 2006.

Berthold, George C., trans., *Maximus Confessor: Selected Writings*, in *Classics of Western Spirituality: A Library of the Great Spiritual Masters*. Mahwah, NJ: Paulist Press, 1985.

Bhagavan Sri Ramana: A Pictorial Biography. Tiruvannamalai, India: Sri Ramanasramam), 1981.

Birch, Charles, *Science and Soul*. Sydney, Australia: University of New South Wales Press, 2008.

Blake, William, "The Marriage of Heaven and Hell" in David V. Erdman, ed., *The Complete Poetry and Prose of William Blake*. rev. ed., New York: Doubleday (Anchor Books), 1988.

Blakney, Raymond B., *Meister Eckhart: A Modern Translation*. New York: Harper and Row, 1941.

Borg, Marcus and N.T. Wright, *The Meaning of Jesus: Two Visions*. San Francisco: Harper, 1999.

Borg, Marcus, *Jesus: A New Vision*. San Francisco: Harper, 1987.

_____, *Meeting Jesus Again for the First Time: The Historical Jesus and the Heart of Contemporary Faith*. San Francisco: HarperSanFrancisco, 1994.

_____, *The Heart of Christianity: Rediscovering a Life of Faith*. San Francisco: HarperCollins, 2003.

Brhadaranyaka Upanisad. 1.4.2. in Patrick Olivelle, trans. and annotator, *The Early Upanisads*. New York: Oxford University Press, 1998.

Browning, Elizabeth Barrett, *Aurora Leigh,* in Kerry McSweeney, ed., *Oxford World Classics*. Oxford: Oxford University Press, 1998.

Brunton, Paul, *A Search in Secret India*. New Delhi: B.I. Publications, 1934, 1970.

Bruteau, Beatrice, "In the Cave of the Heart: Silence and Realization," *New Blackfriars,* Summer 1984.

Burton, Naomi, Patrick Hart and James Laughlin, eds., *The Asian Journal of Thomas Merton.* New York: New Directions Books, 1973.

C

Caputo, John D. "Fundamental Themes in Meister Eckhart's Mysticism," *The Thomist.* 42 (April 1978).

_____, *The Mystical Element in Heidegger's Thought.* Athens: Ohio University, 1978.

Chittick, William C., The *Sufi Path of Knowledge: Ibn al-ᶜArabi's Metaphysics of Imagination.* Albany: State University of New York Press, 1989.

_____, "Belief and Transformation: The Sufi Teachings of Ibn al-ᶜArabi," *The American Theosophist.* vol. 74 (1986) no. 5.

Chödrön, Pema, *Start Where You Are: A Guide to Compassionate Living.* Boston: Shambhala, 2001.

Clark, James M., *Meister Eckhart: An Introduction to the Study of His Works with Anthology of His Sermons.* London: Thomas Nelson and Sons, 1957.

_____ and John V. Skinner, *Meister Eckhart: Selected Treatises and Sermons Translated from Latin and German with an Introduction and Notes.* London: Faber and Faber, 1958.

Clark, Mary T., trans., intro., *Augustine of Hippo: Selected Writings.* in *The Classics of Western Spirituality: A Library of the Great Spiritual Masters.* New York: Paulist Press, 1984.

Colledge, Edmund and Bernard McGinn, trans., intro., *Meister Eckhart: The Essential Sermons, Commentaries, Treatises, and Defense,* in *The Classics of Western Spirituality: A Library of the Great Spiritual Masters.* New York: Paulist Press, 1981.

Colledge, Edmund, "Meister Eckhart: His Time and His Writings," *The Thomist.* 42 (April 1978).

Conze, Edward, *Buddhist Wisdom Books: Containing The Diamond Sutra and The Heart Sutra.* New York: Harper Torchbooks, 1958.

Cousins, Ewert H., trans., *Bonaventure,* in *The Classics of Western Spirituality: A Library of the Great Spiritual Masters.* New York: Paulist Press, 1978.

Crosby, Kate and Andrew Skilton, trans., *The Bodhicharyavatara.* Oxford: Oxford University Press, 1996.

Cutsinger, James S., comp., ed., *Not of This World: A Treasury of Christian Mysticism.* Bloomington, IN: World Wisdom, 2003.

D

Dalai Lama, The, *Dzogchen: The Heart Essence of the Great Perfection.* Geshe Thupten Jinpa and Richard Barron (Chokyi Nyima), trans., Patrick Gaffney, ed., Ithaca, NY: Snow Lion Publications, 2000.

Danner, Victor, trans., *Ibn 'Ata'illah's Sufi Aphorisms.* Leiden: E.J. Brill, 1973.

Deming, Wilbur S., *Selections from Tukaram*. Madras, India: Christian Literature Society for India, 1932.

Deutsch, Eliot, trans., The Bhagavad Gita. New York: Holt, Rinehart and Winston, 1968.

Douglas-Klotz, Neil, *The Hidden Gospel: Decoding the Spiritual Message of the Aramaic Jesus.* Wheaton, Ill: Quest Books, 1999.

Dudjom Jigdral Yeshe Dorje, *Wisdom Nectar: Dudjom Rinpoche's Heart Advice.* Ron Garry, trans., Ithaca, NY: Snow Lion Publications, 2005.

Dumoulin, Heinrich, *Zen Buddhism: A History.* vol. 2, James W. Heisig and Paul Knitter, trans., New York: Macmillan Publishing Co., 1988, 1990.

Dupré, Louis and Don E. Saliers, eds. *Christian Spirituality: Post-Reformation and Modern.* vol. 18, *World Spirituality: An Encyclopedic History of the Religious Quest.* New York: Crossroad Publishing Co., 1989.

E

Eckhart, Meister, *Parisian Questions and Prologues.* Armand A. Maurer, trans., intro., Toronto: Pontifical Institute of Mediaeval Studies, 1974.

el-Eflākī, Shemsu-'d-Dīn Ahmed, *Legends of the Sufis: Selected Anecdotes from the Work Entitled "The Acts of the Adepts".* J.A. Redhouse, trans., Wheaton: Theosophical Publishing House, 1976.

Eliade, Mircea, ed-in-chief, *The Encyclopedia of Religion*. New York: Macmillan Publishing Co., 1987.

Erdman, David V., ed., *The Complete Poetry & Prose of William Blake*. rev. ed. New York: Doubleday (Anchor Books), 1988.

Eswaran, Eknath, trans., The Dhammapada. Petaluma, Ca: Nilgiri Press, 1985.

F

Fa-tsang, "A Brief Commentary on the 'Heart of the Sutra of the Perfection of Wisdom'", in Francis H. Cook, *Hua-yen Buddhism: The Jewel Net of Indra*. University Park: Pennsylvania State University, 1991.

Feuerstein, Georg, *Holy Madness: The Shock Tactics and Radical Teachings of Crazy-Wise Adepts, Holy Fools, and Rascal Gurus*. New York: Paragon House, 1991.

——————, trans., *The Yoga-Sutra of Patanjali: A New Translation and Commentary*. Rochester, Vermont: Inner Traditions International, 1989.

Flew, Anthony, ed., *A Dictionary of Philosophy*. rev. 2nd ed. New York: St. Martin's Press, 1984.

Forman, Robert K. C., *Meister Eckhart: The Mystic as Theologian*. Warwick, NY: Amity House, 1991.

Fox, Matthew, intro., comm., *Breakthrough: Meister Eckhart's Creation Spirituality in New Translation*. Garden City, NY: Image Books, 1980.

Franck, Frederick, trans., *The Book of Angelus Silesius.* Santa Fe, NM: Bear and Company, 1985.

Friedlander, Ira, *The Whirling Dervishes.* New York: Macmillan Publishing Co., 1975.

Friedlander, Shems, *Submission: Sayings of the Prophet Muhammad.* New York: Harper & Row, 1977.

G

Gebser, Jean, *The Ever-Present Origin.* Noel Barstad and Algis Mickunas, trans. Athens, OH: Ohio University Press, 1985.

Glassé, Cyril, *The Concise Encyclopedia of Islam.* San Francisco: Harper & Row, 1989.

Goldstein, Joseph, *The Experience of Insight.* Boston: Shambhala, 1983.

Goleman, Daniel, *The Meditative Mind: The Varieties of Meditative Experience.* New York: Putnam/Tarcher, 1988.

Govinda, Anagarika, Lama, *A Living Buddhism for the West.* Maurice Walshe, trans., Boston: Shambhala, 1990.

_____, *Buddhist Reflections.* Maurice Walshe, trans. York Beach, ME: Samuel Weiser, Inc., 1991.

_____, *Creative Meditation and Multi-Dimensional Consciousness.* Wheaton, IL: Theosophical Publishing House, 1976.

_____, *Foundations of Tibetan Mysticism: According to the Esoteric Teachings of the Great Mantra, Om Mani Padme Hum*. New York: Samuel Weiser, 1960, 1969.

_____, *Insights of a Himalayan Pilgrim*. Berkeley, CA: Dharma Publishing, 1991.

_____, *The Way of the White Clouds: A Buddhist Pilgrim in Tibet*. Berkeley: Shambhala, 1966, 1970.

Guenther, Herbert V., trans., *The Royal Song of Saraha: A Study in the History of Buddhist Thought*. (Berkeley: Shambhala, 1973.

Gunaratana, Henepola, *Mindfulness in Plain English*. updated and expanded ed., Somerville, MA: Wisdom Publications, 2002.

H

Haeri, Fadhlalla, *The Elements of Sufism*. Rockport, MA: Element, 1993.

Hakim, Khalifa Abdul, *Islamic Ideology*. Lahore: Institute of Islamic Culture, 1961.

Hanh, Thich Nhat, *The Heart of Understanding: Commentaries on the Prajnaparamita Heart Sutra*. Peter Levitt, ed., Berkeley, CA: Parallax Press, 1988.

Harvey, Peter, *An Introduction to Buddhism: Teachings, history and practices*. Cambridge: Cambridge University Press, 1990.

Henri Le Saux/Abhishiktananda, *The Eyes of Light*. André Gozier and Joseph Lamarié, eds., Danville, NJ: Dimension Books, 1983.

Hillman, James, *The Soul's Code: In Search of Character and Calling.* New York: Random House, 1996.

Hixon, Lex, *Heart of the Koran.* Wheaton, IL: Theosophical Publishing House, 1988.

Holt, Bradley P., *Thirsty for God: A Brief History of Christian Spirituality.* 2nd ed., Minneapolis: Fortress Press, 2005.

Hoyland, John S., *An Indian Peasant Mystic.* London: H. R. Allenson, Ltd., 1932.

http://thinkexist.com/quotes/st._francis_of_assisi/

Hymnal of the Church of God. Anderson, IN: Gospel Trumpet Company, 1953.

Hymnal of the Church of God. Anderson, IN: Warner Press, 1971.

I

Integral Institute, The, www.integralinstitute.org.

Ipema, Peter, "Muammad as Intercessor according to the Qur'ān and Hadīth," Unpublished M.A. thesis, Hartford, CT: Hartford Seminary Foundation, 1969.

Isāq, Muammad ibn, *The Life of Muhammad: A Translation of Isāq's Sūrat Rasūl Allāh.* A. Guillaume, trans., Lahore: Pakistan Branch of Oxford University Press, 1955, 1967.

Izutsu, Toshihiko, "Ibn al-ᶜArabī," in Eliade, *The Encyclopedia of Religion.* vol. 6, 556.

J

Jeffery, Arthur, "Ibn al-ʿArabī's Shajarat al-Kawm," *Studia Islamica.* vol. 11 (1959).

—————, ed., *A Reader on Islam.* The Hague: Mouton and Co., 1962.

Johnston, William, *Mystical Theology: The Science of Love.* Maryknoll, NY: Orbis Books, 2004.

—————, *Silent Music: The Science of Meditation.* New York: Harper Row, 1974.

Jones, Cheslyn, Geoffrey Wainwright and Edward Yarnold, eds. *The Study of Spirituality.* New York: Oxford University Press, 1986.

K

Kabat-Zinn, Jon, *Wherever You Go, There You Are: Mindfulness Meditation in Everyday Life,* New York: Hyperion, 2005.

Katie, Byron and Stephen Mitchell, *Loving What Is: Four Questions That Can Change Your Life.* New York: Three Rivers Press, 2002.

Kavanaugh, Kieran and Otilio Rodriguez, trans., *The Collected Works of St Teresa of Avila.* vol. 1, Washington, DC: Institute of Carmelite Studies, 1987.

Keating, Thomas, *Intimacy with God: An Introduction to Centering Prayer.* New York: Crossroad Publishing, 2006.

Keenan, John P., *The Meaning of Christ: A Mahayana Theology.* Maryknoll, NY: Orbis Books, 1989.

Kelley, C.F., *Meister Eckhart on Divine Knowledge.* New Haven, Conn.: Yale University Press, 1977.

Kenney, John Peter, *The Mysticism of Saint Augustine: Rereading the Confessions.* New York: Routledge, 2005.

Kertz, Karl G., "Meister Eckhart's Teaching on the Birth of the Divine Word in the Soul," *Traditio.* 15 (1959).

Khan, Muhammad Zafrulla, trans., *Gardens of the Righteous (Riyadh as-Salihin of Imam Nawawi).* New York: Olive Branch Press, 1989.

Khan, Vilayat Inayat, *Toward the One.* New York: Harper & Row, 1974.

Khyentse, Dilgo, *Enlightened Courage: An Explanation of Atisha's Seven Point Mind Training.* The Padmakara Translation Group, trans., Ithaca, NY: Snow Lion Publications, 1993.

Kieckhefer, Richard, "Meister Eckhart's Conception of Union with God," *Harvard Theological Review.* 71 (July-October 1978).

Kierkegaard, Soren, *Purity of Heart is to Will One Thing.* New York: Harper and Row, 1956.

King, Ursula, *Christian Mystics: Their Lives and Legacies throughout the Ages.* Mahwah, NJ: Paulist Press/HiddenSpring, 2001.

Kyabgon, Traleg, *The Practice of Lojong: Cultivating Compassion through Training the Mind.* Boston: Shambhala, 2007.

L

Ladinsky, Daniel, trans., *Love Poems from God*. New York: Penquin Compass, 2002.

Lal, P., trans., The Dhammapada. New York: Farrar, Straus & Giroux, 1967.

Lambdin, Thomas O., trans. "The Gospel of Thomas," in James M. Robinson, gen. ed., *The Nag Hammadi Library in English*. 3rd rev. ed. San Francisco: Harper, 1990.

Lane, Belden C., *The Solace of Fierce Landscapes: Exploring Desert and Mountain Spirituality*. Oxford: Oxford University Press, 1998.

Lawrence, Brother and Frank Laubach, *Practicing His Presence*. vol. 1, *The Library of Christian Classics*. Seedsower, 1988.

Lawrence, Brother, *The Practice of the Presence of God*. New Kensington, PA: Whitaker House, 1982.

Leonard, George and Michael Murphy, *The Life We Are Given: A Long-Term Program for Realizing the Potential of Body, Mind, Heart, and Soul*. New York: Jeremy P. Tarcher/Putnam, 1995.

Levy, Reuben, *The Social Structure of Islam*. Cambridge: University Press, 1962.

Lings, Martin, *A Sufi Saint of the Twentieth Century: Shaikh Ahmad al-ᶜAlawī*. Berkeley: University of California Press, 1971.

_____, *What is Sufism?*. Berkeley: University of California Press, 1977.

Lopez, Donald S. Jr., "Sanctification on the Bodhisattva Path," in Kieckhefer, Richard and George D. Bond, eds., *Sainthood: Its Manifestations in World Religions*. Berkeley: University of California Press, 1988.

_____, *The Heart Sutra Explained: Indian and Tibetan Commentaries*. Albany: State University of New York Press, 1988.

Luibheid, Colm, trans., Paul Rorem, forward, notes, Paul Roques, preface, *et al.*, *Pseudo-Dionysius: The Complete Works*. in *The Classics of Western Spirituality: A Library of Great Spiritual Masters*. New York: Paulist Press, 1987.

Lutyens, Mary, *Krishnamurti: The Years of Fulfillment*. New York: Farrar Straus Giroux, 1983.

M

Macdonald, Duncan B., *The Religious Attitude and Life in Islam*. Beyrouth: Khayats, 1965.

Macnicol, Nicol, *Psalms of Maratha Saints*. Calcutta, India: Association Press, 1919.

Macy, Joanna, *Mutual Causality in Buddhism and General Systems Theory*. Albany, N.Y.: State University of New York Press, 1991.

Marion, Jim, *Putting on the Mind of Christ: The Inner Work of Christian Spirituality*. Charlottesville, VA: Hampton Roads Publishing Co., 2000.

Matics, Marion L., trans., *Entering the Path of Enlightenment: The Bodhicharyavatara of the Buddhist Poet Shantideva*. New York: Macmillan, 1970.

McCarthy, Richard J., trans., *The Theology of al-Ash'arī*. Beyrouth: Imprimerie Catholique, 1953.

McGinn, Bernard, John Meyendorff and Jean Leclercq, eds. *Christian Spirituality: Origins to the Twelfth Century*. vol. 16, *World Spirituality: An Encyclopedic History of the Religious Quest*, New York: Crossroad Publishing Co., 1988.

McGinn, Bernard, "Meister Eckhart: An Introduction," in Paul E. Szarmach, ed., *An Introduction to the Medieval Mystics of Europe*. Albany: State University of New York, 1984.

——————, "The God beyond God: Theology and Mysticism in the Thought of Meister Eckhart," *Journal of Religion*. 61 (January 1981).

——————, ed., *Meister Eckhart: Teacher and Preacher*, in *Classics of Western Spirituality: A Library of the Great Spiritual Masters*. New York: Paulist Press, 1986.

——————, ed., intro., *The Essential Writings of Christian Mysticism*. New York: The Modern Library, 2006.

——————, *The Foundations of Mysticism*. vol. 1, *The Presence of God: A History of Western Christian Mysticism*. New York: Crossroad Publishing Co., 1991.

_____, *The Growth of Mysticism.* vol. 2, *The Presence of God: A History of Western Christian Mysticism.* New York: Crossroad Publishing Co., 1994

McGuckin, John Anthony, *Standing in God's Holy Fire: The Byzantine Tradition.* Maryknoll, NY: Orbis Books, 2001.

Merton, Thomas, *Conjectures of a Guilty Bystander.* Garden City, NJ: Doubleday, 1966.

_____, *New Seeds of Contemplation.* New York: New Directions Publishing Corp., 1961.

_____, *The Seven Story Mountain.* New York: Harcourt, Brace & World, 1948.

Merzel, Dennis, Genpo, *Big Mind, Big Heart: Finding Your Way.* Salt Lake City, UT: Big Mind Publishing, 2007.

Miller, Roland E., "The Muslim Doctrine of Salvation," *The Bulletin of Christian Institutes of Islamic Studies* (Hyderabad, India). vol. 2, nos. 1-4 (Jan.-Dec. 1980).

Mirchandani, Bharati, ed., *Heart is Thy Name, O Lord: Moments of Silence with Sri Ramana Maharshi.* Tiruvannamala, India: Sri Ramanasaramam, 2006.

Mitchell, Stephen, trans., Tao Te Ching. New York: Harper & Row, 1988.

Morris, James E., "The Spiritual Ascension: Ibn ʿArabī and the Miʿrāj," pts. 1 and 2, *Journal of the American Oriental Society.* vol. 107 (1987), no. 4; vol. 108 (1988), no. 1.

N

Nasr, Seyyed Hossein, ed., *Islamic Spirituality: Foundations.* vol. 19, *World Spirituality: An Encyclopedic History of the Religious Quest.* New York: Crossroad, 1987.

——————, ed., *The Essential Writings of Frithjof Schuon.* Amity, N.Y.: Amity House,   1986.

——————, *Ideals and Realities of Islam.* Boston, Beacon Press, 1972.

——————, *Islamic Life and Thought.* Albany: State University of New York Press, 1981.

——————, *Knowledge and the Sacred.* New York: Crossroad Publishing Co., 1981.

——————, *Sufi Essays.* New York: Schocken Books, 1977.

——————, *Three Muslim Sages.* Cambridge: Harvard University Press, 1964.

Newman, Helen, "The Teacher Speaks on Methods: A partial account of Lama Govinda's weekend seminar at HDI," *Human Dimensions.* vol. 1, no. 4, Buffalo: Human Dimensions Institute, 1972.

Nicholson, Reynold A., *Studies in Islamic Mysticism.* Cambridge: University Press, 1921, 1967.

——————, trans., *The Mathnawi of Jalaluddin Rumi.* vol. 6, Cambridge: University Press, 1982.

Nourbakhch, J., "Le Soufisme, Son But et Sa Methode," in *God and Man in Contemporary Islamic Thought*. Charles H. Malik, ed., Beirut: American University, 1972.

Nyoshul Kenpo Rinpoche and Lama Surya Das, *Natural Great Perfection: Dzogchen Teachings and Vajra Songs*. Lama Surya Das, trans., Ithaca, NY: Snow Lion Publications, 1995.

O

Obermiller, E. "The Doctrine of Prajñaparamita as Exposed in the Abhisamayalamkara of Maitreya," *Acta Orientalia*. vol. 11 (1932), parts I-II.

Osborne, Arthur, ed., *The Collected Works of Ramana Maharshi*. London: Rider, 1969.

Osho, *The Book of Wisdom: Discourses on Atisha's Seven Points of Mind Training*. 2nd ed., Pune, India: Tao Publishing, 1993.

Outler, Albert C., ed., *John Wesley*. New York: Oxford University Press, 1964.

P

Panikkar, Raimundo, "Letter to Abhishiktananda—On Eastern-Western Monasticism," *Studies in Formative Spirituality*. 3, no.3 (1982).

Patten, Terry, *et al. My ILP Handbook: Getting Started with Integral Life Practice*. Version 1.0, www.integralinstitute.org: Integral Institute, 2005.

Pennington, Basil, *Centering Prayer: Renewing an Ancient Christian Prayer Form*. New York: Doubleday, 1980).

Philips, Abu Ameenah Bilal, *Salvation Through Repentance (An Islamic View)*. Riyadh: Tawheed Publications, 1990.

Pickthall, Marmaduke, trans., *The Meaning of The Glorious Koran: An Explanatory Translation*. New York: Alfred A. Knopf, 1930.

Ponticus, Evagrius, *The Praktikos [and] Chapters on Prayer*. John Eudes Bamberger, trans., intro., notes, Cistercian Studies Series, no. 4.

Powell, Mark Allan, *The Jesus Debate: Modern Historians Investigate the Life of Christ*. Oxford, England: Lion Publishing, 1998; also published in the USA as *Jesus as a Figure in History*. Louisville, KY: Westminster John Knox Press, 1998.

Price, A.F. and Wong Mou-lam, trans., *The Diamond Sūtra and the Sūtra of Hui-neng*. Boston: Shambhala, 1990

R

Radhakrishnan, Sarvepalli and Charles A. Moore, eds., *A Sourcebook in Indian Philosophy*. Princeton, N.J.: Princeton University Press, 1957.

Ranade, R.D., *Mysticism in India: The Poet-Saints of Maharashtra*. Albany, N.Y.: State University of New York Press, 1933, 1983.

Ranke-Heinemann, Uta, *Putting Away Childish Things: The Virgin Birth, the Empty Tomb, and Other Fairy Tales You Don't Need to Believe to Have a Living Faith*. Peter Heinegg, trans., New York: HarperCollins Publishers, 1994.

Richardson, Alan and John Bowden, *eds.*, *The Westminster Dictionary of Christian Theology*. Philadelphia: The Westminster Press, 1983.

Robinson, Richard H. and Willard L. Johnson, *The Buddhist Religion: A Historical Introduction.* 3rd ed., Belmont, CA: Wadsworth Publishing Co., 1982.

Royster, James E., "The Meaning of Muammad for Muslims: A Phenomenological Study of Recurrent Images of the Prophet." Unpublished Ph.D. dissertation, Hartford, CT.: Hartford Seminary Foundation, 1970.

Rubenstein, Richard E., *When Jesus Became God: The Struggle to Define Christianity during the Last Days of Rome.* San Diego: Harcourt, Inc., 1999.

Ryōmin, Akizuki, "Christian-Buddhist Dialogue," *Inter-Religio*, no. 14 (Fall 1988).

S

Sangpo, Gyelsay Togmay, *The Thirty-seven Practices of Bodhisattvas.* Geshe Sonam Rinchen, comm., Ruth Sonam, trans., ed., Ithaca, NY: Snow Lion Publications, 1997.

Santideva, *The Bodhicharyavatara.* Kate Crosby and Andrew Skilton, trans., New York: Oxford University Press, 1996.

Schimmel, Annemarie, *Mystical Dimensions of Islam.* Chapel Hill: University of North Carolina, 1975.

Schumann, H. Wolfgang, *Buddhism: An Outline of its Teachings and Schools*. Georg Feuerstein, trans., Wheaton, IL: The Theosophical Publishing House, 1974.

Schurmann, Reiner, "The Loss of the Origin in Soto Zen and in Meister Eckhart," *The Thomist.* 42 (April 1978).

—————, *Meister Eckhart: Mystic and Philosopher.* Bloomington: Indiana University Press, 1978.

Sengstan, The Third Zen Patriarch, "Hsin Hsin Ming" ("Verses on the Faith Mind"). Virginia Beach, VA: privately published as a pamphlet by Alan Clements, 1980.

Shafii, Mohammad, *Freedom from the Self: Sufism, Meditation and Psychotherapy.* New York: Human Sciences Press, 1985.

Shantideva, *Guide to the Bodhisattva's Way of Life: How to Enjoy a Life of Great Meaning and Altruism.* Geshe Kelsang Gyatso and Neil Elliott, trans., Glen Spey, NY: Tharpa Publications, 2002.

—————, *The Way of the Bodhisattva.* The Padmakara Translation Group, trans., Boston: Shambhala, 1997.

Shaw, R.D.M. and Wilhelm Schiffer, trans., "Yasen Kanna: 'A Chat on a Boat in the Evening' by Hakuin Zenji," *Monumenta Nipponica* (Tokyo). vol. 13, nos. 1-2 (1956).

Shrady, Maria, trans., foreword, and Josef Schmidt, intro., notes, *Angelus Silesius: The Cherubinic Wanderer*, in *Classics of Western Spirituality: A Library of the Great Spiritual Masters*. New York: Paulist Press, 1986.

Skutch, Robert, *Journey Without Distance: The Story behind A Course in Miracles*. Berkeley: Celestial Arts, 1984.

Smith, Huston, *Tales of Wonder: Adventures Chasing the Divine, an Autobiography*. New York: HarperCollins Publishers, 2009.

Smith, Jonathan C., *Meditation: A Sensible Guide to a Timeless Discipline*. Champaign, IL: Research Press, 1986.

Spong, John Shelby, *A New Christianity for a New World: Why Traditional Faith is Dying and How a New Faith is Being Born*. San Francisco: Harper, 2001.

_____, *Here I Stand: My Struggle for a Christianity of Integrity, Love, and Equality*. San Francisco: Harper, 2000.

_____, *The Sins of Scripture*. San Francisco: Harper, 2005.

_____, *Why Christianity Must Change or Die: A Bishop Speaks to Believers in Exile*. San Francisco: Harper, 1998.

Steindle-Rast, David, *Bulletin of the North American Board for East-West Dialogue,"* no. 30, October 1987.

Streng, Frederick J., *Emptiness: A Study in Religious Meaning*. Nashville, TN: Abingdon Press, 1967.

Stuart, J.D.M., "Abhishiktananda on Inner Awakening," *Vidyajyoti*. (Delhi), 46.

Sunim, Mu Soeng, commentator, *Heart Sutra*. Cumberland, RI: Primary Point Press, 1991.

Surya Das, Lama, *Buddha Is as Buddha Does: The Ten Original Practices for Enlightened Living.* New York: HarperSanFrancisco, 2007.

Suzuki, D.T., "The Buddhist Conception of Reality," in Frederick Frank, ed., *The Buddha Eye: An Anthology of the Kyoto School.* New York: Crossroad Publishing Co., 1991.

T

Tagore, Rabindranath, *Sadhana.* London: Macmillan, 1957.

Tenzin Gyatso, The Fourteenth Dalai Lama, *A Flash of Lightening in the Dark of Night: A Guide to the Bodhisattva's Way of Life.* The Padmakara Translation Group, trans., Boston: Shambhala, 1994.

_____, *Essence of the Heart Sutra: The Dalai Lama's Heart of Wisdom Teaching.* Boston: Wisdom Publications, 2002.

Thurman, Robert A. F., trans., *The Holy Teaching of Vimalakīrti: A Mahayana Scripture.* University Park, PA: Pennsylvania State University Press, 1976.

Tillich, Paul, *Systematic Theology: Three Volumes in One.* New York: Harper & Row, Publishers, 1967.

Tweedie, Irina, *The Chasm of Fire: A Woman's Experience of Liberation through the Teaching of a Sufi Master.* Tisbury, Wiltshire, England: Element Books, 1979.

Tyson, John R., ed., *Invitation to Christian Spirituality: An Ecumenical Anthology.* New York: Oxford University Press, 1999.

V

Vandana, *Gurus, Ashrams and Christians.* Madras: Christian Literature Society, 1980.

Vattakuzhy, Emmanuel, *Indian Christian Sannyasa and Swami Abhishiktananda.* Bangalore: Theological Publications in India, 1981.

Venkataramiah, Managala S., (Ramanananda Saraswati), comp., *Talks with Sri Ramana Maharshi.* Tiruvannamalai, India: Sri Ramanasramam, 1978.

Visser, Frank, *Ken Wilber: Thought as Passion.* Albany, NY: State University of New York Press, 2003.

von Balthasar, H. Urs: "The Metaphysics and Mystical Theology of Evagrius," in *Monastic Studies.* vol. 3, 1965.

W

Waddell, Norman, trans., "Talks by Hakuin Introductory to Lectures on the Records of Old Sokkō," *The Eastern Buddhist.* vol. 24, no. 1, New Series (Spring 1991).

Waddell, Norman, trans., "Wild Ivy: The Spiritual Autobiography of Hakuin Ekaku," *The Eastern Buddhist.* vol. 15, no. 2 (1982).

Wakefield, Gordon, S., ed., *The Westminster Dictionary of Christian Spirituality.* Philadelphia: The Westminster Press, 1983.

Walker, Brian, *Hua Hu Ching: The Unknown Teachings of Lao Tzu.* rev. ed., New York: HarperCollins, 1994.

Wallace, B. Alan, *The Seven-Point Mind Training.* Zara Houshmand, ed., Ithaca, NY: Snow Lion Publications, 1992.

Walshe, Maurice O'Connell, trans., ed., *Meister Eckhart: Sermons and Treatises.* 3 vols. Dorset, England: Element Books, 1978.

Warren, Henry Clarke, trans., *Buddhism in Translation.* New York: Atheneum, 1963.

Watt, W. Montgomery, *Free Will and Predestination in Early Islam.* London: Luzac and Co., 1948.

Wei Wu Wei, *Ask the Awakened: The Negative Way.* Boulder, CO: Sentient Publications, 2002.

_____, *Open Secret.* Boulder, CO: Sentient Publications, 2004.

Wensinck, A.J. *The Muslim Creed: Its Genesis and Historical Development.* London: Frank Cass & Co., 1932, 1965.

Wilber, Ken, *Integral Psychology: Consciousness, Spirit, Psychology, Therapy.* Boston: Shambhala, 2000.

_____, *Integral Spirituality: A Startling New Role for Religion in the Modern and Postmodern World.* Boston: Integral Books, 2006.

_____, *No Boundary: Eastern and Western Approaches to Personal Growth.* Los Angeles: Center Publications, 1979.

_____, *Sex, Ecology, Spirituality: The Spirit of Evolution.* Boston: Shambhala Publications, 1995.

_____, *The Atman Project: A Transpersonal View of Human Development*. Wheaton, IL: The Theosophical Publishing House, 1980.

_____, *The Collected Works of Ken Wilber*. 8 vols., Boston: Shambhala Publications, 1999, 2000.

_____, *The Eye of Spirit: An Integral Vision for a World Gone Slightly Mad* in *The Collected Works of Ken Wilber*. vol. 7, Boston: Shambhala Publications, 2000.

_____, *The Spectrum of Consciousness*. Wheaton, IL: The Theosophical Publishing House, 1977.

Winkler, Ken, *A Thousand Journeys: The Biography of Lama Anagarika Govinda*. Longmead, England: Element Books Ltd., 1990.

Woodring, Carl and James Shapiro, eds., *The Columbia Anthology of British Poetry*. New York: Columbia University Press, 1995.

www.thework.com.

Y

Yampolsky, Philip B., trans., *The Zen Master Hakuin: Selected Writings*. New York: Columbia University Press, 1971.

Yeats, William Butler, "To Lady Elizabeth Pelham" in Allan Wade, ed., *The Letters of W.B. Yeats*. London: Rupert Hart-Davis, 1954.

Z

Zelliot, Eleanor and Maxine Berntsen, eds., *The Experience of Hinduism: Essays on Religion in Maharashtra.* Albany, N.Y.: State University of New York Press, 1988.

Zolondek, L., trans., *Book XX of al-Ghazālī's Ihyā' ᶜUlūm al-Dīn.* Leiden: E.J. Brill, 1963.

Index

of the Lord)

Ar-Rūmī, Jilāl ad-Dīn, 37, 60, 255, 256, 259, 261

Arunachala, India, 121, 123–124, 430

Arya Maitreya Mandala, 204

Asana (bodily posture), 104

Asanga, 144

Ash-Shaykh al-Akbar. *See* Ibn al-ᶜArabī, Muhyid Din

Ashtanga yoga (eightfold path), 103–106

Assumption of the Blessed Virgin Mother, 304–305

Athanasius of Alexandria, 298, 311

Atheism, 46–47

Atisha, 141, 459

Atman (the Self), 100–101, 119, 125–126, 129, 436–437

Augustine, Saint, 370, 381–388, 394, 397–398, 412, 424

Austin, R.W.J., 263, 264

Australian Aborigines, 23

Authentic religion, overview, xiv–xvi, 3–4, 6, 52–53, 64

Avadhuta Gita, 111–112

Avalokiteshvara, the Bodhisattva of Compassion, 151, 203

Averroes. *See* Ibn Rushd (Averroes)

Awareness (meditation/contemplation/prayer), 462–464

B

Bache, Christopher, xiii

Baker, Roshi, 457

Basil the Great, 369–370

Baumer-Despeigne, Odette, 442, 443

Being present, 16

Belief

Arabic translation of term, 267

distinguished from faith, 318–319, 335, 343

idolatry and, 43

saints and sages, difference between, 353

unreflective, 4

Benedict of Nursia, 370, 439

Bernard of Clairvaux, 392–399

The Bezels of Wisdom, 259, 262, 266

Bhagavad Gita (Song of the Lord), 61, 79–81, 92–106

bhakti yoga, 98–100, 108

jnana yoga, 100–102, 108

karma yoga, 92–98, 108

Krishna and Arjuna, 79–80, 94, 95, 98–99, 110–111, 461

quotations from, 83–84, 105, 455

Bhai Sahib. *See* Lal, Radha Mohan/Bhai Sahib

Bhakti yoga, 98–100, 108, 113–116, 118–120

Bible

as final authority, 43

form and redaction criticism scholarship and, 312–314

Gospel of Thomas, 314–315

Jesus Seminar, 316–317, 352–353

mystical study of, 366

New Testament, xiii, 214, 290, 310–317, 337, 339, 340, 346, 356, 466

Old Testament, 310, 335, 367, 372–373, 395

Protestantism and, 305, 307, 309

Protestant/Roman Catholic, different interpretations, 303, 305–307, 309, 310, 313

quotations from, xiii, 46,

Heart Sutra, 61, 181–182
Hinduism, distinguished from, 177
Lama Anagarika Govinda, 154–155, 163, 175, 195–205
meditation and, 69
as religion of practice, 458
Sangha and enlightenment ideal, 135–156
  arahant in Theravada Buddhism, 135–139, 155
  bodhisattva in Mahayana Buddhism, 136, 139–152, 155
  mahasiddha in Vajrayana Buddhism, 152–156
six perfections of bodhisattvas (paramitas), 142–150
  concentration/contemplation, 147–149
  generosity or giving, 142–143
  morality, 143–145
  patience/tolerance, 145–146
  vigor, 147
  wisdom, 149–150
three bodies doctrine, 152
tonglen (sending and receiving), 467–470
See also Buddha; specific schools/traditions

C

Calvin, John, 306
The Cappadocian Fathers, 369–373, 380, 385
Cassian, John, 286, 375
Caste system. See India
Cat school of liberation, 99, 116
Catechetical School, 363–364, 365
Catherine of Siena, Saint, 37, 354–355
Catholic Church. See Roman

Catholic Church
Causal state of consciousness. See Unity mysticism
Cause and effect, law of (karma), 87, 92–94
The Celestial Hierarchy (Dionysius), 389
Chaduc, Marc/Ajatananda, 429, 442
Chakras (psychospiritual centers), 107
Chandrakirti, 150
Change, distinguished from transformation, 51
Change and impermanence, 42
Chapters on Prayer (Evagrius), 377–378
Charismatic Movement (Christianity), 303
Chastity/continence stage (Hinduism), 90, 92
Chekawa, 459
Chenrezi, 151, 203
Chidananda, Swami, 442
China, 93, 136, 151, 214, 289
  See also Tao Te Ching
Chisti Order (Sufism), 270
Chittick, William, 263, 283n89
Chödrön, Pema, 467–468
Christ Consciousness, 337, 360
Christianity, the mind of reconciliation, 285–351
  author's faith and methodology, 285–292
  Charismatic Movement, 303
  doctrine as experiential realities, 334–348
  Eastern Orthodox Church, 297–300, 310, 353–354, 360, 369–370
  evangelism and, 294
  as exoteric/conventional

either/or fallacy, 52
enlightenment and, 21
existence of God, 24
experience-expression
relationship, 53–56
implicit dualism in, 57
limitations and distortions of,
52–56
navel-gazing error, 52
over-valuation of the spiritual
pole error, 52
prayer, 464
sense of superiority error, 52
stages of development, 64–70
as transformational via
transcendence, 50–51
as transverbal realization, 48–49
union mysticism, 49–50, 68,
72–73, 98–100
unity mysticism, 50–51, 68,
72–73, 353, 366
words and written descriptions
of, 70–73
See also specific world religions
Eternal, defined, 28–29
Eternal Now, 14–16
Evagrius Ponticus, 286, 355,
373–381
Exoteric/conventional religion, 38–47
absolutizing the relative, fallacy
of, 43
as complementary to esoteric
religion, 52–57
conflation fallacy, 41–43, 45–46
disjunctive/dissociative fallacy,
44–47
examples of, 38–39
fixity and finality fallacy, 42–43,
55
formation of personal identity
and, 44–45

limitations and distortions of,
40–47
materializing the spiritual,
fallacy of, 43
personal change in, 51
prayer, 464
purpose of, 39
spiritual and mystical sources
of, 55–56
stages of development, 64–70
words and written descriptions
of, 70–73
See also specific world religions
Experience-expression
relationship, 53–56

F

Faith, distinguished from belief,
318–319, 335, 343
Fa-tsang, 61, 173–174
Fiqh Akbar I/II, 220, 242, 248
Five Pillars of Islam, 232–241
Fixity and finality fallacy, 42–43,
55
Flatland view, 36
Forest dweller stage (Hinduism),
91, 92
Formless mysticism, 68
"Forty Traditions" (an-Nawawī),
246
*The Foundations of Tibetan
Mysticism* (Govinda), 203
The Four Noble Truths
(Buddhism), 160–163, 164, 176,
460
Four Quartets (Eliot), 2
Fox, George, 286
Francis of Assisi, Saint, 37, 354–
355, 470, 477
Fundamentalism, religious, 43, 45,
294, 309

Fundamentals of the Middle Way
(Nagarjuna), 179–180

Heart Sutra, 61, 181–182
Hebrew Bible, 214, 321
Here and not here, 16–17
Herod the Great, 320, 333
Hinduism, mind of liberation,
  77–133, 455
  the Vedas, 29, 78–81, 93
  bhakti yoga, 98–100, 108
  buddhi yoga, 108
  Buddhism, distinguished from,
    177
  caste and gender, beliefs about,
    90, 93–94, 99, 115
  gods, God and Ultimacy, 23,
    82–86
  human predicament as bondage,
    86–90
  jivan mukta (liberated while
    alive), 106, 109–112, 116
  jnana yoga, 100–102, 108
  karma yoga, 92–98, 108
  kundalini yoga, 107
  laya yoga, 106–107
  Mahabharata, 79
  mantra yoga, 107
  maya (illusion/appearance), 61,
    83, 88–90, 102, 120, 127
  no other/no fear, 59
  parallels to Incarnation and the
    Trinity within, 339
  raja yoga, 103–106
  satchitananda (existence/
    consciousness/bliss), 68, 83,
    125, 441
  teacher-disciple relationships,
    108–109
  Tukaram, 85, 112–120
  Upanishads, 79, 102, 437, 440
  worldview and, 80–81
  See also Advaita Vedanta;
    Bhagavad Gita (Song of the

Lord); Krishna; Maharshi,
  Ramana
Hoffman, Ernst Lothar. See
  Govinda, Lama Anagarika
Hogan, Ben, 456–457
Holograms, 86
Holons (Koestler), 18–19
Holy Spirit as Ultimacy, 346–348
Hopkins, Gerald Manley, 425
Hortensius (Cicero), 381–382
Householder stage (Hinduism),
  90–91, 92, 102
Hua-yen Buddhism, 173–174, 199
Hui-neng, 142, 155, 162, 163, 182
Humility, religious principle of,
  114–115, 237, 265, 323, 330,
  332, 343, 348, 354, 360, 393,
  397, 405, 465–467
Huss, John, 306

I
I and me, 12–13
Ibn ᶜAtā'illāh, 60, 256
Ibn al-ᶜArabī, Muhyid Din, 250,
  259–269
  metaphysics of, 262–264,
    283n89
  psychospiritual process of,
    260–261
  quotations of, 231, 260–261,
    268–269
  Ultimate Realization, 264–269,
    276
  writings of, 259, 262, 266, 267,
    268
Ibn Rushd (Averroes), 260
Idolatry, 28, 43, 56, 217
The Imitation of Christ (Kempis),
  424
Immaculate Conception, 304–305
Inaction in action (Bhagavad Gita),

318–319, 338–341, 342, 346–348, 370–371, 373–374, 393, 441

Evagrius' second creation and, 379–380

as expression of God's love for mankind, 292–293

first-century descriptions of, 29–30

Koran as parallel to, 229

Maharshi's interpretation of crucifixion/resurrection, 131

mission to dispossessed, 321–322

Muhammad, prophetic lineage and, 218, 219

as revolutionary/reformer, 288, 294, 332

as Teacher, 323–331

trial/crucifixion/resurrection, 331–334, 342, 344–346

as Ultimacy for Christians, 28–29

as Ultimacy for Muslims, 60

See also Bible; headings under Christianity

Jihad (Muhammad), 221

Jinn (subtle beings), 225

Jivan mukta (liberated while alive), 106, 109–112, 116

Jnana yoga, 100–102, 108

Jodo Shin Shu Buddhism, 151

Jodo Shu Buddhism, 151

John of Damascus, 297

John of the Cross, Saint, 286, 439, 473

John Paul II, Pope, 304

John the Baptist, 219, 294, 320

John XXIII, Pope, 295, 302

Joseph of Nazareth, 320

Journey to the Lord of Power (Ibn al-ʿArabī), 268

Judaism, 23, 77, 214, 217, 219, 289, 304, 314, 356

Judeo-Christian-Islamic tradition, 214

Julian of Norwich, 354–355

K

Kama Sutra, 91

Kamalashila, 141, 150

Kannon, the Bodhisattva of Mercy, 23, 151, 187

Karma (law of cause and effect), 87–88, 92–95

Karma yoga, 92–98, 108

Kashyapa, 160

Kataphatic/cataphatic theology, 33–34

Katie, Byron, 476

Kempis, Thomas à, 418, 419, 424

Kierkegaard, Søren, 324

King, Martin Luther, Jr., 37

Knowledge, distinguished from wisdom (Augustine), 386

Koan study, 189–194, 467

Koestler, Arthur, 18–19

Koheleth (Ecclesiastes), 88

Koran, 213–214, 217, 218, 227–232, 256, 278n2

Arabic language version, 227, 229

quotations from, 222, 223, 224–226, 231, 233, 234–235, 237–239, 242–248, 253, 258, 268, 455

Kosmos centric stage, 66

Krishna, 61, 81, 84–85, 98

See also Bhagavad Gita (Song of the Lord); Hinduism, mind of liberation

Krishnamurti, J., 61

216–217
Night Journey and Ascension,
218–220
Opening of the Chest event, 215
political opposition to, 220–221
psychospiritual process of,
215–220
roles of, for Muslims, 222–226
as Ultimacy for Muslims, 29
See also Allah (submission and
salvation); Hadith; Islam, the
mind of submission; Koran
Multiplicity and consciousness,
9–10
Murphy, Michael, 474–475
Muslims
identity as, 245, 248
origin of term, 242
relationship to Muhammad and,
222–226
See also Islam, the mind of
submission
Mystical experiences, four
progressive types of, 68
The Mystical Theology
(Dionysius), 389, 391–392
Mysticism. *See* Esoteric/mystical
religion
Myth, 318
Mythical stage (Gebser), 67

N
Nag Hammadi, Egypt, text
discoveries, 311, 314
Nagarjuna, 179–180
Namadeva, 113
Name changes, in religious life, 91
Naqshbandi Order (Sufism),
270–271
Nasr, Seyyed Hossein, 227, 230,
232, 236, 238

Nataraj (King of the Dance),
84–85
Native Americans, 23
Natural mind (rigpa), 186
Nature and Spirit (Patanjali), 103
Nature mysticism, 68
Navel-gazing, 52
Negation, 32–34, 72, 101, 129–
130, 182, 402
Negative emotions, 87, 153, 163,
239, 342, 375, 471
Neoplatonism, 289, 365–369, 370,
382, 388–390, 400
Neti, neti (not this, not that), 82
Nicene Creed, 296–297, 338–339
Nirmanakaya (transformation
body), 152
Nirvana (liberation), 10, 61, 134,
137, 139, 143, 148, 150, 153,
155, 159, 160, 168–169, 170,
183, 184, 186
Nirvikalpa samadhi, 106, 118,
123–125
Nobody training, 51, 59
Nonattachment. *See* Detachment
Nonduality
Christianity on, 319, 329, 347
Dzogchen school on, 184–186
Gnosticism on, 315
Mahayana Buddhism on, 143
nondual mind, 17–18
nondual mysticism, 68
Qualified Nondualism
(Ramanuja), 99–100
Sufism on, 250–251, 257–258
union mysticism, 49–50
See also Advaita Vedanta;
Duality; Metateric/
nondual religion; Ultimacy,
introduction to; *specific saints
and sages*

Non-returners (Theravada Buddhism), 137
Non-violence (ahimsa), 91, 104, 165–166
Northern Buddhism. *See* Mahayana Buddhism
Now and not now, 14–16, 29
Now and now, 15
Nyanatiloka, Thera, 195
Nyoshul Kenpo Rinpoche, 184–186

O

Obermiller, E., 148
Object permanence, 18
Occult powers, 107
Om Mani Padme Hum (mantra), 203
On Detachment (Eckhart), 407
On the Love of God (Bernard), 394
Once-returners (Theravada Buddhism), 137
Oneness of Being, 258, 263
Origen, 355, 365–369, 380–381, 385, 395
Original sin (Christianity), 301, 304–305, 340–341
Otto, Rudolf, 3

P

Padmasambhava, 37, 184
Panduranga, 118–119
Panikkar, Raimundo, 429, 443
Paradox, 26–29, 41–42
Paramitas. *See* Buddhism, the mind of enlightenment
Part/parochial/fragmentive view, 35
Pascal, Blaise, 27
Patanjali, Yoga Sutra, 103–106
Patience, 102, 145–146, 257, 299,

459, 471
Paul, Apostle, 88, 288–291, 295, 299, 312, 337, 343, 344, 356–363, 382–383, 388, 467
Paul VI, Pope, 302
Perfection of Wisdom in 8,000 Lines (Prajnaparamita texts), 181
Personal holiness, xvii–xviii
Peter, Saint, 288, 295, 298, 333, 335
Pilate, Pontius, 333
Pius XII, Pope, 305
Platform Sutra (Hui-neng), 142
Plato, 289, 364, 365–366, 368, 371, 390, 400–401
Plotinus, 364, 365–366, 382
Pluralistic stage (Gebser), 67
Poetry, 54, 56
The Practice of Lojong: Cultivating Compassion through Training the Mind (Kyabgon), 467
The Practice of the Presence of God (Brother Lawrence), 464
Prajnaparamita (Perfection of Wisdom) texts, 181–182
Praktikos (Evagrius), 374–375
Prayer, 235–237, 462–464
  See also Meditation
Preconventional/conventional/postconventional stages, 66
Pregnant with Nothing (Eckhart), 400
Prejudice, 35–36
Prepersonal/personal/transpersonal stage, 66
Pre/post fallacy (Wilber), 66
Private, distinguished from public self, 24–25
Process Thought (Whitehead), 460–461

and sages

Spirituality, as distinguished from religion, 63–64

Splitting of reality. *See* Dichotomizing principle of thinking mind; Duality; Time and space

Spong, John Shelby, 290

Spontaneity (sahaja), 154

Stages of development (Gebser), 67

Stages of religio-spiritual development, 66

States, distinguished from stages of consciousness, 67–68

Steindle-Rast, David, 460

Stream-winners (Theravada Buddhism), 137

Stuart, J.D.M., 429

Subject and Object (samkhya), 103

Suffering. *See* The Four Noble Truths (Buddhism)

Sufis, Islamic mysticism. *See* Islam, the mind of submission

Sugiyama Iwajiro. *See* Hakuin Ekaku

Super-integral stage, 67

Suprarational way of knowing, 27

Suzuki, D.T., 181, 182

T

Tagore, Rabindranath, 61

Tantric Buddhism. *See* Vajrayana Buddhism

Tao Te Ching, 33, 54

Taoism, 23

Taylor, Jeremy, 418

Teacher-disciple relationships. *See* Gurus/spiritual teachers

Teilhard de Chardin, Pierre, xviii

Tennyson, Alfred Lord, 85

Teresa of Avila, Saint, 286, 354–355, 411–418

That art Thou (jnana yoga), 100

Theistic religions, union mysticism and, 49–50

Theologia Germanica (anonymous), 336–337

Theology
apophatic/negative/mystical, 34, 373, 379
kataphatic/cataphatic, 33–34

Theosis (deification/divination), 298, 337, 360, 364, 368

Theosophical Society, 269

Theravada Buddhism, 134–139, 155, 164, 179, 195, 206n4

Thich Nhat Hanh, 19, 174–175

Thinging and thingness, 19–20

Thinking mind
absolutizing the relative, fallacy of, 43
conflation fallacy and, 41–43, 45–46
dichotomizing principle of, 10–17, 19–20, 27, 32
either/or fallacy, 52
entitizing feature of, 19–20
intuition of Ultimacy and, 27, 33
Maharshi on thoughts as obstacles to seeing, 127
metateric/nondual religion and, 59
object permanence, 18
paradox and, 26–29
past and future, 15–16
transcendence of, 27
waking state and, 19–20

The Thirty-seven Practices of Bodhisattvas (Sangpo), 471

Three bodies doctrine (trikaya), in Buddhism, 152

CPSIA information can be obtained
at www.ICGtesting.com
Printed in the USA
FFOW02n0540140217
32405FF

9 781452 572741